Cold War Redux Amidst Great Power Rivalry

Victor Teo

Cold War Redux Amidst Great Power Rivalry

China and the Rise of the Global Right

Victor Teo
CRASSH
University of Cambridge
Cambridge, UK

ISBN 978-981-97-3732-1   ISBN 978-981-97-3733-8 (eBook)
https://doi.org/10.1007/978-981-97-3733-8

© The Editor(s) (if applicable) and The Author(s), under exclusive license to Springer Nature Singapore Pte Ltd. 2024

This work is subject to copyright. All rights are solely and exclusively licensed by the Publisher, whether the whole or part of the material is concerned, specifically the rights of translation, reprinting, reuse of illustrations, recitation, broadcasting, reproduction on microfilms or in any other physical way, and transmission or information storage and retrieval, electronic adaptation, computer software, or by similar or dissimilar methodology now known or hereafter developed.
The use of general descriptive names, registered names, trademarks, service marks, etc. in this publication does not imply, even in the absence of a specific statement, that such names are exempt from the relevant protective laws and regulations and therefore free for general use.
The publisher, the authors and the editors are safe to assume that the advice and information in this book are believed to be true and accurate at the date of publication. Neither the publisher nor the authors or the editors give a warranty, expressed or implied, with respect to the material contained herein or for any errors or omissions that may have been made. The publisher remains neutral with regard to jurisdictional claims in published maps and institutional affiliations.

Cover illustration: eng.chinamil.com.cn/Photo by Zhang Lei

This Palgrave Macmillan imprint is published by the registered company Springer Nature Singapore Pte Ltd.
The registered company address is: 152 Beach Road, #21-01/04 Gateway East, Singapore 189721, Singapore

If disposing of this product, please recycle the paper.

Acknowledgements

One of the most significant changes in recent times is how nationalism has evolved from an academic discipline we study in the classroom mostly to become such an important force in our lives. It affects how we view and interpret the problems that afflict the world, and how we conceive of the solutions to them. Arguably, nationalism has once again become the most important ideology that influence the societies we live in. The social realities for many of us have changed drastically. Chinese students once again are finding themselves having their visas denied and ejected from their studies in the United States, while many Russians overseas are caught in the cross-nets of sanctions imposed on Russia and have their savings and property confiscated. Likewise, Americans are met with increased hostilities when they travel abroad. We no longer hear much about the global village we were supposed to living in, but rather we are learning from the Leader of Free World that walls should be built (literally) between nations, and just as ironically, from the Secretary-General of the world's largest Communist Party (which had been inducting capitalistic entrepreneurs into the party ranks) advocating for free trade. Geopolitical alignments now appear to be dictating our lives once again even as on a daily basis, we hear daily that a new Cold War is not brewing. The developing Great Power rivalry is now being enshrouded in Cold War language by the politicians in United States and her allies on one hand, and in China and Russia on the other, to rally support and drive a new understanding of who our enemies are or should be. The forces that divide our world now appear to be much stronger than the forces that unite us. Like the generations before us, we are now presented with little choice as the world heads towards a strange sort of bifurcated globalisation where the interaction of nations is once again divided into blocs, even as the fighting in Ukraine and the Middle East rages on and the confrontation in the Taiwan Straits and South China Sea escalates. The academia has unfortunately not been spared from this phenomenon as career networking, research funding and academic freedom are being increasingly compromised whether in Asia or America. The "you are either with us or against us" mindset has taken root even in the free world that many of us live in. This book therefore hopes to be a contribution to the growing literature on the international relations of the Indo-Pacific, as a possible kind of introspection that can help us understand why we have gotten to this point today.

The ideas for this book were conceived when the author was an Academic Research Associate at Harvard Program for US–Japan Relations and a Visiting Scholar at Harvard Law School. For the most part, the research and writing of the book was done with the support of a Fellowship from The Beyond the Cold War project based at the University of Cambridge's Centre for Arts, Social Sciences and Humanities when the Covid pandemic was in full swing. The author wants to acknowledge the support of the Academy of Korea Studies Grant (AKS-2016-LAB-2250005) and the encouragement of Professor Heonik Kwon, The Beyond the Cold War Project leader at the University of Cambridge's Center for the Research in Arts, Social Sciences and Humanities. The author is also grateful to his family and close friends for all the love and support through this project. Needless to say, all errors contained therein are the responsibility of the author.

CONTENTS

1	**Cold War Redux Amidst Great Power Rivalry: The Rise of the Global Right, the Quad and China**	1
	The Problematic	1
	Aims and Objectives	10
	Theoretical Framework	12
	Main Arguments	15
	Domestic Politics and the Rise of Global Right Agenda	15
	Emergence of Charismatic Illiberal Leaders	18
	Great Power Rivalry and Systemic Change	20
	China's Resistance	22
	Cold War Redux	27
	Assumptions and Limitations of the Research	31
	Chapters Overview	34
	Chapter 1: The Cold War and the China Challenge	34
	Chapter 2: Japan	34
	Chapter 3: The United States	35
	Chapter 4: Australia	37
	Chapter 5: India	39
	Chapter 6: Cold War Redux	41
	References	43

vii

viii CONTENTS

2 Japan's Resurgence as a Neoconservative State: Towards Constitutional Revisionism and Great Power Status — 49

Level One: The Leader — 50

Shinzo Abe: The Making of Japan's Foremost Conservative and QUAD Idealogue — 50

Family Legacies: Pedigree, Networks and Transgenerational Aspirations — 51

The Second Coming of Shinzo Abe, the Global Right and Quad 2.0 — 57

Level II: Domestic Politics — 63

Political Nationalism in Japan: National Identity and Historical Evolution — 63

Economic Decline and LDP's Quest for Continued Relevance and Dominance — 65

Normalising Japan in the Post-Cold War World — 67

Overcoming Resistance to LDP's Continued Dominance: Factionalism, Bureaucracy and the Media — 70

The Rise of New-Age Conservative Politics: From Koizumi to Abe — 77

Frustrated Electorate: The Rise of the Abe School and Japan's National Security Agenda — 85

Level III: The International System — 88

The Rise of China and Japan's Global Role — 88

The China's Challenge: Irredentism, Strategic Threat, the Erosion of Japanese Regional Influence and Leadership — 94

Japan's Concerns Over the US–Japan Alliance: Inaction, Credibility and Abandonment — 96

Countering China's Global Clout: Asymmetricity Reduction, Alternate Developmental Narrative and Manufacturing Relocation — 103

References — 112

3 The United States' Neoconservative Turn: America First, Preserving U.S. Hegemony and the Containment of China — 123

Level I: The Political Leadership — 123

Donald Trump: The Unlikely Conservative — 123

A Pragmatic and Transactional Political Chameleon — 125

CONTENTS   ix

Unconventional Politics and the Embracement
of the Global Right Agenda   130
Level II: Domestic Politics   135
Electoral Concerns and the Changing Tone of US
Nationalism   135
Trump's Hostile Takeover of the Republican Party   140
Using Foreign Policy to Fight Domestic Political Battles:
The Role of Russia and China in the 2016 Presidential
Elections   142
The Trump Doctrine: Operationalising the Global Right's
Agenda   144
The Rightwards Shift of US Politics and Its Impact
on the Biden Administration   149
Democratic Hedging and Biden's Doubling Down
on Trump's Policies   153
Level III: International System   155
The United States and the Asia–Pacific in the Pre-Trump
Era   155
The Belt and Road Initiative: Chinese Style "Marshall
Plan" and "Fukuda Doctrine"   169
The Trump Doctrine: The Indo-Pacific Strategy
and Preservation of US Hegemony   172
Promoting Human Rights, Democracy and Freedom:
Xinjiang, Taiwan and Hong Kong   174
The Kim-Trump Summit: Pre-emptory Neutralisation
of a Possible Chinese Proxy   177
On the Offensive: The United States' Trade and Tech
War on China   180
The COVID-19 Pandemic and the Quad's Quest to Secure
the Supply Chain   189
"America First" Biden Style   191
From Unilateral Decoupling to Multi-lateral De-Risking:
Prioritising Security Goals Before Economic Interests   195
Biden's Doubling Down and Trump's Return: Great
Power Hegemonic Struggle and Cold War Redux   196
References   199

4 The Era of the Conservatives and Australia's Relations
with China and the United States   219
Level One: The Political Leadership   221
The Rise of Conservatives   221

x CONTENTS

The Liberal-National Prime Ministers	227
Level Two: China in Australia's Domestic Politics	242
Australia's Cultural Heritage and its Strategic Affinity for the United States	243
Australian National Identity and Nationalism: Human Rights, Freedom and Values	246
China's Economic Ascendance and Its Impact on Australian Domestic Politics	253
China and the Chinese in Australia Domestic Politics: Scapegoating, Strategic Industries and Democratic Participation	255
When the Commercial Becomes Political: Stopping the Growth of Firms and Barring Purchase of Domestic Strategic Assets	258
Ports, Utilities and Cattle Ranches	259
Political Interference and Party Politics	261
The Conservative Methodology: Cultural Nationalism, Racial Tarring and Identity Politics	264
Level III: The International System	268
Systemic Drivers and Australia's Conservative Turn	268
The Need for a Rejuvenated San Francisco System: Hard Pivot to the United States	271
Securing Australia's National Interests and Addressing Security Concerns South China Sea and Australia's Defence	274
South Pacific and Australia's Role as Regional Hegemon Cum Watchman	276
Australia, the Quad and AUKUS	279
Course Adjustment in the Post-Conservative Era	285
References	288
5 India's Global Right Moment and Its Grand Strategy	307
Level I: The Political Leadership	308
The Rise of Narendra Modi	308
Anti-Corruption Fighter, Development Advocate and the "Hindu First" Doctrine	310
The Pragmatic Nationalist	313
Level Two: Domestic Politics	315
The Primacy of Local Politics: Anti-Colonialism, Statism and Rightwards Drift	315

Majoritarian Politics, Pakistan and the Muslim Question	318
BJP's Economic Conundrum: Grassroots Politics,	
Distributive Justice and Job Creation	323
The Spectre of Comparison: Civilisational Enemy, Model	
Neighbour or Competitor	328
India's Question for Great Power Status: China	
as a Political Football	331
Level Three: The International System	333
India's Historical Relations with China: Estrangement,	
Indifference and Détente	333
China's Rise as a Power in India's Neighbourhood	338
Joining the Global Right Fraternity: Bandwagoning	
with the United States and Japan	341
Territorial Disputes, Threat Perceptions and Chinese	
Irredentism	346
China's BRI, Pakistan and India's Sovereign Sensitivities	350
The Indian Ocean and Resecuring India's Role	
as the Regional Hegemon	353
The Global Right: Reorienting India for Global Influence	
and Great Power Status	356
The "Weak" Link: India's Propensity for Strategic	
Independence and Ties to Russia	360
References	366

6 The Rise of the Global Right, Great Power Politics and The Revival of the Cold War — 379

China, Russia and the West in the Era of Globalisation	382
Multipolarity, Return of Great Power Politics and Cold	
War Narratives	385
Capitalistic Disparity, Dysfunctional Politics and Economic	
Difficulties	392
Conservative Leaders, Innovative Campaigning	
and the Aggravation of the China Problem	393
The Strategic Need for Re-balancing and the Strengthening	
of the San Francisco System	398
Trajectory for Cold War Redux	400
References	408

Index 409

ABOUT THE AUTHOR

Victor Teo is a Political Scientist specialising in the International Relations of the Indo-Pacific. He was a faculty at the University of Hong Kong for 13 years and was most recently Beyond the Cold War Visiting Fellow at the Center for Research in Arts, Social Sciences and Humanities at the University of Cambridge and Wang Gungwu Visiting Senior Fellow at Yusof-Ishak Institute Singapore.

CHAPTER 1

Cold War Redux Amidst Great Power Rivalry: The Rise of the Global Right, the Quad and China

THE PROBLEMATIC

Over the past decade, international relations scholars have intensely debated whether there is a new or renewed Cold War brewing between the United States and China. This was even before the Trade and Tech War, when the United States launched against China after Trump came to power in 2016 (Wade, 2009). The debate on whether we are entering a period of renewed Cold War complex has multifaceted views, but there is one consensus that all scholars and policymakers agree upon: that is, the Sino-US relations have plunged to a new low, never before since Washington and Beijing reconciled in 1972 at the height of the Cold War. There is also an agreement that there is certainly some truth in the idea that some form of Cold War is beginning to envelope us all. As early as 2014, the US Army War College published a paper that spoke to the beginnings of "The New Cold War". Prophetically, the paper begins by stating that "The New Cold War will be long and deep only if the current Sino-Russian entente turns into an alliance. A hostile Russia alone can cause mischief but compared to the old Soviet Union, is weak and sufferable. Russia and China's together are a much tougher challenge. The Sino-Soviet split … marked the end of the original Cold War" (Roskin, 2014). A cursory survey of the developments in US relations with Russia and China and regional politics in Asia, Europe and the Middle East provides us with much food for thought as to where we are heading.

© The Author(s), under exclusive license to Springer Nature Singapore Pte Ltd. 2024
V. Teo, *Cold War Redux Amidst Great Power Rivalry*,
https://doi.org/10.1007/978-981-97-3733-8_1

1

Just as US relations with Russia and China are at their lowest points in contemporary history, Sino-Russian relations have never been stronger in their history. Roskin's thinking is turning out to be very prescient today.

A new or a renewed Cold War between China/Russia and the United States is, however, still far from being a certainty (Christensen, 2011), but it would be safe to assume that it would be impossible for US–Russia or US–China relations to revert back to relatively positive relations, such as those during the late 1980s and the early 1990s. If is hard to see at first how the war can become bifurcated into two blocs competing over every sphere of human activity as it once was (Hendrix, 2018). As the United States heads into the election season of 2024 at the time of the book's publication, this question becomes more prescient than ever. Graham Allison observed, "[2024] promises to be a year of danger as countries around the world watch US politics with a combination of disbelief, fascination, horror, and hope" (Allison, 2024). Donald Trump's election could mean a decisive moment for the United States that would seek complete decoupling from China and a world where many countries would be asked to do the same. Likewise, the fate of Ukraine and Palestine would likely be decided by the same election. It could also decide whether a full-scale Cold War would be revived.

Insofar where Sino-US relations are concerned, there has been a massive avalanche of viewpoints and narratives over the last decade, ascribing Chinese foreign policy behaviour to a few reductionistic traits: China is ambitious (Manning, 2020), expansionist (Sankei Shimbun 2020; Venkataraman, 2020), irredentist (Buruma, 2023; Chang, 1998; Chen & Huang 2015; Roy, 2019), deceptive (Ching, 2016), assertive (Christensen, 2011; Zhao, 2011), resource hungry (Cáceres & Ear, 2013; Tracy et al., 2017), nationalistic (Chang 1998; Hu, 2023) and always keen to broadcast their propaganda (viewpoints) worldwide (Asada et al. 2022, Christensen, 2011; Liu & Ma, 2018). Whether intentional or not, Chinese development is now regarded as a "threat" in almost every conceivable dimension, from strategic to economic to environmental. If these narratives are to be believed, China is a threat to the post-war global order and in the words of American and Japanese politicians, a threat to a "free and open Indo-Pacific". In the words of US Navy Admiral Samuel Paparo (Head of US Indo-Pacific Command), and General Brawner from Philippines (Chief of Staff, Philippines Armed Forces), China's claims in South China Sea are "illegal, coercive, aggressive and deceptive" (Moriyasu, 2024). China also stands accused of "bullying" Taiwan and

Philippines by politicians and the media in the United States and her allied partners. China, in a nutshell, must be stopped, and consequently, there is no alternative, except for the complete vanquishing of China. America's competition with China must be won, not managed, according to Matt Pottinger and Mike Gallagher (Pottinger and Gallagher 2024) in a piece published in Foreign Affairs. There are those who argue that the problems we see today are all because of China's leader Xi Jinping (Kleine-Ahlbrandt, 2013; Branigan, 2017); others have argued for over two decades, the West has made wrong assumptions about China, such as that economic growth will eventually lead to democracy, and the way the Chinese would regard authoritarianism, Western way of life and values when they grow rich (Mitter & Johnson, 2021). The question of self and public perceptions is a difficult one, and is often subjected to misinterpretations (Tamamoto, 2005). It is hard to see how politicians in Quad countries are able to put themselves in the shoes of the leaders in China and imagine accurately what it is they are thinking, imaging or desiring. Very often, it is just gross speculation and one-sided presumption of what the other wants. Whether it is a question of leadership, system, values, outlook, or way of life, much of the information online in the Quad countries suggests that most of the ills in the world today traces back to China. There are also those who argued that if the US played her cards wrongly, the US could actually lose this new Cold War (Stiglitz, 2022). These arguments while muted in large American discourse have effectively hardened the political mood and strategic attitudes in Washington, Tokyo, New Delhi, Canberra and London.

It would be prudent to remind ourselves that the United States, along with most of her allies, cultivated very amicable relations with Beijing only after 1978, before which bilateral dynamics were far more egregious and tenuous. At every level, China has undergone unprecedented liberalisation since it embarked on economic reforms and built intensive commercial linkages with the region and the world. For almost three decades (from 1992 to 2012), US–China bilateral relations were relatively good, but it took a drastic change for the worse. Why has the world we are so familiar with changed drastically over the last decade? It is important to understand that many of the skewed opinions on China are presented in online forums and catchy short media puff pieces written by non-specialists, but the interesting question is why are many learned scholars so quick to jump on the anti-China bandwagon? How did US–China relations deteriorate so quickly to the extent that so many scholars are convinced that we have gone "back to the future" with the Cold War playing out again? Did this begin with Obama's "pivot" to Asia or was it Trump whose Trade and Tech War had so destroyed the foundations of US–China relations? Alternatively, was it Biden's who doubled down on Trump's policies and challenged both Russia and China that got us to where we are today?

Further questions follow: Why did the United States, along with her allies, Japan and Australia decide to overturn decades of fruitful and rewarding economic relations with China to seek out a confrontational policy with China? Was this really because China had fundamentally changed since Xi Jinping came to power in 2012? Is it as many who suggest that Xi's irredentist agenda or worse because of "values" differentiation between the Chinese and American nations. If the latter were to be responsible, then surely one would question why the Americans and her allies are discovering this now. Where did this source of information come from—would it be because all media reports on Xinjiang, Tibet and Hong Kong are to be believed without exception? Has it anything to do with the perceptual lens by which we are using to scrutinise China are in fact provided or affected by our changing media environment or political climate? China was a country with whom the United States, Japan, India and Australia had all but worked closely for the past four decades. The Communist Party of China has been more or less the same, even though the government has grown more insecure over the past few years owing to several stress factors. Those who study China professionally would certainly agree that all these issues hyped up in the press in recent years have existed since the PRC was founded. Whether its human rights transgressions, minority protection issues in Tibet and Xinjiang, difficulties in Central-Hong Kong relations, reunification challenges with Taiwan or South China territorial disputes, none of these challenges are "new". The dynamics may have changed, but the substance of the issues remains fundamentally similar. Why has the mood changed so radically in the United States, Japan, Australia and India against China to the extent that these countries have now revived the Quad, an institution that is manifestly "anti-China" in nature against their most important trading partner?

Relationships between nations are always driven by human behaviour. Whether it is the thinking of the nation's top leader translated into policy or prevailing domestic consensus shaped by bickering political factions or problem-framing and option-selection by bureaucrats, there is always someone whose decisions or outlook has the most consequential (direct or indirect) impact on the eventual course of a nation-state's diplomacy. While a strong leader can dictate foreign policy, there will be ideational and material structures within each society that will ameliorate his policy choices: political factions/parties and public opinion, bureaucratic inertia and departmental agendas, commercial interests and economic constraints and vagaries of international politics. These structures and forces work in tandem to shape and reshape policy initiatives and responses enacted and often elicit unintended results and policy responses.

To that extent, this volume takes a three-tier approach towards understanding the shift against China in the decade from 2012 to 2022 by examining the political leadership within each country, the domestic context and the international system of the Quad countries as they struggle to reframe their China policy against their broader foreign policy. 2012 marks an important turning point in global and regional history; however, in our case, it also represents an important watershed in the politics of the countries concerned. This is not only because Xi Jinping became the General Secretary of the Chinese Communist Party in November 2012 but also because Shinzo Abe became the Japanese Prime Minister for the second time in December 2012, as well as Australia electing the first of three Conservative Prime Ministers, Tony Abbott, in September 2013. In May 2014, Narendra Modi, the ardent Hindu nationalist leader, became Prime Minister. For the United States, 2012 represents a "watershed" year as President Obama undertook an Asia trip in November 2011 to announce the American "pivot" back to Asia after a decade-long War on Terror. In November 2016, Trump was elected US President.

It is important to understand where the above-mentioned politicians mentioned above are situated in the concept of the "Global Right". Politicians who use nationalism as a platform to national power are hardly new. The Global Right represents a new wave of political parties and politicians who often share common characteristics and objectives, and campaign on similar strategies and populist platforms of national identity, anti-globalisation and protectionist tendencies, climate change scepticism as well as national security (including anti-immigration). Of course, there will be differences in what they articulate, but by and large, they do have similar strategies and coordinated networks. Many of these global right politicians claim to be for freedom, democracy and liberal international order, but often reflect authoritarian tendencies. Since 2010, there have been many successful examples such as Victor Orban of Hungary (elected 2010), Recep Erdogan of Turkey (elected 2014), Boris Johnson (elected London Mayor 2008, Prime Minister 2019) along with other populist regimes in Poland, Mexico and Hungary.

For the purposes of this book, 2012 is a significant year because it marks the beginning of the rise of the "global right" in Quad countries. The rise of these conservative politicians and regimes, as well as their particular domestic circumstances, is certainly responsible for the rapid rise of anti-China sentiments in these countries, which is pushing the United States, Japan, Australia and India to come together to confront China. It is important that we understand this as much as we understand what is happening elsewhere, such as in China and Asia in general. China has become an important foreign policy adversary as Beijing is being used as a nationalistic piñata of sorts to rally domestic political support and consensus. Standing up to China became an important rallying cry for fledging political parties and politicians to gain national attention and boost wavering political support (Hibbing, 2020). The list of politicians who have utilised this is long: think Junichiro Koizumi of Japan to Tsai Ing-wen of Taiwan to Bongbong Marcos in Philippines today.

These four countries came together to revive the Quadrilateral Security Dialogue (i.e. the Quad) proposed by Japan in 2006. Essentially, the Quad is a strategic community that aims to encircle and contain China. In Western and Japanese narratives, the Quad has been lauded by many scholars as evidence of an emerging manifestation of how key countries in the Indo-Pacific region are attempting to cope with a stronger and supposedly more assertive China. Conceptualised initially by Shinzo Abe in 2006, the concept suffered a stillborn fate when Kevin Rudd of Australia pulled out of its membership and Abe stepped down after a year as Prime Minister. The concept was revived only by Japan during Abe's second term and implemented with vigour when Trump came to power. The dominant narratives that explain the emergence of the Quad in Western and social media can be mostly distilled down to a singular version: that Quadrilateral Security Dialogue emerged to prevent an "aggressive" China under the leadership of Xi Jinping from challenging the status quo, to keep peace and to ensure that the Indo-Pacific region remains "free and open". The Quad is therefore seen as a multilateral response to a plurality of challenges, beginning with maritime security, and has expanded to realms such as cyber security and non-conventional security challenges such as the Covid pandemic over time (Jha, 2021).

This expansion has allowed members to legitimise their grouping internationally as they grow beyond their original remit of being an anti-China posture to adopt the mantle of a more innocuous institution aimed at addressing a wide variety of security challenges and regional crises, such as vaccine production or supply chain protection. The Quad has also expanded to peacetime cooperation, particularly in the economic and technological realms, to help expand and fight the US trade and tech war against China. It is clear that the Quad aims to reinforce the dominance of the United States in the Asia–Pacific region. To reiterate, it is the new kind of Conservatism and virulent nationalism that is taking root in the politics of these countries that is driving developments such as the "Quad" initiatives, as politicians use national security agenda to grapple and frame China policies that has stimulated the ongoing route towards a new confrontation with China (and Russia). Conservatism manifests itself in the form of institutions, and cooperation envisages and operationalises.

The reason why the volume argues that Global Right Quad countries are taking the lead in stoking the Cold War is simple. Increasingly difficult economic circumstances accompanied by the rise of sophisticated Conservatives skilled in electoral politics in the age of social media against the larger backdrop of a rising China has created the perfect combination of factors that is singularly driving global politics towards a renewed Cold War. Conservative political methodology in the rallying of domestic nationalism and geopolitical realpolitik are the real driving forces of this new global conservatism. The identity politics and explicit targeting of China as a basis for membership could not be clearer from 2012 onwards. Lead by Shinzo Abe, the Quad has been explicit in that its membership is predicated on their political system of liberal democracies that have shared "values", that their people champion a "rules-based" international order. This membership criteria therefore naturally posits the People's Republic as the political "other" (along side Russia, Iran and North Korea) with a radically different ideology and values, a naturally "aggressive" entity with strategic bloodlust that aims to upset the "rules-based" international order (Mazza, 2023). Repeated often and enough times through international corporate and social media, the message is amplified across the world that Beijing is the party causing injury to peace and stability in the Asia–Pacific region. Thus, the strong voices emanating from the Quad countries cast China as the new "evil" empire, an irredentist one that is dissatisfied with the current post-1945 international system, hell bent on changing the status quo and destroying Western values and ways of lives.

While language has become more subtle over the years, this subtext is deeply embedded in the logic and script of the Quad narrative.

Observers have labelled the Quad as "timely", "imaginative", and "essential", "critical" amongst many positive ways. As a dialogue mechanism and defense institution, there is nothing wrong with making more friends and reinforcing relations with like-minded partners. In the era of Great Power rivalry, particularly when the conception of the dialogue is targeted at a particular country, the rewards reaped and costs would be different for the participating countries. Naturally, how one reacts to the emergence of the Quad certainly reflects a person's professional affiliation, nationality and political outlook. There is, of course, a degree of commonality if one speaks to the strategic community or diplomatic corps from the Global Right Quad countries. It would be difficult to find anyone within the Beltway think tanks in D. C. or in the allied capitals who would say anything different. Most of these institutions are, after all, related to or funded by national security or foreign policy establishments and are headed by former government officials. This is also true for those working in Canberra, Tokyo or other Asian countries that are nominally part of the San Francisco system. Likewise, the same sort of "official" but a contrarian narrative is found in Beijing or for that matter in Moscow. In the United States, Japan, India, Australia and China, saying anything contrarian openly the against country's position would risk the author being ostracised and branded publicly as a "traitor".

Beijing's reaction to the Global Right and Quad is also expected. China has angrily denounced the Quad as an anti-China platform, and there are muted discussions amongst Chinese strategists that the Quad is possibly the beginning of an Asian NATO aimed at China (Zhu, 2020). For Beijing, the narratives surrounding the Quad are simply beautiful rhetoric masking the US's containment policy, which is underpinned by the revival of Washington's Cold War politics to maintain its hegemony. Even as China understands that many regional countries are clearly disturbed by the rapidly changing balance of power in the region due to the rise of it's influence and capabilities, Beijing views this situation as no fault of its own and one that regional countries should get accustomed to.

Amidst all the denials, the "anti-China" mission of the Quad grouping is clear. The Quad is trying to expand its membership and reach by enacting Quad Plus, enticing other regional countries, such as Vietnam, New Zealand and South Korea, to participate in its activities (Panda, 2022). The members are also seeking new ways to expand its function through new initiatives and missions. Regardless of how the narrative has been spun or language toned down, there is hardly anyone in either camp who disagrees that, in essence, the Quad is aimed at China.

Chinese scholars have argued that the PRC's general foreign policy position has remained constant since Deng Xiaoping embarked on modernisation reforms. Beijing has primarily focused on meeting its own modernisation goals and has generally been risk-adverse in her strategic posture in order to maintain a favourable strategic environment free of conflict. China is therefore all for "peace". The Quad countries of course would vehemently disagree as their idea of regional "peace" would be very different from what the Chinese version. Naturally, the Quad of course would prefer that Beijing does not become assertive in any manner or form in her territorial disputes, whether land or maritime, and be acquiescent to the wishes of the Quad community. This of course is a non-starter for China. Beijing also has always preferred a peaceful strategic environment that is conducive for stable strategic relations with its neighbours, but today sees very little incentive to shy away from defending her territorial claims or political position over Taiwan in the face of increasing provocations by the United States.

When China talks about stability, it usually refers to the conditions that have enabled China to achieve its economic growth at the high growth rate that it has become accustomed to. It is the same conditions which continued Chinese modernisation is predicated upon, which in turn facilitates it's rapidly modernising military force. When the US and Japanese scholars talk about "stability", it inevitably refers to a situation where China should not "upset" the regional equilibrium that both Washington and Tokyo are used to in the 1970s and 1980s where Beijing's territorial claims, political dreams of reunification or becoming a middle-income country remain just a political aspiration. Increasingly, their perception and understanding of what "peace and stability" means in Asia are becoming divergent. For the United States and its allies, China's authoritarian political system with very opaque decision-making coupled with its exponentially growing power is now on the verge of creating a systemic change that might alter regional dynamics and political patterns they are unaccustomed to. It is however the fact that China is beginning to have clout, the capacity and the will to enact and enforce its aspirations that the Quad countries find so disturbing rather than China's ambitions. The trajectory of this systemic change, if left unchecked, might mean that a new world order may emerge, something that many in the

West and the developed world are very uncomfortable with. This discomfort, however, has not been translated into a very clear and concrete policy prior to 2012, even though the Asia–Pacific countries have been debating on the emergence of a "China threat" immediately after the collapse of the Soviet Union. The Quad 1.0 dissipated in 2007 because domestic politics, political leaders and the foreign policy outlook of the United States, India and Australia did not meet the conditions for its sustenance (Flitton, 2020). From 2012 onwards, there appeared to be a concerted movement spurred by the rise of conservative politicians across the world that prompted a toughened consensus on China. This book examines the rise of the global right regimes that have come to power with the election of Abe in Japan, Modi in India, Trump in the United States and Liberal Prime Ministers (Arbott, Turnbull and Morrison) in Australia, and how these leadership changes spurred by domestic and international politics continue to stoke regional tensions. The Great Power rivalry has now spurred a renewed and reinvigorated Cold War, as the old fault lines have reappeared. Russia, North Korea and China are banding together as the Ukraine War and the Israel-Hamas conflict rages on. The world it would appear is heading back to the future, where a renewed Cold War awaits. American politicians, officials and scholars have argued that only the United States is capable of leading the world towards a new world (whatever that might be) (Power 2021; Pottinger & Gallagher, 2024; Clinton 2020; Kagan 2021).

Aims and Objectives

This volume begins with the premise that the Cold War had, in fact, ended in Europe with the collapse of the USSR but not in Asia. Communist regimes in China, along with those in Vietnam, Laos and North Korea, had not only survived this catastrophic event but had, in fact, reformed their economies to take advantage of the opportunities offered by the globalised world of the 1990s. Regardless, these countries were prepared to work with the United States and their allies. The rise of the PRC had its roots in the 1972 strategic reproachment facilitated by Nixon and Kissinger's grand strategy, which in effect allowed the PRC to switch sides to the US camp against the USSR. After China emerged from the disastrous lost decades of the Great Leap Forward and Cultural Revolution, the Chinese people rallied behind Deng Xiaoping in 1978, who argued that China had to make drastic changes to survive. China's opening-up and economic reforms have enabled Beijing to ditch the Soviet-style command economy and adopt market-centric practices. Overtime, China had in essence became a "de facto" (rather than de jure) member of the San Francisco system, by joining the wider political and economic network of the United States with the major economies of Asia–Pacific region, including Japan, South Korea, Hong Kong, Singapore and New Zealand. Likewise, Vietnam and, to a lesser extent, Laos joined the economic reform bandwagon. China's participation helped not only the United States overcome the challenge of the Soviet threat but also helped East Asian countries become more prosperous. By the turn of the century, China had become so successful in her capitalistic reforms that she now threatened the hegemonic status of the United States, accentuating the geopolitical tensions towards full fledged Great Power rivalry.

This volume presents an introspective assessment of the conditions that have led to the increasingly bifurcated world we live in today. The emergence of conservative regimes in the United States, Japan, India and Australia has raised questions about the assumptions and policies made by preceding governments with regards to economic growth and national security, as well as the respective country's China policy. To answer these questions, it is necessary to examine the historical, political and economic factors that contributed to the rise of conservatism in these nations and to assess the impact of conservative governance on their foreign policies, particularly with regard to China. By analysing the interplay between political leadership and domestic and international dynamics, a comprehensive understanding of the role of conservative regimes in shaping China's policies can be achieved.

Utilising three traditional Waltzian "images of analysis", the book explains the conditions that prompted the United States, Japan, India and Australia to securitise their relations with their trading partner, China, over the past decade (2012–2022). Against the backdrop of rapidly growing disparities and increasingly untenable political-economic conditions, this decade witnessed the emergence of a populist, right-wing, conservative political movement on a global scale. China's rapid economic ascent, coupled with its ability to cultivate asymmetrical influence with its trading partners, intensified anxieties as it closed the gap in capabilities with the United States, further exacerbating insecurities in the international system and at home in the Quad countries. This set the stage for political figures such as Abe, Modi, Trump and Morrison to capitalise on the perceived China threat to gain political power and prominence. This book contends that, beneath the veneer of advocating for democracy and freedom, these leaders share notable similarities in their political ideologies and methodologies with China's Xi Jinping. While their rhetoric often emphasises the promotion of rights and values in their respective narratives, the reality is a deep-seated realpolitik struggle for dominance in the Indo-Pacific region. Paradoxically, this situation has arisen because of China's remarkable success in becoming a de facto (rather than de jure) member of the San Francisco system in the second half of the Cold War through a very successful adaptation of capitalistic reforms. The adjustments that are being brought about by the Quad leaders today are actually a collective attempt to stoke conditions for the Cold War to re-emerge so that structurally the PRC can be isolated if not banished from the San Francisco system. A significant takeaway is that unless the Quad countries can recalibrate their relations and adapt to a significantly more influential China, the region's insecurities are likely to intensify as the conditions fuelling nationalism persist and globalisation becomes increasingly bifurcated, leading to a possible collapse of the San Francisco system itself. This is on top of the many challenges that this 75 years old institution faces (Hara, 2001). This is a humble addition to a string of interesting and strong discussions on the emergence of a new Cold War (Christensen, 2021; Mueller, 2004; Steinbruner & Lewis, 2002; Kupchan, 2023; Abrams, 2022; Furuoka, 2002; Ash, 2020; Hack, 2009; Wang, 2023; Kim et al., 2023; Lebrow, 1994; Leonard, 2023; Friedberg, 2020; Layne, 2020; Koh, 2023).

THEORETICAL FRAMEWORK

Kenneth Waltz's seminal work "Man, the State, and War: A Theoretical Analysis" (1959 [2018]) is a significant contribution to the field of international relations theory, which aims to explain the root causes of international conflict and war by focusing on three levels of analysis. In this work, Waltz presents a three-tier theoretical framework for analysing the behaviour of states, which includes (i) the individual leadership of each country, (ii) the prevailing domestic politics and circumstances and (iii) the international relations of each country in relation to China during the period under study. The adoption of this theoretical framework determines the methodology used in the research, which involves scrutinising the leadership, domestic politics and international relations of the

Quad countries in each chapter. Ultimately, the rise of conservatism and the Quadrilateral Security Dialogue (Quad) between the United States, Japan, India and Australia is a clear result of the dialectical relationship between these factors, as much as the publicly stated reasons for China's "assertiveness" or "aggressiveness".

The primary objective of the first image analysis (focusing on the country's leader) is to investigate the leadership of Shinzo Abe in Japan, Narendra Modi in India and Donald Trump in the United States, as well as the tenures of conservative leaders Tony Abbott, Malcolm Turnbull and Scott Morrison in Australia. These leaders have played a significant role in solidifying their respective countries' political agendas, promoting anti-China sentiment, and working together diplomatically to advance security initiatives, such as the Quad. This study aims to address the following key questions: under what circumstances did these leaders rise to power? What factors prompted them to adopt a drastically different China policy from their predecessors and how successful have they been? Are these leaders driven by ideological or realpolitik considerations? In examining the role of China in each leader's domestic political context, this book provides an analysis of how it has influenced the country's foreign policy. By utilising a combination of qualitative and quantitative evidence, the project will explore long-term strategic planning for each country's China policy and its impact on the emergence of the Global Right collective and world politics. Ultimately, this study seeks to shed light on the relationship between these leaders' thinking about China and their respective countries' foreign policies, as well as the implications for global politics.

In Waltz's theoretical framework, the second image focuses on the study of domestic politics. This image presents a set of enquiries, including: what were the dominant dynamics and factors (bureaucratic, intra-and inter-party politics and public sentiments) that impacted the nation's framing of international political issues and domestic priorities? What were the broader political processes in each country that facilitated the rise of conservatism and emergence of right-wing charismatic leaders? How was China perceived and debated by the elite and the public in each country? In this volume, the second image analysis focuses on the development of internal political dynamics such as intra- and inter-party interactions, as these are the primary channels through which parliamentary or congressional politics are played out. Since the initiation of economic reforms by the People's Republic of China (PRC) in 1978, the United States, Japan, Australia and India have established varying degrees of functional relationships, if not amicable ties, with Communist China. Political leaders in the United States, Japan, Australia and even India have spent much of the late twentieth century persuading their citizens that economic cooperation with China is crucial to their national interests. How did the politics in each country evolve to the point where China is now perceived as the primary security threat to American, Japanese, Australian and Indian nations in an era of heightened capitalistic division and transnational insecurity? What role did social and traditional media play in this, and to what extent is a country's foreign policy influenced by special interest groups, such as the military-industrial complex and the national security establishment? Is this really about defending freedom from communism or is it more about rekindling Cold War tensions to gain domestic political advantages and realpolitik goals?

The third image in the Waltzian framework focuses on the nature of the International System. The emergence of China as a dominant power in the international system presents a significant strategic challenge for Quad countries, as the disparity in capabilities between these countries and China has narrowed significantly. The management of China has long been an important but contentious issue, but it was not until 2017 when the consensus to confront China emerged. From a neorealist perspective, Australia, Japan and India appeared to align with the United States to balance against China, adjusting against the PRC's growing power *and* potential threats. The narratives of "like-minded" countries banding together based on certain values suggest that identity politics and ideology played a critical role (Lemann), but at the same time, Japan's efforts' in cajoling the other Quad countries and the reinvigorated alliance politics decisively shaped this consensus. In short, the analysis in this image considers questions such as What were the external geopolitical developments that prompted the Quad countries to come together so decisively? Was it because Beijing has now grown to a point that would yield more political, economic and strategic influence to rewrite the rules of the international system? Or was it because China was directly impinging on their national interests and intruding into their sphere of influence by cultivating asymmetrical economic relations with their neighbours? Or could it be because China's growing strength and ties with key members of the San Francisco system undermine the ability of the system to act against China should the need arise? The third image focuses on the analysis of individual Quad countries' strategic thinking vis-à-vis the external environment. A key explanation offered by this "third image" is that even though there was relative "peace" in the era after the collapse of the USSR, the prevailing concern states have with systemic mechanisms and national interests never went away. As Waltz (2000) argued even though the factors that many scholars have argued are changing international relations have expanded (i.e. through the spread of democracy, increased interdependency and increasing adaptation of institutions), these in themselves do not constituted evidence that States would always subordinate their interests to international concerns. Here, the four Quad states are actively responding to China's changing role in the international system to pro-actively "balance" the PRC. In this imagery, the "intent" or "desires" of China really does not matter.

Main Arguments

Domestic Politics and the Rise of Global Right Agenda

First, after decades of intense globalised economic growth, structural inequalities and ills associated with the capitalist economic system have emerged in China and most other Quad countries. The relative high Gini coefficient data reflects the inequality in the various countries concerned. See Table 1.1. While the specific conditions and challenges for each country might be different, most of the ills (such as stagnant wages, inflation, pollution and environmental degradation) had a disproportionate impact on the burgeoning middle and working classes in these societies. As exploitation increases, the size of the working class as well as those in the middle class that feel dissatisfaction with the status quo grows exponentially. Today, even though many elites would deny it, the living standards of a significant number of their fellow citizens have fallen, even if economic indicators might show that the economy has grown. Even as national elites often justify their agenda with politically correct and progressive narratives, a plurality of factors (deep-seated institutional interests, enduring prejudices and growing economic disparity) have come together to ensure a surge in distrust of the international, globalist political agenda of liberal elites. Domestically, most of these developed West have seen an influx of immigrants from the third world, including China. Naturally, it goes without saying that there is a strong undertone of racism in these politics. Radical nationalism has adhesive powers beyond imagination, often bringing together disparate groups that might otherwise never be related in real life. Cold War alliance politics and

16   V. TEO

the all encompassing competition between two camps become once again important frames of reference for the global right conservative politicians.

This has engendered nostalgia for "better good old times" of a past golden age where life was slower, kinder and more affordable. During such times of dissatisfaction and insecurity, nationalism often becomes the

Table 1.1   Economic Indicators (2012–2022) for Quad Countries and China

Country	Year	GDP (Current US$)	GDP per Capita (PPP)	Average growth rate (%)	Unemployment rate (%)	Gini coefficient	Inflation rate (%)	Govt. debt (% of GDp)
United States	2012	$16.2T	$52,984	2.2%	7.9%	41.7	2.1%	102.6%
	2014	$17.5T	$55,982	2.4%	6.2%	41.4	1.6%	105.2%
	2016	$18.6T	$57,466	1.6%	4.9%	41.3	1.3%	106.8%
	2018	$20.5T	$65,280	2.9%	3.9%	41.4	2.4%	108.7%
	2020	$21.4T	$68,309	−3.4%	8.1%	41.4	1.2%	127.1%
	2022	$22.7T	$75,271	2.3%	3.6%	41.4	3.5%	129.1%
Japan	2012	$6.2T	$36,484	1.5%	4.3%	32.1	0.0%	198.7%
	2014	$4.8T	$37,652	−0.1%	3.6%	32.2	2.8%	203.6%
	2016	$4.9T	$311,958	1.0%	3.1%	32.5	0.5%	218.4%
	2018	$5.0T	$43,118	0.3%	2.4%	32.9	1.0%	231.3%
	2020	$4.9T	$44,587	−4.6%	2.8%	32.9	0.0%	256.9%
	2022	$4.9T	$45,565	1.0%	2.6%	32.9	2.5%	263.1%
Australia	2012	$1.5T	$42,822	3.4%	5.2%	34.9	1.8%	27.6%
	2014	$1.4T	$45,867	2.6%	6.1%	34.6	1.5%	31.4%
	2016	$1.2T	$48,407	2.8%	5.7%	34.6	1.3%	35.6%
	2018	$1.4T	$53,818	2.8%	5.3%	34.4	1.9%	41.4%
	2020	$1.4T	$54,760	−2.4%	6.9%	34.4	0.9%	55.1%
	2022	$1.7T	$56,966	2.6%	3.5%	34.4	3.0%	58.6%
India	2012	$1.8T	$5,167	5.1%	5.6%	35.4	10.2%	67.1%
	2014	$2.0T	$5,795	7.4%	5.4%	35.7	6.6%	68.5%
	2016	$2.3T	$6,700	8.3%	5.0%	35.7	4.9%	68.9%
	2018	$2.7T	$7,161	6.8%	5.3%	35.7	3.9%	69.6%
	2020	$2.6T	$6,946	−6.6%	8.0%	35.7	6.2%	74.1%
	2022	$3.1T	$8,358	6.1%	8.0%	35.7	6.8%	80.4%
China	2012	$8.5T	$10,429	7.9%	4.5%	42.5	2.6%	35.6%
	2014	$10.4T	$13,135	7.3%	4.7%	43.5	1.8%	41.6%
	2016	$11.2T	$14,541	6.8%	4.6%	44.1	2.1%	45.8%
	2018	$13.6T	$16,097	6.6%	4.9%	46.5	2.1%	50.6%
	2020	$14.7T	$16,842	2.3%	5.0%	46.5	2.4%	61.7%
	2022	$17.7T	$19,338	6.6%	5.1%	46.5	2.2%	64.3%

Source World Bank Data

sole political currency to assuage and rally the nation. Populist conservative rhetoric becomes like a warm blanket in the depths of winter, providing the emotional support across a disparate number of groups across the political spectrum. The coalescence of popular opinion in favour of conservative politics cannot be achieved without the mechanisms of online and social media. The transnational influence of websites and apps such as Facebook, YouTube and instant messaging software such as WhatsApp has united people across nations to feed content according to online algorithms. During times of national crisis or political challenges, the nationalist fervour tends to be swept up and aided by social media apps. Likewise, media, both traditional and online, play a reinforcing role in shaping popular and public opinion.

The rise of conservative politics that capitalise on such sentiments is a hallmark of the politics of Quad countries over the past decade or so. In the Quad countries, political discourse frequently identifies China as the primary or secondary cause of various problems related to past policies. These issues include economic stagnation, a decline in manufacturing industries, unemployment, loss of competitiveness, lack of R&D momentum, environmental degradation, inflation and diminished economic and diplomatic influence. Compared to the rise of Chinese influence domestically and internationally through trade and finance, the picture becomes even more frightening. Thus Conservative leaders in Quad countries argue that the key to national rejuvenation and enhancement of national interests almost dwells exclusively on the rolling back of an open, globalist agenda and this often translates into the cutting back on international commitments and the eschewing of international cooperation (apart with certain "like-minded" friends). Along with the help of certain segments of domestic actors usually associated the national security establishment, there is also an overwhelming push by the Conservatives to dominate the national security discourse. This enables the global right politicians to rally support, pacify the "deep state" actors and sideline their political opponents by making them look like traitors to the nation if they disagreed with their agenda. Externally, the grouping's key strategy is to isolate China and prevent third parties from affiliating, trading, or accepting China's advances in any form or manner through the promotion of a discourse. For instance, the "vaccine" diplomacy waged against China's offer of vaccines is a good example. The emphasis is often on the defending of "values" and democracy from China, but ironically during the period under study, the Quad countries themselves are in some ways degrading into more authoritarian and less democratic ways instead. The reality is that stoking competition with China often harms, rather than comprehensively benefitting each nation's material interests. While domestic developments are likely to spur the Quad's institutional development through innovative new schemes, the underlying difference in the Quad countries' own relations with China is likely to offset the Quad's overall effectiveness in achieving more security for these countries.

Emergence of Charismatic Illiberal Leaders

The emergence of "strong" charismatic leaders has been facilitated, by current domestic conditions. Despite differences in their narratives, demeanours and political styles, there are striking similarities in the political methodology of leaders such as Trump, Abe, Modi, Morrison and Xi. Even though these Conservative politicians' daily discourse is peppered with references to "freedom", "democracy" and "values", they political practices leaned towards illiberalism and autocracy. Additionally, these Conservative elites often disguise their political ambitions and personal policy preferences by presenting their decisions and policies in line with the pursuit of national interests which are often narrowly defined. This of course is not unique to them, but their tendency to prioritise personal and/or party interests under the guise of the exigencies of national interests should not go unnoticed. All of these conservative leaders utilised imageries of China for their domestic political methodology, often eschewing decades of cordial relationships built by their predecessors with China. The justification, of course, is a variant of the explanation that the character of China has changed for the worse (more aggressive, scheming repressive, authoritarian, irredentist, dishonest, ambitious, etc.) and has therefore become inimical to their country's national interests, regional peace and global order. These Conservative leaders were therefore obliged to "stop" Chinese schemes, in order to protect their nation and preserve their interests. The narratives of these leaders thus overwhelmingly focus on "national security" and reinforce the message of the importance of working with their traditional security partner, the United States.

Amongst all leaders, Shinzo Abe stands out as the prime example of an influential conservative leader exerting tremendous influence by riding on "anti-China" sentiments. In the decade before (2000–2010), Shinzo Abe's predecessor, Junichiro Koizumi, achieved great electoral success with his carefully crafted public image, fiery-nationalist rhetoric and tough stance against China. Abe successfully emulated Koizumi's approach, paying particular attention to his image management and public rhetoric, resulting in unprecedented political longevity in his second term in a country known for frequent changes in Prime Ministers. Abe's tactics also served as an inspiration for leaders such as Modi, Trump and the Australian conservatives in their respective political careers. For a leader such as Shinzo Abe, his personal beliefs, family legacy and formative experiences truly inform his worldview. He genuinely believes in what he preaches, given the environment he grew up in and his experiences as a younger politician. Narendra Modi unlike Abe did not grow up in a privileged background, but rather is similar in profile to Shinzo Abe's Chief Cabinet Secretary and successor Suga Yoshihide. Modi spent a large part of his formative years working in India's underground opposition and most of his life in grassroots politics. He was a political fixer well-versed in retail politics across Indian states and was for a better part of his life an ardent Hindu nationalist. Modi understood the importance of using religion and ethnicity in political mobilisation in his conservatism and put it to good use. Unlike Abe, China did not figure hugely in his political methodology until after his 2014 election, when he realised he needed to redefine the role of China in his political strategy and alter India's strategic choices ahead. The same can be said for Donald Trump. Trump was not a lifelong Conservative, having been affiliated with the Democratic Party earlier in his career. In fact, in his earlier interviews (available online), he only expressed critical views on Japan regarding how the Japanese were ripping Americans off. Nonetheless, Trump as Presidential candidate gained prominence attacking the "establishment" position, arguing how the Democratic Party had sold out Americans by striking deals with Beijing. In essence, Trump blamed China for a slate of domestic problems that afflicted contemporary America. His cure to "Make America Great Again" of course was his trade and tech war against China within months of taking office. Of the four Quad powers, the Australia Prime Ministers present the most curious case, given that Australia has very little quarrel with China. In succession, Tony Abbott, Malcolm Turnbull and later on Scott Morrison adopted an increasing tough posture towards China both within and outside of Australia. Motivated by conservative ideology and their traditional proclivity to side with the United Kingdom and the United States, their "tough" posture is underlined not only by calculations against their domestic political opponents who favoured cooperation and collaboration with China and Chinese-linked businesses. In reality, these leaders all have their own political agenda and calculus vis-à-vis domestic politics and found a winning formula in combining nationalism with xenophobia in their campaigning methodology.

In terms of foreign policy, these Quad Global Right elites often eschew broad international cooperation and lean towards alliance politics. The primary strategy of Quad countries is to identify China as a strategic and existential threat. By positioning themselves as defenders of freedom, these politicians garnered significant public support for their stance on China. Beneath this veneer, it is evident that domestic protectionism, realpolitik considerations and alliance politics (Christensen, 2011) are the primary motivators of their actions. The political longevity of conservative, charismatic leaders in the Quad countries has greatly influenced both the tone and substance of domestic political debate and international politics and diplomacy. Initially, the tough talk and political rhetoric were intended to gain political capital and enhance electoral success, but it has now led to a downward security spiral between these countries and China. This has also resulted in the rejuvenation of the US-led alliance in the Asia–Pacific region.

Great Power Rivalry and Systemic Change

The notion of a China threat has been a topic of intense discussion since the fall of the Berlin Wall and the collapse of the Soviet Union. The victory of the United States over the Soviet Union was largely facilitated by the Nixon administration's enlistment of China to confront the Soviet Union along its vast 6759 km border. The American rapprochement and normalisation of relations with China was a significant but understated contribution to Cold War literature. In essence, China was an unspoken but de facto ally of the United States and was integrated into the San Francisco system as a key economic partner. This allowed the United States not only to surmount the challenge posed by the Soviet Union but also helped advert the economic challenge posed by Japan in the 1980s. As Chinese economic reforms progressed, they also enhanced the role of the United States' economic strategy around the world. Due to the exigencies of the Cold War, outstanding issues such as Taiwan, North Korea and even the dispute in South China were therefore established and set aside as each country focused on their development. US–China relations were also harmonious, largely because there was a huge gap in strategic capability between them. Today, with China's rise, the capability gap between the PRC and the United States is narrowing at an alarming pace (at least from Washington's perspective). This is evidenced by a number of indicators (such as projected GDP growth, force and power projection capabilities and manufacturing processes, especially in high-tech sectors in AI and telecommunications to diplomatic sway). The size and clout of China's economy, as well as her tradition of working with countries not in the US orbit, ironically increased her global prominence in Africa, Latin America and the Middle East.

From the perspective of Waltz's third image, whether China intends to displace the United States is not so important. Most US strategists and analysts take this as a given and regard China as the single power capable and willing to challenge its global supremacy, and in the process creating an inordinate amount of strategic stress for the United States (Chua, 2020). China's rise cannot be anything but a systemic threat to the structural dominance of the United States in the international system. There is plenty of evidence to suggest that the US is in the decline internationally (Cooley & Nexon, 2020). The determination of US strategic planners to "contain" China and helm the Chinese into the first island chain therefore continues to be the dominant thinking in Washington (Clinton, 2020). This has resulted in the United States lobbying her allies—Japan, South Korea, Taiwan and the Philippines—as well as Quad partners such as India (Babones, 2020; De Castro, 2014; Clinton 2020; Curran 2018) and South Korea to confront China. This has become particularly important as the US power gap vis-à-vis China (and Russia) has diminished.

The fact that China's transformation has been much quicker and more comprehensive than what the United States and her allies have predicted is creating a serious security dilemma for Washington. If the balance of power theorists is to be believed, the United States and her allies would need not only balance China but also work to ensure that China would never be in a position to be influential enough to pose a systemic threat. It is no longer just about keeping China in check but to comprehensively set back Chinese developmental goals across the board. From Beijing's perspective, her "threat" to the United States is a direct consequence of her development, and consequently, it is almost impossible for any Chinese leader to agree to accept the "rolling" back or the "capping" capping of China's rise. China and the United States are in a classical security dilemma, as they begin to define their relationship in competitive rather than cooperative terms. The globalised world that we are supposed to live in appears to become increasingly bifurcated as US–China bilateral competition is taking a toll on the relationship countries have with each of the giants. The Quad 2.0 is a small but significant move as the United States, Australia, Japan and India have taken significant steps to "securitise" their political and economic relationship with China in the period discussed (Singh, 2020; Stavridis, 2021; Dobell 2019; Madhav, 2020; Curran 2018; Chanlett-Avery, 2018; Clarke, 2021; Jaishankar, 2017; Huong, 2019; Lalwani, 2019; Dreyer, 2021). Although Australia has somewhat softened her stance (upon the Labour party's return to power under Prime Minister Albanese) (Tyler, 2020), the United States, Japan (Tsutsui, 2020) and India appeared to continue with the Trump era policies insofar as China is concerned. This institutionalisation of the Quad is, of course, lauded as a positive development by those who see it vital to contain China, but in reality, the main effect would only accentuate security competition in the region (Rudd, 2021). This security competition is increasingly expanding to resemble the emergence of a new Cold War bloc as Quad countries do their utmost to entice target countries such as the Philippines, South Korea or even New Zealand to join Quad just as Russia, China and North Korea are consolidating their alliance.

China's Resistance

Just because the Global Right is able to come up with an agenda to contain China does not mean they will succeed, for the simple reason China is not a static entity. The global right's collective calls to "decouple" and reduce trade with China did have an impact on China, as demand from the developed West was drastically reduced, leading to very difficult economic conditions across China. Coupled with the impact of the Covid pandemic, the PRC probably faced one of the most onerous periods in decades of economic growth. There is however a significant opportunity for the Chinese leadership. This period has allowed the Chinese government a period of "calm" to address many of the challenges within and "reset" some of the issue areas that are central to their concerns. From raging disparity to runaway inflation to the restive problems in Xinjiang and Hong Kong, the turn of international events has provided a relief valve from the pressure built up over the years. Many past policy failures can now be attributed to external causes (such as factory closures in

Guangdong and the bursting of the real estate bubble that has plagued the Chinese economy). Unfortunately, contrary to the expectations of the Global Right, China's economy has not spiralled out of control.

Beijing has shown that it would not flinch in the face of threat, and if anything, she had doubled her resolve to resist the Global Right as strongly as possible. First, as China has become a critical player in the global economy, Beijing has already built asymmetrical relations and a disproportionate influence with many countries, including the United States. As the recent (and ongoing) Trade War has shown, the United States cannot confront China without inflicting pain on herself, her allies and the wider region. Even with the limited "de-risking" (the "light" version of forced decoupling proposed in the Trump era), there is evidence that the United States has not achieved the desired outcomes. The deficit that the United States wanted to reduce actually increased. The deficit with China in 2022 was greater than that in 2017 when Trump became President (Huang and Slosberg, 2023). The overall deficit for the United States had increased from $ 593.08 billion in 2018 to $ 861.71 billion in 2021, indicating that the United States was importing more even though direct imports from China might have been reduced. The tariffs from the trade war have led to an increase in the cost of imported goods, leading to higher prices for consumers and businesses, both of which contribute to the basket of factors that create inflation in the United States. Global supply chains adjusted to the tariffs and imports from China actually rebounded, particularly if we take into account exports done via third countries. The broad impact is felt across the world via the global economy as global supply chains disrupted along with adjustments in economic strategies, investment decisions, and trading routes. To say that there have been very few such "shocks" in the global economic system is an understatement. Even though the United States and its allies are now adjusting their global trading alliances based on identity politics, it is unclear whether the balance of power in economics and trade is tilting to them decisively.

Collectively, the Quad is formidable, as it consists of the United States, the largest economy, Japan's third-largest economy, and India, the most populous nation with a fast-growing economy in the world. Despite this, China's manufacturing capabilities remain critical for Quad countries. China fills an important gap in terms of meeting what these economies are unable to or unwilling to manufacture. The United States and her allies realised this in the aftermath of their calls to "decouple" from

China's economy, and consequently, the politically correct term is now known as "de-risking" shows a certain acknowledgement of this fact. China's Renminbi is slowly and steadily internationalising, and Beijing has steadily reduced its holdings of US Treasury debts while increasing its stockpile of gold. China's economy appears to be growing, and selected industries, such as the Electric Vehicle and telecommunications industries, are doing very well. Even the semiconductor industry which has been severely impacted by US efforts to restrict chip-making machines to China, appears to be growing stronger by the day. China has increased its trade with other regions in the world, notably Russia, the Middle East, Southeast Asia and Latin America and this has put considerable pressure on the United States as well. It is an understatement to say that there have been very few instances of such "shocks" in the global economic system. As the United States and her allies adjust their global trading alliance based on identity politics, it is uncertain whether the balance of power in economics and trade is shifting decisively in their favour.

Second, while the PRC is not a global military power like the United States, the Chinese have managed to build their capabilities to the extent that it has now narrowed the gap between themselves and the United States in the Western Pacific. Beijing has now "pockets" of excellence, notably in hypersonic missile technology, naval and ariel asset construction and projection power. China also appears to be pulling ahead in the space race. This would include China's new navigation system Beidou, its rival to the Global Positioning Satellite Technology (GPS), and the space infrastructure it is currently building. Although China's nuclear arsenal comprises a small fraction of the United States, it is still capable of balancing the US strategic arsenal with its delivery systems that can accurately deliver its payload efficiently and accurately across the United States. China has also built up its naval capabilities and missile forces that would allow it to mount a credible challenge to US carrier groups entering the first island chain, even though the PLA is largely an untested military, apart from its limited skirmishes with Vietnam, Korea and India. This is not to suggest that China has decisively better capabilities than the United States. Far from this, China has no certainty of outright victory if it chooses to engage in direct hostility with the United States in distant waters, especially if the latter is being helped by Japan and South Korea. What the Chinese are capable of, however, is their ability to project power overwhelmingly into the two principal areas of strategic concern to Beijing and Washington, namely the Taiwan Straits and the South China

Sea. The United States no longer has overwhelming advantages, as it has for the better part of the last century.

What is also clear, however, is that the Cold War fronts of Taiwan, Korea and territorial disputes in the South China Seas have been reinvigorated. The Global Right is now increasing its rhetoric and policy focus on these Cold War fronts, articulating that it is necessary to remilitarise to defend against North Korea, Taiwan and the Philippines from Communist China. Beijing has a geographical advantage over the United States in the region. This is not even taking into consideration that for their own reasons, Russia and North Korea might step in to help China. As an economic juggernaut and a political giant right on their doorstep, confronting the Chinese in their own backyard is a no-win proposition for any Asian country, US ally or not. The problem with the global right government's determination to reinforce the US alliance creates a security dilemma for both China and themselves, particular since a very tight alliance is inherently dangerous for partners as there is often little room to manoeuvre (Christensen, 2011).

Thirdly, the rhetoric of the Global Right regimes in Quad countries does not currently hold much sway with other countries in the international system. While the European community may be more receptive to the Global Rights' claims of moral superiority, many countries in the Middle East, Latin America and Africa remain sceptical. The United States' stated goals of defending freedom and democracy or preserving a "Free and Open" Indo-Pacific have not been enough to overcome the counter-narrative that US interventions are primarily motivated by self-interest. Even in the Asia–Pacific region, there is evidence to suggest that many people in staunch US allies such as Taiwan and Japan have increasingly expressed doubt about the credibility of the United States (Kirshner, 2021; Kagan, 2021; Mainichi Shimbun, 2023), and across the board, there is a growing desire across East and Southeast Asia for the governments not to allow the United States not to drag the region into conflict with China. This is not only because of these countries' distaste for large scale strategic adventurism that will come at the cost of development, but also because of the nature of authoritarian regimes that are in power (Hutt, 2021). There is also the question of how various electorates are becoming more savvy as the population becomes more educated and wary of global developments. Various opinion polls conducted in Taiwan in 2023 revealed that most Taiwanese do not believe that the United

States would actively fight for Taiwan in the event of a Chinese invasion. Even in Japan, where attitudes towards the US–Japan alliance are deeply reverential and the public opinion of China is at an all-time low, there is a sense of unease about US saber rattling and military posture in Asia and beyond. This means that, for the most part, countries in the region might pay diplomatic lip-service and make political gestures, to maintain cordial relations with the Americans, most will remain cautious about fully challenging China without carefully considering its potential consequences. After all, for developing countries, economic development is a far more pressing concern than the promotion of freedom and democracy. Consequently, the narrative of needing to "balance" China is now slowly and surely taking an additional dimension: there is every necessity to "restrain" the United States and Japan to prevent an Asian Ukraine situation from happening.

For Washington, Beijing's "corrosive" effect in various regions and on her allies' unwavering support is clear. The San Francisco system that Washington put in place in 1951 is at a crossroads because the cost of challenging China is particularly high. The Quad arrangement was supposed to ensure that there was a "hard-core" inner cycle of states that would band together and reinforce the San Francisco system. While Australia and Japan are allied with the United States, India is not. The Quad would enable India to be roped in, and in the future, perhaps states such as Vietnam, New Zealand and the Philippines. This not only provides legitimacy to the grouping but also in effect could potentially help overcome the regional reluctance precisely because smaller regional states would not be willing to partake in any anti-China alliance. This phenomenon already manifested itself in Philippines during the rein of Rodrigo Duterte (Periez, 2016). Unfortunately, from Beijing's perspective, intra-regional concerns (regardless of whether it is coming from Japan, the Philippines, or other actors) are now subsumed under and viewed through the lens of US–China relations. Beijing would interpret any moves by the Philippines in the South China Sea as coming from Washington rather than Manila (Fravel, 2011), or for that matter, any policy by the DPP ruling party as Washington-sponsored actions. This may or may not be accurate, but insofar as China is concerned, such an interpretation would be "correct". Beijing is also convinced that Japanese strategic developments are sure signs of a militarist resurgence led by the LDP elites "auto-cruising" on an Abe-set agenda.

Deep-seeded insecurities, misguided mutual perceptions and increased cross-linking of issues would only stimulate a downward political spiral in Asia. This also presents a security dilemma that disrupts the fragile strategic balance that has anchored stable US–China relations since 1972. Historically the confrontational and collaborative tendencies of Sino-US relations have been cyclical, but today it is looking like the "trough" of the downward cycle of this confrontation is going to be deeper and longer than any time before. The world is approaching a dangerous tipping point, where both the United States and China perceive an over the horizon "critical" threshold where they might be defeated in their rivalry. The United States fears that it would lose its unrivalled global and regional leadership position, while Beijing dreads that its storied growth miracle would end up with China being caught in the middle-income trap perpetually rather than the vision laid out in the Chinese Dream. Countries in the region must prepare for a prolonged period of intensifying strategic competition between the United States and China for the foreseeable future. The key to overcoming crisis and international challenges lie in the ability of states to take precautions and plan ahead (Fukuyama, 2020).

Cold War Redux

What does this mean for regional and international security? China's first line of defence is diplomatic. China's strategy to deal with the Global Right in the Quad countries has been to ridicule the Quad as a Cold War institution designed to contain China's legitimate rise in order to preserve the hegemony and imperialistic system that the Americans had built and achieved after the war. The United States is deeply committed to contain China's rise and neutralise PRC's ascendance before it becomes strong enough to challenge. In order to preserve its hegemonic position, the US-Japanese strategy is to reinstitute the Cold War politics by identifying China as its principal challenger and reinvigorate its alliances by labelling the effort as an ideological and normative struggle to preserve democracy, freedom and human rights. Washington is desperately keen to prevent her allies from "defecting" (or become neutral) and other states from interacting, trading and indirectly "helping" China. The key to doing this is to prevent any change in the status quo in East Asia, including stopping any process that would strengthen China domestically or boost its status globally. This narrative has unfortunately not succeeded in areas such as Middle East, Latin America, Africa and not even in Southeast Asia. China's BRI, trading and development-focused orientation has been helpful here. More importantly, it is because of the attitude towards US policies towards various issues that have created difficulties for the Americans themselves. Unfortunately, as the United States intensify her efforts to reinforce this her strategy manoeuvres in Ukraine, South China Sea, Taiwan and Philippines would further fuel Sino-Russian strategic cooperation. If regional countries are not careful, Asia and Europe will find their security circumstances deteriorate further.

This book is an introspective study of why conservatism has arisen in the Quad countries (the United States, Japan, India and Australia) by looking at the changes in political leadership and domestic politics within and external strategic environment faced by these countries. Utilising the Waltzian three-tier analysis, the book argues that it is likely that the Cold War will be reinvigorated going forward as the United States and her allies will reinforce the existing bilateral alliance structure and build new ones such as Quad, where extra-regional players are invited to partake in the security discussions and potentially reinforce the existing security architecture. The rise of the global right Conservative governments and the development of the Quad would like to spur rather than deter China's military buildup, strengthen China–Russia cooperation and provoke greater reactions from China. Even as the Global Right attempts to institutionalise the Quad from mere dialogue into a military-economic entity that ostensibly upholds "free and open" Indo-Pacific, it would essentially still be more symbolic than real in nature for a few reasons, the principal being that the cost of outright confrontation with China is too high. Other than that, no other nation other than the United States has the capability and interest to do so. China's second line of defense of course is to speed up her military modernisation in accordance with the famous Maoist maxim that "Political power grows out of the barrel of a gun". There is a certain truth in that US preponderance in the Western Pacific stems principally from her military might, and the Chinese have been working towards fulfilling this aspiration for the past few decades.

The next logical stage of Quad's development is to expand membership by including more members such as the Philippines and Vietnam. There is therefore much discussion of whether Quad is an Asian NATO or, in reality, an eastward expansion of NATO. The Quad would provide a new layer of security enmeshment between Americans' Asian allies and external ones, and some have argued that this "mini-lateralism" would prove to be an extremely positive development. This in effect plants the seeds of building a larger network that would supplement the existing San Francisco Treaty. While this is not a formal arrangement, there is increasing evidence that US allies in Europe (Germany, France and the UK) are starting to adopt an Indo-Pacific strategy and are taking part in naval sorties and exercises in the Western Pacific. These extra-regional countries have mostly also adopted a common position vis-à-vis China in the period concerned. US allies such as Japan in the region are also expanding their footprint to engage in Europe: Japan is beginning to attend NATO meetings; South Korea has sold 50 KF21 Borame fighter jets and 1600 tanks to Poland and takes on a more proactive approach to further its value as a US ally.

All these activities might look like a good idea at first, as the San Francisco system could actually co-opt extra-regional actors to "balance" or "contain" China. This ensures that the US hub-and-spoke system which forms the basis of the region's architecture, will function properly with extra-regional support that helps counter balance the impact of a rising China. Roping in potential new members such as South Korea, Taiwan, the Philippines and possibly even Vietnam, into a loose military coalition that would see coordination in the event of a China contingency amongst them. As it expands, the Quad could even become more "legitimate" in the eyes of the international community and provide a mechanism to socialise various States that it is a "normal" turn of events and that its activities are perfectly innocuous. In an ideal world or a "make-believe" one, the imagery painted by Western narratives could become true.

In reality, how this might play out is not certain, particularly in a world ravaged by the COVID-19 pandemic and plagued by geopolitical tensions and wars in Europe and the Middle East. The security dilemma faced by both the Global Right (Quad) countries and China is creating echo chambers in each capital, where moderate voices are down out by the shrill nationalistic calls often dressed in liberal rhetoric (e.g. defending freedoms). It is important to recognise that China and its friends also have options. The Ukraine War is pushing China and Russia closer than ever before. The eagerness of the ROK's Yoon government to please (or support) the United States by sending weapons to Ukraine has backfired now because Moscow has largely decided to support North Korea's military modernisation program across several fields that should be alarming for everyone in Asia. Even as Japan advocates for ASEAN Centrality, Southeast Asian countries are committing to NOT antagonising China.

The Global Right envisions that Quad's existence is, therefore, meant to supplement this weakness. In the short to medium term, China is likely to remain relatively cautious to avoid provoking a war with the United States. However, it is likely to accelerate its plans for Taiwan contingency as evidenced by the recent military exercise in the Taiwan Strait (de facto blockade) after Pelosi visit. Even though the United States appears to have prevented the dominance of the Western Pacific by the PLA, China today has been shrewd enough to recognise the immediate weaknesses of US forces in the Asia–Pacific and has made great strides forward in its strategy and military modernisation priorities.

Beijing's strategy is to prevent the Global Right, and specifically the Quad, from further success in terms of (b) recruitment, (b) formal institutionalisation and (c) operational success in military terms. While Beijing cannot work on telling what Quad can or cannot do, what they can do is to entice and ensure that potential members would consider very carefully their participation. To date, Beijing has had limited success in this regard. There are liberal democracies that have been unwilling to join the Quad crusade outright—New Zealand, South Korea and Indonesia, to name a few even though these countries also have their own issues with Beijing. The Quad members themselves, however, show greater determination to institutionalise the body. In particular, the United States and Japan are keen to continue to utilise the Quad as an additional tier of network to shore up what it perceives as the weakness of its security architecture in the Asia–Pacific region. Yet the dynamics of this might lead to greater tensions between the US and China. The escalation of US–China tensions would likely accentuate the conflict in the Taiwan Straits and in the South China Sea especially if extra-regional players are brought in to help shore up the alliance against China.

Building on the Quad, therefore, stokes the regional security dilemma even more and is likely to push China and the United States into a renewed Cold War, the likes of the world have never seen before. The US is not lobbying against China in Asia, but across the world where the Chinese are desperate to make economic inroads such as Latin America and the Middle East. Despite many arguments against the possibility of a renewed Cold War (as even the Chinese people themselves have forsaken the practice of communism in their daily lives), this book maintains that such a notion cannot be written off. The contestation between China and the United States is still ideological, with the leadership and elites of both countries believing that their system and governance are superior and viable in the long run. Just as Americans believe in their manifest destiny, China regards her rise and rejuvenation towards the realisation of the Chinese dream as an unstoppable journey.

Judging by the numerous op-eds and articles being published about the global leadership of the United States by American and European officials on how the United States should continually build up its military forces against China to maintain peace, the world today is closer to what we are seeing in the latter half of the 1940s (rather than the early 1930s, as these elites assert) when Washington elites decided to contain the Soviet Threat. Today, the traditional Washington outlook and mindset is conjuring up a similar China threat that would no doubt lead to a renewed (rather than a completely new) Cold War. The Western strategic community is striving to promote its own interests and power (such as NATO expansion) rather than recognising the realities on the ground in Asia. The Indo-Pacific region faces a plurality of threats: environmental degradation, relative and absolute poverty, increased social tensions due to even development and capitalistic divide, increased occurrences of natural disasters due to climate change, such as bushfires due to prolonged droughts, floods and landslides from excessive torrential rainfall, typhoons, as well as increased frequency of volcanic eruptions and earthquakes. In these trying times, when most of the world, including Asia, is trying to shake off the ill effects of the Covid pandemic and the associated hyperinflation resulting from the Ukraine conflict, few have appetites to fight the new (or renewed) Cold War. For most Asians and Americans, the existential threat is not China. The endearing question is whether a renewed Cold War would really serve the security of residents of the Indo-Pacific and of Americans themselves.

Assumptions and Limitations of the Research

At the onset, this book makes three important clarifications regarding some of the assumptions made in this study. They pertain to the nature of China's domestic politics, the positions undertaken by national think tanks and academia, and the roles of corporate and social media. The first assumption pertains to the nature of China's domestic politics. The project constraints do not allow the volume to delve deeply into the development of China's domestic politics. This volume agrees with the general literature that, since 2012, the domestic political environment has become increasingly complex and political governance has become more authoritarian than at any time in the past two decades. This is not only due to Xi Jinping's political philosophy and governance style. The year 2012 marks a new stage in Chinese political development as the two prevailing factions that have dominated all aspects of China's political system, economy and society in previous decades entered an unprecedented era as their patrons (former leader Jiang Zemin and Hu Jintao) were being eased out. Tensions also escalated because of Xi's determined efforts to tackle corruption (and by extension, the war against entrenched interests). This power struggle comes on top of the massive developmental challenges that have manifested across all aspects of Chinese society, ranging from environmental degradation to an overheated economy to shocking disparity that is threatening to tear China's social fabric apart. In response to the revelation of the aborted coup by Bo Xilai and the attempted assassinations of Xi Jinping, the Central Government tightened its grip on the people's daily lives. The volume, therefore, fundamentally agrees with the fact that China's Communist Party boosted its conservative nationalistic discourse both within and outside China to boost its legitimacy and to fend off attacks by political opponents within and without. Needless to say, its foreign policy has been adjusted to address the challenges presented by the external environment, including the Quad.

The second assumption the volume makes is regarding the nature of think tanks and academia in both China and the Global Right Quad countries. Regardless of whether the think tanks are in China or in the Global Right countries, most are allowed to debate intensely and freely within their institutions. However, externally, these think tanks often mostly adopt an ultimately "patriotic" posture since they are often fully funded in part by the government (or corporate donors that are too government-linked) and often are led and heavily staffed by former members of the intelligence or national security bodies. Whether it is in Beijing, Washington or Tokyo, these bodies are often more hawkish and take on propaganda and echo chamber functions. For the most part, the think tanks are politically constrained, ideologically restricted and are functionally restricted to raise very critical pieces that run counter to their national government's current position. The biggest difference is, of course, in China or Russia; they would never criticise the existing leadership, that internal censorship exists and that published pieces are "one-sided" pieces critical of the other side. At the end of the day, there are clear red lines that all analysts in these think tanks understand should not cross.

Unlike in general science or humanities research, this problem of "toeing the line" afflicts the discipline of international relations, particularly as it relates to defence or foreign relations. Scholars who speak against the power of the day would often find themselves marginalised or worse, exiled or locked up. To that effect, the foreign policy community is deeply ethnocentric, as scholars often jostle with journalists and social media influencers for their attention, funding and impact. Whether in Beijing, Washington, Tokyo or New Delhi, analysts will write according to fit their pieces into the national narrative. In an increasingly birfurcated world, moderate and contrarian voices are drowned out by shrill calls of nationalism and identity politics. Conversely, uninformed or misinformed views justify tough and self-righteous hawkish politics and policies on a competitive basis. It is therefore extremely important that a certain amount of introspection be taken into how the world now stands at the precipice of another Cold War.

The third assumption pertains to the role of corporate and social media in propagating populist and nationalistic discourse and narratives, not just in China, but also in the West. Transnational companies and special interest groups often work together to obtain their messages across social and corporate media, often polarising domestic politics. Attention-grabbing headlines and short videos perform better than lengthy articles, which often leads to a skewed distribution of content that primarily aligns with the positions adopted by national governments. This media community comprises individuals with diverse backgrounds, very often many with no expertise in foreign affairs, international security and limited knowledge or interest in the region they are writing about. The quality of analysis varies significantly, with some good pieces being grounded in the historical context and deep insights into the country, while others are mere opinion pieces lacking substance and analysis. The propagation of misinformation (intended or otherwise) creates an overabundance of videos, posts and articles on platforms such as YouTube, TikTok, Facebook and Instagram, which amplifies bias and inaccuracies in the portrayal of events and personalities. This has, in fact, helped promote nationalistic and conservative agendas in both the Global Right Quad States and China.

Chapters Overview

Chapter 1: The Cold War and the China Challenge

This chapter lays out the basic research problematic, aims and objectives, theoretical framework and methodology, as well as the main arguments for the book. This chapter establishes the research assumptions and limitations before providing an overview of the arguments advocated by the project. The basic question that is being scrutinised in each of the empirical chapters is why conservative politics have taken root in the country, and what is the role of China in the country's domestic politics and security outlook and international politics. The chapter then presents a brief chapter by chapter synopsis.

Chapter 2: Japan

This chapter traces the genesis of the Quad directly to Prime Minister Shinzo Abe's intellectual efforts early in his first term as Prime Minister to establish an "arc of freedom and democracy", a value-based alliance designed to keep Communist China at bay. Beijing's remarkable rise has overshadowed Japan's phenomenal economic rise during the 1970s, and by the turn of the century, China has emerged as the primary threat both in the strategic and existential threat in the eyes of neoconservatives in Japan. Tokyo perceives that a richer China is not only a more capable power, but also a more belligerent one, more likely to be a status quo challenger in the years to come. Japan's immediate concerns over security interests include sovereignty over the Senkaku/Diaoyu Islands and border demarcation in the East China Seas. Japan is at risk of losing its esteemed position as the leader of Asian countries and eminent power in the Asia–Pacific region. In addition, the maintenance of China as a threat is a useful exercise for Japan to bolster domestic support to erode pacifism, amend the Constitution and strengthen Japan's global reach within and outside the US–Japan alliance. The chapter argues that the real but unstated goal of Japan's intent is to promote the Quad to prevent the possibility of a grand-bargain being struck between China and the United States, insuring against a scenario where Japan faces possible strategic estrangement if not outright abandonment by the United States. To that end, Shinzo Abe has been extremely successful in persuading the Western alliance and the world of the real prospects of a China threat. Domestically, China has provided the neoconservatives with a renewed policy platform that has enabled them to chip furiously away at the Peace Constitution, all along encouraged by the Americans, because of the perceived looming strategic US–China competition. The question, however, is whether Japan would inevitably adopt nuclear arms as it faces the prospects of bearing the brunt of Chinese retaliation should US–China relations deteriorate into actual hostilities. This scenario now haunts the Japanese people as the prospects of a Cold War era like hostility becomes very real. Internationally, China has helped Japan, in her quest to become a normal nation. In that respect, the Quad has become another important avenue to help legitimise Japan's ambition to become a global military power and a political giant. Abe's vision of the Quad actually reinstituted the strategy that Gobarchev took when he wanted to enhance ties with China, as the Quad effectively encircles China. This approach has several important advantages for Japan. This shows China that Tokyo is not alone; it drums up permanent support for Tokyo politically and diplomatically. It also enabled Japan to distract China from her singleminded economic expansion and military modernisation and put China on defense. This move would also permanently bind regional countries from becoming too close to China and alleviate the political pressure these countries might face from Beijing as China's strength grows from day to day. It would also remind China that her expansion not only threatens Tokyo but the majority of her neighbours as well. The problem, however, is that the response from China might be unexpected in Tokyo's calculations, leading to further deterioration in Sino-Japanese relations. This would actually increase Japan's reliance on the United States and further degrade Tokyo's ambition to become a "normal" power in all senses of the word.

Chapter 3: The United States

This chapter examines how the advent of the Trump Administration saw a radical shift in the politics and foreign policy of the United States through the new President embracing a new Conservatism that essentially upended most of the assumptions that US Foreign Policy was based on since the Cold War. Notwithstanding Obama's pivot to Asia and increased tensions in the South China Sea from 2010 onwards, relations between Washington and Beijing were relatively cordial. The Obama administration, emerging from the 2008 subprime financial crisis—weakened, humbled and emboldened, and in a geopolitical environment where the prospect of the United States losing its pre-eminence became a very real possibility. Even as Washington had to work closer with Beijing and Tokyo, the Obama administration however was wary of the tensions between China and Japan, principally because Washington did not want to be chain-ganged into a conflict with China due to the perceived historical revisionist excesses in Japanese domestic politics. The Obama administration assiduously avoided embracing the Quad initially because the US President appreciated the high economic stakes in US–China relations even as he ordered a "pivot" to Asia. The lukewarm relations the United States had with India was another important reason why the Quad did not take off in a big way previously, even as Tokyo had assiduously tried to play an important role in persuading the United States and ASEAN to cultivate close relations with India. Things took a radical turn with the election of Trump.

The new Trump Administration saw several important benefits (rightly or wrongly) in ratcheting tensions and magnifying the China threat: reducing trade deficits, stopping unfair trade practices, excluding Chinese communication companies from globalising their 5G technology, cultivating better relations with Russia, increasing weapons sales to East Asia, extracting concessions/contributions from allies and gaining a political edge in the 2016 elections. Trump's trade war had evolved into a no-holds bare across the board competition with China. Seasoned US–China relations watchers who attributed much of Trump's agenda and rhetoric to the President's desire to win a second term were left surprised by the radicalness and forthrightness of anti-China sentiments that broke out, particularly during the pandemic. The Quad was therefore one of the institutions that the Trump administration, personified by Secretary of State Mike Pompeo, chose to pontificate and promote the administration's policy agenda through. Through the Quad, Trump and Pompeo lobbied for increased defence contributions, weapons sales and the tightening of alliances in the Indo-Pacific and Southeast Asia (Hiebert 2020; Jaishankar 2017).

A significant reason why Trump's trade and tech war had stayed the course even with the election of Biden was that the Republicans had securitised most China-related issues. In politicising and attacking the neoliberal trade policies that previous Democratic administrations had pursued, Trump had effectively labelled these policies as unpatriotic and responsible for the plight of Americans who were suffering hardship. This political "football" is used by the Republicans to taint the Democrats in retaliation for the labels they had attached to Trump, the Republican Party and Putin. This development is not just only intra-party politicking but stems from the long historical animosity that had developed between the Russian leader Vladimir Putin and Hilary Clinton when she was Secretary of State. The "anti-China" rhetoric has grown so prevalent in US official circles that the Biden Administration has very little reason or choice, politically and strategically to modify Trump's policy, plunging US–China relations to be the lowest ever since 1972. The Democratic Party and the Biden administration decided to "double down" and opened up a new front with Russia in the Ukraine War. Today, there is every reason to expect the US–China confrontation to escalate, particularly if Trump is re-elected. The intent of the United States and her allies, particularly to confront the Russians and the Chinese together and vice versa, would reinvigorate the Cold War tensions that many have presumed to have been over since the 1990s. In turning to a classical strategy (invoking a Cold War enemy), the United States turned to a 1940s playbook to confront a twenty-first-century enemy of a very different makeup, ignoring much of the realities on the ground. The prospects of a Cold War look real, going forward.

Chapter 4: Australia

This chapter dissects Canberra's strategic U-turn in embracing the global conservative turn against China and joining the Quad alliance. Driven in part by the rising domestic security concerns of China's strategic reach and accentuated by an increasingly rightward shift in the tone and narrative of Australia's political debate, in part due to the perceived inability of the Chinese to respond to Australia and global criticisms of various issues, Canberra's position hardened over the last decade or so. Australia–China relations began a downward spiral from the Abbott administration (2013–2015) through to the Turnbull administration (2015–2018), and subsequently Morrison's administration (2018–2022). Unlike Japan, the United States and India, Australia's case is unique because her geographical location meant that there have been no conflicting interests with China, such as territorial spats, border demarcation issues, or the burden of history. Australia has never been part of the Western bloc such as the G7 or NATO (Australia is an enhanced opportunities partner) with outstanding disagreements with China and has been for the most part enjoyed an unprecedented and strong commercial relations with Beijing.

Three important drivers account for this phenomenon. The first is the increased disaffect that ordinary Australians face over the socio-economic tensions at home. While the economy has grown over the years, particular sectors have become very reliant on China—for example, mining, wine exports and education. The growth of China's influence has become somewhat disconcerting for the country which has dominantly adopted a conservative position on race and immigration. These policies were attributed to left-wing Labor Party, and China became a central "weakness" by which the Conservatives used to attack those in power. Second, these conditions allowed the emergence of United States or Eurocentric politicians who admired their conservative counterparts in the United Kingdom and Japan, who privileged identity politics and values as part of their nationalist campaigns. Third, at the international level, the Trump administration's rise and success gave Australia the opportunity to play a greater global role. In part because of his personal ambition and in part because of inexperience, Prime Minister Morrison played an exception role in reversing of Australia–China relations. Morrison's decision to spearhead the call for an enquiry into China's responsibility for the ongoing pandemic was the proverbial straw that broke the camel's back and triggered a massive reaction from Beijing—the basis for Canberra's hardening rhetoric. This appears to be a far cry from previous Australian administrations, and often is linked to the bitter rivalry in Australian domestic politics (Hartcher, 2009). For instance, the Australian Prime Minister, such as Kevin Rudd, has steered away from the Quad, seeing such an organisation as inimical to Australia's interests. Canberra's recent enthusiastic embrace of the Quad was a surprising and costly decision that marked a turning point in Australia–China relations. Unlike other Quad states that have genuine clashing realpolitik challenges with Beijing, Australia appeared to have undertaken this move out of "solidarity" with the United States and Japan more than anything else. While Australia might not necessarily come out for the worse, Canberra learned that it would be difficult to wean Australia off the lucrative Chinese market that she had relied on in the long run. The Liberal Party Prime Ministers have made a big deal out of their national security, which would undoubtedly cement Australia's alliance credentials. Fortunately, the Australian public saw fit to vote in the Labour Party, and Australia seems to have reversed its China policy even as it sought to reinvigorate her alliance with the United States.

Chapter 5: India

Of the four Quad countries, India's rise as a conservative global power joining the United States, Japan and Australia to contain China is hardly surprising. Assiduously courted by Japan's Shinzo Abe, India's membership in the Quad provided much resources, muscle and legitimacy the group needed. As the world's most populous country, a member of the non-aligned movement and a South Asian power that straddles the Indian Ocean and Himalayas, India brings a lot to the strategic table (Haidar, 2020). India's participation allows the Quad to avoid looking like it is a rich white club dominated by the United States and rich allies that target China. New Delhi not only could help encircle China, tie PLA forces down in the Himalayas and disrupt China's Belt and Road initiatives in South Asia but also potentially "replace" China's role in providing the United States, Japan and their allies an alternative market with preferential access, a cheaper source of labour and resources for their enterprises.

The question of a certain India–China confrontation is not definite. While history has shown that New Delhi has always been willing and able to challenge and fight China (as shown by the 1962 border war and skirmishes in 1967, 1987, 2017 and 2020), both countries have great commonalities and do get along fine in terms of trade and general global politics. Modi and Xi have conducted mutual visits, even though communications between India and China in general are relatively limited. Sino-Indian relations have a very different dynamic from Sino-Japanese and Sino-US relations. While these two nations have a long history of close interaction, they have never actually become intimate in any sense of the word. India has legacy territorial issues with China, but the conflict has always been seen principally as a foreign policy issue, as opposed to being linked to domestic politics and nationalism in either country.

Until the ascendance of Narendra Modi as Prime Minister in 2014, India's foreign policy largely remained somewhat non-aligned. Despite this, Russia has always been eager to transfer weapons systems to New Delhi, often balancing China as an unstated aim. Since its independence, India has always insisted on maintaining its own path. Notwithstanding this, many officials have felt that this non-aligned position has cost India greatly and that many in India's foreign policy establishment have argued that New Delhi should seek to build better relations with the West. It was only when the BJP's Modi came to power that such aspirations were realised. Modi's ascendance provided the nudge necessary to enable

New Delhi to reorient its foreign policy. Domestically, Modi's methods, like his conservative counterparts, relied on stoking a brand of nationalism premised on Hinduism that many commentators blamed for the communal riots that had broken out in the country. China had never been an important consideration until it became clear that adopting such a tough position against China would rehabilitate Modi's international image and provide India with new strategic and economic opportunities with its partners.

The Indian decision to join the Global Right Conservative moment and the Quad was prompted by two major geopolitical considerations. First, New Delhi's primary concern was to counter the growing power disparity between herself and China. In particular, New Delhi is concerned with what she perceives as China's increasing encroachment on South Asia and the Himalayas. In both areas, China's economic expansion through its much-lauded One Belt One Road (OBOR) also known as Belt Road Initiative (BRI) projects in India's immediate backyard did not sit comfortably with New Delhi. With the exception of Bhutan and Sikkim, almost all of India's South Asian neighbours are involved in BRI projects. The success of these projects would likely increase Beijing's influence in South Asia and relieve South Asian countries of New Delhi's dominance and influence over them. With an economy four times the size of India, the extending reach of Beijing cannot possibly be ignored by New Delhi, never mind if the BRI projects are really developmental rather than strategic. Second, the Quad presents India with an opportunity to further ingratiate itself with the United States and Japan and accords India's maximum political and geostrategic advantages given New Delhi's warm relations with ASEAN, Russia and members of the Shanghai Five Organisation (SCO). This not only helps with countering China but also increases New Delhi's diplomatic manoeuvrability, accord India with significant opportunities to enhance her national interests and boost her global status. This would also give Modi more leverage in his dealings with China. Internationally, this would greatly boost India's strategic importance and enable New Delhi to have unprecedented access to the Western and Japanese technology, investment and military cooperation that she craves. India's recent border clashes with China were opportune, as it only reaffirmed domestically that Modi's policy posture was politically righteous. The problem, however, is that India's recent behaviour with Russia in the recent Ukraine War has left the allies wondering about her commitment during times of crisis, and if India could be truly relied upon in the event of a confrontation with China.

Chapter 6: Cold War Redux

This chapter surveys how Beijing views its respective relations with the United States, Japan, India and Australia through the prism of a renewed Cold War. Recent developments have forced the Chinese and Russians to come together strategically to confront the United States and her allies. There is no question that Cold War structures, such as NATO and the San Francisco System, are being reinvigorated over the course of the last decade even as China contemplates its geopolitical trajectories. Even though the PRC views that the downturn in relations is principally led by the Global Right leaders for their own political ends, there is increasing recognition in Beijing that the long-term system realpolitik factors (as opposed to changing political leadership or domestic politics) will continue to drive the deterioration of US–China relations. Beijing cannot accommodate Washington's desire to preserve her hegemony at the expense of her own national development. Regardless of who or which party is in power in the White House or Congress, America's geopolitical ambition would drive Sino-US security competition. This realpolitik understanding of Sino-US relations is making the Chinese a nation more determined to stay ahead and meet the US challenge head-on. China's response has so far been defensive and rhetorical, but there is evidence that Beijing is preparing for conflict with the United States and Japan in the years ahead. This explains why China believes that the Quad is the beginning of an Asian NATO.

Regardless of what Beijing says or does, the Global Right regimes only choose to interpret these actions to reaffirm China's "aggressive" nature or global ambition. This has much to do with domestic politics, mass and social media and vested interest groups in Quad countries. However, China bears a huge responsibility in the sense that it has been unable to maintain its image and soft power abroad. The principal handicap in China's case is structural: (1) China's system inhibits most ordinary Chinese people from engaging with Western traditional and social media and provides the impression that Chinese people do not value freedom or human rights; (2) The system also meant that PRC's presence and representation in the international society and civil societies in Quad countries are heavily circumscribed because whatever comes out of China is being dismissed as "propaganda" as China lacks the requisite soft power; (3) Many groups who are advocating a "tough" China policy posture in the Quad and advance countries are made up of exiled diaspora who are staunchly anti-Communist Party, i.e. Hong Kong democrats, pro-independence Taiwanese, exiled Uyghurs in Germany and Tibetans in India are some of the most anti-China groups. The inability of the Chinese government to reconcile the differences in society and negotiate the exigencies of citizenship has created this phenomenon.

Fundamentally, the growth of China's economy, rather than any irredentist agenda, tops Beijing's foreign policy goals. China is now carefully calibrating its political response and diplomacy to prevent sanctions by the United States and is striving to build resilience in trading relations in a bid to ensure that its economy remains open, vibrant and free. It is adopting an extremely "tough" approach towards Taiwan and increasingly asserting its presence in East and South China Seas. However, China appears to be working hard to maintain its relations with the ASEAN cordial, notwithstanding what is going on with the Philippines and the South China Sea. It is continuing to work on BRI projects in the Middle East, Central Asia, Eastern Europe and the Americas. China's "dual circulation" strategy has yet to manifest as something that would enable it to get herself out of its economic quandary, but there are pockets of excellence as some Chinese companies are doing very well globally. Beijing is emerging as a leader in Green Tech such as Electric Vehicles and Solar Energy products, as well as the production of low-priced quality industrial and consumer products which has benefited most people globally.

Even as these countries (Quad countries and China) try their level best to "contain" each other, it is clear from hindsight that they would benefit immeasurably if they returned to the era of cooperation. The conclusion summarises the findings of the individual chapters and presents answers to the primary questions raised in the introductory chapter. It provides a summary of the three images (leaders, domestic politics and international circumstances) and argues that a renewed Cold War is imminent, at least until one of the two powers prevails in their struggle. There is every reason to believe that this competition would like to inhibit the next two decades in the medium term and would increasingly affect most countries in the Indo-Pacific region. Despite the negative prognosis, this chapter argues that this outcome is not inevitable, as Asian countries such as those in Southeast Asia can help play an important balancing role to ensure that neither the United States nor China oversteps their realpolitik manoeuvres. Collectively, the region can ensure that regional diplomacy can be calibrated in such a way as to restrain the great powers involved in preventing a renewed Cold War from breaking out, reversing decades of peace and prosperity that the region has built up.

REFERENCES

Abrams, Eliott, "The New Cold War, National Review", Council on Foreign Relations, 4 March 2022, https://www.cfr.org/blog/new-cold-war-0

Allison, Graham, "Trump is Already Reshaping Geopolitics: How U.S. Allies and Adversaries Are Responding to the Chance of His Return", Foreign Affairs, January 16 2024, https://www.foreignaffairs.com/united-states/trump-alr eady-reshaping-geopolitics

Ash, Timothy Garton, "Cold Days Ahead: As We Seek to Manage Our Newly Frosty Relationship with China, Lessons from the Cold War Can Help", Hoover Digest, Issue 4, Fall 2020

Asada, Kenji, Munakata, Aiko, Zhou Marrian, Zhou, Cissy, & Li, Grace, "Inside China's Online Nationalist Army", Nikkei Asia, 29 December 2022, https://asia.nikkei.com/Politics/Inside-China-s-online-nationalist-army

Babones, Salvatore, "What the West Needs From Modi", Foreign Policy, 11 September 2020, https://foreignpolicy.com/2020/09/11/india-modi-china-quad-military-alliance/

Branigan, Tania, "Xi Jinping: Has China's Strongman Forgotten the Perils of Power?" The Guardian, 24 October 2017, https://www.theguardian.com/world/2017/oct/25/xi-jinping-has-china-strongman-forgotten-the-perils-of-power

Buruma, Ian, "China's Autocracy in Crisis", Project Syndicate, 9 January 2023, https://www.project-syndicate.org/commentary/china-xi-jinping-zero-covid-authoritarian-by-ian-buruma-2023-01

Cáceres, Sigfrido B., & Ear, Sophal, How China's Resource Quest is Reshaping the World, London: Routledge, 2013

Chang, M. H. (1998). Chinese Irredentist Nationalism: The Magician's Last Trick. *Comparative Strategy* 17, no. 1: 83–100. https://doi.org/10.1080/01495939808403133

Chanlett-Avery, Emma, "Japan, the Indo-Pacific, and the 'Quad.'" Chicago Council on Global Affairs, 2018. http://www.jstor.org/stable/resrep17325

Chen, Boyu, & San Yih Huang, "Senkaku/Diaoyu Islands Dispute and Taiwan's Netizens' Sentiments Toward Japan and China." *East Asia* 32, no. 4 (December 2015): 385–99. https://doi.org/10.1007/s12140-015-9245-3

Ching, Frank, "China Has All But Ended the Charade of a Peaceful Rise", South China Morning Post, 26 August 2016, https://www.scmp.com/comment/insight-opinion/article/2008900/china-has-all-ended-charade-peaceful-rise

Christensen, Thomas J., "There Will Not Be a New Cold War", Foreign Affairs, 24 March 2021

Christensen, Thomas J., Worse than a Monolith: Alliance Politics and Problems of Coercive Diplomacy in Asia, Princeton, NJ: Princeton University Press, 2011

Christensen, Thomas J., "The Advantages of an Assertive China", Foreign Affairs, Vol. 90, Issue 2, March/April 2011

Chua, Amy, "Divided We Fall: What Is Tearing America Apart?", Foreign Affairs, July/August 2020, https://www.foreignaffairs.com/reviews/review-essay/2020-06-01/divided-we-fall

Clarke, Ryan, The Evolving Nature of the Quad: American Strategy, ASEAN Centrality and Chinese Responses, EAI Background Brief No. 1614

Clinton, Hillary, "A National Security Reckoning; How Washington Should Think About Power", Foreign Affairs, Vol 99, Issue 6, 2020

Cooley, Alexander, & Daniel H Nexon, "How Hegemony Ends: The Unraveling of American Power", Foreign Affairs, Vol. 99, Issue 4, 2020

Curran, James, "All Shot and No Powder in the Quadrilateral Security Dialogue", East Asia Forum, 28 January 2018, https://eastasiaforum.org/2018/01/28/all-shot-and-no-powder-in-the-quadrilateral-security-dialogue/

De Castro, Renato Cruz, "The Aquino Administration's Balancing Policy against an Emergent China: Its Domestic and External Dimensions." *Pacific Affairs* 87, no. 1 (1 March 2014): 5–27. https://doi.org/10.5509/2014871005

Dobell, Graeme, The Quantity and Quality of Quad Questions, The Strategist, Australia Strategic Policy Institute, 25 February 2019, https://www.aspistrategist.org.au/the-quantity-and-quality-of-quad-questions/

Dreyer, June Teufel, The Quad: Form Without Substance? Foreign Policy Research Institute, 12 February 2021

Fravel, Taylor M., "China's Strategy in the South China Sea", *Contemporary Southeast Asia* 33, no. 3 (2011): 292–319

Flitton, Daniel, Who Really Killed the Quad 1.0? Lowry Institute, 2 June 2020, https://www.lowyinstitute.org/the-interpreter/who-really-killed-quad-10

Fukuyama, Francis, "The Pandemic and Political Order: It Takes a State", Foreign Affairs Vol. 99, Issue 4, July–August 2020

Friedberg, Aaron L., "An Answer to Aggression: How to Push Back Against Beijing", Foreign Affairs, Vol. 99, Issue 5

Furuoka, Fumitaka, "Challenges for Japanese Diplomacy After the End of the Cold War." *Contemporary Southeast Asia* 24, no. 1 (2002): 68–81. http://www.jstor.org/stable/25798580

Hack, Karl, "The Origins of the Asian Cold War: Malaya 1948." *Journal of Southeast Asian Studies* 40, no. 3 (October 2009): 471–96. https://doi.org/10.1017/S0022463409990038

Haidar, Suhasini, "The Confluence of Four Powers and Two Seas", The Hindu, 25 July 2020

Hartcher, Peter, To the Bitter End: The Dramatic Story Behind the Fall of John Howard and the Rise of Kevin Rudd, New South Wales: Allen & Unwin, 2009

Hara, Kimie, "50 Years from San Francisco: Re-Examining the Peace Treaty and Japan's Territorial Problems." *Pacific Affairs* 74, no. 3 (2001): 361. https://doi.org/10.2307/3557753

Hendrix, Cullen S., "Cold War Geopolitics and the Making of the Oil Curse." *Journal of Global Security Studies* 3, no. 1 (1 January 2018): 2–22. https://doi.org/10.1093/jogss/ogx022

Hibbing, John R., *The Securitarian Personality: What Really Motivates Trump's Base and Why It Matters for the Post-Trump Era.* 1st ed. Oxford University Press, 2020. https://doi.org/10.1093/oso/9780190096489.001.0001

Hiebert, Murray, Ciorciari, John D., and Associate Professor and Director of the Weiser Diplomacy Center and International Policy Center at the Gerald R. Ford School of Public Policy, University of Michigan. "Under Beijing's Shadow: Southeast Asia's China Challenge." *Contemporary Southeast Asia* 42, no. 3 (10 December 2020): 431–33. https://doi.org/10.1355/CS42-3f

Huang, Yukon, and Slosberg, Genevieve, "What Exactly Does Washington Want From Its Trade War With Beijing?", Carnegie Endowment Commentary, 11 April 2023, https://carnegieendowment.org/posts/2023/04/what-exactly-does-washington-wantfrom-its-trade-war-with-beijing?lang=en

Hutt, David, "Post-Pandemic Southeast Asia Faces a Crisis of Authoritarianism", The Diplomat, 22 January 2021, https://thediplomat.com/2021/01/post-pandemic-southeast-asia-faces-a-crisis-of-authoritarianism/

Huong, Le Thu, ed., "Quad 2.0: New Perspectives for the Revived Concept: Views from The Strategist." Australian Strategic Policy Institute, 2019. http://www.jstor.org/stable/resrep23015

Hu Yanweanan, "The Rising Tide of 'Imperial Han' Nationalism in China", The Diplomat, 2 December 2023, https://thediplomat.com/2023/12/the-rising-tide-of-imperial-han-nationalism-in-china/

Jaishankar, Dhruva, "It's Time to Resuscitate the Asia-Pacific Quad", Brookings Institution, 9 January 2017

Jha, Ashish, "System Failure: America Needs a Global Health Policy for the Pandemic Age", Foreign Affairs, March/April 2021

Johnson, Simon, "The Next Stage of the Hot Cold War", n.d.

Kagan, Robert, "A Superpower, Like It or Not: Why Americans Must Accept Their Global Role", Foreign Affairs, March/April 2021

Kleine-Ahlbrandt, Stephanie, "China: New Leaders, Same Assertive Foreign Policy", International Crisis Group, 8 March 2013, https://www.crisisgroup.org/asia/north-east-asia/china/china-new-leaders-same-assertive-foreign-policy

Kim, Patricia M., Matthew Turpin, Joseph S. Nye Jr, Chen Weiss, Eun A. Jo, Ryan Hass & Emilie Kimball. "Should the US Pursue a New Cold War with China?", Brookings Institution, 1st September 2023, https://www.brookings.edu/articles/should-the-us-pursue-a-new-cold-war-with-china/

Kupchan, Charles, "A New Cold War Could Be Much Worse Than the One We Remember", The Atlantic, 3 June 2023, https://www.theatlantic.com/international/archive/2023/06/cold-war-china-risks/674272/

Kirshner, Jonathan, "Gone But Not Forgotten: Trump's Long Shadow and the End of American Credibility", Foreign Affairs, Vol. 100, Issue 2, March–April 2021

Koh, Fabian, "China and US Already in Early Stage of a New Cold War, Have to Choose Either Peace or Escalation: Analysts", Channel News Asia, 7 March 2023

Lalwani, Sameer, "Reluctant Link?: India, The Quad and the Free and Open Indo-Pacific", in Sharon, Stirling, Mind the Gap: National Views of the Free and Open Indo-Pacific German Marshall Fund of the United States, 2019, http://www.jstor.org/stable/resrep21474.8

Layne, Christopher, "Coming Storms: The Return of Great-Power War", Foreign Affairs, Vol. 99, Issue 6, 2020

Lebow, Richard Ned, "The Long Peace, the End of the Cold War, and the Failure of Realism". *International Organization* 48, no. 2 (1994): 249–77. https://doi.org/10.1017/S0020818300028186.

Leonard, Mark, "This Cold War Is Different", The Strategist, Australian Strategic Policy Institute, 3 September 2023

Liu, Chuyi, & Ma, Xiao, "Popular Threats and Nationalistic Propaganda: Political Logic of China's Patriotic Campaign." *Security Studies* 27, no. 4: 633–64. https://doi.org/10.1080/09636412.2018.1483632

Madhav, Ram, "Quad Must be Built on Agendas, Not Emotions. Can't Afford to Become Another NATO", The Print, 16 October 2020, https://theprint.in/opinion/quad-must-be-built-on-agendas-not-emotions-cant-afford-to-become-nato/524749/

Manning, Robert, "These 10 Things Could Help Subdue Power-Hungry China", The National Interest, 6 December 2020, https://nationalinterest.org/feature/these-10-things-could-help-subdue-power-hungry-china-173797

Mainichi Shimbun, 1,600 People March Through Naha Protesting Japan's Defense Buildup in Okinawa, 27 February 2023, https://mainichi.jp/english/articles/20230227/p2a/00m/0na/009000c

Mazza, Michael, "The Axis of Disorder: How Russia, Iran, and China Want to Remake the World", Global Taiwan, 13 December 2023, https://globaltai wan.org/2023/12/the-axis-of-disorder-how-russia-iran-and-china-want-to-remake-the-world/

Mitter, Rana, and Johnson, Elsbeth, "What the West Gets Wrong About China", Harvard Business Review, May–June 2021, https://hbr.org/2021/05/what-the-west-gets-wrong-about-china

Moriyasu, Ken, China's Territorial Claims Illegal, Deceptive: U.S. Indo-Pacific Chief, 4 May 2024, https://asia.nikkei.com/Politics/International-relati ons/Indo-Pacific/China-s-territorial-claims-illegal-deceptive-U.S.-Indo-Pac ific-chief

Mueller, John, "What Was the Cold War about? Evidence from Its Ending." *Political Science Quarterly* 119, no. 4 (2004): 609–31. http://www.jstor.org/stable/20202432

Panda, Jagannath, "Making Quad Plus a Reality", The Diplomat, 13 January 2022, https://thediplomat.com/2022/01/making-quad-plus-a-reality/

Periez, Jane, "Philippines' Deal with China Pokes a Hole in US Strategy", The New York Times, 2 November 2016, https://www.nytimes.com/2016/11/03/world/asia/philippines-duterte-southchina-sea.html

Pew Research, Most Americans Have 'Cold' Pew Research Center, "Views of China. Here's What They Think About China, In Their Own Words", 30 June 2021, https://www.pewresearch.org/global/2021/06/30/most-ame ricans-have-cold-views-of-china-heres-what-they-think-about-china-in-their-own-words/

Pottinger, Matt & Gallagher, Mike, "No Substitute for Victory", Foreign Affairs, May/June 2024, https://www.foreignaffairs.com/united-states/no-substitute-victory-pottinger-gallagher

Power, Samantha, "The Can-Do Power: America's Advantage and Biden's Chance", Foreign Affairs, 100, no.1, January–February 2021

Roskin, Michael G., "The New Cold War". *The US Army War College Quarterly: Parameters* 44, no. 1 (1 March 2014). https://doi.org/10.55540/0031-1723.2792

Roy, Denny, "Assertive China: Irredentism or Expansionism?" *Survival* 61, no. 1: 51–74. https://doi.org/10.1080/00396338.2019.1568044

Rudd, Kevin, "Short of War: How to Keep U.S.-Chinese Confrontation From Ending in Calamity", March/April 2021

Sankei Shimbun, China's Preposterous Claim, Greedy Ambitions Over Senkaku Islands Disturb Peace, (originally published as 尖閣諸島 中国の主張は荒唐無稽だ in), Sankei Shimbun Editorial, 26 May 2020, https://japan-forward.com/editorial-chinas-preposterous-claim-greedy-ambitions-over-senkaku-isl ands-disturb-peace/

Sangjoon Lee, "The Asia Foundation's Motion-Picture Project and the Cultural Cold War in Asia." *Film History* 29, no. 2 (2017): 108–37. https://doi.org/10.2979/filmhistory.29.2.05.

Singh, Swaran, "What Tokyo Ministerial Holds for the Future of Quad", The Straits Times, 5 October 2020

Stavridis, James, "Four Ways a China-US War at Sea Could Play Out", Bloomberg, 26 April 2021, https://www.bloomberg.com/opinion/articles/2021-04-25/u-s-china-sea-war-could-spread-to-japan-australia-india

Steinbruner, John, & Jeffrey Lewis, "The Unsettled Legacy of the Cold War." *Daedalus* 131, no. 4 (2002): 5–10. http://www.jstor.org/stable/20027801

Stiglitz, Joseph E., "How the US Could Lose the New Cold War", Project Syndicate, 17 June 2022

Tamamoto, Masaru, "How Japan Imagines China and Sees Itself." *World Policy Journal* 22, no. 4 (2005): 55–62. http://www.jstor.org/stable/40209995

Tracy, Elena F., Shvarts, Evgeny, Simonov, Eugene, & Babenko, Mikhail, "China's New Eurasian Ambitions: The Environmental Risks of the Silk Road Economic Belt." *Eurasian Geography and Economics* 58, no. 1 (2017): 56–88. https://doi.org/10.1080/15387216.2017.1295876

Tsutsui, Kiyoteru, "How Japan's Suga Can Build an Alliance to Counter China", Nikkei Asia, 6 December 2020, https://asia.nikkei.com/Opinion/How-Japan-s-Suga-can-build-an-alliance-to-counter-China

Tyler, Melissa Conley, "Australia Can Repair Its Relationship with China, Here Are 3 Ways to Start", The Conversation, 1 December 2020, https://theconversation.com/australia-can-repair-its-relationship-with-china-here-are-3-ways-to-start-150455

Venkataraman, N., "Expansionist Greed of Chinese Government: A Pain in the Neck for the World", WION News Online, 30 July 2020, https://www.wionews.com/opinions-blogs/expansionist-greed-of-chinese-government-a-pain-in-the-neck-for-the-world-317063

Wade, Geoff, "The Beginnings of a "Cold War" in Southeast Asia: British and Australian Perceptions." *Journal of Southeast Asian Studies* 40, no. 3 (October 2009): 543–65. https://doi.org/10.1017/S0022463409990063

Waltz, Kenneth, Man, The State and War: A Theoretical Analysis, New York: Columbia University Press, 2018 (First published 1959)

Waltz, Kenneth N., "Structural Realism after the Cold War." *International Security* 25, no. 1 (2000): 5–41. http://www.jstor.org/stable/2626772

Wang, Jisi, "America and China Are Not Yet in a Cold War", Foreign Affairs, 23 November 2023

Zhao, Suisheng, "China's New Foreign Policy "Assertiveness": Motivations and Implications", ISPI Analysis, Istituto per gli Studi di Politica Internazionale, no. 54, May 2011

Zhu, Ying, "Containing China: Will the Quad Become an Asian Mini-NATO?", ThinkChina, 6 October 2020, https://www.thinkchina.sg/containing-china-will-quad-become-asian-mini-nato

CHAPTER 2

Japan's Resurgence as a Neoconservative State: Towards Constitutional Revisionism and Great Power Status

If there is one country to be credited for the idea and genesis of the Quad, it has to be China's closest neighbour, Japan. From Tokyo's perspective today, the rise of China as a political and economic power has brought about unprecedented challenges. This challenge is presented across all realms, from political-military to economic-social identity crises, to the point that China's rise is viewed as an existential crisis. China has not just spurred strategic anxiety for Japan but has also opened unprecedented opportunities for politicians and political parties to rejuvenate and reinvent their public persona and private agendas, extend their domestic influence and build their reputation. Collectively, at the individual and societal levels, these changes have brought about a sea change in the way Japanese people and elites view and interact with their closest neighbours.

Viewing international events through international and Western-influenced local outlets, a new generation of Japanese people is seeing China in a very different light from their parents. With the war generation dying out, the post-War generation (those born in the 1950–1970s) have a very different vision of how they see themselves as a nation surviving in post-war Asia and a globalised world. Their vision of course is mediated by the incessant stream of interpretations and opinions put forth by mainstream media. These narratives offered by international and Western-influenced media outlets and reinforced by social media discussions and prevailing nationalistic discourse contributes to the overall

© The Author(s), under exclusive license to Springer Nature Singapore Pte Ltd. 2024
V. Teo, *Cold War Redux Amidst Great Power Rivalry*, https://doi.org/10.1007/978-981-97-3733-8_2

49

political climate within the country. In Japanese narratives today, if the United States is the saviour of the Japanese nation, then the People's Republic of China is the devil spawn. Of course, things in reality are not all that binary and a lot more complicated, but understanding how Japan's political leadership, domestic politics, and external environment have evolved would help one appreciate how the rise of the conservatives has resulted in this development.

LEVEL ONE: THE LEADER

Shinzo Abe: The Making of Japan's Foremost Conservative and QUAD Idealogue

It would not be possible to understand the genesis and evolution of neo-conservatism and the emergence of Quad without first understanding former Japanese Prime Minister Shinzo Abe's political philosophy, outlook and goals. The latter is also particularly important for anyone wanting to understand the intricacies of the LDP's strategy in Japanese politics and its impact on Japan's foreign policy. At both party and national levels, Abe has had an unprecedented influence on the evolution of Japan's domestic politics, foreign diplomacy and international politics. The Prime Minister did not create the international political environment he operated in, but his decisions and choices certainly shape the times we live in today.

Of the politicians scrutinised in this book, Shinzo Abe must rank as the most genuine right-wing politician in the Quad countries. His ultra-conservatism stemmed from a generational legacy as well as deep-seed beliefs drawn from his formative experience of growing up in post-war Japan and later refined through his quick defeat after one year in office as Prime Minister. By the time he came to power a second time in 2012, Shinzo Abe could be considered the most formidable and politically skilled conservative in contemporary Japan (Nilsson-Wright, 2020). While hardly the first leader to adopt a staunch anti-China posture (think of his former boss Junichiro Koizumi for instance), his ascendance has not gone unnoticed in the global conservative movement and has certainly inspired foreign leaders to emulate his political ideas and methodology. Tony Abbott of Australia has openly declared his admiration for Abe, and other conservative politicians such as India's Modi, Australia's Scott Morrison and the United States' Donald Trump have certainly adopted some of Abe's political methodology (particularly with regard to China) to boost their own political career.

Family Legacies: Pedigree, Networks and Transgenerational Aspirations

Japan is known for its love for tradition and craftsmanship. Be it leather goods, tofu or electronics, the biggest brands in Japan are synonymous with quality, skills and values transmitted over generations. The Japanese love for brands extends from everyday life products to politics. Abe's family background carried an immense amount of legitimacy and capital to Abe's career, and it would not be wrong to say that his status in Japanese society and politics is well-cemented from birth. Shinzo Abe was born to Shintaro Abe (1924–1991), a Japanese politician, and Yoko Kishi (1928–). The Abe family hailed from Heki, Yamaguchi Prefecture, and was a prominent landowning family in the Edo period who were also soy sauce and sake brewers. Shinzo Abe's paternal grandfather Kan Abe (1928–1946) attended Tokyo Imperial University before going on to run as an independent candidate who opposed Tojo government in the 1942 election. He married a general's daughter and went on to serve in the Japanese legislature until he died of a heart attack in 1946. Abe Kan's son Shintaro Abe, also became a Japanese politician who served as Japan's Foreign Minister from 1982 to 1986 in the Nakasone Cabinet. Shintaro Abe married Yoko Kishi, who is the daughter of Japanese Prime Minister Nobusuke Kishi (1896–1987). Nobusuke Kishi was a towering and controversial figure in Japanese politics.

Shinzo Abe's paternal grandfather was a legislator and a contemporary of Tojo, while his maternal grandfather Kishi served in Tojo's cabinet as Minister of Commerce and Vice Minister of Munitions and subsequently Japan's Prime Minister from 1957 to 1960. Kishi's younger brother (Abe Shinzo's granduncle) was Japanese Prime Minister Eisaku Sato (1964–1972). Shinzo Abe's father did not become Prime Minister but served as Minster of Agriculture and Forestry (1974–1976) in the Miki cabinet, Chief Cabinet Secretary (1977–78) for the Fukuda Cabinet, Minister of International Trade and Industry (1981–1982) in the Suzuki Cabinet and finally as Foreign Minister in the Nakasone Cabinet (1982–1986). Shinzo Abe has also a younger brother Nobuo Kishi (adopted by Nobukazu Kishi as his own child and lived with Nobusuke Kishi till ten). This younger brother Nobuo Kishi eventually also became Defense Minister. Shinzo

Abe therefore had familial relations with two Prime Ministers, a Foreign Minister and a Defense Minister. His nephew also appeared to be running for office (Maeda, 2023). This form of dynastic politics is not unique to just Japan or Abe's family but is found across many polities.

Shinzo Abe's political career was greatly influenced and helped by his family's long involvement in politics and government. He also benefited from the prestige and legitimacy conferred by his familial connections, and he had an "insider" track knowledge of how things were done. The brand recognition that Abe inherited from his grandfathers, granduncle and father provided him with an immediate sense of awe and respect amongst the electorate, an important advantage which few of his contemporaries had. Abe's family's linkages offered him a distinct political branding, similar to the Kennedys, Bushes and Clintons in the United States. His family legacy also essentially means that Abe could draw upon his family's connections across generations of LDP politicians. Shinzo Abe's network is unparalleled. Abe's father led a major LDP faction (Seiwa Seikaku Kenkyukai) sponsored by Kishi who also mentored Fukuda (*Seiwa Seikaku Kenkyukai*). This faction was headed by Machimura Notbutaka until 2015, succeeded by Hososa Hiroyuki until 2021 when Abe took over. This nationalist-conservative faction is currently the largest faction in the LDP and is now known as the Abe faction. Prime Minister Mori, in fact, was a junior member of Shintaro Abe's faction and helped propel Shinzo Abe's career greatly. The importance of factional politics will be elaborated later, but for now, suffice it is to say that such a network provided Abe with important social capital for realising his political vision later.

To understand Abe's politics and ideological orientation, it is important to understand the influences of Kishi Nobusuke his grandfather has on Abe's political vison and ideals (Fujita, 2015). Born during the Meiji Restoration in 1896, Kishi was a Japanese politician and bureaucrat who served the successive Japanese governments. He was most well-known for his atrocious behaviour and involvement in the exploitative governance of Japanese puppet state of Manchukuo in Northeast China in the 1930s, and was euphemistically known as the "Monster of Showa" (Iwami, 1994). As someone who openly touted the policies of Nazi Germany, Kishi called for the elimination of capitalist competition and subject all economic activities, particularly in Manchukuo, to the benefit of imperial Japan. This heavily guided economic policy underlined the basis for the philosophy behind the developmental state model in post-war Japan. When the Second World War came, Kishi served in the Cabinet of Wartime Prime Minister Hideki Tojo, holding portfolios in the Commerce and Munition Ministry. As a member of the cabinet, he co-signed the Declaration of War on the United States on 7 December 1941. He was subsequently imprisoned as a Class A War Criminal, but eventually rehabilitated by the American Occupation Forces and identified as someone who could lead post-war Japan in a pro-American direction. Kishi was a member of the Liberal Party and a political enemy of Yoshida Shigeru whom he felt had been too deferential to the Americans and opposed Article 9 of the Constitution. He led a revolt and left the Liberal Party to found the Democratic Party eventually and eventually won the election. By then, Yoshida had already stepped down and he sought a merger with the Liberals. As one of the *Genros*, Kishi was instrumental in helping shape post-war Japanese politics by constructing the 1955 system that guides Japan until this day. The smaller parties in Japan consolidated into two major parties, the Japan Socialist Party (JSP) and the Liberal Democratic Party (LDP).

By and large, Kishi felt that his imprisonment and judgement that were cast on the Japanese wartime leaders were essentially "victor's justice". As a staunch traditionalist, he was a strong supporter of the Chrysanthemum Throne as well as the war waged in its name. Even though he was imprisoned, it is evident from his politics that he did not regard Japan as having done wrong. This historical revisionist view is certainly inherited and shared by Abe as well, given his controversial position on history-related issues, such as the comfort women controversy and visits to Yasukuni shrines (Fujita & Hiroki, 2020). Kishi's nationalist ideology and "imperial" sense of politics can be found in Abe's political ideology and outlook.

One aspect that Kishi was very unhappy with in post-war Japanese politics that he thought needed correction was the sense of pre-war confidence in Japan. This is the basis for what many regard as masochistic politics—Japan had developed a negative sense of self, resulting in a polity that was always insecure, apologetic and reliant. Abe's manifesto, "The Beautiful Japan" was therefore key to understanding how a strong, secure and prosperous can be restored. The key to restoring confidence was to cultivate a younger generation that had a less masochistic sense of history and a narrative that befits a confident Japan that could be proud of her history. Early in his career in the 1990s, Abe was part of a study group that denied that the Nanjing Massacre had happened; during his first term in 2006–2007, he also refuted the claims of Comfort Women and took a full-page advertisement in Washington post only to be refuted by a non-binding resolution by the US Congress asking Japan to atone its role (Dudden cited in Chotiner, 2022). Abe was one of the leaders of Nippon Kaigi, a shadowy group that appeared to become the real power behind the throne in contemporary politics, almost analogous to the Tea Party in the United States. Abe's pandering to the conservative constituents and his active attempts to helm in critical educators and academics, civic activists and journalists are therefore parts of his attempt to achieve his vision. The critical and watchdog functions of these professions are extremely important in ensuring that autocracy, misinformation and the abuse of power are kept in check in any society. The problem with Abe was that he often spoke about the need to maintain peace, but his ideas to achieve this was based on strengthening Japan's military, restoring Japan's rightful place in the world and was never about reconciling with her neighbours or acknowledging Japan's misdeeds. Abe thought that this brand of history was "masochistic" and was damaging to Japan's future generations and should be thoroughly abolished. Abe's politics was based on age-old nineteenth century imperial nation rather than any contemporary idea of achieving liberal peace through reconciliation. This is one of the significant reasons why so many Japanese are reluctant to come fully onboard with Abe's political ideas, even though they might recognise and respect his commitment to the Japanese nation. In the eyes of the generations of defenders of Japan's Constitution and civic defenders who have worked hard to prevent Japan's rearmament, Abe's politics was actually a big step backward from what post-war Japan had achieved.

Shinzo Abe had also inherited and shared Kishi's deep understanding of the nature of Japan's relations with the United States. It is a well known fact that Kishi had in the face of widespread protects pushed through the revision of the US–Japan Security Treaty in the 1960s. Pardoned as a War Criminal by the Americans, Kishi was elevated to the position of Prime Minister and was widely viewed as Washington's man in Japan. An alternative view of Kishi's role was that his support for the revised US–Japan Treaty cultivated more equal ties with the United States, rather than the subjugation of ties of Japan to the United States. This interpretation is debatable, but the fact of the matter is that, by ramming through the revised Treaty, Kishi had tired Japan to the United States structurally for the foreseeable future, binding Japan to follow where the United States might go strategically or diplomatically. Likewise, Abe understood that in order to further loosen the political and legal shackles imposed by the United States on Japan after the war, it was vital that Tokyo continue to gain the trust of the Americans, and in doing so, benefit from the protection and the favoured status Japan has to enhance its political, security and economic interests.

Kishi's influence on Abe therefore cannot be underestimated. There is considerable evidence that Abe framed many of his policies as a "continuation" of Kishi's ideals and work. In his foreign visits, he would often make reference to his grandfather's journey before, and how he intends to continue the work that has been taken by him. There are too many coincidences in which Abe has been caught referring to significant dates for his later father and grandfather when setting his official schedule (Fujita, 2015). For one, Abe was keen to ram through the National Security Bill by 15 July 2015 in order to avenge his grandfather's political defeat. This date was the date that Kishi's cabinet was forced to resign the renewal of Japan–US Security Treaty anniversary 55 years ago. Abe also referenced his grandfather's visit on 31 July 1959 to Chile on his own visit on the same day in 2014 (Fujita, 2015). Likewise, Abe appeared to have been influenced by his grandfather's thoughts about India. In 1957, Kishi visited India. Abe understood India well through his grandfather's assessment of India and the country's potential and made India a central pillar, reinforcing the efforts of his predecessors Yoshiro Mori and Junichiro Koizumi (Jain, 2022).

The Prime Minister is also known to have despised people who were protesting for him to step down, as they appeared to remind him of his grandfather's political defeat displayed by his consistent combative attitude towards those who oppose him, maybe academics, reporters or political opposition (Koga, 2022). Abe also professed to be a democrat, but like his grandfather, he spared no effort in taking down his critics or opponents in centralising power in his hands. In his rhetoric casting himself as a defender of freedom and liberty, he continuously defended the righteousness of imperial Japan, becoming a chief-revisionist in suggesting that the atrocities that Japan committed in Korea and Southeast Asia never happened before. Abe has a "Jekyll and Hyde" quality about him (Park, 2013), but this of course conveniently overlooked most of the time by his like-minded friends who shared his revisionism and anti-China views.

Shinzo Abe's worldviews were also significantly shaped by his formative years and experiences. He grew up when Japan was under occupation and witnessed one of the greatest economic revival stories in human history after the devastating war. Abe studied at Seiki University and the University of California, where he immersed himself in American culture and society. Upon returning to Japan as a young man, he worked at Kobe Steel, as the company sought to expand its presence overseas. In 1982, he landed a new position in the Foreign Ministry and the ruling Liberal Democratic Party. This period coincided with the rise of Japan as a significant economic power and the US–Japan economic tensions. By 1993, Abe was elected as an LDP Legislator representing the prefecture of Yamaguchi and eventually led the LDP's largest faction, Seiwakai (previously headed by his father who died in 1991). (Associated Press, 2022).

As he evolved and grew as an LDP politician, Abe developed the required skills for backroom dealing in inter-party politics and acquired the knowledge to build and expand his own faction within the Party. He also learnt how the United States maintained its dominance in the economic competition with Tokyo in a world where Japan was emerging as an economic power. With increasing US–Japan tensions during the 1980s, a new generation of nationalistic politicians, including Shinzo Abe, emerged. He demonstrated a strong sense of national pride and advocated for a more prominent global role for Japan, pushing for a robust defense policy and reevaluating Japan's Constitution as he climbed the political ladder in a Japan grappling with the utility of the US–Japan alliance and the strategic future of the nation.

When Junichiro Koizumi, the popular Prime Minister, appointed Abe as the Chief Cabinet Secretary in 2005, Abe's political standing significantly increased. Abe's strong stance against North Korea on the abductee issue had made him popular. As the Chief Cabinet Secretary, Abe used the North Korea issue to promote a more muscular foreign policy, with an eye on China and the goal of making Japan more independent of the United States. After Koizumi stepped down in September 2006, Abe became Prime Minister with an obsession on national security, constitutional revision and foreign policy. Due to declining public support and poor health caused by ulcerative colitis, Abe resigned after a year in office. Abe used his downtime to reflect upon how he could come back a stronger politician and a better leader. He realised that as Prime Minister, he would have stronger public support if he had focused more on domestic priorities, particularly economic growth, and toned down his ideology with more sensible approaches such as international diplomacy. Abe also realised that his singular focus on North Korea and China, particularly his call to construct a "diamond of democracies" that was aimed at containing China did not go down so well with the United States that was trying to strike a balance in managing her relations with China. This made him look like a raving nationalist than a statesman; he should have instead focused on strengthening Japan's role in regional and global affairs and on Tokyo's role in the US–Japan alliance. In Japanese culture, there appeared to be some admiration for figures whose ultimate failure was ennobled by the purity and sincerity of their ideals, and Abe proved to be such a model of failure after he stepped down in September 2007 (Levidis, 2012).

The Second Coming of Shinzo Abe, the Global Right and Quad 2.0

Shinzo Abe capitalised on the lessons learnt, displaying an acute political acumen and a confident image to the nation. In order to prepare Abe to be nominated as leader of the LDP prior to his re-election, his advisors and public relations team "remould" his image by promoting three important aspects that are related to history: Abe needed to complete his great work of Constitutional Revisionism from his first term, that he needed to restore Japan as a "beautiful country" and "take back" Japan in terms of restoring its economic vigour (Toh, 2020).

Abe was very well advised by Suga Yoshihide, an LDP grassroots fixer, and later his Chief Cabinet Secretary to ensure that he delivered the two messages that the electorate wanted. The first was that Abe would no longer overtly fixate on his ideological obsession to revise the Constitution, but instead adopt a realistic and sensible attitude and deal with all the political problems then, including foreign policy challenges in his next term as leader. The second was that Abe will prioritise and address the economic malaise that Japanese nation faced. Abe's image presented was that he would be the democratic and responsive Prime Minister that the nation badly needed and would deliver the leadership and continuity that the DPJ could not. In other words, Abe needed to be more statesmen-like and democrat (real or otherwise) that the nation had expected. As a masterful storyteller, the Prime Minister and his team were able to construct a political narrative that promises all that and more. After all, Abe had written a book in Japanese called "Toward a Beautiful Country" (*Utsukushii Kuni E*). Abe will not only address the external challenges faced by Japan with a firm hand butwill also restore Japan to its rightful place in the world and become Japan's greatest global advocate.

When voters elected to vote out the DPJ in 2012, Abe was elected Prime Minister once again. His return was not so much that the voters liked the LDP or him per se but had a lot to do with the DPJ's disappointing performance in responding to the economic malaise, political instability and perceived inability to handle deteriorating external circumstances poised by North Korea and China. To that end, he was able to capitalise on the existing public sentiment within the country and strategic climate and offer assurances to the Japanese nation that he would decisive leadership, prioritise and tackle Japan's economic challenges using the three arrows of Abenomics (monetary easing, fiscal stimulus and structural reforms). Abe was also able to consolidate his power within the party, leveraged on his hawkish reputation to assure voters that he would act decisively to address the challenges that Japan faced. For ordinary folks on the street, Abe promised to be a pair of "stable" hands in a time of great uncertainty (Estevez-Abe, 2014). As Nakahara (2021) notes, "Abe capitalised on the language of 'Take Back Japan' to reconstruct and legitimise LDP's long-term rule and one-party dominance … and used the slogan and crisis rhetoric to construct a sense of deprivation and build public support for "new" policies that were a recycling of what the conservative LDP had been pursuing before the DPJ interregnum".

Abe was more careful about not expounding a very aggressive anti-China agenda from the get-go this time round. Even though keeping the China threat alive and exaggerated was necessary for his political agenda, Abe realised that Japan needed a stable strategic environment and working relationship with Beijing to prevent the escalation of conflict in order to achieve its political and economic goals. The difficult relationship with China began to improve after Abe's meeting with Chinese leader Xi Jinping at the APEC Summit in Beijing.

There is no question that Abe was the intellectual leader of the Global Right, and the Quad was a reiteration of his ideas that were promoted during his first term. Abe had spoken extensively about building the "Arc of freedom and democracy" and values-based diplomacy in his first term, a concept that was widely interpreted as an anti-China conception in his first term. Beyond the intellectual framework, Abe also repackaged and reframed his anti-China military alliance into a quintessential liberal concept that speaks to defending liberty and democracy by emphasising a vision for a "Free and Open Indo-Pacific" (FOIP) that became the guiding principle for the Quad so that a "rules-based" order can be maintained (Smith, 2021a, 2021b; Hosaya, 2017; Siow, 2022). Abe articulated his vision for Japan's foreign policy in a speech he gave entitled "The Bounty of the Open Seas" in Jakarta 2013 where he conceptualised the notion of "Indo-Pacific" and argued that Japan would strengthen ties with the United States and maritime Southeast Asia based on Five Principles: (1) protection of freedoms of thought, expression and speech; (2) ensuring that high seas and global commons are governed by laws and rules; (3) protect free and interconnected economies and encouraging flows of trade, investment, people and goods; (4) promote intercultural exchanges and (5) promoting exchange among younger generations (MOFA 2013).

Abe also sought to build a consensus over the Quad and to attempt to legitimise and normalise the idea by expanding the Quad dialogue to other partners such as ASEAN, Vietnam and the Philippines. The importance of this cannot be underscored, as Abe has implicitly through the concept of the idea that China is against a "Free and Open Indo-Pacific", and by extension must be stopped with military force built and centred around the US–Japan security alliance. What had essentially begun as a realpolitik Abe-inspired Japanese strategic and military attempt to balance its neighbour is now a repackaged larger diplomatic and strategic concept that provides justification for a strategic alliance that encircles China.

Under Abe's leadership, Japan served as the driving force behind the Quad concept and worked towards operationalising it. Through increased diplomatic engagements with the United States, Australia and India at various levels, including summits, Abe successfully fostered a sense of "comfort" in working with these "like-minded" partners across different domains, such as economic cooperation, technology protection and infrastructure development. All of these efforts were aimed at countering China's growing influence within the Quad countries, as well as in third countries and global south regions where China's Belt and Road Initiative was being implemented.

Abe endeavoured to integrate and legitimise his personal worldview and advocated for a more robust defense policy for Japan by asserting that it was necessary for Tokyo to increase its defense and security cooperation with the Quad countries. This involved not only deepening Tokyo's defense relationships with the United States but also with Australia and India. It required harmonising their strategic goals wherever and whenever feasible and addressing a range of security issues, such as maritime security, weapons procurement and cybersecurity. Initially, these discussions were intended as a dialogue mechanism, but they have since been institutionalised into real-life training exercises and operations, realising Abe's long-cherished plans. Without Abe's leadership, the concept of the Quad would not have been realised. Abe's conceptualisation and rhetoric were successfully replicated in policy statements and media narratives across the Quad countries and the region. What is more impressive is that Abe often utilised personal diplomacy to build strong relations with leaders, such as Trump, Modi, Abbott, Turnbull and Morrison. Abe went about reinvigorating the concept slowly and stealthily, gradually building the coalition of the Global Right.

If Abe's pedigree and ideological tendencies had helped elevate him to his first Prime Ministership, it's his finely honed political skills that ensured his political longevity. Recognising that even within the LDP, there are politicians with a wide variety of views, one of the most important tasks for Abe was to appoint people with either a similar political background, pedigree or political outlook with regard to history. Beyond ensuring that his strongest direct political rival is sidelined (such as Shigeru Ishiba) (Siripala, 2018; Gallagher & Sieg, 2000, 2020), Abe ensures that "like-minded" individuals from different factions are appointed to his Cabinet. Taro Aso, a former Prime Minister with a similar pedigree who leads another powerful faction. Aso also shares Abe's policy views strongly and vested interests in whitewashing history, military rearming and Constitutional Revisionism remained his Deputy Prime Minister during his second stint. Most Cabinet Appointees are drawn from *Nippon Kaigi*, the openly right-wing revisionist organisation. With the exception of Taro Kono (Glosserman, 2021b, 2021d, 2022), all Abe's ministers were members of *Nippon Kaigi*.

The drastic turn towards conservatism would have not been possible if Abe was not able to focus on maintaining his image well and sustaining high hopes for the Japanese public hoping to arrest the spate of troubles domestically and externally that was affecting Japan. His stints as Koizumi's chief cabinet secretary and lessons from his downfall as Prime Minister after 2007 have taught him that it was critical to maintain tight control over his political messaging and image maintenance carefully to ensure political longevity and support. Abe announced that he would step down on 28 August 2020 for health reasons. He achieved many goals, apart from a full-fledged constitutional revision. He has also become Japan's longest serving Prime Minister in the process, a feat that cannot be that easy. He had far exceeded where Koizumi left when it came to security. Japanese society had moved further right, the US–Japan alliance was reconfigured and strengthened, and China had indeed become more of a threat in the eyes of the Japanese public and elites. In real terms, Abenomics did not bring down debt or reduce structural problems such as reducing excessive bureaucracy (Kaya, 2022), and despite all the official pronouncements, Japan was not as secure as it once was in the early 1990s.

There has been debate on his legacy, with many claiming that he is possibly the most consequential of post-war Prime Ministers (Kato et al., 2022) . For many in the West, Abe's promotion of democracy and freedom, particularly in his stance against China and advocacy for a rules-based order and a "Free and Open Indo-Pacific", is seen as his greatest legacy. His rhetoric and outlook mirrored as well as were embraced by mainstream and social narratives in the global right countries (Chacko & Jayasuriya, 2018). However, it is important to note that Abe was in fact full of contradictions (French, 2022) and he was neither very liberal nor democratic. While he was not as brash as the Philippines' Duterte or bigoted as Turkey's Erdogan, Abe shares more similarities with these autocrats than with US leaders such as Barack Obama. Perception is often more important than reality in politics. Abe's true talent lied in his ability to repackage his grandfather's ultra-right-wing attitudes and beliefs, dressed them in liberal rhetoric and marketed them both at home and abroad. This liberal veneer helped him erode the guardrails of liberalism and democracy at home and convinced his supporters and many detractors that it was necessary to abandon the post-World War II framework and rearm Japan. He was however not all that popular in reality but his political skills in factional politics endowed him with a certain political longevity (McCurry, 2022; Sim, 2022). Diplomatically, Abe's liberal democratic image vis-à-vis China enabled him to sell his repackaged policies to international audiences. His true talent as a politician was his remarkable cleverness in interpreting and translating his family legacy and personal beliefs into a larger political doctrine and methodology, operationalising it into a larger Japanese realpolitik aimed at stifling China's growing power and promoting Japan's prospects as an independent strategic power. During this process, Abe also persuaded the Americans not only that Japan be allowed to overcome the legal and political latches they had put on Japan since the Second World War but to realign against their most important economic and trading partner

(China) in the name of national security. His role in advancing anti-China containment is much understated but remains critical if one wants to understand the international politics of the Asia–Pacific. (Harris, 2020; Siow, 2022)

Abe's ability to reconfigure regional and global politics was done through the demonstrative success of his political methodology for conservatives globally and his proactive diplomacy. Abe exerted significant influence on Tony Abbott, who spoke fondly of his admiration for Abe. Coming to power in the aftermath of Labour's Kelvin Rudd who had questioned the real significance of the Quad, Abbott took the first step of securitising Australia's relations with China. Abe also successfully enticed Turnbull, once a Sinophile to continue his political enemy's (Abbott) policies vis-à-vis China, by emphasising the need for a values-based diplomacy. Abe also actively courted the Indian Prime Minister Modi and actively acted as the bridge that brought India into the fold of the US–Japan alliance cooperation. Lastly, it was through his persistence and personal diplomacy that he was able to win over Trump in a manner that he was never able to, with Obama, to lean towards his policies, particularly over China. In a sense, if Washington thinks that Abe is their man in Tokyo, they might not have it entirely correct. If anything, Trump could be construed as Abe's man in the United States.

Abe also sought to engage and build relations with other powers beyond the United States. For instance, he also did try to mend Japan's relations with Russia, having met Vladimir Putin many times over, even though it was clear that Russia would *not* ever return the Northern Four Islands that Japan claims. Insofar as many Russian Japan specialists were concerned, dialogue was necessary, but in their personal opinion, it would take a lot for Russia to come to such an agreement with Japan. He was active in the Global South, trying to counter China's BRI efforts even as he lobbied for Japan's allies to do the same.

For all intents and purposes, as a revisionist, Abe has been able to get other leaders to overlook his personal ideological proclivities or his domestic agenda and achieved de facto but limited remilitarisation. The problem, however, for Abe, regardless of how the threat of China was magnified, it did not provide him with enough domestic support for the constitutional revision that he sought. It also was not enough to persuade the Obama or Trump White House to support his goals in this respectHowever, even if this might be due to large political realities, Abe's ideas and rhetoric have certainly provided Trump with a blueprint to radically and drastically accelerate the demise of contemporary US–China relations. However, this might not necessarily lead to the outcome that Abe was hoping for, given that the trajectory of what had transpired had not necessarily weakened China or, for that matter, strengthened Japan strategically in the way Abe envisaged. Trump had withdrew from the Trans-Pacific Partnership (TPP), threatened Japan with tariffs and generally contravened the liberal spirit that Japanese people admired. While Japan might have tightened her relations with the global right-quad countries, the escalated tensions with China hardly bode well for regional and global security. With Abe's passing, his ideas remain influential even though his legacy is still being intensely debated (Gunangurunathan, 2022; Harris, 2022). Be that as it may, Japan's politics do not look as purposeful as it did during Abe's reign, as his successors such as Suga (Ichihara, 2021), Kishida and Ishiba looked like they have much difficulty consolidating support to govern after the demise of Japan's foremost nationalist. Abe only managed to formulate all these bold policies that laid the foundation for the Quad because he was able to keep himself in power for a long while (Mukai, 2022)

Level II: Domestic Politics

Political Nationalism in Japan: National Identity and Historical Evolution

The emergence of Conservatism in Japan cannot be attributed solely to the efforts of Shinzo Abe alone. Japan's political climate shifted significantly to the right well before Abe's second Prime Ministership. The Quad 2.0 is an embodiment and expression of this conservatism. The rise of conservatism is the result of a convergence of various factors, including generational change and the corresponding shifts in long-standing societal norms and post-war political culture. This is, in part, stimulated by external challenges and domestic politics that prompted a substantial shift in national identity. The prevalent narrative in both Japan and the West today is that China's "aggression" poses a threat to the peace and stability of East Asia. Thus, the shift in Japanese national identity and worldview as well as the nature and tone of nationalism is seen as a response to this.

The roots of contemporary Japanese nationalism have historically been traced back to a few important influences. Japan's political system had limited exposure to liberalism or democracy until the early twentieth century, when the Taisho era (1912–1926) brought about reforms in the nation-state structure to emulate emerging political ideals in the West. Japan's attempts to establish liberal democracy during this time were paradoxically accompanied by colonial experiments in Korea and Taiwan. In the 1930s, power struggles between military elites from the Army and the Navy took place due to Japan's imperialistic ambitions in China and against the backdrop of the Great Depression. The establishment of the Peace Constitution and Japan's transformation into a liberal democracy by occupation authorities led to the birth of contemporary Japan. Since then, Japan has had a series of Prime Ministers, but only a few have been noteworthy: Shigeru Yoshida, Ichiro Hatoyama, Nobusuke Kishi, Eisaku Sato, Yasuhiro Nakasone, Junichiro Koizumi and Shinzo Abe. These leaders not only served for extended periods but also shared a commonality; many were descendants of Samurai families and exhibited tough personalities with a confrontational approach to domestic politics. Traditionally, strong leadership signals the ability of leaders to protect themselves and their communities. With deep-held strength and conviction, strong leaders are almost always capable of leading with determination and resilience and likely succeed in overcoming difficulties in adversity. The key criteria for political success, whether in the 1950s, 1980s, or 2010s, was therefore not only how well any party or politician responded to the challenges of the day, but also whether the politician could be trusted to preserve the Japanese way of life and vigorously defend, protect and enhance Japan's national interests. The most charismatic leader often is one who does the best job persuading the electorate that he would be able to implement all his agenda and rejuvenate his nation to greatness. In post-war politics, perhaps no one does this better than Shinzo Abe and Junichiro Koizumi.

The second important historical influence of Japanese nationalism is related to how Japan defines itself. The basis of any identity, whether ethnic, gender or national, presupposes an "other" reference where members of the group can use markers to map out the boundaries of the group and distinguish those who are members of the group from those who are not. For a long time, the most important "other" reference groups were her closest neighbours—Korea and China. The historical connections between East Asian nations are extensive. These nations have been profoundly impacted by a wide range of influences, resulting in a shared cultural foundation. Buddhism, Confucianism, literary and culinary practices, economic systems, social hierarchies and political structures are only a few examples of the common historical influences that have shaped the region. However, each nation has developed its own distinct cultural and linguistic traditions that contribute to its unique identity, outlook and daily life. The nationalisms that exist between these East Asian nations are therefore part of a long-standing social conversation between them that has persisted for centuries, often manifested through narratives of economic, cultural and moral superiority, as well as regrettably, through invasions, colonialism and warfare. The progress made by these nations has often been achieved through observation, emulation and indigenisation. One only needs to examine the evolution of writing systems, such as the shift from Chinese characters to contemporary Japanese *hiragana* and *katagana* systems, or the development of hangul in Korea. For these nations, the desire to distinguish themselves from and claim superiority over their neighbours has historically been a major driving force behind their progress and the foundation of international relations. The Meiji Restoration was a significant turning point in the Japanese history. One of the primary reasons for this event was the Japanese elite's desire to prevent and overcome what they saw as the decline of Qing China. This marked the beginning of Tokyo's determination to learn from the West and modernise its society. This process marked the beginning of an era in which Japan's self-reference and identity began to relate to Western imperial powers. As a result of this modernisation process, Japan gained the technological advantages and ambitions of the nineteenth-century imperial power. However, this also marked the beginning of a tragic history of the Japanese colonisation of its supposed inferior neighbours, which created a host of problems that contemporary Japan had to live with. The nationalism between Japan and its neighbours, particularly China and Korea, is plagued with negative sentiments and extreme emotions. These historical influences are deeply embedded in today's formulation of Japanese statist nationalism and fundamentally remain at the heart of Japanese conservatism, continuing to affect ways that underpin their social cohesiveness and progress as a nation.

Economic Decline and LDP's Quest for Continued Relevance and Dominance

After emerging from the "lost decades" of the Great Leap Forward and the Cultural Revolution, China embarked on economic reforms in the post-Mao era. By this time, Japan's economy had grown to the extent that Tokyo was challenging the United States' economic prowess as she had become the world's second largest economy. At the convening of the 12th Chinese Communist Party Congress in 1982, China was still largely an agriculture-based economy. World Bank Statistics indicate that Japan's economy was approximately $1.084 trillion and the US economy was $2.7 trillion. Owing to data transparency issues, China's GDP was estimated to be around $303 billion (Penn World Table), which meant that Japan's economy was 3.43 times that of China's GDP. By 2012, World Bank data shows the United States had a GDP of $16.16 trillion, China $8.22 trillion and Japan $6.16 trillion. China has now overtaken Japan as the world's second largest economy. In 2020, United States' GDP was $21.42 trillion, China's GDP was $16.08 trillion and Japan's $5.01 trillion. The situation has now reversed, as China's economy is approximately 3.2 times the size of Japan. However, the use of GDP is not a good measure. If we look at the numbers on a per capita PPP basis using data from the World Bank, the United States is $76,329.60, Japan $45,583.80 and China $21,482.60. The average American is almost 3.55 times and the average Japanese 2.1 times richer than the average Chinese person. Of course in reality, the real picture could be a lot more grim, given the disparity that exists in these three countries, but the per capita data suggest that China has yet to catch up with the United States or Japan's standard of living.

The miraculous rise of Japan after World War II is an important source of pride for many Japanese born in the aftermath of the war. This success was attributed to both the LDP as well as the bureaucracy (Fulcher, 1988). The post-war generation that grew up during this period now controls the levers of Japanese politics, society and economy that underwent the lost decade from the 1990s to the 2000s, when Japan's economy faced deflationary pressures, banking crises and prolonged slow economic growth and stagnation. Like most other developed economies was seeing increasing signs of slow growth and widening disparity. When Koizumi took over from Mori at the turn of the century, Japan's economy was in deterioration particularly in its fiscal policy. Koizumi had to restore fiscal health through cuts, and not to raise consumption tax. The Prime Minister was of the view that there will be "no growth without reform", that Japan should "allow the private sector do what it can" and that "local government should handle what it can" (Komine, 2007). Quintessentially, Koizumi was an advocate of minimum government intervention in the likes of Ronald Reagan and Margeret Thachter. Koizumi's agenda of eradicating pork barrel politics (Saito, 2009) and implementing neoliberal economic reforms had led to economic prosperity of a small handful of firms without the trickle-down reform as envisaged. Abe had rolled back some of the reforms that Koizumi made and reinstituted much of the pork barrel politics that LDP has so used to. Juxtaposed against China's economic reforms, this undoubtedly created different sentiments within Japan amongst different societal segments. There is, of course, a sense of economic opportunities amongst businesses, as well as a positive impact on the daily lives of people with the influx of cheaper and higher-quality consumer goods. At the same time, as the economic gulf widens, this has created intense concern amongst the Japanese regarding the competition China would pose for Japanese industries, technological rivalry and impact on Japanese industries domestically and overseas. Over the last decade as the gulf between China and Japanese widens, this economic disparity has been translated into a national security issue for Japan. China's economic strength has been translated into strategic influence, military modernisation and political clout that threatens to undercut Japan's interests in third countries and issue areas that have never been observed before.

Normalising Japan in the Post-Cold War World

The economic rise of China did not look all threatening to Japan in the early 1990s, even though there was a fair amount of strategic soul-searching that was going on in Tokyo, just as it did in Canberra, London and Washington D.C. After all, the collapse of the USSR was a seismic event in international relations and even though the Soviet Union dissolved without much fanfare, there was still much consideration as to what to do after, as well as the fate of the institutions born during the Cold War, such as the North Atlantic Treaty Organisation (NATO) and the US bilateral alliances system in Asia. In the Asian capitals of US allies such as those in Tokyo and Seoul, the strategic angst is clear as governments debated whether there might be a strategic withdrawal from the region since the Soviet threat had clearly dissipated. The "peace" that the US strategic presence purported underpinned in the region was built on the backs of two long and prolonged wars in Asia, the Korean War and the Vietnam War. From the perspective of the allies and partners in the region, the relationship with the United States goes back a long way for the many parties involved. Whether it is the Kuomintang in Taiwan or the Liberal

Democratic Party in Japan, the regime's partnership with the Americans has also helped confer both legitimacy and often assistance to help with the regime's political prospects, insuring them against domestic opposition, particularly those from left-wing. Thus, even with the dissolution of the USSR, the United States retains an important interest in ensuring that politicians and regimes in the region enact policies that would lean towards the United States.

During the 1990s, despite the unipolarity of the international system, the strategic community in the United States and its allies engaged in a rigorous debate on the potential threat posed by China. The Japanese nation's attitude towards China at the time however was ambivalent. Likewise there were also still residual anti-American sentiments in Japan (as well as the Koreas) too (Smith, 2003). However, as the decade progressed, various issues emerged in Japan–China relations, such as China's nuclear tests, the Senkaku Islands, Taiwan missile tests, history textbooks, the demarcation of the East Sea, the division of carbon resources and the intrusion of Chinese naval vessels into Japanese territorial waters. The previously golden era of Sino-Japanese relations appeared to have given way to a decade of unprecedented acrimony in their bilateral relationship. Concurrently, politicians and policymakers within Japan started to focus on the possibility of the United States scaling down or abandoning its presence and what this might mean for Japan. There is no question that should the US–Japan Security alliance, Japan would be drastically affected as the alliance is the fundamental cornerstone of Japanese defence and foreign policy. Thus, the LDP elites were extremely keen to undertake tackle two issues. The first was how to retain the US strategic presence in the region and ensure that Japan worked with Washington more effectively to facilitate and transform the US–Japan alliance to better address emerging challenges facing Japan and the region. The Liberal Democratic Party (LDP), led by Hashimoto Ryutaro, had reached an agreement with the Clinton administration by 1997 to reaffirm the US–Japan Security Alliance, which included fine-tuning defense arrangements, logistical support and enacting legal amendments to better support US operations. This was done to ensure that the alliance was equipped to deal with the emerging challenges posed by China.

The second major aspect of this development is a renewed discussion of how Japan can become a "normal state". This became an important and significant domestic debate amongst the Japanese domestic politics, as they ponder whether the United States can be reliable enough to back

Japan in all scenarios. The concept of Japan as a "normal state" typically refers to the idea that the country should adopt a more proactive stance in international affairs, particularly in defense and strategic matters. Japan's constitution, which renounced the use of war and imposed restrictions on its military, has historically shaped its pacifist position. However, the concept of a "normal" state suggests a shift towards a more conventional military posture, similar to other sovereign nation-state. This concept is often debated in the context of Constitutional reinterpretation or amendment, with the aim of expanding Japan's Self-Defense Forces' scope and enabling the country to participate more actively in international security efforts. The subtext of this relates to Japan's contingency planning in the event of US strategic abandonment or worse choosing to privilege ties with China at the expense of Japan. While remote, these possibilities look like they would happen since the insecurities drove Japan elites to debate vigorously about the nature of their relations with both the United States and China even as they sought to tighten the US–Japan alliance. This debate is not without controversy, as it raises concerns about potential regional tensions and doubts about Japan's commitment to pacifism. Even though public opinion is divided, the democratic impulses of Japan during the 1990s however did not allow this quest for normalcy to dictate Japanese foreign policy entirely. It did however become an important platform for politicians and the basis for LDP's political agenda from the late 1990s onwards (International Viewpoint, 2002).

In a large part, these discussions and debates are driven by changing notions of what it means to be secure in such challenging times, as well as the continued relevance of these post-war arrangements put in place. The necessity of these debates is not only due to the changing external environment but also the generational change within Japan. Each generation has its own formative experiences, worldview and identity and employs different values, priorities and criteria for framing challenges encountered. Consequently, as new generations mature to take the reins of the nation's leadership, they inevitably challenge the worldview and frame of reference of the previous generations. This is evident in the criticism of the baby boomers for a variety of social ills, such as generational wealth, national debt and the environmental crisis (Avenell, 2023). The differences in how historical events should be dealt with and whether policies instituted seventy-five years ago after the War are still relevant and suitable for today's Japan have become a subject of debate. This conversation naturally extends to include the discussion on national defense

70   V. TEO

and Japan's prospects as a normal nation-state. A significant segment of the baby boomers grew up and witnessed Japan's economic ascendance, experienced the Vietnam War and lived through the US–Japan economic antagonism during the 1970s and 1980s. During that period, Japanese nationalism was often framed against the United States. The later generations grew up in a period where Japan's economy experienced stagnation and saw a sharp downturn in relations with China, whose economy was growing very briskly (Fig. 2.1).

Overcoming Resistance to LDP's Continued Dominance: Factionalism, Bureaucracy and the Media

In order to comprehend the reasoning behind the receptiveness of Japanese society towards Shinzo Abe's conservative nationalism from 2012, one has to understand the role played by political nationalism, economic decline and generational change in raising questions about Japan's governance and the continued relevance of its post-war institutions. The direction and tone of this debate were primarily shaped by the country's ruling elites. This debate also involves traditional actors within the Japanese political establishment who have historically served to provide a measure of balance to the ruling party, albeit with diverse and often self-interested motivations. Their resistance, expressed through open questions, challenges and non-compliance, has frequently hindered the Liberal Democratic Party (LDP) from being able to act with impunity for their agenda. From 2012 onwards, the LDP under the leadership of Abe was able to increasing erode the power of these institutions and actors to rein in the LDP, enabling the LDP elites to become even more powerful than before.

The essence of multiparty democracy lies in party politics, and the Liberal Democratic Party (LDP) has been the dominant ruling party in Japan since its two-party system emerged in 1955. The political opposition had little chance of gaining power due to the LDP's success in securing the nation during the Cold War through its alliance with the United States and overseeing Japan's rapid economic growth, which made it the world's second largest economy. This resulted in decades of peace and stability that the electorate highly valued. The LDP has always been favoured by the United States for her own purposes, and this itself provided a certain measure of electorate advantages for the Party. The LDP's ability to project an image of being the most capable of protecting

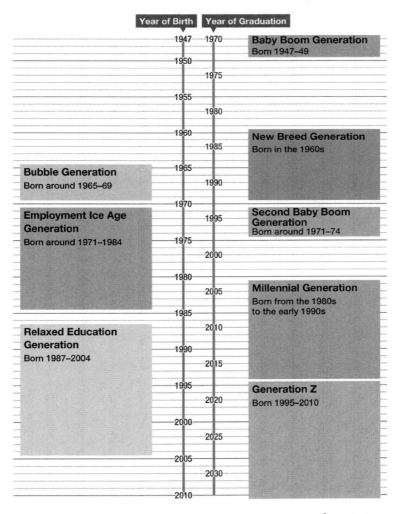

Fig. 2.1 Japanese generations adopted from Nippon.com (Nippon, 2022)

the nation and adapting to changing internal dynamics and external challenges has contributed to its success. Since 1955, the LDP has only been out of power twice: 1993 to 1994 (ten months) and then again from 2009 to 2012. Since then, the LDP and its coalition partner, Komeito has won seven successive elections.

When the Liberal and Democratic parties decided to merge and form the LDP in 1955 at the behest of the CIA in response to the consolidation of the left-wing politicians into the Japan Socialist Party (JSP), the structural arrangements created tremendous difficulty for the left-wing parties to be able to win votes and get traction in Japan's political system. At the same time, the United States actively shaped and ally Japan to US interests, using formal policy pronouncements, administrative guidance and soft power cultural influences (Kushner & Sato, 2005). It was virtually not possible for an independent power base to emerge in Japan under the watchful eye of the Americans. As such, since the LDP took power in 1955, political change has always traditionally come from within the party (The Economist, 2021) through factional politics, instead of genuine democratic checks and balances and power transfer between parties. Factionalism therefore has been a dominant force that has held sway over Japanese domestic politics. Echoing Martin Luther King, former Prime Minister Tanaka Kakuei said "Politics is about numbers, and numbers are power" (Bosack, 2022). This is particularly important in Japan's political system as the largest faction controls the intra-party debates and decision-making and wins internal elections to seize power through the acquisition of important administrative positions like the President and Secretary General of the Party and in turn, assumes the Prime Ministership.

Prior to the reforms of 1994, factions wielded significant influence over a politician's career. Factional leaders were instrumental in negotiating with other factions to secure grand bargains, recruiting and promoting factional candidates and fundraising for their campaigns. They also lent their prestige and influence to endorse these candidates. In an election, losing candidates in single-district races may have the opportunity to be included on the proportional candidate ticket, which can potentially revive their chances of winning. However, due to the limited number of proportional seats, party leaders must engage in discussions and make decisions on which candidates will be given preference. Factional members, in theory, were expected to be loyal and support their leader in gaining power, manufacturing support and seeking cabinet and party posts. Shifting faction allegiances often create opportunities for change and leadership renewal. For instance, regime change was only possible when factional leaders rebel and break off from the LDP as demonstrated in 1993 when 39 members of the Hata-Ozawa faction along with Watanabe group broke off from the LDP (Jain, 1993).

Electoral reform undertaken in 1994 over voting rules enabled the institution of a new system that gave citizens two votes, one for the party and one for the candidates allowing for the breaking of the stranglehold of the LDP in Japanese politics and the emergence of the DPJ. (Krauss & Pekkanen, 2011). Although the 1994 reforms reduced the influence of factional heads over their ability to whip votes or negatively impact the careers of their members, factions continue to play a crucial role in the continued success of a politician's career. Often, political resistance towards the ruling establishment comes from within rather than outside the LDP in policy debates. This is of course accentuated by the clientelism that has grown within the LDP over the years as different groups of politicians have developed networks and patron-client relationships with various interest groups. Factions emerged in importance from 2012. Once LDP returned to power under the leadership of Shinzo Abe, his faction became even more dominant as Abe implemented a series of measures to expand its influence and co-opt members across the LDP, ensuring that support for his conservative agenda grew and remained strong. As the head of one of the largest factions in LDP, Abe's faction does exert tremendous influence on intra-party decision-making and became increasingly influential in terms of recruitment, funding and mobility opportunities. When it came to the LDP Presidency, only factions with large enough members would enable the faction leaders to run for Party President. Noda Seiko, for instance, tried to run for Party President multiple times but never had the faction support necessary to get nominated until 2021 when she lost to Fumio Kishida (Takahara, 2021). Abe's political skills has ensured that his faction became the dominant faction in the LDP and this reduced any resistance to his agenda. This dominance eventually translated into a succession problem after his death (Langley Esquire, 2022).

There are other sources of resistance to LDP's dominance of course. One important source is the power of the bureaucracy in Japan. The strength and power of the bureaucracy in Japan is a well-studied subject to the extent that they are often regarded as the people with the real power in Japan. One author had observed as early as 1947 that neither

74 V. TEO

the elimination and barring of influential bureaucrats from public office nor sweeping changes in the structure of the Japanese government have been enough to alter the basic character of the bureaucracy there (Maki, 1947: 391). Bureaucrats were one of the three pre-war governing classes not punished by the even as the Occupation government sought to dislodge militarists and eradicate the influence of *zaibatsu* (monopoly capitalists) that were deemed to be responsible for Japan's domestic and foreign policy decisions before and during the war. Japan's bureaucrats were in reality a governing class and operated with little restrain or reform even from the pre-war days (Maki, 1947: 405). In the post-war world, the bureaucrats played a central role in the planning and implementing of so many of the major changes in Japan and are to be seen favourably as agents of change. For instance, Japan's MITI representing the State has been seen as a critical force behind the economic development and expansion in Japan, and the success was genuinely devised and implemented by a limited number of elite bureaucrats in the central agencies (Johnson, 1982). A small number of former bureaucrats who were supporters of Prime Minister Yoshida Shigeru were elevated to stand for office, and in the first twenty-five years, after the formation of the 1955 system, the office of the Prime Minister was held for twenty years by former bureaucrats (Pempel, 1992: 23). Consequently, the bureaucracy became dominant force in Japanese politics for a better part of post-war Japan and continues to become problematic and difficult for the Japanese Prime Ministers to rein in. Japanese bureaucratic elites have a far greater staying power than assumed as they cannot be easily replaced; additionally, bureaucrats often procrastinate over acute problems (particularly with regard to economy problems) both politicians and bureaucrats value social cohesion and harmony over the economy (Drucker, 1998). In short, they are inimical to change and unaccountable to the electorate. By the mid-1990s, the bureaucrats' influence on politics was on the wane because increasingly they were no longer recruited for top positions within the political hierarchy. The Japanese political class was increasingly united in their view that the bureaucrats should be beholden to the agenda of the executive branch, rather than the other way around. Koizumi introduced and later Abe continued to enforce the measures that ensured that the bureaucracy would be reined in and remained responsive to changing times.

The media serves as the third significant group that should technically provide resistance and checks on the Japanese government. Japan has indeed a sheer number of newspapers, magazines, radio stations and television stations, the media functions quite differently from the media in Western democracies. The relationship between the media and the government is complex and often less adversarial than assumed, as the press tends to be more polite and accommodating than their Western counterparts. The media model in Japan has been characterised in the 1980s by Oxford Japanologist J. Stockwin to be in a symbiotic relationship with the LDP. The LDP relied on the bureaucracy for technical expertise and legislative work, and the bureaucracy depended on the LDP for their parliamentary support and access to national resources upon the bill's passing as well as cushy jobs upon retirement, known popularly as "amakudari" (descent from heaven literally). The LDP also depended upon big businesses for electoral funding and in turn, the business depended on the LDP for political endorsement, favourable policies and political stability. The business, in turn, relies on favours from the bureaucracy in drafting and implementation of legislation, as well as in discretionary application of powers (Stockwin 1980: 10). The role of the media is often to disseminate and pass messages that would harmonise public opinion for the LDP, the bureaucracy and the business. The media in Japan has never been a monolithic bloc even though dominant newspapers might exist, exercising a sort of controlled environment for new big players as the newspapers only differ in "matters of degree and emphasis". Whereas outside of Japan, the personal views of newsmen might influence the tone of the article and direction of reporting, within Japan, the newsmen (while most of whom are left of centre), are actually conformist to their companies' external policies and expectations (Nester, 1989). From the early 2000s, the media landscape evolved and the media began to play a greater role in uncovering government scandals and holding officials accountable. The media does occasionally function in a supervisory capacity by exposing scandals and raising critical questions through editorials. Even though the media has become more assertive in holding the government accountable, particularly in cases of political scandals and nuclear energy policy, the reach of the state has become a concern for many in the industry.

As Shinzo Abe ascended for the second time in 2012, his government weakened press freedom in Japan and the ability of the media to criticise and question the LDP's policies, even as sought to ensure that the narratives crusade against China remains steadfast. During his tenure, journalists are being pressured and punished for reporting on sensitive issues, and often those who write in the "correct" tone and direction are allowed access. There are concerns over how reporters are socialising with politicians and bureaucrats of ministries they are assigned to and maintaining a relationship with them. This has two important consequences. There will be an inclination to prioritise access over investigative journalism and self-censorship to eradicate critical reporting and file only stock-positive narratives for publication. This greatly reduced the journalists' integrity as such practices only encouraged self-censorship, increased corporate influence and compromised government advertising on media independence. Moreover, the government's control over information, especially during times of crisis or national security concerns, remains a subject of debate.

In 2014, the Japanese government also implemented the Protection of Specially Designated Secrets Act that impeded the freedom of information rights of Japanese nationals and in the process targeted whistle-blowers (Bosack, 2022). Over the summer that year, Asahi Shimbun had actually withdrew its both its comfort women coverage and its investigations into Fukushima following harsh right-wing attacks, led by Abe himself, on missteps in some of its articles. On the 3rd of October 2014, Abe criticised the Asahi for harming Japan's reputation, following the newspaper's admission that their previously published stories about comfort women were based on a discredited Japanese army veteran's sourcing. Abe emphasised to the lower house budget committee that the newspaper's misreporting had caused numerous individuals to experience hurt, sorrow, suffering and outrage and had significantly damaged Japan's image (Fackler, 2016).

In March 2016, Japan removed the most outspoken TV anchors on three different networks that were making comments on high-profile critics of Abe's agenda, including restarting nuclear power and the erosion of post-war Pacificism. One of Abe's ministers, Sanae Takaichi had declared in parliament that the government had power to shut down the newspapers if they were deemed to be politically biased, effectively subduing the largest newspaper Asahi Shimbun. There were others (such as Abe's advisor Yosuke Isozaki) who interfered with the media, by asking them to rework and adjust their notions on the fairness of political talkshows and reports, and essentially strong-armedthem to change their rules and adjust their behaviour (Narazaki & Sasagawa, 2023). Affected outlets included the Japan Times, Asahi Shimbun. Abe also empowered institutions such as Nikkei to ensure that the editorial direction remains staunchly anti-China. There is no question that the collective opinion has swayed again China. Additionally, the algorithms on Japanese social media (akin to Western social media) in both countries are completely unified in cyberspace to promote the statist nationalistic narrative that has significantly changed public opinion against China.

The education sector also came under the scrutiny of the State (Asahi Shimbun 2020). Abe directly addressed the writing of what he perceives as masochistic history, allowing the state to maintain greater control of textbooks thereby enabling the younger generation of Japanese to have a greater sense of patriotism. The bureaucrats at the Education ministry as well as academics who question either Abe's or the LDP's greater political posture are sidelined or removed. Additionally, the Abe government has been criticised all roundly on how they have disregarded policy experts' views to the public. To that end, the Abe government has not really been receptive to these criticisms, and in that respect, the effort to remove "harmful" history continues. This focus on eradicating however did not start from Abe, but really can be traced back to Abe's predecessor Koizumi.

The Rise of New-Age Conservative Politics: From Koizumi to Abe

By the time Koizumi handed his Prime Ministership to Shinzo Abe in 2006, three important developments in Japanese politics had occurred. First Koizumi had broken several taboos in Japanese domestic politics and foreign policy thereby becoming one of the most popular Prime Ministers in post-war Japan. His advisors had carefully crafted his image in the traditional and social media, showcasing him as a tough and determined patriot determined to reform Japan and take on vested interests that are impeding the nation, including his own party. Second, the events of September 11 and the consequent War on Terror had diverted the attention of the United States away from Asia. This neglect provided the LDP to assume some measure of alliance management and more assertive in security enhancement methods. This allowed the LDP to become more vocal in asserting their resistance to China, both symbolically (with Yasukuni visits and political barbs and accusations against the China or the Chinese government) (Shibuichi, 2005). In doing so, the LDP set off a downward security hysteria that saw the rapid deterioration of Japan's relations with China that eventually paved the way for Japan's current security trajectory. Third and most consequent for Japan is the fact this created the dynamics for the rise of a significant shift in Japanese conservatism and nationalism.

The rise of Junichiro Koizumi in the LDP is abnormal in LDP politics. Although his grandfather was a former Minister of Post and Communications and his father a former director of the Japan Defense Agency under the Ikeda and Sato administrations in the 1960s, Koizumi's family influence cannot be compared to the likes of Shinzo Abe or even Yukio Hatoyama. Koizumi had also served in the Cabinet-level positions since 1988, holding the Health and Welfare portfolio (twice), the Post and Telecommunications portfolio, and even though he was part of the Shinseki Faction otherwise known as the "YKK" Faction, led by Taku Yamasaki and Koichi Kato and Koizumi himself, he was not as prominent as other Ministers. Initially considered as an "outsider" candidate, he nevertheless scored a victory over Ryutaro Hashimoto.

His electoral popularity was due to his uncanny ability to exhibit the kind of toughness and strength that the Japanese public appreciates in their leaders. There is of course nothing tougher than taking on the establishment, particularly in promising to remove pork barrel politics, revamp party politics and tame the power of the bureaucrats. His brand of right-wing populism was much appreciated by the electorate (Lindgreen, 2012). This strategy as he had hoped helped enhance the LDP's electoral success and allowed him some measure of credibility to undertake his neoliberal market reforms. Koizumi's government also inherited important legacies started by Ryuraro Hashimoto in terms of streamlining the bureaucracy and electoral process, which had in effect put in place a system where the bureaucracy would be more responsive to the Cabinet Office. The Prime Minister's grassroots popularity should give him the credibility and backing he needed to take on power interests within the LDP and wrestle power from both the *genros* and the establishment bureaucrats. In 2005, Koizumi did even better by scoring one of the great triumphs of modern Japanese political history essentially promising the same thing, even after failing to deliver to advance a reform agenda in his first term. In 2000, the LDP won 41% of votes and secured 50% of seats, while in 2005, the LDP had won 48% of votes but secured 73% of seats. Koizumi's team was extremely skilled in cultivating Koizumi's image, as he was immensely popular with his flamboyant hairstyle and swashbuckling style that is reminiscent of a modern-day Oda Nobunaga. Koizumi was able to rally mass support because of the strength and determination he showed, particularly those who were disenfranchised or unemployed, as he is seen as really "cool" in their dark and drab world (McCormack, 2005). Yet, as ANU Professor McCormack notes, Koizumi's reign had several "illusory" impacts. The "new" LDP had become more fundamentalist and clique, intolerant of criticism; the exercise to get rid of factions had turned into one where he expanded his own faction at the expense of others and while he had reduced the power of the "*zoku*" or functional tribes, Koizumi had actually given the business community unimpeded access to the halls of power (McCormack, 2005). Koizumi was therefore the most "LDP" of LDP leaders.

Most paradoxical of all was that in advocating his brand of nationalism by visiting Yasukuni Shrine five times in his official capacity as Prime Minister five occasions (April 2001, April 2002, October 2003, January 2004 and October 2005). As a nationalist and/or a populist politician, Koizumi shared a conservative and somewhat mainstream view that those that died for Japan during the War needed to be honoured. Observing this tradition appealed to the Conservative voters, a mainstay of the LDP and cements Koizumi's role in the polity. In doing so, he showed little sensitivity to their neighbours. This of course infuriated China and to a lesser extent Korea so much that it even alarmed the Americans. It was also the same nationalist Koizumi who completely embraced the United States utterly and wholeheartedly without the slightest hinge of embarrassment. In doing so, Koizumi completely eradicated the balance that post-war Japan had achieved in the calibration of their policy towards China and the United States.

Koizumi was ferocious in his nationalistic gestures to convey his political toughness and resistance to the Japanese people in actual fact battling the old-school LDP Nationalists. He was able to purge or retire most of the old-school nationalists, many of whom targeted the United States in their nationalisms. During this same period, many LDP lawmakers who belonged to the faction founded by PM Takana Kakuei and a breakway faction led by PM Noburo Takeshita had either died or vanished politically (Kitazume, 2005). This is the beginning of the demise of the human bridge that had existed between China and Japan as the real advocates of pro-China or cordial relations disappeared with the Tanaka and Takeshita factions.

In making public the discussions on previously taboo subjects such as nuclear weapons, the future of US–Japan alliance, the fate of Article 9 and the revision of the Japanese Constitution, Koizumi introduced a competitive platform by which the right-wing politicians could debate publicly and showcase their patriotism as to who was more "concerned", "loyal" or "advocated" for strong Japan. This debate naturally evolved into more conversations on how Japan could become more "normal" as well as showcase a discussion on how the US–Japan security alliance could be further strengthened. It also opened the gate towards "unrestrained" narratives on China as the dominant new understanding "war atrocities" guilt should no longer burden Japan any longer since the Japanese have "apologised" many times before. The political left as represented by the opposition was of course completely sidelined in this debate. The Social Democratic Party, under the leadership of Murayama Tomiichi, had acknowledged the constitutional legitimacy of the Self-Defense Force (SDF) and supported the US–Japan security treaty (Mukae, 1996; Liff, 2017), as well as the use of the Hinomaru and Kimigayo as the national flag and anthem (Bruaset, 2003). Consequently, there was little that could be done to change this stance. Koizumi's behaviour and the Chinese reactions pushed Sino-Japanese relations on a downward trajectory that has never recovered. This is partly because both countries were unable to establish a proper and respectful independent relationship; both thought that with the United States, they will be able to manage each other; without the United States but in reality, their interactions reinforce the nationalisms as the opportunity for nationalisms drastically reduced.

The War on Terror had netted an additional unforeseen benefit for the United States in Asia. The US neglect in Asia during this period and Bush's trust in Koizumi had given the leader tremendous latitude in handling Japan's foreign policy. The Sino-Japanese tensions that had resulted had led both Tokyo and Beijing wanting to ensure that the Americans were drawn closer. For Beijing, it was to handle and rein in the difficult LDP nationalists, and for Tokyo, it was to hedge and balance against increased Chinese aggressiveness. Koizumi's official Yasukuni Shrine visits as well as nationalist comments vis-à-vis her neighbours had raised concerns in Washington about the new "brand" of LDP politics; after all, there are some in the United States who remembered that it was the Japanese that the Americans fought during the Second World War. There were also concerns on actually chain-ganging of the United States into a conflict with China and disrupting the effective function of the overall US bilateral alliance system in Asia since the Koreans were as aggrieved with Japan as the Chinese were. The critical question for the United States was how to further modify or tweak the alliance revolves not so much on whether to retain an old alliance, but instead on how to modernise that alliance so as to align it more closely with Asian societies that have evolved dramatically since the two alliances were created half a century ago (Smith, 2003). This period therefore also saw an increase in the number of defense hawks that rode on the wave of anti-China sentiments in the Japanese Diet and policy circles since such a posture did help and facilitate the moment of LDP cadres into important positions with the dominance of the right-leaning factions. This of course was made only possible by the fact that the corporate (traditional) and social media has become more important amongst the electorate. Competitive nationalistic posturing, quick sound bites and tough policies made for good political theatre, which in turn was good for political fortunes. Koizumi's lessons in using image management and media manipulation to broaden his own power base to over traditional LDP factional politics provided instructive lessons. Even though his neoliberal reforms was effectively dismantled after he stepped down, and LDP went about back to its traditional ways, the LDP politicians did benefit from Koizumi's time in office as his political methodology in campaigning and rallying public opinion became instructive. The other significant aspect about Koizumi's time was the co-opting of Shinzo Abe as his Chief Cabinet Secretary to boost his faction's appeal and government's popularity. Shinzo Abe was popular because of his outspokenness against the DPRK's kidnapping of Japanese nationals.

After Koizumi stepped down, many of his supporters who helped him get elected in the previous elections (including his "assassins") lost power even though Abe was technically Koizumi's anointed successor. Abe in his first term (2006) faced tremendous problems because the LDP was essentially at war with itself with intense factional infighting. Koizumi's neoliberal reforms had upset the proverbial applecart where many LDP old-timers were reeling from due to the loss of traditional pork barrel politics. Abe lost power after a year not only because of the anger amongst the traditional rank-and-file who felt betrayed by Koizumi's policies but also because Abe's political vision and ambitions of Constitutional revisionism, the eradication of "masochistic history" did not find traction amongst the politicians or the people. The instructive lesson Abe learnt was that it was absolutely necessary to grow his faction as numbers were key to power and he needed to speak to his base even if he maintained a more approachable public persona. The key to power is therefore to grow a faction to grow a strong base and cross-sectional appeal. The end of the Koizumi era marked what is now known as the era of the "revolving door" Prime Ministers—Shinzo Abe (9/2006–9/2007), Yasuo Fukuda (9/2007–9/2008), Taro Aso (9/2008–9/2009), Yukio Hatoyama (9/2009–6/2010), Nato Kan (6/2010–9/2011) and Yoshihiko Noda (9/2011–12/2012). For the second time since the 1990s, Japan came under the governance of the opposition party, the Democratic Party of Japan (DPJ).

The 2009 elections were held against a slew of domestic problems which the LDP had failed to address: economic stagnation, rising unemployment, spiralling national debt, a rapidly aging population and declining external environment. The DPJ came to power because voters were disillusioned with the LDP's and inability to deliver results and respond to electoral demands, as with the return of pork barrel politics and corruption. Taro Aso's personal gaffles did not help, but the DPJ as the alternative party has never looked better to the Japanese electorate. It was ironical because this democratic exercise of the people's power in effecting regime change proved to be a divine intervention for the political fortunes Liberal Democratic Party (LDP). The three DPJ Prime Ministers governed for approximately 39 months. Over the course of this period, the Japanese people too became disappointed with the DPJ. The inexperience of the DPJ as both a political party as well as a governing party however proved to be a blessing in disguise for the Liberal Democratic Party in 2012.

As a new governing Party, Yukio Hatoyama was nominated to become the Prime Minister as Ichiro Ozawa due to a political donation scandal. Ichiro Hatoyama was, in fact, another scion of Japan's political families. Yukio Hatoyama is the grandson of former Prime Minister Ichiro Hatoyama, who was the first President of the Liberal Democratic Party in 1956. Hatoyama's promise to rebalance Japan's relations with the United States and build better relations with China and Korea promised to herald an era that was very different from that of the LDP reign. Both Beijing and Seoul were interested in this curious and very "unjapanese" politician and had great hope for the DPJ. This however did not last very long.

In truth, the DPJ under Hatoyama's leadership was immensely unprepared for the rough and tumble world of Japanese politics nor the herculean task of reining in the Japanese bureaucracy and the media. The new Prime Minister appeared to have little interest or knowledge in handling the press and bureaucracy and showed no inclination to listen to the advice of his advisors or heed the guidance of his bureaucrat handlers. His bold comments about the need to redistribute Japan's relationship with the United States and cultivate closer ties with China and Korea made many in the Japanese political establishment uneasy. Although this was a remarkably courageous and farsighted move for the region, it might not have been the most astute given the political climate in Japan at the time. Consequently, the public narratives of him were unflattering. He was reviled as someone who did not understand what "politics" or "governance" meant, even by his own advisors.

Over the next 30 months, Hatoyama's successors, Prime Ministers Kan and Noda faced severe governance challenges in both their domestic and foreign policy. On 9 August 2010, Tokyo announced that Japan's economy was valued at about $1.28 trillion in the second quarter, slightly below China's $1.33 trillion, suggesting that China's economy would overtake Japan's as the second largest economy in 2010 (Barboza, 2010). The official response from the DPJ government was a calm reaction, but there was a quiet discomfort on the part of the Japanese public. The news that China had surpassed Japan as the world's second largest economy was a source of concern for many Japanese people. It was not just a matter of national pride, but a genuine sense of crisis that was fuelled by the potential economic impact of a strong and wealthy China. For those who grew up after World War II, such as Shinzo Abe, this blow was particularly hard as they had only known a Japan that challenged the United States economically, not one that could possibly be overtaken by an Asian neighbour no less. China has long been viewed with apprehension and often disdain in Japan. This negative perception is linked to the country's sense of superiority that dates back to the Meiji Restoration. During this time, Japanese elites sought to distance themselves from Asia and align with Europe in order to gain equal status with the great powers of the global system. Japan's victory in the 1895 Sino-Japanese War and the 1905 Russo-Japanese War allowed Tokyo to become the dominant power in the region, but this did not allow Japan to become the regional hegemon. Tokyo was instead challenged by both the United Kingdom and Russia for supremacy in her own backyard.

Ironically, it was the external environment, particularly Japan's near skirmishes with China that provided the rallying effort domestically for Japan to rise to the China challenge. The following month on 8th September 2010, a China fishing trawler collided with the Japanese Coast Guard boat in waters near the Senkaku island. While the international and Japanese media labelled this as an incident where the Chinese captain Zhan Qixiong rammed his vessel against the Japanese boat, the narrative from the Chinese side was radically opposite. It resulted in the deten-, tion of the Chinese captain and his crew (Branigan & McCurry, 2010), and the tit for tat of the arrest of Japanese nationals in China alleged to be spies (Fackler & Johnson, 2010). China also suspected the export of rare earths to Japan and Tokyo eventually released the Chinese skipper. The DPJ had wanted to demonstrate resolve in confronting the intrusion of Chinese vessels that approached the Senkaku islands, but in the end, it ended up losing both the diplomatic battle with China and the public relations war at home. The political opposition argued that the DPJ could not be relied upon to protect Japan or her interests and that its positions on "improving ties within Asia" and reduce Japan's reliance on the United States were flawed. This substantially hardened the sentiments on the ground. While this was eventually defused, it laid the background for greater difficulties in 2012. In the run-up to the 2012 elections, Tokyo governor Ishihara Shintaro announced that he was going to approach the private owners of three out of the five Senkaku islands (Uotsurishima, Kita-Kojima and Minami-Kojima) to buy them over so that Tokyo can develop infrastructure on islands which was announced during a visit to the Heritage foundation in the United States (McCurry, 2012). By May, the Tokyo Metropolitan government had received ¥951 million ($12 million) from roughly 67,000 people in contributions to be spent for purchasing the islands from a private Japanese owner (Hayashi, 2012). By July, this amount has already grown to JPY 1.4 billion in public contributions to fund the purchase of the island. Ishihara's incendiary rhetoric against China (calling a derogatory name "Shina" etc.) further aggravate a tense situation. The Noda administration saw that they had little choice but counter Ishihara's offer by offering JPY 2.05 billion to buy the islands. Japan agreed that there will be no new construction on the Senkakus and only minimal repair to existing infrastructure to be carried out. This decision triggered reactions from both Taiwan as well as China, even as Taiwan reached out privately to assure Japan that Taiwan-Japan relations remain strong. From mid-August to mid-September, this dispute became a full-blown diplomatic and security crisis that involved several interrelated and overlapping developments that shocked and rallied the Japanese.

The Liberal Democratic Party (in opposition) saw an immediate opportunity to attack the government in their response to China. The politicians took this opportunity to lob political firebombs at the DPJ government for its inability to defend Japan, with then-Tokyo governor Shintaro Ishihara joining forces with then-Osaka Governor Hashimoto Toru to form a new party for the 2012 elections. Ishihara's campaign to "buy" Senkaku back from China leveraged the DPJ government badly. The various factions, including those led by Shinzo Abe stepped up their attacks on the DPJ's handling of the incidents with China in order to gain the upper hand in elections. With the assistance of Suga Yoshihide and an excellent Public Relations and media team, Shinzo Abe managed to force two rounds of elections to narrowly beat Shigeru Ishiba to once again win the premiership.

Frustrated Electorate: The Rise of the Abe School and Japan's National Security Agenda

The electorate clearly chose to support Abe's LDP again in 2012 due to his tough demeanour and previous experience as Prime Minister, which conveyed a sense of confidence and leadership that the electorate believed Japan needed after six years of revolving Prime Ministership and 39 months of perceived incompetent governance by the Democratic Party of Japan. Abe's years in political wilderness allowed for soul-searching and self-reflection, leading him to accurately deduce the reasons for his failure to hold onto power in his first term. He learned that he needed to appear less dogmatic and ideological, grow his own faction at all costs, even if it meant becoming less collegial, and reinstate pork barrel politics that Koizumi sought to eliminate. Most importantly, he developed an economic agenda that was missing from his previous tenure, which led to the birth of Abenomics. Abe also benefitted immensely from the DPJ's perceived bungling of foreign policy challenges Japan faced over the territorial disputes with China, Japan and Russia. The China Threat has been well debated over the last two decades but by 2012, the Japanese public was incredibly frustrated and anxious, in no small part prompted by the daily onslaught of negative coverage in the press and social media. The consistent attacks by the right-wing elements such as Ishihara and Toru's faction during the run-up to the election had enabled Abe's LDP to look more reasonable than ever. Shinzo Abe adapted his agenda and leadership style to appeal to Japanese tradition and nationalism. His faction expounded his vision such as the ideas contained within his book (the 2013 republication of his 2006 book "Towards a Beautiful Country". Despite this, he maintained his image as a responsible and forward-looking democrat and statesman. The Liberal Democratic Party (LDP) returned to power rejuvenated and more determined than ever to maintain its grip on power. Over the next eight years, the LDP secured three additional electoral victories. The rise of the Abe School and Japan's new conservatism can be attributed to Abe's political longevity and the mainstreaming of his political ideas from 2012 onwards. During this time, the Kantei was able to overwhelm and increase its control over the democratic institutions that had previously played a role in checking and resisting government overreach, including the media, bureaucracy, political opposition and other factions within the LDP.

Within the Diet, the key to Abe's success was to marginalise his main challengers within his own party. A central strategy was to spread his political influence by making important concessions to other factional leaders and political opponents to ensure that the LDP forms the government and that his hold on power would remain stable. The LDP under Abe's leadership was able to negotiate and co-opt the leaders of other factions in the Cabinet and convince these like-minded faction leaders (such as Taro Aso, Kishida Fumio, Toshimitsu Motegi) of their common mission and outlook. The LDP restored some of the more traditional practices of the LDP in order to ensure that even the greatest detractors are also offered an appointment (such as Ishiba). With a cabinet united in outlook, the next important aspect was to prevent the Diet from creating obstacles to the LDP's bills. In 2012, Abe formed a coalition government with New Komeito. Abe had appointed Akiro Ota, the former Komeito leader who had previously served in the Democratic Party of Japan (DPJ) government, as Minister in charge of National Land, Infrastructure, Transport and Tourism. Abe's appointment of Ota was a strategic move to solidify the coalition government, as both men shared a view on the importance of incorporating disaster prevention measures into building design. This partnership between the LDP and Komeito endured throughout Abe's four cabinets, as well as those of his successors, Yoshihide Suga and Fumio Kishida. By forming the coalition government, Abe was able to establish a two-thirds majority in the House of Representatives and overturn most matters that were subject to upper house veto. The appointment of moderate Kishida as foreign Minister in 2012 made Abe's government appear moderate even as he assembled a team to implement his national security agenda with full force. With the appointment of politicians such as Taro Aso (Deputy Prime Minister), loyalist Tomomi Inada as Defense Minister and Suga Yoshihide as Chief Cabinet Secretary and Minister for strengthening National Security, Abe had total control of the national security agenda. Abe's faction had cleverly used the external challenges posed by China and the internal weakness of the opposition to completely dominate the national security discourse. The more Abe hyped up the "China threat" and the need for national security reform, the more mainstream his politics became. In the 2014 election, Abe replaced his defense minister, Akinori Eto, who was embroiled in a significant political funding scandal, with Gen Nakatani, the former head of the Japan Defense Agency. From 2014 to 2020, the LDP under Abe's leadership controlled both the upper and lower houses of the National Diet. Abe's faction was able to grow more popular by staying true to its roots—privileging the base's agenda through recruitment and grooming of politicians of the same shade (i.e. from the *Nippon Kaigi*) and appointing them into high-profile positions. Abe was also able to deftly balance the interests and mask the divide between the conventional conservatives and the reformist conservatives within the LDP though the proposal of Abenomics, which appeared to have something for everyone (Ohi, 2018). Factional leaders tend to bring on politicians who share their vision and outlook as patronage is still an important aspect. Abe's faction grew quickly and became more influential to the extent that it was able to defeat intra-party challengers for the LDP Party Presidency, such as the former Defense Minister Shigeru Ishiba in 2012 and then again in 2020. As Abe has consolidated power to such a degree, it was almost impossible for anyone challenger, domestic or external to challenge his place within the Party (Kingston, 2017). Towards the end of his tenure, even though Abe was not very popular within Japan (BBC, 2017), he was still irreplaceable as he had successfully sidelined the emergence of any plausible opposition or successor. By the time Kishida Fumio took over, Shinzo Abe chaired the largest faction in the LDP, with Deputy Prime Minister Aso helming the second largest faction (53 members) and Kishida as the fifth largest faction. Abe also has a close relationship with Sanae Takaichi who runs the Party's Research Council Chairperson and is an arch-political rival of Kishida Fumio (Yomiuri, 2021). Abe's factional influence was so dominant that even Kishida could not change it without losing majority support. This ensured that the LDP maintained its continuity of its policy agenda and implementation.

Under the LDP, the Abe Administration focused on a single-minded pursuit of enhancing Japan's national security. He campaigned on a platform that promised to safeguard Japan's national interests, by emphasising their credentials as protectors of Japanese sovereignty and territorial integrity. The proposals floated at this time included the establishment of an American-like National Security Council, the pursuit of the right to collective self-defence, boosting of the JSDF and itemised a list of 38 detailed policy agenda as opposed to the 24 items in 2009 (Jimbo, 2013). While it is true that factions have never been the dominant influence on LDP's policy-making as this is really often a function of a cross-factional representation group of lawmakers with special interests and focus (*zoku* or policy tribe), most lawmakers are deeply aware of how successful the respective factions have been in appealing to their constituents in winning votes, swaying public opinion and gaining power. The rhetoric, outlook and political strategy of Abe's faction therefore become worthy of emulation (Frum, 2022). Even if Kishida ran the policy council and is publicly known as a "dove", he was in many ways under the influence of Abe, even after his death. The Abe School's agenda cannot be rid of so easily as politically it could backfire on anyone trying to do so, including the current Prime Minister Kishida who is actually less ideologically driven and more pragmatic than Shinzo Abe.

The rise of this new Conservatism had been two decades in making, and in a large part has been driven forward by both Koizumi's and Abe's political vision and methodology. The peculiarities of politics that saw the emergence of a more dominant and powerful LDP any time before in its history. Upon returning from the opposition, the Abe faction successfully consolidated political power and overcame all manners of checks and balances within and outside the Party, subduing the media, bureaucracy and other elements of civil society such as the education system to serve its purpose all in the name of national security. This is achieved largely not only through intense politicking and smart political campaigning, but also by narratives of a rapidly deteriorating external environment.

Level III: The International System

The Rise of China and Japan's Global Role

The dynamics of Japan's domestic politics are in a large part driven by how political leaders and public opinion shifted in view of Japan's external security environment. The demise of the USSR in December 1991 elicited a mix of celebration and apprehension in Tokyo. While people were relieved, they also grappled with the uncertainty of the US's global presence and the future of the US–Japan alliance. The implications of American isolationism spurred intense discussions on China's rise and its impact on the region and individual countries. From Tokyo to Jakarta and Washington, politicians and strategists debated the effectiveness of their current approaches to managing US relations. Japan has long considered the US–Japan Security alliance to be the cornerstone of its foreign and security policy. Initially, Prime Minister Nobuske Kishi faced domestic protests while reaffirming the Treaty in 1960. However, over time, the Japanese government shifted from merely tolerating the alliance to fully embracing it. Today, the Liberal Democratic Party views Kishi's legacy as crucial to the well-being of Japan and the Japanese people, with the exception of Okinawa. The Yoshida doctrine and the three nuclear principles guided Japan during the Cold War, allowing it to benefit from the US–Japan alliance's extended nuclear umbrella and long-term military assurances. In return, the US gained financial and technological support for its military presence in Asia and beyond. Despite occasional grievances on both sides, there is an acknowledgment in both Washington and Tokyo that the relationship has always been asymmetric, with Japan heavily reliant on the United States. This asymmetry has been a source of political discontent in Japan, earning the country the unflattering image of a political dwarf. In the mid-1990s, both the United States and Japan sought to strengthen the alliance when President Bill Clinton and Japanese Prime Minister Ryutaro Hashimoto met. The primary objectives of Japan's reforms were to bolster the US–Japan alliance in three key areas. First, Japan has enacted legislation to strengthen its defense capabilities and take on a more active role in the alliance. Second, there is a growing awareness within the LDP establishment of the need to improve the military's logistical, personnel and organisational capabilities to enhance its fighting effectiveness. Third, Japan recognises the need to adapt to changing circumstances outside of its borders.

In the view of Tokyo, a series of external events occurred that Tokyo perceived as negative developments, necessitating Japan to enhance its external security posture. The majority of these events involved the People's Republic of China (PRC) directly or indirectly. In 1995, China conducted nuclear tests, and in response to Lee Teng Hui's visit to Taiwan for the country's first presidential elections, China conducted missile exercises that effectively blockaded the Taiwan Straits from July 1995 to March 1996. Tokyo also expressed concerns about Hong Kong's democratic future in the lead up to the 1997 handover and was frustrated by the frequent attempts by activists to sail to the Diaoyu/Senkaku islands. Additionally, Japan alleged that China disrespected Japan's exclusive economic zone (EEZ) when its ships crossed the median line to survey and prospect for oil in the disputed gas fields. Between 1998 and August 2000, 16 Chinese ships intruded into Japanese waters on 12 different occasions (Harrison, 2005: 4). There were of course attempts to try and enhance Japan's overall security, including Prime Obuchi's attempt to try and persuade Russia to sign a peace treaty. By the turn of the century, there were three important changes to Japan's diplomacy viz-a-viz East Asian Security and a renewed sense of conservatism. Japan had begun to deviate from the deference attitude that it had adopted towards China since the end of the Pacific War and taken a new assertive approach towards Beijing's perceived transgressions. There were incremental steps taken to reinvigorate the US–Japan alliance to cater to the new challenges in Japan's security as Tokyo alluded to new security concerns particularly with her concerns over China and North Korea.

From 2000 to 2012, Japan's external security environment took on important challenges. The most significant incident occurred in March 2001, when a US electronic surveillance EP-3 plane was forced down at Hainan island, which effectively ended the Military Maritime Consultative Agreement signed in 1998 as a Confidence Building Measure (CBM) (CFR, N.D). These events underscore the need for Japan to develop a more robust external security posture to address the challenges posed by the PRC. The United States had by then regarded China as a new threat, but the events of 9/11 reoriented US foreign policy priorities onto the War on Terror for the next decade. Even as US strategic priorities shifted and US–China relations improved moderately when Beijing announced they would support US efforts, the threat perception in Tokyo did not ameliorate. This period is also significant in that China and Japan began to operate in an environment where the United States did not deploy significant resources to guide their mutual interactions and antagonisms. In short, for the first time, Japan and China began to interact with each other more independently than they had any time before in their post-war relations.

The principal challenge that Japan stated openly during this period was actually the DPRK. North Korea was ideologically opposed to Japan, both as a former imperialistic power and now a staunch ally of the United States that is still at War with the DPRK. Pyongyang had conducted nuclear tests and missile tests, including two that overflew Japan and splashed into the Sea of Japan. The most egregious issue for Japan however is the seventeen Japanese nationals kidnapped and brought to North Korea for leverage, espionage, and training reasons. Abe's tough rhetoric against Pyongyang won him the popularity and paved his way in the Koizumi cabinet. Even though the threat from Pyongyang was real, the real source of strategic anxiety was China. Japan's external environment became even more challenging after Koizumi stepped down. Shinzo Abe, Koizumi's popular Chief Cabinet Secretary took over as the natural successor during a particularly turbulent period. In his first year as Prime Minister, Shinzo Abe fixated on his political agenda to normalise Japan. Abe proposed the "Arc of Democracy" in an effort to bring together "like-minded" countries that share Japan's values and outlook. This is the genesis of the Quad. Shinzo Abe spent a great deal of political capital and attention on setting up his theory and operationalising the concept. Unfortunately, Abe's political platform did not appeal to the existing Diet members nor the public who were actually more concerned about the economy. By 2008, the LDP was in trouble politically. Like Koizumi, Shinzo Abe, Taro Aso, and other LDP politicians' gestures and statements on history were viewed ambivalently by policy elites in Washington D.C. Even though Japan was an important ally, historical revisionism was generally frowned upon by American policymakers. Beyond the fact that such statements rile US veterans domestically and Asian countries occupied by Japan during the Second World War, it also weakens the prospects of Korea and Japan working alongside as security partners.

The DPJ of course is not solely to be blamed. Since Junichiro Koizumi left office, Japan has had a series of "revolving door" Prime Ministers with very short stints: Shinzo Abe (09/06–09/07), Yasuo Fukuda (09/7–09/08), Taro Aso (9/08–9/09), Yukio Hatoyama (9/09–6/10), Naoto Kan (6/10–9/11) and Yoshikiko Noda (9/11–12/12). This pattern was only interrupted by Shinzo Abe in his second election. From hindsight, while the common theme for their downfall was that these Prime Ministers were unable to address the important domestic concerns of the voters, the singular continuity in their policies was their attempts to address the exigencies of the external environment. Apart from Hatoyama's rhetoric on DPJ's aims to recalibrate the balance with the United States and reset relations with China and Japan, most of the other Prime Ministers in effect undertook measures to strengthen the US–Japan alliance. Yet, the external challenges the DPJ faced in their China policy considerably restricted the latitude of the successive DPJ governments to do anything else other than to reaffirm the US–Japan alliance. The very fact that the United States decided to face down China when Hillary Clinton became

Secretary of State over South China Sea only complicated matters (Chang, 2010), and this had major repercussions in terms of how ASEAN and China reacted, as well as the repercussions of how events are interpreted in Japan.

The biggest challenge during the DPJ era was the perceived encroachment and infringement of Japanese territorial rights over the Senkaku/Diaoyu islands. After Koizumi's very nationalistic posture that was well-publicised across the Chinese-speaking world, the Senkaku/Diaoyu issue became an even more important issue in Chinese nationalism. The motivations behind the actors using this issue are varied. Hong Kong democrats, Taiwan pro-independence politicians as well as a wide variety of actors with different attitudes and goals towards the Chinese state and the Chinese Communist Party all might want to stoke tensions between China and Japan over this issue. The problem however is that the extent of this nationalism has put the Chinese government under immense pressure to "act" to protect this disputed territory. Japan's unwillingness to admit that this is "disputed" has provided an opportunity for anyone opposing the Chinese government to utilise this issue to its advantage. Hong Kong pan-democrats and other pro-China groups have set sail time and again joined by their compatriots from Taiwan. Naturally, these sailings have presented themselves as a political problem for Beijing trying to build better ties with Japan. Tokyo's defence of these islands and its "deportation" of Chinese who landed there is a demonstration of international law that Beijing cannot be allowed to stand. The Japanese right-wing groups naturally organised their own outings. The dynamics of such tit for tat civic nationalism over the Senkaku/Diaoyu "visits" in 2010–2012 escalated beyond what was seen in the previous decades. Right-wing nationalists politicians such as Ishihara Shintaro who promised to buy over the Senkaku Islands from her owners like the political opposition in China used the issue to wedge the DPJ government. This popularisation of this issue takes on an extremely emotive angle that threatens to derail sensible handling of this issue on all sides. Nationalism has therefore become a potent and independent force that drove foreign and security on both sides.

The amplification of this incident has real and important implications. It inflated the Senkaku/Diaoyu islands from a minor issue to a central one. Inflamed nationalism popularised hard-core responses which in turn stoked similar reactions from the other side. In China itself, the issue brought out angry protestors onto the streets in over 150 cities across

China. This wrought destruction to Japanese -owned (real or perceived) properties and businesses in China and showcased a very ugly side of Chinese sentiments that completely shocked the Japanese. The official response on the Japanese side was as hard as it was provocative, rallying the domestic public opinion around the LDP. The ramifications of the Senkaku/Diaoyu Islands dispute played in support of the Conservative agenda in both China and Japan and led to a downward spiral in Sino-Japanese relations.

Japan's hard-nose attitude towards the Senkaku/Diaoyu dispute was understandable. The LDP has for years maintained that there is "no" sovereignty dispute—even now it fully knows that the "administration" of the islands was transferred to Japan by the Americans who in turn acknowledged that they do not arbitrate on the sovereignty of the islands. By "nationalising" the islands, China had little choice but to "demonstrate" its ownership by dispatching PLAN ships to the islands. The CCP also had to "act" to pacify domestic nationalistic sentiments, given how the Party always argued that it was the sole guardian of Chinese sovereignty. This measure of course in turn provoked increased Japanese coast guard and naval sorties. The Chinese also began to patrol the waters surrounding Senkaku/Diaoyu, as they had explicitly claimed them to be Chinese waters, which in turn upset the Japanese. Both sides began to view the other side as "upsetting" the traditional balance. Beijing became more assertive since it viewed that the Japanese were no longer upholding the 1978 agreement to leave the settlement of the issue to the wiser "next generation". Japan in turn began to argue that no such agreement existed. This divisive issue began to boost the interests of domestic and international actors to stand to gain from an increase in tensions between Japan and China.

It also paved the way for an entire generation of politicians to come forward and advocate a tougher posture towards the other side. China had also little choice but allows for more support for those constituents who wanted to sail to the islands. The Japanese were confident that the protests domestically were led by CCP affiliates or officials in disguise and that the Chinese government was using the issue to extract political concessions from Japan. It is certainly conceivable as the security forces worldwide often infiltrate and lead protests to control these movements from going astray. However, such views often dismiss the genuine anger felt at the grassroots level and channel blame to the government instead. Japan perhaps does not realise that Chinese leaders have very little room to manoeuvre insofar when the Japanese are concerned. The reign of Koizumi and the revolving door Prime Ministers (Abe, Fukuda, Aso, Hatoyama, Kan and Noda) had all but guaranteed that Sino-Japanese relations spiralled to a new low.

The China's Challenge: Irredentism, Strategic Threat, the Erosion of Japanese Regional Influence and Leadership

By 2012, it had become clearly evident to both the Japanese people and the government that China's rise have implications that would have made the previous mode of "co-existing" with Beijing more difficult. Beyond the question of China's irredentism, it was clear to Tokyo that it would be increasingly more difficult to deal with China politically and strategically. A strong China is severely at odds with Japan's interests in four respects. Regardless of the intentions of a country's leaders, the transformation of the said country into a geostrategic and economic behemoth would engender insecurities even for the most secure neighbours. China in translating her economic gains into a more confident defence capability, also created a more intimidating environment for Japan, whether Beijing wills it or not. The modernisation of the PLA had, in fact, created strategic angst in neighboring countries where governments grappled with how their strategic interests could be defended. Whether it is in Hong Kong, Taiwan and the Taiwan Straits or for that matter in the South China Sea, the strategic disparity that the United States and Japan enjoyed had shrunk immensely. With a rapidly modernising aircraft fleet as well as naval assets, the US–Japan alliance no longer enjoys the overwhelming dominance it once did in the 1980s and 1990s. China could now effectively threaten the sealines of communications that are vital to Japan and disrupt the interests of not only Japan but also the United States and South Korea. In particular, the waterways stretching from the Indian Ocean through to the Straits of Malacca, through the South China Sea right up to the Taiwan Straits which the US alliance interdiction operations in the event of a contingency involving China cannot be taken for a given. This has two immediate implications for Japan. Japan's strategic comfort zone has always built on a China that is incapable of mounting serious military challenges to her direct interests. The very fact that the PLA was increasingly capable of mounting operations with her blue water navy and resisting the US–Japan alliance is cause for concern. An increase in capability could well translate into a never before strategic boldness that would enable Beijing to further assert her rights and realise her plans. There is no reason for Tokyo to believe that the peace that has pervaded much of Asia from the 1980s onwards will continue to exist.

From Tokyo's point of view, China also appeared to be becoming more assertive or aggressive. Since Koizumi's very public display of paying homage to Japanese nationalism through his Yasukuni Shrine visits and signalling his "resistance", Japan's relations with China and Korea have become exceedingly difficult. This new "normal" of his domestic political exercises have eroded the little restraint and goodwill that had underlined bilateral relations before. Koizumi had argued his Shrine visits are a purely domestic Japanese matter just as it is consonant with Japan's values of freedom of speech and worship, and bilateral relations should not hinge on whether he visits the Yasukuni Shrine or not. While this might look right from the Japanese viewpoint, the fact of the matter is that it has led to considerable public anger and embarrassment in both Beijing and Seoul. Koizumi and many of the LDP politicians also held the view that even if the visits stop, the criticisms of Japan and the call for apologies would not end. What the Japanese leadership however did not consider is how this conservative politics and nationalistic expressions would also have a similar kind of galvanising effect against Japan and the public pressure it would have on both the Chinese and Korean government. This nationalistic anger prevented any sort of easy reconciliation and increasingly tied the hands of both the Chinese and Korean governments. By 2009, it was evident that China had become a lot less intolerant of Japan than in previous years (this is read of course as Beijing had become a lot more aggressive or assertive outside). The detention of the Chinese Trawler and subsequent and frequent episodes of high seas confrontation between Chinese, Japanese and even the Taiwanese coast guard and naval vessels are thus taken as evidence of this. China became increasingly willing to challenge any kind of line in the sand that Tokyo has drawn, whether it is Senkaku/Diaoyu and the East China Sea, or Taiwan or South China Sea. The anger in both Tokyo and Beijing cannot be underestimated, and this in turn puts the US in a precarious position (Thayer, 2012).

China is also displacing Japan as Southeast Asia's dominant power and regional hegemon. While many might argue that it is the United States that is the dominant power, the key to Tokyo's influence is enshrined in the Fukuda doctrine that Japan's Southeast Asian policy is premised upon. Tokyo's economic assistance (and hence influence) was unparalleled. Even though Obama's pivot was largely welcomed by many countries in the region, including Japan. There was a deep sense of unease in the Japanese strategic community as to the resolve of the United States to commit and help Japan defend against China. The issue for Japan was the reliability of the United States to defend Japan's interests in Senkaku, whereas for the United States, it was an issue of a nationalistic Japan that would chain-gang Washington to fight China over the islands which were not significant enough for the United States to go to War with China.

Japan's Concerns Over the US–Japan Alliance: Inaction, Credibility and Abandonment

Even as Japan went about normalising its defense posture and military capabilities, Tokyo elites were suspicious about the United States' commitment to "defend" Japan at all costs. During a State visit to Japan in 2014, Obama had, in fact, reiterated that Article 5 of US–Japan security Treaty covers the Senkaku islands since it is under Japan's administration, but had also emphasised the fact that the United States did not take a position over its sovereignty and value a peaceful resolution of the matter (McCurry, 2014). Washington had stressed that the United States opposes all attempts to alter the current state of affairs through the use of force, it is noteworthy that no senior US official has ever explicitly stated that the United States would support Japan in the event of China occupying the Senkaku islands, or made any similar statement (Takahashi, 2014). This absence of a clear commitment from the US has heightened suspicions in Tokyo about the value of the security alliance between the two countries. The dynamics of "chain-ganging" of a patron state by a client state is well-known problem in alliance dynamics, whether it's between street gangs or nation-states. The patron state is unlikely to agree to unconditionally defend Japan, particularly if it is Tokyo that is involved in the provocation. In this sense, Obama's statement is both a reassurance to Japan and at the same time a "hedging" signal that it won't condone Japan's enthusiasm to entrap the United States into fighting the Chinese over Senkaku.

The essence of the problem is that there is a gulf with regard to how Washington and Tokyo view the Senkaku issue, and how central these islands are to the US and Japanese national interests. For the United States, these islands held by Tokyo in "administration" do not warrant an all-out confrontation with China as the value of these islands in US national interests is limited to the extent that it acts as a divisive wedge that keeps Japan, ROC and PRC perpetually apart. For Japan, Abe had by this time completely ignored the fact that Senkaku is still considered a "disputed" territory by both China and Washington (Kwan, 18 December 2012). By refusing to give lip service and acknowledge the Senkaku/Diaoyu islands as being "disputed", the chest-thumping nationalistic LDP politicians have actually undercut the understanding of the peace they have had with the Chinese since 1978. This of course is not how it is interpreted in Tokyo, but deep down, most Japanese politicians understand that there is a wide gulf in value ascribed to Senkaku islands by the United States and Japan. Today, even when united in their vision to contain China, the Obama Administration and the Abe government might actually have very different end goals and interests. Shinzo Abe probably realises this but in forcing the Americans to make this commitment (on Article 5 of US–Japan Treaty covering Senkaku) publicly, he would at least force the issue onto the foreign policy agendas of both China and the United States and at the same time bolster the case for his remilitarisation agenda at home.

From 2012 to 2016, there was therefore a sense of unease and a growing scepticism amongst conservative political circles in Tokyo that despite the "pivot", the Obama White House was only concerned with American interests (rightly so). The Japanese politicians felt that the Americans seemed to have increased their tolerance or even acceptance on the increased number of patrol vessels and aircraft intrusion into the waters and airspace surrounding Senkaku, which the Japanese regarded as a violation of its sovereignty. The most aggrieving fact was that Washington did not appear to have condemned these activities (Takahashi, 2014). Many conservative politicians were concerned that Obama's pivot to Asia was motivated primarily by the US's burgeoning economic interests in China's substantial markets, rather than for Japanese national security concerns. The issue for Tokyo was the perceived unwillingness of the Obama administration to go to bat for Japan at all costs. The basis for doubting the United States is well founded even if it is unspoken mostly. This prompted a public discussion with Japan and provided powerful domestic justifications as to why Japan's post-war pacifism are no longer suited for our times. It was therefore incumbent upon Japan to think of ways to bolster the US–Japan alliance to ensure that Japan's security interests were met. It was therefore not just about China's aggression (perceived and real) but also whether the United States can be that all-weather ally that Japan can expect in her looming confrontation with China, particularly as Beijing becomes exponentially more powerful.

This growing power is not only impinging on Japan's interests directly but also eroding Tokyo's influence in third countries and regions such as Southeast Asia where Japan has exercised much economic leadership since the 1970s. China's rise and the intensification of Beijing's linkages through trade and now through assistance has seen China displacing or diluting Tokyo in Southeast Asia. Even though Japan is still hugely respected and viewed as an important source of economic aid and investment, one can no longer conclusively say that Japan is now as influential as China in Southeast Asia. The developmental stages of many Southeast Asia countries would see them finding more utility in cheaper goods and services from trade with China than with Tokyo, Beijing naturally becomes the partner of choice. Japan understands this and knows that when push comes to shove, Tokyo would have a much harder time rallying Southeast Asia to become more sympathetic to Tokyo in the event of a Sino-Japanese clash. In order to compensate and balance the growing Chinese power and threat, the Japanese government has implemented several sets of policies to ensure that Japan would be able to match China's growing power and influence. The first set has to do with Japan's own economic strength, military capabilities and soft power through the reinforcement of the US–Japan alliance system. Japan would also build on the existing sets of bilateral and multilateral relations with another complex set of security centred on US alliances to further bolster Japan's position and defence.

To enhance Japan's own military capabilities and reinforce the working of US–Japan alliance, Japan embarked on a series of different steps towards the "normalisation" agenda (Hanada, 2022). In essence Abe instituted a series of policy initiatives that amounted to a new direction in Japan's security policy (Sakaki, 2015). Japan established a National Security Council in December 2013 following the passing of a law establishing the National Security Council the previous month. Building on what previous LDP governments did, Japan went even further in undertaking legislative reforms to further loosen the shackles that the post-war Peace Constitution had imposed on her military capabilities. Tokyo reinterpreted her Pacificist Constitution in 2015 so that she could partake in collective defence. This essentially means that Japan could defend the United States even if Japan herself was not directly attacked. Japan also revised and upgraded the status of her military following the reforms undertaken. During Shinzo Abe's first term in office, Japan upgraded the Defense Agency to a full-fledge cabinet-level ministry, officially becoming the Ministry of Defense (MOD) on 9 January 2007, bringing both symbolic and substantive changes to Japan. With representation at the Cabinet level, the Defense establishment and the military now have a greater voice in governmental affairs and would be able to project their aspirations, interests and plans into the overall government. Japan has also steadily increased the budget of its military, and expanded its operating range through the participation of international peacekeeping missions, including deployments to South Sudan and the Gulf of Aden. Based on these deployments, the JSDF would have the opportunity to work with external alliance partners ensuring greater interoperability between Japanese and allied forces, reinforcing the regular military exercises and drills they conduct. Japan also began stealth and steady qualitative upgrade of her armed forces, marking acquisitions in very capable defense weapons such as the Aegis Ballistic Missile Defense System and the Patriot Advanced Capability-3 (PAC-3), as well as cutting edge ariel and naval power projection assets such as the F35 Joint Strike Fighters as well as the Soryu class submarines. These weapons are inherently offensive in nature. These large ticket items come on top of other improvements and upgrades to existing capabilities and assets such as surveillance drones and anti-submarine capabilities. The Japanese government has also strengthened the JSDF capability on the islands near the Senkaku Islands and established an Amphibious Rapid Deployment Brigade in Nagasaki, with additional aviation support units in Kyushu armed with Longbow and Apache attack helicopters (Kyodo News, 2018). For the first time, since World War II, Japan has now seen fit to establish these marine battalions with a mission to recover "lost islands" from the enemy. This sort of preparation reinforces Japan's increased surveillance and patrols in the troubled waters of the East China Sea. Additionally, Japan also increased existing R&D efforts in other domains, such as Cybersecurity, space defense, stealth capabilities and hypersonic missiles which Japan considers to be necessary in light of evolving security threats. This rearming exercise was in tune with US policyand was exactly what the Abe government as well as the Trump administration wanted for Japan. This tightening of military cooperation has, in fact, continued in the post-Abe era. Both Suga and the Kishida cabinet had ensured that Japan's defense rejuvenation and military modernisation kept pace even though they both have had trouble rallying the kind of domestic support Abe had. Suga had needed the help from the Genros such as Toshiro Nikai to secure the top spot (Yora, 2021; Johnston, 2020). The problem with Abe's successors is that they too faced challenges in being able to draw support from hardliners and right-wing elements. This however did not mean that these forces have disappeared in Japanese politics (Hurst, 2018). What these might mean is instead there is a possibility that the LDP would lose control over these right wing groups. This does have ramifications for Japan's domestic politics. Regardless, the LDP has show a focus on pursuing Abe's normalisation agenda, particularly in acquiring sufficient military capabilities to fend for itself. For instance in 2022, the Kishida cabinet announced that Japan has for the first time announced it is acquiring capability to strike enemy bases as a "bare minimum" gesture, since neighbouring countries have "significantly reinforced its missile forces" (Nakamura, 2022).

Japan's strategy, from 2013 onwards was to ensure that the United States would be refrained from moving towards accommodating China. The credibility of the United States has come into question over the past few years, particularly over her inaction in places such as Syria when Washington decided that rhetoric more than action was conductive to her national interests. Japan's first priority is to ensure that the United States would never be able to sacrifice her interests by striking a grand agreement with China. At the same time, to prevent inertia or unwillingness on the part of the United States to help Japan (as in the Senkaku's case), the Japanese leader felt that they must be ready to act on her own to defend her own interests or fail Japan when Sino-Japanese confrontation actually takes place. The key for Japan was of course extremely keen to strengthen relations with the United States. However, the then-President Obama and his advisors had a rather jaundiced view of Abe Shinzo as a raving nationalist from his first term. In January 2013, the Obama White House had dispatched a team of Asian specialists consisting of Kurt Campbell, Daniel Russel and Mark Lippert to calm tensions between Tokyo and Seoul over the simmering tensions over then President Lee Myong Bak's visit Dokdo/Takeshima islands in the previous summer, as well as to advise Abe not to undertake nationalist policies (Chen, 2013). In 2015, Japan began to revise the guidelines for Japan–US Defense cooperation that expanded its scope for cooperation with the United States across different domains. It was clear that even though Japan had their reservations about the Obama White House, they nonetheless sought to undertake quiet diplomacy to try and shore up the alliance. In an address to the Joint meeting of the US Congress entitled "Toward an Alliance of Hope" which was steeped with expressions of gratitude for the democracy and freedom that America had brought to the shores of Japan, the then-Prime Minister highlighted several aspects of Japan's new foreign policy orientation. Japan would support unconditionally the "rebalancing" by the US in order to enhance the peace and security of the Asia–Pacific region, deepen its strategic relations with Australia and India, enhance cooperation with ASEAN and Republic of Korea and provide US\$2.8 billion dollars in assistance to help improve US bases in Guam (MOFA, 2015). Further, Japan would uphold three principles with regard to the state of Asian waters: (1) States shall make their claims based on international law; (2) that States shall not use force or coercion to drive their claims and (3) to settle disputes, any disputes, they shall do so by peaceful means (MOFA, 2015). In order to rehabilitate Abe's revisionist image in the United States(Graham, 2015) and internationally and make US–Japan cooperation look more "forward-looking", both countries undertook exchange visits to address amongst other things, the lingering question of "history". President Obama, on a State Visit in May 2016, laid a wreath at Hiroshima Atomic Bomb Memorial as in Abe's words "a gesture of condolences" (The White House, 2016a, b). The hope of course was that the public relations effect would soothe those in Japan who were upset at how Abe was trying to work with the very power who had used nuclear weapons against the Japanese people. Abe then paid a return visit to Pearl Harbour in December 2016 where he offered "sincere and everlasting condolences". In all the speeches, the visits were labelled prominently as historic gestures of reconciliation as where both leaders spoke of the need to remember the horrors of wars and to avoid them. These exchange visits were regarded important symbols for the transcendence of recriminatory impulses that weighed down bilateral relations. These visits also softened Abe's international image as a nationalist and revisionist, and Obama's appearance likewise was meant to provide some measure of comfort to the stark social memories of Hiroshima and Nagasaki in Japan. Ideally, the visits would have made US–Japan alliance more palatable to both the US and Japanese public, as for this talk of peace and reconciliation, there was a strong subtext of preparing the alliance for war. There were a series of important steps undertaken by Tokyo to ensure that the US–Japan alliance worked smoothly. The problem of course was such a strategy was really more about ameliorating Abe's image in the United States and

Obama's image in Japan, but did not fundamentally alter the nature and tone of Japanese conservatism.

A second important Japan strategy was to put into effect a containment strategy quietly that would encircle China. Having strong ties with countries that are China's close neighbours that have tensions would help reinforce Japan's agenda through policy legitimation, enhance the JSDF's capabilities and most importantly backstop Tokyo's escalating confrontation with China. From Tokyo's perspective, Southeast Asia as a whole can no longer be counted on to counter China, and strengthening ties with states not yet under the undue influence of the PRC remains critical. Lobbying "extra-regional" powers outside of the Asia–Pacific such as India to partake more actively in the alliance made sense strategically for the alliance. It would enhance the strength and the capabilities of the alliance even more. In order to have any global influence and power projection, Chinese naval assets, including Submarines would have to transverse the India Ocean and Australia. Both India and Australia have important continental and oceanic powers that have influence over large sways of waters that are far away from the Chinese mainland. Japan's calculus was to involve as many extra-regional powers as possible as Asia's security problems would also become a global security problem. Given that these countries too have competing interests with China in their respective spheres of influence, it becomes much easier for Japan to pull them closer strategically. Additionally having strong political relations and communications with all the other US allies would dissuade the United States from making deals with China at Japan's expense. To put it bluntly, Tokyo would be able to leverage on a "social pressure" to ensure that the United States acted with prudence, since how Washington acts might have ramifications in the eyes of the rest of her allies. There would always be strength in numbers, and as long as these partners' interests were more aligned with Japan's against China, then it probably is advantageous for Japan in the long run. The political and diplomatic fury in Japan's external activities helps to build the foundation of the Quad. By 2016, policy documents and media narratives switched to the use of the term "Indo-Pacific" replacing the phrase "Asia–Pacific" to signify the rise of the Quad framework.

Countering China's Global Clout: Asymmetricity Reduction, Alternate Developmental Narrative and Manufacturing Relocation

No other country understands the concept of economic asymmetry better than Japan. The Fukuda doctrine put in place by Tokyo in 1977 presents one of the most important instruments of Japan's foreign policy doctrine. Japan was able to exert political and strategic influence across a variety of target countries and markets, by leveraging on her trade ties and developmental assistance distribution. China, once a recipient of Tokyo's aid, is now enacting its own version of this doctrine across the world. As the world's factory with one of the world's largest market, Beijing's trading influence and economic clout is staggering. Across the globe, Chinese companies, private or state-affiliated, are engaged in trading and the provision of goods and services to cities big and small. Whether it is in Africa, Latin America or the Middle East, the Middle Kingdom has become one of the most important powers seen as concretely improving the lives of the people in developing states. China's cheap consumer goods along with its long-standing history of interactions with these regions have seen China's influence grow by leaps and bounds. Unless something drastic happens, it would be almost impossible for Japan to reduce much less stop Chinese economic influence in these areas. Even if India emerges as an OEM and consumer goods manufacturer envisaged by the Quad, there is no guarantee that Indian companies can displace the Chinese trading network. For Tokyo, the willingness of the United States to privilege, work and reap the benefits of its economic ties with China has always carried an inherent risk for Japan's long-term strategic goals. Therefore in order to preserve Japan's autonomy and competitiveness, the Japanese have tried to rival China globally, often competing with the Chinese for infrastructure projects, the provision of loans and developmental assistance.[1] Yet, such competition might not be sustainable if economic trajectories then persisted. For Japan, just as concerning was the prospects of Trump assuming the office of the President.

Like most of Liberal America, Trump's election shocked and dismayed Japanese elites. For Abe in particular who had spent the last four years

---

[1] This eventually became formalized in 2023 as Japan's Development Cooperation Charter where Tokyo's new blue print for developmental assistance is linked to security and rule of law in additional to traditional goals (Kaizuka, 2023).

to be a better ally to the United States, Trump's rhetoric as Presidential candidate thoroughly jolted Tokyo: "If somebody attacks Japan, we have to immediately go and start World War III, okay? If we get attacked, Japan doesn't have to help us ... Somehow, that doesn't sound so fair" (Sieg, 2016). Additionally, Trump had also accused Japan of stealing jobs and attacked the US-led Trans-Pacific Partnership Trade pact that Japan regards as vital for her economic and strategic well-being. There are concerns that the United States would turn isolationist, coming at a time when Japan was facing what she considers the most extenuating circumstances at home. This is particularly distressing when Trump has neither political nor military experience, appears to be unpredictable and has a lack of clearly defined policy goals, principles and values (Kubo, 2017). Itsunori Onodera, who served as defense minister under Prime Minister Shinzo Abe suggested that Trump's comments on security brought about a great anxiety for allied countries (Onodera cited in Seig, 2016). Japan's principal security concerns stem from issues directly involving or directly from China. There is a deep sense of strategic frustration, anxiety and fear of how her huge neighbour would affect her own security needs and interests.

Japan however was able to parley Trump's victory into a win for the Conservative's agenda. Through his personal diplomacy, Japan's Prime Minister Abe was able to please Trump in a way few other leaders could. Soon after the election, Abe journeyed to the President-elect's office in New York, bearing a golden Honma golf driver as a token of appreciation, along with an invitation to Trump's Mar-a-Lago residence. This relationship between the two golf enthusiasts subsequently led to a series of summit meetings, which continued until Trump's state visit to Tokyo in May 2019 and his attendance at the G20 summit in Osaka in June 2019. There is no question that Abe and Trump are on a first-name basis, a "bromance" relationship that has only been observed in the past between US presidents and Japanese Prime Ministers Reagan and Nakasone, and Bush and Koizumi (Fujiwara, 2019). One has to admire Japan for her fidelity to the US–Japan alliance, or in Abe's case to cement his family legacy and his vision into Japanese mainstream politics.

Upon taking office, Abe was able to negotiate promptly and quickly with the Trump administration with issues that the then-President was concerned about, specifically the trade imbalances and tariffs on certain classes of products such as automobiles and agriculture products. Trump had, in fact, gained politically by emphasising how his threats had forced

Japan into trade talks (Japan Times, 2018). By 2019, Abe and his chief trade negotiator Toshimitsu Motegi declared that they have managed to strike a "win–win" deal that delivered positive outcome for both Tokyo and Washington, even though Trump in reality had made significant gains and Tokyo made all the concessions (Mulgan, 2019). The United States managed to keep on the US tariffs on Japanese cars and car parts on national security grounds, and got Japan to eliminate or lower tariffs on 7.2 billion yen worth of American agricultural products (Mulgan, 2019; Sieg & Kaneko, 2019). This negotiation concession was probably made by Japan to ensure that Trump had a huge political victory for his base, but the subtext of this means that Abe had hoped that this de facto cooperation with Trump would soften him and make him amenable to Abe's more important priorities in the realm on national security. This turned out to be far more complicated than what Japan had expected.

The first area of challenge was North Korea. Tokyo was terribly displeased when they first learned of Trump's intended high-profile engagement with North Korea's Kim Jung-un (Hurst, 2018) Japan felt that they would be short-changed by any possible US reconciliation with North Korea because of Japan's long-standing position in the complete denuclearisation and halting of missile tests and the accounting of kidnapped Japanese nationals before any sort of deal could be made. This approach was largely in agreement with those of the previous US administrations. The Trump White House of course had other ideas on how to approach North Korea. For the President himself, the particular prospect of making a "big score" on foreign policy, of making a movement in an area which previous administrations were not able to and of sharing the media glory with Kim Jung-un topped with the prospects of a possible Nobel Peace Prize nomination was certainly more appealing than following the dictates of the State or Defense Departments.

Trump only communicated the American overtures to North Korea to Japan in April 2018 during the Japanese Prime Minister's visit to Mar-a-Lago. Japan was also extremely concerned that the United States might strike a deal with the DPRK on the decommissioning of only long-range missiles, leaving Tokyo at the mercy of DPRK's medium- and short-range missiles which might be nuclear-tipped. The very fact that Japan was informed after the fact had left Tokyo deeply concerned (Teo, 2019: 4–5). It was clear, however, that nothing was going to dissuade the American President from meeting DPRK's Kim Jung-un despite the objections of his national security team, from Japan's Shinzo Abe and

Shatoro Yachi and Singapore's Foreign Minister Balakrishnan (Bolton, 2022). When Japan's efforts to dissuade Trump and his national security team to call off the meeting failed, Abe spoke at length to Trump about DPRK's nuclearisation program, kidnapping of Japanese nationals and their general untrustworthiness (Bolton, 2022). The United States President nonetheless went ahead with meeting Kim, even as members of his National Security team had suggested that "South Korea's interests were not their interests". By the end of their "meetings" in Singapore (2018) and Vietnam (2019), North Korea's Kim had gained the necessary credentials that he had hoped for in this regime building efforts at home, and established some momentum for his economic cooperation with South Korea's Moon Jae-in. While foreign policy experts in Washington and allied countries laughed at Trump's supposed "antics", what they failed to highlight was the fact that Trump has pacified the North Koreans with a couple of meetings and photo-ops. In doing so, Trump had deftly neutralised a possible nuclear-armed proxy that China could influence or use. Perhaps at that point, few had realised that Trump's foresaw an all-rounded confrontation with China in the near future. For Japan, this nonetheless remained a problem because even though a temporary "understanding" with North Korea has been reached, there are still complications with this scenario down the road as Tokyo's concerns were not addressed. Japan is still vulnerable to North Korea's nuclear and missile threats. The prospect of a united Korea is never in Tokyo's interests, and with Moon's South Korea and Kim's North Korea talking about economic cooperation, this might not necessarily be a good thing for Japan, given that South Korea might detract from US alliance goals. Additionally, the political benefits for Kim meant the perpetuation of a regime that was fundamentally hostile, although Japan's choices were not better even if the Kim regime collapsed. With the United States safe and secure, Japan might be left alone to face Pyongyang alone with her allies (the United States and South Korea dragging their feet) if tensions with DPRK increase. Beyond that, little has been done to address the issue of the kidnapped victims. Moon Jae-in's efforts to reconcile with DPRK could potentially leave a "crack" in the alliance structure, since the Moon government was actively trying to take back control of the command of its military under the auspices of the US-ROK. The increased antagonism with South Korea over Comfort Women row therefore impacts the smooth functioning of US–Japan alliance from Tokyo's perspective.

From the vantage point of Tokyo, Japan's security environment had grown from bad to worse. Two decades ago after the collapse of the USSR, Japan had relatively amicable relations with North Korea, China, Russia and South Korea, notwithstanding the territorial disputes and disagreements over history. By 2016, Japan's relations with all her four East Asian neighbours had deteriorated considerably. Following the Trump White House's willingness to have better relations with Russia and North Korea, Shinzo Abe also announced his intentions to try and have his own diplomacy with North Korea. This of course was a non-starter for North Koreans and only remained part of the administration's rhetoric. Shinzo Abe was able to meet Russia's Vladimir Putin on several occasions but did not make much headway in terms of being able to move beyond the stalemate in their negotiations over the Kurile islands. While such diplomacy did seem futile, Japan was able to keep its relationship with Russia cordial, at least until they became deeply entrenched on the side of the United States during the Ukraine War during the Biden Administration.

The greatest success that Japan had with the United States was China. The Trump administration's willingness to implement it's across the board containment policy against China was a political godsend come true, even a severe fracture of economic Sino-US ties would have negative implications for Japan's economy. Yet, even as the US–China tech and trade war escalated, it was disrupted by the outbreak of the Covid pandemic. The Covid outbreak essentially created a never-before-seen upheavals across the world. On top of the trade and tech war, the United States was engaged in a high-profile political campaign against China aimed at turning international public opinion against Beijing. There were daily reports on how Beijing was threatening Taiwan's independence advocates, rolling back Hong Kong democracy, conducting genocide in Xinjiang and manufacturing the Covid Virus in their bid to manufacture bio weapons lab. The very public exchange was fought out between China's foreign ministry against the Trump White House but in reality against the entire Western media. Tokyo partook in this global campaign too, as many newspapers published editorials as well as refiled Western media reports. All official pronouncements out of China became interpreted as "Wolf Warrior" diplomacy. There is no question that China's image began to take a beating as Beijing began to impose a crippling quarantine on its citizens across the country to combat the Covid outbreak.

It also led to the "flow" of hot money out from China (including Hong Kong and Macau) either via licit or illicit means.

For Japan and the other Quad countries, this dependence on China for manufactured and other materials is a long term strategic dilemma, even though the question of supply chain security became an immediate one. China's closing of the economy had severe repercussions as they have come to rely on China for the manufactured products as well as critical supplies vital to the effective functioning of their economy. This however was *not* just China per se, as the logistics chain virtually across the world had been disrupted. Whether it was importing vegetables or food stuff, or for that matter medical masks and other cheap daily consumer goods, things had by then become exponentially difficult (Glosserman, 2021a, 2021c).

Tokyo in joining the Trump Administration's announcement of it's across the board countering China effort was an important step forward. The coming of Trump, in fact, was a godsend for Japan's Shinzo Abe's personal ideology and politics. Japan's lobbying efforts to counter China's global ambition and growing power had finally found an eager audience in the White House. Trump's efforts to contain China provided political backing, policy justifications and international legitimacy to Abe's policy agenda. While this was good news for those in the Kantei, the problem in reality was much more complicated. Japan's good fortunes as an economic power have been achieved on the basis of the free trade system that the United States and her allies had built over the decades after the War. Trump's protectionist instincts did not fly well with Japan, or for that matter, most of the Asian allies such as Seoul and Singapore that were concerned about what or how the US economic and trade war might impact them and what also meant for other important trade and economic projects in the pipeline. The withdrawal of the United States from the Trans-pacific Partnership (4th February 2016) which had been in negotiation for a long time dealt a blow to the neoliberal hopes of the Pacific economy elites who were convinced that the TPP would help substantiate their economic expansion. China's eagerness to join would showcase Beijing as becoming the most important power in upholding the liberal international trading order—something that both upset and infuriate the Japanese elites. Most of the nations (Australia, Brunei, Canada, Chile, Japan, Malaysia, Mexico, New Zealand, Peru, Singapore, Vietnam) that were in the TPP agreed to stay on, initiating what is known as the

Comprehensive and Progressive Agreement for Trans-pacific Partnership (CPTPP).

This development poses an important dilemma for Japan. Should Tokyo go all out to back the United States in all her policies enacted particularly towards China or should the Japanese elites remain selective and only endorse policies that work for Japan? Arguably, Japan has an even more interdependent relationship with China. Beijing's economic prowess and influence cannot be significantly reduced unless most countries opt to decouple from its economy, but that one comes at a price. From the "strategic" vantage point of the Trump camp, the preservation of the San Francisco system might look only feasible if China's central economic role is to be extricated from the system. This is the essence of the "decoupling" movement that pervaded the thinking of the Global Right—but this is actually fallacious in conceptualisation and fraught with difficulty in implementation.

Even before Trump came into the picture, the Abe administration had, in fact, encouraged Japanese enterprises to relocate their manufacturing to third countries such as India, Vietnam and other Southeast Asian countries with subsidies. This movement to "decouple" was taken with gusto by the Trump administration, as well as encouraged by New Delhi who saw that it had much to gain from companies relocating its manufacturing and services to India. The realities on the ground however were quite different from what the politicians were envisaging. Many global firms had spent decades trying to build a presence in China and were either making a healthy profit or on the verge of doing so. To have them abandon this huge market was extremely problematic from a commercial point of view. There are additional issues of course such as the practical problems of being able to find the requisite conditions necessary to be able to replicate their supply chain or produce their products. For well over decades, China has realised that it's role as the world's factory had become threatened due to rising costs and had, in fact, encouraged factories to move inland and westwards (in China) to take advantage of cheaper manpower costs. The government had also increased incentives for various firms particularly in the Pearl River Delta region as well as the Eastern seaboard to move up the global value chain in anticipation of the scenario that the costs would become too expensive for firms. Chinese firms have, in fact, taken advantage to move their operations offshore to third locations including Southeast Asia but also globally to be nearer to their markets.

While the Quad governments might point to India or Vietnam as the ideal place for the relocation of manufacturing—the fact remains that these locations still lag behind China in many aspects of infrastructure, particularly in utility provision or port facilities. The second problem is that the impact this "decoupling" has is an important impact on the economies of countries that had come to rely on China. In Australia, Canberra has had its wine, seafood iron and mineral industry devastated after the Chinese unilaterally stopped imports in response to the narratives coming out of Australia. Morrison's insinuation that China be held responsible for the Covid pandemic after he suggested the idea that the "root cause of the Covid" needed to be investigated. The Australians then learned the hard way that the Americans exporters had, in fact, filled their quota instead. This became an important but unspoken lesson in Quad countries. Tokyo had, in fact, tried its best to compete with China in a number of years for infrastructure projects such as building of high-speed rails in Laos, Vietnam, India and Indonesia. Even though Japan had worn in some instances such as in Vietnam and India, there were a number of difficulties that saw very slowed progress. The Chinese have had better luck in Laos and Indonesia, but they were not without problems as the locals were keen on technology transfer and the indigenisation of the project.

During the Covid pandemic, Japan had, in fact, partnered with the United States and other Quad countries to manufacture and distribute vaccines and urged countries to cooperate to establish an alternate supply chain outside of China. Japan's JICA worked closely with the United States to create an alternate infrastructure plan to counter China's One Belt One Road project. This alternative was meant to "protect" developing countries from falling into China's "dept trap" diplomacy. Japan understands how powerful the Chinese narrative of its support for global development and its claims to be the world's factory is for Beijing's economic clout. By undermining both through offering an alternative to the developing world, Japan hopes to be able to counter China's increasing influence. The problem however is that one of China's strengths lies in areas in which the Quad nations have very little ability to compete. The global demand for cheap and good quality consumer goods or industrial products cannot be replaced overnight through manufacturing by India or Southeast Asian countries. Beijing's economic ties with nations in Middle East, the Americas and Africa cannot be supplanted easily by the Quad nations just as her ability to manufacture cannot be taken away overnight. Further, Chinese manufacturers have stealthily "globalised" their operations to third countries, including favoured destinations such as Vietnam or Thailand in hopes of avoiding allied sanctions. It has become more difficult to be able to "stop" Chinese trade because of the very entrepreneurial nature of the businessmen themselves in reinventing or disguising themselves What the United States cannot

In the Post-Abe world, Japan's Suga and Kishida have guided Japan in the direction that Abe had set, even there are those in China who wished that Japan would take a step back and mend fences with Beijing (China Daily, 2022). Abe's legacy is viewed grimly in China in both national and geopolitical terms (Lo, 2022). From China's perspective, it would appear that it is Japan's right-wing nationalism and sense of racial superiority as well as the LDP's staunch allegiance to the United States that are driving its security policy to create sustained animosity towards China. It is Japan's desire for Great Power status that is reviving Japanese militarism that the LDP is guising through its liberal rhetoric and democratic narratives. From Japan's perspective it is China's authoritarianism, strategic ambitions and opaque military modernisation that is upsetting the strategic balance and creating regional insecurities. Japan has passed and enacted further laws to loosen the shackles of its Pacifist Constitution (Smith, 2022) and increased its defence budget to further rearm the JSDF (Smith, 2021a, 2021b) into a military capable of independent war-waging capacity under the auspices of "tightening" the alliance. In effect, Abe had set the course for a new security policy (Sakaki, 2023), and his legacy in its purest ideological terms might live on well after him (Sneider, 2022). Abe's rhetoric and policy are threefold—to get the United States to Japan and South Korea has appeared to grow closer because of the political outlook of Prime Minister Kishida and ROK President Yoon, but this is unlikely to last because it is not a genuine reconciliation between the two nations (Kamata, 2023). Japan is now increasingly seeing itself at the forefront of a new struggle against China, and to that extent, "resisting" and "containing" China are now central keywords in Japanese public narratives and strategic discussions. Tokyo also now occupies a central role in the West's strategic rivalry with China by not only cultivating the United States, but also other partners such as ASEAN and Europe (Pohlkamp, 2023). Even though all these are done in the name of security, it raises the question if this is a proverbial situation of the tail wagging the dog. The problem with such focused thinking on "containing" or "balancing" China is that it uncritically abandons the value of engagement with Beijing in order to achieve what right wing factions such as those under Abe wanted. Being fixated and going all out in highlighting the China threat would almost definitely invite a response from China. Japan also cannot assume that in all cases her partners would unconditionally back Tokyo's ambition and play. Furthermore, in the United States led by the very unpredictable President Trump, there is no guarantee that Japan would not be chain-ganged or made to front a proxy conflict that it does not wish to take part. The question now remains if the Japanese government under the newly elected centrist Shigeru Ishiba is able to balance what Japan really needs politically and strategically with the interests of the United States and China going forward. A second-term Trump administration is likely to be bolder, more focused and less reasonable in their dealings with the perceived geopolitical competitor—the United States. An outright confrontation between the United States and China cannot be in Japan's interests, particularly if a conflict breaks out in the Taiwan Straits or in the South China Sea. Would the post-Abe Japan be able to define their national interests with more pristine accuracy in a clear-eyed and independent manner and formulate a better China strategy to ensure their security rather than become a proxy and new frontline in the United States' renewed Cold War with China?

References

Asahi Shimbun, "Shambolic Approach to Education Under Abe's Tenure", Asahi Shimbun, 5 September 2020, https://www.asahi.com/ajw/articles/13699568

Abe, Shinzo, Towards a Beautiful Country (revised and complete edition), *Atarashii kuni e : utsukushii kuni e kanzenban* (2006, Revised 2013), Tokyo: Bungel Shunjul

Associated Press, "A Timeline of the Career of Former Japanese PM Shinzo Abe", Voice of America, 8 July 2022, https://www.voanews.com/a/a-timeline-of-the-career-of-former-japanese-pm-shinzo-abe-/6650480.html

Avenell, Simon, "Generational Tensions Flare as Japan Faces the Economic Reality of Its Ageing Baby Boomers", The Conversation, 15 November 2023, https://theconversation.com/generational-tensions-flare-as-japan-faces-the-economic-reality-of-its-ageing-baby-boomers-217289

BBC, "Why is Japanese Prime Minister Shinzo Abe So Unpopular?", BBC News, 24 July 2017, https://www.bbc.com/news/world-asia-40701810

Barboza, David, "China Passes Japan as Second-Largest Economy", The New York Times, 15 August 2010, https://www.nytimes.com/2010/08/16/business/global/16yuan.html

Bolton, John, "The Death of Shinzo Abe is a Loss to the U.S. and its Allies", The Washington Post, 8 July 2022

Bosack, Michael, "The Evolution of LDP Factions", Tokyo Review, 4 January 2022, https://tokyoreview.net/2022/01/the-evolution-of-ldp-factions/

Branigan, Tania, & McCurry, Justin, "Japan Releases Chinese Fishing Boat Captain", The Guardian, 24 September 2010, https://www.theguardian.com/world/2010/sep/24/japan-free-chinese-boat-captain

Bruaset, Marit, "The Legalisation of Hinomaru and Kimigayo as Japan's National Flag and Anthren and its Connections to the Political Campaign of "Healthy Nationalism and internationalism"", University of Oslo Thesis, 2003 https://www.duo.uio.no/bitstream/handle/10852/24202/bruaset.pdf?sequence=1

CFR (Council For Foreign Relations) n.d., China Maritime Disputes 1895–2020 Timeline, Entry on 1998, https://www.cfr.org/timeline/chinas-maritime-disputes

Chang, Gordon, "Hillary Clinton Changes America's China Policy", Forbes, 28 July 2010, https://www.japantimes.co.jp/opinion/2022/07/13/commentary/world-commentary/anti-americanism-problems/

Chen, Guangjin, "US Delegation Looks to Mend Fences", The China Daily, 16 January 2013, http://usa.chinadaily.com.cn/epaper/2013-01/16/content_16125545.htm

Chotiner, Issac, "How Shinzo Abe Sought to Rewrite Japanese History", The New Yorker, 9 July 2022, https://www.newyorker.com/news/q-and-a/how-shinzo-abe-sought-to-rewrite-japanese-history

Chacko, Priya, & Jayasuriya, Kanishka. 2018 "Asia's Conservative Moment: Understanding the Rise of the Right", Journal of Contemporary Asia 48, no. 4: 529–540, https://www.tandfonline.com/doi/full/10.1080/00472336.2018.1448108

China Daily, "Abe's Death May Transform Japan's Political Landscape", China Daily 9 July 2022, China Daily, https://global.chinadaily.com.cn/a/202207/09/WS62c90746a310fd2b29e6b6db.html

Drucker, Peter F., "In Defense of Japanese Bureaucracy", Foreign Affairs, September–October, 1998, Vol. 77, Issue 5 (September–October, 1998), pp. 68–80, https://www.jstor.org/stable/20049051

Estévez-Abe, Margarita, "Review of Feeling Triumphalist in Tokyo: The Real Reasons Nationalism Is Back in Japan, by David Pilling". Foreign Affairs 93, no. 3 (2014): 165–71. http://www.jstor.org/stable/24483416

Fackler, Martin, & Johnson, Ian, "Japan Retreats With Release of Chinese Boat Captain", The New York Times, 24 September 2010, https://www.nytimes.com/2010/09/25/world/asia/25chinajapan.html

114   V. TEO

Fackler, Martin, "The Silencing of Japan's Free Press", Foreign Policy, 27 May 2016, https://foreignpolicy.com/2016/05/27/the-silencing-of-japans-free-press-shinzo-abe-media/

French, Howard, "The Many Contradictions of Shinzo Abe", Foreign Policy, 18 July 2022, https://foreignpolicy.com/2022/07/18/shinzo-abe-history-japan-diplomacy-contradictions/

Fujita, Taisuke, & Hiroki Kusano. "Denial of History? Yasukuni Visits as Signaling." *Journal of East Asian Studies* 20, no. 2 (2020): 291–316. https://doi.org/10.1017/jea.2020.2

Fujita, Testuya, "Memory of Kishi Seen Behind Abe's Political Agenda and Calendar", Nikkei Asia, 24 July 2015, https://asia.nikkei.com/Politics/Memory-of-Kishi-seen-behind-Abe-s-political-agenda-and-calendar

Fujiwara, Kiichi, Abe-Trump Bromance Yet to Bring Rewards, Brief, East Asia Forum, 1 November 2019 (Article Appeared Originally in East Asian Forum Quarterly as "Japan's Leadership Moment", Vol. 11, No. 3, https://eastasiaforum.org/2019/11/01/abe-trump-bromance-yet-to-bring-rewards/

Fulcher, James. "The Bureaucratization of the State and the Rise of Japan." *The British Journal of Sociology* 39, no. 2 (1988): 228–54. https://doi.org/10.2307/590782

Frum, David, "Shinzo Abe Made the World Better", The Atlantic, 8 July 2022

Gallagher, Chris, & Sieg, Linda, "Ex-Defence Minister Ishiba is People's Choice for the Next Japan PM: Polls", Reuters 31, August 2000, https://www.straitstimes.com/asia/east-asia/ex-defence-minister-shigeru-ishiba-is-peoples-choice-for-next-japan-pm-polls

Gallagher, Chris, & Sieg, Linda, "Ex-Defence Minister Ishiba is People's Choice for Next Japan PM: Polls", Reuters, 31 August 2020, https://www.reuters.com/article/us-japan-politics-abe-idUSKBN25R07X

Glosserman, Brad & Schaede, Ulrike, "Japan's Fractured Polity by Covid 19 Crisis", Nikkei Asia, 8 August 2021a, https://asia.nikkei.com/Opinion/Japan-s-fractured-polity-exposed-by-COVID-19-crisis

Glosserman, Brad, "Taro Kono Faces Intractable Opposition—From His Own Party", The Japan Times, 28 September 2021b, https://www.japantimes.co.jp/opinion/2021/09/28/commentary/japan-commentary/kono-faces-ldp-opposition/

Glosserman, Brad and Schaede, Ulrike, "Japan's Fractured Polity Exposed by COVID-19 Crisis", Asia Nikkei, 8 August 2021c, https://asia.nikkei.com/Opinion/Japan-s-fractured-polity-exposed-by-COVID-19-crisis

Glosserman, Brad, "Taro Kono Faces Intractable Opposition—From His Own Party: Quietly Some Senior LDP Officials Worry About His China Policy", 28 September 2021d, https://www.japantimes.co.jp/opinion/2021/09/28/commentary/japan-commentary/kono-faces-ldp-opposition/

Glosserman, Brad, "Anti-American Sentiment Throws a Long Shadow Over Geopolitics", The Japan Times, 13 July 2022, https://www.japantimes.co.jp/opinion/2022/07/13/commentary/world-commentary/anti-americanism-problems/

Graham, David, "Shinzo Abe Bets on America's Fading Memories", The Atlantic, 30 April 2015

Gunangurunathan, A.D., "Abe's Legacy is Not All Glowing", Deccan Herald, 22 July 2022, https://www.deccanherald.com/opinion/abe-s-legacy-is-not-all-glowing-1128862.html

Harrison, Selig, Seabed Petroleum in Northeast Asia: Conflict or Cooperation, Woodrow Wilson International Center for Scholars, https://www.wilsoncenter.org/sites/default/files/media/documents/publication/Asia_petroleum.pdf

Harris, Tobias, The Iconoclast: Shinzo Abe and the New Japan, London: Hurst & Company, 2020

Harris, Tobias, "Why Shinzo Abe Will Continue to Govern Japan for Years After His Death", Time Magazine Online, 14 July 2022, https://time.com/6196551/shinzo-abe-legacy-after-death-japan/

Hanada, Ryosuke, "Abe's Drive To "Bring Back Japan"", The Interpreter, 26 July 2022, https://www.lowyinstitute.org/the-interpreter/abe-s-drive-bring-back-japan

Hayashi, Yuka, "Ishihara Unplugged: China a 'Thief', America 'Unreliable'", The Wall Street Journal, 29 May 2012, https://www.wsj.com/articles/BL-JRTB-12141

Hosaya, Yuchi, "Why Abe's Global Strategy Is Important: Japan's Foreign and Security Policy under Prime Minister Shinzo Abe", Italian Institute for International Studies Newsletter, 11 January 2017, https://www.ispionline.it/en/publication/why-abes-global-strategy-important-japans-foreign-and-security-policy-under-prime-minister-shinzo-abe-16181

Hurst, Daniel, Japan Frets About Trump's Looming Talks With North Korea, 2018, https://www.nbcnews.com/news/north-korea/japan-frets-about-trump-s-looming-talks-north-korea-n869201

Ichihara, Maiko. "Japanese Democracy After Shinzo Abe." *Journal of Democracy* 32, no. 1 (2021): 81–95. https://doi.org/10.1353/jod.2021.0002

International Viewpoint 2002, "Japan: Militarisation Under the Koizumi Administration", International Viewpoint Socialist Online Magazine, November 2002, https://internationalviewpoint.org/IMG/article_PDF/Japan-militarisation-under-the-Koizumi-Administration_a326.pdf

Iwami, Takao, The Monster of Showa, Asahi Sonorama Publications (now Asahi Shimbun Publications Inc): Tokyo, 1994 published in Japanese as 岩見隆夫昭和の妖怪 岸信介』 朝日ソノラマ、1994 年 (first published) ISBN 4-257-03390-8

Jain, Purnendra, Shinzo Abe's Legacy and Japan's India Engagement", National University of Singapore Institute of South Asian Studies (ISAS) Insights, 13 July 2022, https://www.isas.nus.edu.sg/papers/shinzo-abes-legacy-and-japans-india-engagement/

Jain, Purnendra C., "A New Political Era in Japan: The 1993 Election." *Asian Survey* 33, no. 11 (November 1993): 1071–82. https://www.jstor.org/stable/2645000

Jain, Punendra, "Smooth Sailing for Abe in LDP Leadership Contest", East Asia Forum, 5 September 2015, https://www.eastasiaforum.org/2015/09/05/smooth-sailing-for-abe-in-ldp-leadership-contest/

Jain, Purnendra, & Akimmoto, Daisuke, "Hereditary Politicians Remain Dominant in Japan", East Asia Forum, 28 February 2023, https://www.eastasiaforum.org/2023/02/28/hereditary-politicians-remain-dominant-in-japan/

Jimbo, Ken, & Tatsumi, Yuki, "From The JDA To The MoD—A Step Forward, But Challenges Remain", Stimson Institute Commentary on Indo-Pacific Affairs, 27 January 2007, https://www.stimson.org/2007/jda-mod-step-forward-challenges-remain/

Johnston, Eric, "Meet the 'Shadow Shogun' Behind the Making of Japan's Next Prime Minister", The Japan Times, 11 September 2020, https://www.japantimes.co.jp/news/2020/09/11/national/politics-diplomacy/ldp-kingmaker-toshihiro-nikai-suga/

Johnson, Chalmers, MITI and the Japanese Miracle: The Growth of Industrial Policy, 1925–1975, Stanford, CA: California University Press, 1982

Kaizuka, James, "Japan's 2023 Development Cooperation Charter: The Aid-Security Nexus", The Diplomat, 14 June 2023, https://thediplomat.com/2023/06/japans-2023-development-cooperation-charter-the-aid-security-nexus/

Kamata, Jio, "The Japan-South Korea Thaw Is Far From a Done Deal", The Diplomat, 14 March 2023, https://thediplomat.com/2023/03/the-japan-south-korea-thaw-is-far-from-a-done-deal/

Kaya, Keiichi, "Abenomics: The Reasons It Fell Short As Economic Policy", Nippon "Politics" Feature, 19 January 2022, https://www.nippon.com/en/japan-topics/g01236/#

Kingston, Jeff, "Shinzo Keeps Winning", The Atlantic, 21 October 2017

Kingston, Jeff, "Curbing Academic Freedom In Japan." *The Asia-Pacific Journal*, 15 February 2023, https://apjjf.org/2023/2/kingston

Kitazume, Takashi, "Sino-Japan Policy Dialogue Held Hostage by Nationalistic Fervor: A Presentation by Huang Jing", Brookings Institute, 24 December 2005, https://www.brookings.edu/on-the-record/sino-japan-policy-dialogue-held-hostage-by-nationalistic-fervor/

Komine, Takao, "How did Koizumi Cabinet Change Japan? Assessment of Koizumi's Economic Policies and Preview of Abe's Economic Stewardship",

Japan Spotlight, May/June 2007, https://www.jef.or.jp/journal/pdf/153 cover%20story01.pdf

Kato, Yuko & Abdul Jalil, Zubaidah, "Shinzo Abe: The Legacy of Japan's Longest-Serving PM", BBC News, 8 July 2022, https://www.bbc.com/news/world-asia-53938094

Koga, Ko, "Memories of Abe Shinzō: The Man Who Reshaped Japan", Nippon, 15 July 2022, https://www.nippon.com/en/japan-topics/g02169/

Krauss, Ellis & Pekkanen, Robert J., The Rise and Fall of Japan's LDP: Political Party Organisations as Historical Institutions, Ithaca: Cornell University Press, 2011

Kwan, Weng Kin, "Abe Talks Tough, Senkaku Belongs to China", The Straits Times, 18 December 2012, https://www.straitstimes.com/asia/south-asia/abe-talks-tough-senkaku-islands-belong-to-japan

Kubo, Fumiaki, "Trump prompts Japan's cautious shift to self-reliance", East Asia Forum, 3 September 2017, https://eastasiaforum.org/2017/09/03/trump-prompts-japans-cautious-shift-to-self-reliance/

Kushner, Barak, & Sato, Masaharu, "Digesting Postwar Japanese Media." *Diplomatic History* 29, no. 1 (2005): 27–48. http://www.jstor.org/stable/249 14783

Kyodo News, "Japanese Self-Defense Forces launch 1st amphibious fighting unit", 7 April 2018, https://english.kyodonews.net/news/2018/04/2f3 bb80eb01b-japan-holds-kick-off-ceremony-for-1st-full-fledged-amphibious-force.html

Langley Esquire, "Abe Faction: A Struggle of the Leadership", Langley Esquire Paper, 3 August 2022, https://langleyesquire.com/abe-faction-a-struggle-for-leadership/

Levidis, Andrew, "Shinzo Abe and the Dream of a Conservative Asia", East Asia Forum, 2 October 2012, https://eastasiaforum.org/2012/10/02/shi nzo-abe-and-the-dream-of-a-conservative-asia/

Liff, Adam P., "Policy by Other Means: Collective Self-Defense and the Politics of Japan's Postwar Constitutional Reinterpretations." *Asia Policy*, no. 24 (2017): 139–72. https://www.jstor.org/stable/26403212

Lindgreen, Petter, "The Era of Koizumi's Right Wing Populism", University of Oslo, Spring 2012, Master Thesis, https://www.duo.uio.no/bitstream/han dle/10852/24218/Lindgren.pdf?sequence=2

Lo, Sonny Shiu Hing, Shinzo Abe's Legacy on Japan's Relations with China, Macau Business Agency, 9 July 2022, https://www.macaubusiness.com/opi nion-shinzo-abes-legacy-on-japans-relations-with-china/

Maeda, Kenta, "Kishi Removes Family Tree From Website Amid Cries of Nepotism", The Asahi Shimbun, 14 February 2023, https://www.asahi.com/ajw/articles/14839247

Maki, John M., "The Role of the Bureaucracy in Japan." Pacific Affairs 20, no. 4 (1947): 391–406. https://doi.org/10.2307/2752543

McCurry, Justin, "Tokyo's Right Wing Governor Plans to Buy Disputed Senkaku Islands", The Guardian, 19 April 2012, https://www.theguardian.com/world/2012/apr/19/tokyo-governor-senkaku-islands-china

McCurry, Justin, "Obama Says US Will Defend Japan in Island Dispute with China", The Guardian, 24 April 2014, https://www.theguardian.com/world/2014/apr/24/obama-in-japan-backs-status-quo-in-island-dispute-with-china

McCormack, Gavan, "Koizumi's Kingdom of Illusion", The Asia-Pacific Journal: Japan Focus, 24 November 2025, https://apjjf.org/-Gavan-McCormack/1924/article.pdf

McCurry, Justin, "Shinzo Abe: Man Sets Himself Alight in Protest at State Funeral for Killed Japan PM", The Guardian, 21 September 2022, https://www.theguardian.com/world/2022/sep/21/shinzo-abe-man-sets-himself-alight-in-protest-at-state-funeral-for-killed-japan-pm

MOFA (Ministry of Foreign Affairs, Japan) "Toward an Alliance of Hope", Address by Prime Minister Shinzo Abe to a Joint Meeting of the U.S. Congress, 29 April 2015, https://www.mofa.go.jp/na/na1/us/page4e_000241.html

MOFA (Ministry of Foreign Affairs Japan), The Bounty of the Open Seas: Five New Principles for Japanese Diplomacy, 2013, https://www.mofa.go.jp/announce/pm/abe/abe_0118e.html

Mukai, Yuko, "Abe's Death Puts Focus on Kishida's Contrasting Leadership Qualities", The Japan News, 15 October 2022, https://japannews.yomiuri.co.jp/editorial/political-pulse/20221015-64465/

Mukae, Ryuji, "Japan's Diet Resolution on World War Two: Keeping History at Bay." *Asian Survey* 36, no. 10 (1996): 1011–30. https://doi.org/10.2307/2645631

Mulgan, Aurelia George, "The 'Trump Factor' in the US–Japan Trade Deal", East Asia Forum, 13 October 2019, https://eastasiaforum.org/2019/10/13/the-trump-factor-in-the-us-japan-trade-deal/

Nakahara, Junki, "Deconstructing Abe Shinzo's "Take Back Japan" Nationalism", *The Asia-Pacific Journal: Japan Focus* 19, no. 24 Number 1|Article ID 5658|December 15, 2021, https://apjjf.org/2021/24/Nakahara.html

Nakamura, Keita, "Japan OKs enemy base strike capability in major defense policy shift", Kyodo News, 16 December 2022, https://english.kyodonews.net/news/2022/12/02fc9015409c-japan-to-vow-to-obtain-enemy-base-strike-capability-amid-threats.html

Nilsson-Wright, John, "Shinzo Abe: Revisionist Nationalist or Pragmatic Realist?" BBC News, 28 August 2020, https://www.bbc.com/news/world-asia-53950704

Nippon, "Japanese Generations: Boom, Bubble and Ice Age", Nippon.com Society Feature, 12 May 2022, https://www.nippon.com/en/japan-data/h00535/japanese-generations-boom-bubble-and-ice-age.html

Nester, William, "Japan's Mainstream Press: Freedom to Conform?" *Pacific Affairs* 62, no. 1 (1989): 29–39. https://doi.org/10.2307/2760262

Ohi, Akai, Two Kinds of Conservatives in Japanese Politics and Prime Minister Shinzo Abe's Tactics to cope with them, Asia Pacific Bulletin (East-West Center), no 114 (December 2018), https://www.eastwestcenter.org/publications/two-kinds-conservatives-in-japanese-politics-and-prime-minister-shinzo-abe's-tactics

Park, Cheol Hee, "The Double Life of Shinzo Abe", Global Asia, June 2013, https://www.globalasia.org/v8no2/feature/the-double-life-of-shinzo-abe_cheol-hee-park

Pempel, T.J., "Bureaucracy in Japan." *PS: Political Science and Politics* 25, no. 1 (1992): 19–24. https://doi.org/10.2307/419570

Pohlkamp, Elli-Katharina, "The New Central Front: Japan's Special Role in the West's Strategic Rivalry with China", Council for Foreign Relations Commentary, 1 June 2023, https://ecfr.eu/article/the-new-central-front-japans-special-role-in-the-wests-strategic-rivalry-with-china/

Sakaki, Alexandra, "Japan's Security Policy: A Shift in Direction Under Abe", SWP Research Paper, German Institute for International and Security Affairs, Berlin, 2 March 2015

Sakaki, Alexandra, "A New Course for Japan's Security Policy: The Historic Decision for Japan's Security Policy", SWP Comment, No. 13 March 2023, https://www.swp-berlin.org/publications/products/comments/2023C13_Japan_SecurityPolicy.pdf

Saito, Jun, "Infrastructure as the Magnet of Power: Explaining Why Japanese Legislators Left and Returned to the LDP." *Journal of East Asian Studies* 9, no. 3 (2009): 467–93. http://www.jstor.org/stable/23418738

Sieg, Linda, "Trump Candidacy Stirs Alliance Angst in Japan", Reuters, 20 March 2016, https://www.reuters.com/article/us-usa-election-japan-idUSKCN0WM017

Sim, Walter, "Japan's Politicians Admit to Ties With Unification Church After Abe's Death", The Straits Times, 26 July 2022

Siow, Maria, "Shinzo Abe: A Political Titan Who Shaped Japan's Policies on China, Defence, Economy", South China Morning Post, 8 July 2022, https://www.scmp.com/week-asia/politics/article/3184587/shinzo-abe-force-behind-japans-policies-china-defence-economy

Shibuichi, Daiki, "The Yasukuni Shrine Dispute and the Politics of Identity in Japan: Why All the Fuss?" *Asian Survey* 45, no. 2 (2005): 197–215. https://doi.org/10.1525/as.2005.45.2.197

Sieg, Linda, & Kaneko, Kaori, "Details on Car Tariffs Fuzzy as U.S., Japan Head for Trade Deal", Reuters, 17 September 2019, https://www.reuters.com/art icle/idUSKBN1W20IP/

Siripala, Thisanka, "After the Presidential Election, What Next for Abe and the LDP?", The Diplomat, 23 September 2018, https://thediplomat.com/2018/09/after-the-presidential-election-what-next-for-abe-and-the-ldp/

Smith, Sheila, "Will Abe's Legacy Be Constitutional Revision?" Council of Foreign Relations, 11 July 2022, https://www.cfr.org/blog/will-abes-legacy-be-constitutional-revision

Smith, Sheila, "Japan, the Quad and the Indo Pacific", The Asan Forum Special Issue, 23 June 2021b, https://theasanforum.org/japan-the-quad-and-the-indo-pacific/

Smith, Sheila, "How Japan Is Upgrading Its Military", Council on Foreign Relations, 24 February 2021a, https://www.cfr.org/in-brief/how-japan-upgrad ing-its-military

Smith, Sheila, "Remarks on "The Making of Anti-American" Sentiment in Korea and Japan", Wilson Center, May 2003, https://www.wilsoncenter.org/event/the-making-anti-american-sentiment-korea-and-japan

Sneider, Daniel, "Will Abe Shinzo's Death Give His Agenda New Life?" The Christian Science Monitor, 11 July 2022, https://www.csmonitor.com/World/Asia-Pacific/2022/0711/Will-Abe-Shinzo-s-death-give-his-agenda-new-life

Solis, Mireya, "Shinzo Abe's Surprising Victory", Brookings Institute, 28 September 2012, https://www.brookings.edu/articles/shinzo-abes-surpri sing-victory/

Synder, Scott, "Japan-South Korea Tensions Are Eroding Security in Northeast Asia", Council on Foreign Relations, Asia Unbound, https://www.cfr.org/blog/japan-south-korea-tensions-are-eroding-security-northeast-asia

Narazaki, Takahashi & Sasagawa, Shohei "Documents: Abe Aide Bullied Ministry Like a 'Loony Yakuza'", The Asahi Shimbun, 8 March 2023, https://www.asahi.com/ajw/articles/14856463

Takahashi, Kosuke, "Japan Frustrated With US' China Policy", The Straits Times, 25 April 2014, https://www.straitstimes.com/opinion/japan-frustr ated-with-us-china-policy

Takahara, Kanako, "Seiko Noda Makes Last-Minute Bid for LDP Presidency", The Japan Times, 16 September 2021, https://www.japantimes.co.jp/news/2021/09/16/national/politics-diplomacy/noda-enters-ldp-race/#:~:text= Noda%20tried%20unsuccessfully%20to%20run,having%20served%20as%20c onstruction%20minister

Stockwin, J.A.A, Dynamic and Immobilist Politics in Japan, Basingstoke: Macmillan Press, 1980

Tajima, Yukio, Prime Ministers in Japan Stronger Than Ever 20 Years After Reforms, 18 July 2021, https://asia.nikkei.com/Politics/Inside-Japanese-politics/Prime-ministers-in-Japan-stronger-than-ever-20-years-after-reforms

Tanaka, Aiji, Why Has the LDP Stayed in Power so Long in Post-War Japan?:Democratic System Support and Electoral Behavior, UC Irvine: Center for the Study of Democracy, 2007. Retrieved from https://escholarship.org/uc/item/5gm0f2jf

Teo, Victor, Japan's Arduous Rejuvenation as a Global Power: Democratic Resilience and the US-China Challenge, Singapore: Palgrave Macmillan, 2019

Thayer, Carlyle, "The Senkaku Islands Dispute: Risk to U.S. Rebalancing in the Asia-Pacific?", USNI News, 16 October 2012, https://news.usni.org/2012/10/16/senkaku-islands-dispute-risk-us-rebalancing-asia-pacific

Tien Ce Joe, Balancing Rivalry and Cooperation: Japan's Response to the BRI in Southeast Asia, https://www.e-ir.info/2022/06/20/balancing-rivalry-and-cooperation-japans-response-to-the-bri-in-southeast-asia/

The Economist, How the LDP Dominates Japan's Politics, 28 October 2021, https://www.economist.com/the-economist-explains/2021/10/28/how-the-ldp-dominates-japans-politics

The White House, Remarks by President Obama and Prime Minister Abe of Japan at Pearl Harbor, 27 December 2016, https://obamawhitehouse.archives.gov/the-press-office/2016/12/28/remarks-president-obama-and-prime-minister-abe-japan-pearl-harbor

The White House, Remarks by President Obama and Prime Minister Abe of Japan at Hiroshima Peace Memorial, 27 May 2016, https://obamawhitehouse.archives.gov/the-press-office/2016/05/27/remarks-President-obama-and-prime-minister-abe-japan-hiroshima-peace

The Japan Times, Trump Brags Auto Tariff Threat Forced Japan into Trade Talks, 2 October 2018, https://www.japantimes.co.jp/news/2018/10/02/business/trump-brags-auto-tariff-threat-forced-japan-trade-talks/

Toh, Lam Seng, Shinzo Abe's Second Term: Was Abe Pro-China? Should the Chinese Miss Him?, 6 October 2020, https://www.thinkchina.sg/shinzo-abes-second-term-was-abe-pro-china-should-chinese-miss-him

Yomiuri, "Abe Increasing Influence at Helm of LDP's Largest Faction", The Yomuri Shimbun, 7 December 2021, https://japannews.yomiuri.co.jp/politics/politics-government/20211207-7080/

Yora Masao, "The 3A-2F War: The Veiled Election-Year Struggle Inside the LDP", Nippon Feature, 18 August 2021, https://www.nippon.com/en/in-depth/d00727/

CHAPTER 3

The United States' Neoconservative Turn: America First, Preserving U.S. Hegemony and the Containment of China

LEVEL I: THE POLITICAL LEADERSHIP

Donald Trump: The Unlikely Conservative

As the President of the United States, Donald Trump's personality, vision and outlook drastically altered the tone and direction of US politics and foreign policy in a manner that from hindsight has fundamentally altered the nature of global politics. Today as the United States engages in a proxy war in Ukraine with Russia and is increasingly challenging China across the Taiwan Straits and South China Sea, the world is on the brink of a renewed Cold War. While the development of global politics can hardly be attributed to a single actor, Donald Trump's ascendance as US President did set off a series of actions that is radically felt across the world, and changed the paradigm of how the United States and her allies have been dealing with Russia and China.

Donald John Trump was born on June 14, 1946, in Queens, New York City. One of the most interesting aspects is how different his upbringing and experiences are from his Presidential predecessors. He grew up in a well-heeled family in a relatively affluent environment where his father Fred Trump made a fortune in the real estate and construction business. His upbringing and formative years proved to have a decisive effect on the moulding of his worldview and his emergence as a businessman and later politician. Trump attended the New York Military Academy, where he was instilled with a sense of discipline, focus and competitiveness and

© The Author(s), under exclusive license to Springer Nature
Singapore Pte Ltd. 2024
V. Teo, *Cold War Redux Amidst Great Power Rivalry*,
https://doi.org/10.1007/978-981-97-3733-8_3

123

went on to study at the Wharton School at the University of Pennsylvania majoring in Economics. Trump started out his career working for his father, and he sought to make a name for himself by striking out on his own in Manhattan where he too engaged in the construction and real estate business with the help of his father and his social circle. By his own admission, his father had given him a US$1million loan to start his career. In this respect, Trump had more in common with Japanese leader Shinzo Abe than Indian Prime Minister Narendra Modi as he was very much born into a privileged background and rubbed shoulders with elites of American society growing up. From his numerous interviews in print and on social media, he admitted that his father was one of the most important influences on his life His avoidance of alcohol and cigarettes is one such indicator, given that his father had died from alcoholism at the age of 43 (BBC, 2021).

In his early career, Trump participated in the transformation of downtown Manhattan by acquiring 100 Central Park South (Howell, 1985) and very controversial refurbishment of the buildings to condominium units in 1981 (Mahler, 2016; Taylor, 2016), before going on to rebuilding the rundown Commodore Hotel to become the Grand Hyatt. He also built the 68-story Trump Tower on the Fifth Avenue. This was followed by a string of other very prominent properties amongst listed on the Trump Organization today as spanning across the US (New York, Florida, New Jersey, Connecticut, Hawaii, Illinois, Nevada) and overseas (India, Philippines, South Korea, Turkey, Indonesia and Uruguay). Trump also invested in the hotels and casinos but had filed bankruptcy (corporate) over these businesses. Like almost every high profile businessmen, Trump was never far from the limelight and high society in his dealings. Other than his high-profile divorces and numerous scandals that graced high society magazine pages, he also built his reputation on a string of high-profile "entertainment" business like modelling events and beauty pageants (Miss USA, Miss Teen USA and Miss Universe). He then became a reality TV Star hosting shows such as the Apprentice for 14 Seasons where he was reportedly paid a sum of US$213 million by the NBC Network (BBC, 2021). Trump has also several books published under his name, with lines of merchandise from Talking Figures on Amazon to his signature red ties and apparel sold at Trump Stores. Forbes estimated Trump was worthed US$2.6 billion in September 2023 (Alexander, 2023). To that end, the exposure Trump had in the media served as a pivotal element in shaping his public image. Oddly enough, it was also his antagonistic relationship with these very institutions that would come to define his candidacy and his Presidency.

During Obama's tenure, Trump's ties with the Republican Party solidified. He, however, has in reality vacillated from Party-to-Party through his career. Trump was known to have a relationship with the Clintons, but in view of how Obama had even beaten Hilary Clinton to clinch the Democratic Party nomination in 2008 (MacAskill & Goldenburg, 2008), there is a chance that Trump might have thought that it was easier to clinch the nomination from the Republican Party. Donald Trump had in fact tweeted over 67 times (ABC, 2017) about the "birther" movement, alleging that Hilary Clinton was in fact the person who started it in a tweet (Trump, 2015). Trump had in fact made 67 tweets on that subject even as Obama had in fact released his birth certificate in 2011. The animosity between Trump and Obama started in 2011 when Obama mocked Trump over the "birther" conspiracy theory at a White House Correspondents dinner, and a few weeks just before the 2016 elections, Obama went on the "Jimmy Kimmel Live!" show, read a series of insulting tweets aimed at him (Obama), including one made by Trump regarding how Obama will go down as the "worse" President. Obama retorted forcibly by saying "Well, @realDonaldTrump, at least I will go down as a President". Obama, then mimicking a rapper dropping the mike, Obama held out the phone and dropped it to the floor (Remnick, 2016). There is no question that the rivalry between Obama and Trump is probably just as intense if not more than Clinton and Trump.

A Pragmatic and Transactional Political Chameleon

Donald Trump is at heart not a right-wing conservative, at least for most of his life. Until the point he ran for President, no one would take the prospects of Trump rising to prominence in nationwide right-wing politics seriously. He was considered the "inside joke" amongst establishment Republicans, and therefore an unlikely candidate for Republican Party leadership. The other Republican competitors did not regard him as a true Conservative or a respected establishment politician like Jeb Bush. The disdain for those that supported Trump was not confined just to the Democratic camp (remember Clinton's "Basket of Deplorables"), they also came from the echelons of the "traditional" Republican Party. This however was a bad mistake on the part of the elites of both parties to have underestimated Trump's abilities as a politician (Lweis, 2021). In the end, it was extremely ironic that it was the New York millionaire who had relied on the neoliberal economic framework for his fortune should become the chief advocate and poster-boy for conservative politics in America. His remarks and positions during the campaign significantly differed from what many would regard as mainstream neo-conservatism thought in the country. Reagan's conservatism would include the following elements: a small government role domestically, a global foreign policy outlook that sought to promote US values such as freedom and democracy abroad that relied on a strategy of promoting American leadership, reinvigorating US alliances and building coalitions globally. While Trump did agree that small governments were necessary, his other agenda items were in fact contrary to what many true-blue Republicans believed. Trump's advocations of America First agenda that focused on domestic issues, particularly economic malfeasance in Red states and the critique of the economic and human costs of US interventions and alliances abroad sounded more like Wilsonian isolationism.

As a businessman, Trump had particularly good instincts in recognising opportunities, and understand the dynamics involved in the competition and the strategy to achieve his goals. For someone to be successful in the cut-throat world of real estate, one of course would also expect Trump to be as calculating and ruthless in his political methodology as the next successful millionaire. With a shrewd appreciation of how important the traditional corporate media as well as social media is in American politics, Trump dominated the airwaves, cable television and print media every day, and in turn also ensuring that a steady stream of Trump's unvarnished messages are delivered his supporters every day on social media. In so doing, Trump acknowledged the anger and dissatisfaction that many voters (GOP or not) in the party machinations as well as those that felt left out, marginalised, or hurt by mainstream policies of the governments. Not only did he stand out in the crowded field of candidates, but his messages resonated with voters across the nation. Trump did not create his doctrine, he merely tapped on existing sentiments that the mainstream Republicans (and probably some Democrats as well) had for a long time failed to capture to lead a movement. This movement later came to subsume the entire Republican Party. As an American academic put it, "[Trump] is above all a salesman and he sells to a constituency – a set of customers, if you will. He is simply able to read them incredibly well, … he has built this enormous following that adores him because he says what they have been thinking but what more mainstream Republican leaders have been dancing around" (Richardson cited in Collinson, 2015). Trump's coalition draws his support from 25 to 35% of the GOP electorate that proved to be extremely loyal to Trump than most pundits predicted, with 68% polled saying that they would vote for him if he created a third party (Collinson, 2015). Trump's appearance had splintered the Republican Party, creating a faction that no longer had faith in the country's leaders and the party leaders. By 2019, Trump had successfully taken over the party as the base of the Party had completely realigned their preferences, and in every institutional sense, the Republican Party had become Mr Trump's party (Burns & Martin, 2019).

Trump's initial securing of the ticket shocked but jolted everyone to take him seriously. The Democrats along with the national media, military-industrial complex balked at the idea of Donald Trump becoming President, as did many neoconservatives. In fact, Trump's foreign policy vision had become extremely horrifying for some conservatives. Robert Kagan, a neoconservative naval historian who was also an intellectual backer of the Iraq War and advocate for Syrian intervention had openly stated that if Donald Trump became the nominee, the only option left was to vote for Hilary Clinton (Jilani, 2016). Trump was also sparred the pro-Israel lobby because he had argued that military invasions of Libya and Iraq had left those countries worse off, but Trump could have been secretly targeting the special interests groups from the military-industrial complex (Jilani, 2016).

Trump was (rightly or wrongly) portrayed as indecent, pretentious, narcissistic, self-serving and manifestly unfit to be President (Galston, 2020). Societal expectations of standards of morality and behaviour of real-estate moguls of course have always been very different from what they would expect from say an ethics professor or in this instance, someone would might become the nation's President. Trump's moral scruples (Walker, 2021; Sisak, 2023) or individual decency (Gass 2015; Fahrenthold, 2016) never mattered much when he was a tycoon, but in unveiling his Presidential ambitions, these traits became very much the foci of the press and the Democratic Party. Amidst the many allegations, the one that stood out was the "Steele dossier", a compendium of allegations that Trump was colluding with the Kremlin, as the Russians have blackmail material on Trump for his supposed interactions, including a golden (urine) shower with prostitutes in a Moscow hotel (Barakat, 2022). Yet, the more these stories were stoked, the more prominent

Trump became, and the stronger the support for him. Most of his supporters believed Trump (and his narratives about the Deep State's attempt to derail him) rather than his opponent's narratives. Thus, Trump's apparent connections with Russia did not hurt him in the way the Democrats hoped for.

The Trumpian narrative during before and during his Presidential campaign was that his story is an American dream made good through individual merit, hard work and the overcoming of adversity against all odds. The counter narratives was of course that Trump was not as hardworking or competent as he made himself out to be, but succeeded largely through his family's money and social connections. Be that as it may, many would agree Donald Trump had in fact actually accomplished a lot in life. Carly Fiorina a rival early on in the Primaries had asked Trump to defend his business record, given that he has had a string of Chapter 11 bankruptcies which had allowed his business to survive even as it is reorganised and debt restructured (Taylor, 2016). The question of how and what Donald Trump did to accumulate his wealth as well as how he went about maintaining his wealth came under scrutiny during the Presidential campaign. Trump's opponents painted him as an immoral politician with a non-existent sense of morality and a narcissistic personality who was really ill-suited to be president (Gass, 2015; Graham et al. 2019). His principal opponent, Hilary Clinton repeatedly spoke about Donald Trump's tax returns, hinting that Trump had either underpaid or not pay any taxes. This of course raises the question of the integrity of Trump as a person, and his genuineness in claiming to want to represent ordinary Republicans since he would very much be behaving like the rest of the billionaires who have tried to avoid paying any taxes. It of course comes as no surprise that recent disclosures in 2022 revealed that the former President paid little to no taxes from 2015 to the 2020 period. As CNBC reported, the Trumps reported a negative income of $31.7 million on their 2015 federal tax return, with no taxable income. They paid $641,931 in federal income taxes. For the 2016 tax year, they reported a negative income of $32.2 million and zero taxable income, paying only $750 in taxes. In 2017, they declared a negative income of $12.8 million with no taxable income and paid $750 in taxes. For 2018, they reported a total income of $24.4 million, with $22.9 million in taxable income. They paid $999,466 in federal income taxes. For 2019, the Trumps reported a total income of $4.44 million, with $2.97 million in taxable income, paying $133,445 in taxes. Their 2020 tax return showed a negative income of $4.69 million, with no taxable income, and they claimed a refund of $5.47 million, paying no taxes (Mangan, 2022).

Even if we assume that all these negative narratives (McAdams, 2016) printed about Trump are true, one cannot deny that Trump had a few traits that make him a formidable politician. First, as a real estate businessman, Trump has an uncanny accurate appreciation of the power dynamics in every situation, and usually acute appraisal of what enticed, motivated or constrained people. His appreciation of how human nature is intricately linked with their interests provides him with a unique and powerful insight into how politicians and actors operate. Second, he understood deeply how the American political system worked, particularly the internal mechanics of both the Republican and Democratic Parties as well as larger inter-party dynamics. During the Reagan years, Trump identified with the Republican Party as an up-and-coming real estate businessman in Manhattan. He has gone on record in several of his interviews, one on CNN's Larry King live speaking his mind about how he believed that US allies are taking advantage of America's generosity in shouldering the defence burden. During the 1990s, his political affiliation switched, and he was closely identified with the Democratic Party and was in fact photographed frequently with Democratic Party elites, including Bill and Hillary Clinton. By 2001, he shifted his allegiances back to the Republican Party. By and large. Trump's party affiliation appears to shift to the party in power. It was only during the Obama administration that Trump shifted his identification back to the Republican Party, espousing more conservative narratives and ideology, and even began joining the movement to question Obama's birthplace. However, like every other magnate in the United States, Trump saw the importance of making campaign donations to both Democratic and Republican candidates, leaning towards the candidates of choice that he believed served his business interests. Trump understood the importance of being able to have friends in both parties and this political elasticity has allowed him to move seamlessly in both Democratic and Republican circles for years. Third, despite what one may think of Trump as a businessman or a politician, one has to agree that he has strong survival instincts. Besides being politically very adaptable, Trump has himself often spoken (boasted) about his perchance for risk-taking and negotiation skills. It is however his ability to withstand criticisms and attacks and to deflect and counterattacks very well that distinguishes him from the other politicians. Like most excellent politicians, Trump often appears unmoved by controversies (probably because he is media savvy and had lots of experiences before). He took little heed of the exploding headlines in the press and went through this period unscathed. His resilience enabled him to withstand periods of intense criticisms and manufactured counter-narratives to secure the support of his base. Trump exhibited much of this during the 2016 elections, surviving through very negative media onslaught orchestrated by those threatened by his agenda. Throughout his campaign he displayed a fine sense of situational awareness, an uncanny ability to mobilise support and resources, and was able to transcend and survive in a very hostile environment. Fourth, Trump usually unburdened by ideology, principles or ethics, has a sense of pragmatism that enhances his political skills and is often underestimated by his opponents. He was often able to make his own assessments with regard to a situation or a person very quickly and come to a decision. In the world of D.C. politics, this of course is an excellent trait to have. Ironically, even though he is politically "adaptable", his nomination as the Republican candidate meant that he has at least on a minimum basis pay lip service to Republican ideals.

Unconventional Politics and the Embracement of the Global Right Agenda

Upon election, Trump did everything he could to ensure that he kept up the popular support. One of his strategies of course was to keep up pressure and cast doubt on the actors that he had always labelled as working against him: may it be the "establishment" (i.e. Congressional democrats, long-time party operatives, Republicans-in name only and socio-economic elites), the "dishonest" media (corporate or social), the "deep state" (unelected government officials past and present), foreign powers (particularly China) and even immigrants. Buoyed by his electoral success, Trump's newfound legitimacy conferred by his electoral victory no doubt gave him a renewed sense of confidence as a politician as well as a sense of mission in implementing his agenda. The narrative that surrounded his presidency did not change just like his obsession with his "greatness". Once President, Trump became more outspoken and direct in his political communication, preferring to use Twitter in an unvarnished manner to express his opinions (as well as to keep dealings oral rather than in written form) despite protests from his staff (Johnson et al., 2018). In doing so, he was often able to provide an image that he was "in charge" often bypassing his White House staff as well as bureaucrats in the State or other Departments that might be trying to "steer" or "handle" him. The upshot of this meant that Trump gave the impression that he was "his own man" in the sense that he did make the decisions on most things and that any impediments to his agenda would be often interpreted by his supporters as a move against Trump, and by extension against his "America First" agenda. This clever tying of his political agenda to a nationalistic mission clearly put Trump at the forefront of the new Conservative moment. America First required everyone to back the President and focus on the pursuit of the United States' interests as opposed to their own agenda and interests. This also allowed Trump to challenge established ideals, norms and conventions in the US political system, particularly in the national security and foreign policy establishment. This sense of "independence" of the President (or dysfunctionality in the Administration) is often derided in the media as it is in the memoirs of those who have worked with him in the Administration, Many of Trump's staff and advisors have written memoirs as National Security advisors such as John Bolton, H.R. McMaster, Chris Christie, Sean Spicer, Cliff Sim, some who believed that the President should be handled (such as McMaster or Bolton) while the other group (the believers) believes that the President couldn't or shouldn't be (Miller, 2020; Green, 2021; Mahdawi, 2021).

Trump's dominant personality led to a high turnover of staff in an administration that found it difficult to place suitable candidates in positions in the first place. This however had the ironic effect that it was Donald Trump who called the shots in most scenarios and that the bureaucrats had found it hard to serve without the pleasure of the President. His approach to politics and foreign policy reflected his ethos as a businessman, often treating issues with a business-focused attitude which various foreign policy commentators have dismissively labelled a "transactional" mindset or approach (Hadar, 2017; Nye, 2020). His close advisors have in private railed at Trump's foreign policy thinking while in office, but often reprimanded him publicly after their stint in office for not having a macro perspective on how United States foreign policy is conducted. Trump had various disagreements over foreign policy with heavyweights such as John Bolton, Rex Tillerson and Jim Mattis over the Iran Nuclear Deal, the Paris Climate Accord, NATO, Syria, Venezuela, Afghanistan, Russian meddling and North Korea (Bush, 2018; Borger, 2018; Finnegan, 2018; Smith, 2019; Sullivan, 2019a, 2019b). Trump however has always been insistent that his decisions reflected the will of the American people, and not those of the establishment or the bureaucracy. On this point, Trump is not wrong as he did indeed have the electoral mandate of the people. Trump has often gone it alone on certain issues such as meeting Kim Jung-un of North Korea or withdrawing from Afghanistan, but his thinking on these issues might be unorthodox and different from the supposed foreign policy experts, but not necessarily less valid. The differences in opinion might have arisen because Trump has felt that existing norms and conventions impede his strategy for his domestic and foreign policies, thus explaining the resistance to follow his staff's suggestions and recommendations. An example would be the meeting with Kim Jung-un. It is evident from John Bolton's memoir that he, most of the State Department as well as certain American allies and partners (such as Japan and interestingly Singapore) considered that Trump was making an epic mistake in making nice with Kim. In effect, the United States was actually giving Kim something for nothing as Trump had waived the United States longstanding insistence that DPRK undertook verifiable denuclearisation before any sort of negotiations began (Bolton, 2020). Trump had obviously thought that this might be a huge public relations win for him at a political level both domestically and internationally, but an alternative but unstated goal could well be that he understood how authoritarian leaders such as Kim and Putin operated, possibly because he is a kindred spirit. It is also plausible that Trump saw that the best way to neutralise the possibility of a "united front" of a nuclear-armed North Korea working as a proxy for China would be to meet Kim and enable him to gain the domestic legitimacy function he sought (with a photo op with a US President) that would reduce his insecurities as much as his reliance on China. This would inevitably help in the ensuing confrontation that Trump was implementing at that time.

Trump's personality and political methods meant that for the first time in the modern history of the United States, an individual unencumbered by traditional political and diplomatic considerations and constraints has ascended to the Presidency. Trump's campaign ideas were not new, as for years he had been saying that the United States has been taken advantage of by allies in terms of unequal burden sharing as well as in terms of defence (Gonyea et al., 2017). To achieve his America First agenda, Trump had framed China to be the principal strategic (FT 2017) as well as economic competitor that was responsible for job losses and trade imbalances that his predecessors let happen. He alleged that China's trade and economic practices posited a threat to the nation because Beijing had "stolen" all the jobs, disenfranchised workers, robbed US industries of its technological edge through intellectual property theft and built up huge reserves through unfair trade practices and currency manipulations. He also suggested that Beijing was also an unparalleled military threat, was oppressing the minorities in Xinjiang as well as the democratic movement in Hong Kong and Taiwan as well as increased assertiveness in East and South China Seas rattling her neighbours. In the Trumpian narratives, the threat that China posed was ideological, political and existential in the sense they diminished American standing in the world. China became Trump's "whipping" target in his political speeches and rhetoric as it rouses right-wing nationalism in the United States itself while appealing to Conservative constituents domestically and regimes elsewhere in the allied countries to do the same. By tapping into existing sentiments on economic and national security concerns within the United States and abroad, Trump was able to hijack the Conservative movement for his own ends (Bennett, 2022).

As a politician, Trump understood that he needed the support of important elements within the American political system. While challenging China certainly dovetailed with Trump's campaign promises, it also had the effect of pacifying the many important actors whose feathers Trump had ruffled during the elections. With his economic sanctions, trade and tech war, the Trump White House showed that the United States was indeed tripping up Chinese economic growth and slowing down her economic ascent. This was good news for most of national security establishment and those that opposed China globally (particularly elites in the Quad countries). Military confrontation naturally meant reinvigorating alliances, which in turn brought increased armed sales. Under Trump's consistent pressure, certain US allies also eventually began a discussion to undertake greater burden sharing in defence arrangements. All these ironically benefitted the actors who were initially alarmed by Trump's rhetoric on US foreign policy. Upon assuming office, Trump exhibited a willingness to order military strikes readily (e.g. at targets in Syria during a dinner with Xi Jinping). This rehabilitated his image as someone who at first appeared to be non-interventionist and isolationist. Neoconservatives, mainstream Republicans, Democrats and most of Washington D.C. love talk of a strong defence. Trump was always there to deliver it. While we may never know, Trump's momentary introspective reconsideration of America's global role could well have been a tactical ploy to provide pause for everyone to contemplate as to just how critical American global leadership is, and also a learning opportunity for everyone to understand that their interests must be subordinated to American ones.

Such a confrontation also helped with the media, given the tradition of portraying a "focused" enemy found in the Islamic world, Russia or China. The 2016 Presidential portrayed Russia as a domestic threat (in terms of electoral interference) and China as an economic and strategic threat (Reuters, 2022a). Trump had consistently pointed out that Democrats (particularly the Clinton administration) were responsible for the export of jobs abroad, and this narrative creates a problem for the neoliberal Democrats since much of their political platform before (and still is) was premised upon free trade, particularly with China. Since Trump's actions were aimed at stopping other nations from taking advantage of the United States and protecting her interests abroad, no one should stop him from exercising the will of the people. Further, Trump even claimed that he had done things no President had ever done, and United States would emerge better from it. This strategy ended up with Trump revitalising the Republican base as his radical, populist and authoritarian approach gave the voters the impression that he really cared about his fellow citizens and that he was going to make America great again. In short, Trump's "America First" policy is an assertive interpretation of American exceptionalism: in order for the United States to become great again, it was necessary to rethink and do things differently from the past. His assertive leadership on emphasising the importance of the Americans at home and the United States abroad cemented his role as the leader of the American nationalist movement that underpinned the new Conservatism in the country. Be that as it may, even though Trump emerges as the undisputed leader of the Republican Party, the bigger problem however is that Trump had departed from traditional Conservatism in a few important aspects. Conservatives worship institutions, Trump took them on. Conservatives are keen to promote democracy and free market overseas whereas with Trump, there was democratic backsliding and protectionism to erode free market in the name of national security.

As the former Australia Prime Minister revealed what he though of Trump's America in his 2020 memoir:

3 THE UNITED STATES' NEOCONSERVATIVE TURN: AMERICA ... 135

[Trump] says America is more respected than ever. It depends what you mean by respect. Strength is respected when it is matched with values consistently advanced. Around the world, Trump's deliberate unpredictability generates fear rather than respect, anxiety rather than certainty. His view of the world is much closer to the "don't tread on me" isolationists of centuries past than it is the neoconservatives who, after the fall of the Soviet Union, sought to remake the world in America's image (Turnbull 2020).

Trump alone did not bring about all the changes to the US domestic political system. The United States has evolved over the decades, and Trump has given a face and a voice to the grievances that had accumulated as he deftly tapped into these pre-existing sentiments. The shifts in domestic politics and international relations since the 1990s had created tremendous unhappiness that no longer be "contained" by political correctness, fancy media spin or feigned ignorance. Trump's ascendance meant that a huge segment of Americans wanted the ways things were done to be changed. It is also important to recognise that Trump was hardly the first opportunistic politician to use negative campaign methodology and tap on populist sentiments to capture power, but his rise to the office of the Presidency meant that his journey to the highest office in the land had great demonstrative effects for the global Conservative moment. His decisions were probably the most consequential in global politics. This had immense consequences for US domestic politics and foreign policy. To contextualise the sharp neoconservative turn that drove America's attitude towards to nosedive, and the consequential chain of events leading us to the brink of a new Cold War with Russia and China, a closer examination of the domestic politics of the pre-Trump era is necessary.

Level II: Domestic Politics

Electoral Concerns and the Changing Tone of US Nationalism

The economic conditions when Obama took office in 2009 were grim. The United States was facing its worst recession since the Great Depression, with record high unemployment that averaged at around eight per cent, with 600,000 American jobs lost in Jan 2009 alone, but by 2016 when Trump was preparing to take office, 178,000 jobs were related with an unemployment rate hovering at 4.6 per cent, adding a total of 15.4 million jobs. (White, 2017) Obama himself has rated his own legacy quite proudly, noting that "by nearly every economic measure, America is better off than when [he] took office. The United States are in the midst of the longest streak of job growth on record. U.S. businesses [had] added 15.6 million jobs since early 2010 … Rising home prices have brought millions of homeowners back above water, [Americans] are less reliant on foreign oil than in nearly three decades, and the United States had cut it's budget deficit by two-thirds as a share of the economy" (White House, 2017). Even though Obama's fiscal spending had contributed to industries, added jobs, extended unemployment insurance available for displaced workers, and granted health insurance to more than 20 million people, others have argued that Presidents rarely have a direct influence and deciding the fate of the economy (Thoma, 2016). The good fortune that America saw during the Obama administration was the making of the markets rather than the President himself.

The effects of unbridled capitalistic globalisation have unfortunately created a wide income disparity gulf in and between countries globally. America was no exception. Unfortunately, even as the United States' image improved and the economy recovered under Obama's Presidency, income inequality has actually increased with the hallowing out of the middle class due to significant changes in the voters demographics (Dimock, 2017). The critical problem is that the narratives within the country are shaped by the dominant economic and political elites that justified the worsening circumstances for the majority premised on neoliberal market discourse. This dominant national narrative is controlled and shaped by the upper class elites who lived blessed lives that enjoy the best of health care, education and all the benefits that wealth brings. Unfortunately, the narrative of free market enterprise also conceals the fact that the moneyed interests compound their wealth by stifling true, dynamic capitalism, crippling growth, undermining the rule of law, and distorting democracy that has resulted in a divided society that is incapable of tackling its most pressing problems (Stiglitz, 2012). By the time Obama left office, the economic situation had not improved at all for many. This voting profile too has evolved dramatically. Democratic voters were becoming less white, less religious and better educated at a faster rate than the rest of the country, while Republicans were aging more quickly than the country and most likely to identify as without a college degree (Dimock, 2017). Many middle-class Americans, particularly those in the Red states had seen better days. There was somewhat of a sense of cultural pessimism with regard to how society seems to have changed. While one can debate or attribute the sorry state of affairs to globalisation, poor governance, the advent of modern technology and the decline of unions in the workplace, the effect for those on the lower strata of society is certainly diminished economic opportunity and social mobility (Horowitz et al., 2020). From 1980s to 2016, income inequality in the United States was found to have increased by about 20 per cent (Horowitz et al., 2020). The same report suggests that even as the middle class which once comprised the clear majority of Americans is shrinking, from 61per cent in 1971 to 51% in 2019, a greater share of the nation's aggregate income is going to upper income households, particularly for the top 5% of the families since 1981.

While Obama's Presidency was historic in symbolism and its message of hope for the American nation, the post-mortem assessment of his tenure was ambivalent (Kamarck, 2024). Obama was regarded as an "effective policymaker but not a successful party builder", indicating the paradoxical Obama as someone who is good a formulating policies but absolutely lacking in politics (Zelizer, 2018). Even though Obama enjoyed high approval ratings towards the end of his term, the Democratic Party lost "more than one thousand seats in state legislatures, governors' mansions and Congress during his time in office (Zelizer, 2018: 1). The bipartisan divide between the Republicans and the Democrats was unlike what Obama believed to be superficial, and cannot be overcome that easily as the Republican machinery had dominated Congress. Along with their own media outlets, Congress has become a Republican stronghold even when they are not in power. Likewise, even when Democrats had a majority in the House of Representatives, Obama was not able to command fully the Congress during his two years in office often simply because the Democrats did not have the outright number of votes in the Senate (Akron Beacon, 2012). By 2014, the Republicans had made incredible gains in the Congressional elections, holding its largest majority since the end of the Second World War thus ensuring that Obama would be a lame-duck President in his last two years in office (Collinson, 2014).

The domestic circumstances of the Republican states mattered significantly for the 2016 elections. The electorate mood in middle America was a critical aspect of the United States' domestic politics that no traditional Washington elites have paid significant attention to until now. The Republican Party's role in the American Civil and abolishing slavery ensured that it dominated US politics until the 1930s when the Democrats, led by Roosevelt whose New Deal programs saw the emergence of a more balanced bipartisan politics and ushered in a new era of growth in the post-war era until the election of Richard Nixon ushered in a new Republican era. Nixon won the 1972 election carrying 520 electoral votes and 49 states, with 60.7% of the popular vote. Yet as elderly Republicans would agree the greatest Republican President would be Reagan. Those that grew up in the 1980s during the Reagan era remember fondly the years of economic boom and of a renewed vigour in the pursuit of individualism, liberty and opportunity that underpins the founding of the United States. Reagan was regarded as the first truly Conservative President in over five decades who pursued domestic policies that spoke to the Conservatives cause. This included the lessening of federal government responsibility in solving social problems, reducing restrictions on business, and implementing tax cuts. In terms of foreign policy, the Reagan White House exhibited a strong opposition to the Soviet Union which he labelled as the "evil empire" (Reagan Library, n.d). American strategist all too often recall with pride the "Starwars" program of the Reagan administration and how eventually Reagan policies enabled the United States to win the Cold War. One of the most remarkable qualities of Reagan was his flexibility. He was willing to negotiate with the Communists regardless of what he thought of them, and that he recognised that even "communists could change for the better". Reagan was flexible in his pursuit of common goals even it meant compromising with his political enemies (Bands, 2015). Trump's political methodology and visions, unfortunately, did not display this sense of tolerance or pragmatism.

In the earliest primaries, Trump only won 36 per cent primary votes, while a majority of 64 per cent voted for his competitors. Trump was no Republican or at least, not in the mould of what a tradition Republican would stand for. Many traditional Republican candidates despised and attacked Trump, that is at least until they realised that Trump's methodology was reviving the fortunes of their party. The Republican Party was able to attract five clusters of voters: American Preservationists, Staunch Conservatives, Anti-elites, Free Marketeers and the Disengaged, but the key that attracted voters towards Trump (and the Party) were their attitudes towards Hilary Clinton, evaluations of the economy, views about illegal and Muslim immigration (Ekins, 2017). The coalescing of such a disparate group of people meant that the Republican Party was able to tap into the dissent on the ground to seek out those trapped by what they perceived as a trap of hopelessness and despair. A large segment of voters had left that the traditional political establishment had not been effectively addressing their concerns, and out of the candidate's field, only Trump was speaking to their concerns directly. In order to emerge from a crowded Republican field, Trump focused his attacks on issues and his opponents during the primaries which he thought could boost his popularity. His methods were by no means conventional or innovative, but he accurately understood the nature of the Republican base. One particular aspect of his message appealed to the constituents—that of economic rejuvenation, and how he was going to bring back economic revitalisation to the Red States. Needless to say, Trump's high-profile strategy located China and the Democratic Party in the cross-hairs of its attack.

In the years of stagnation and declining standards of living for many voters across the United States, the Republican Party's platform was certainly most palatable to voters yearning for a return to a romanticised glorious era of the past, no matter how misguided or unreal this is. The sense of pervasive pessimism and political chasm was deeply felt was also due to a variety of political and social developments that had concretely divided America more than ever before (Pew 2018). The Republican Party itself was able to capitalise on issues that mattered to the electorate in the red states. It was ironic during the tenure of the first black President that the most serious racial problems emerged after a slew of deaths of black Americans that led to the rise of Black Lives Matter movement. In 2015, the Supreme Court ruled to protect same-sex marriage which created considered unhappiness amongst Conservative quarters that provided ammunition for Republican candidates (Lewis, 2015). Likewise, even though there is growing support for bipartisan for the legalisation of soft drugs like Marijuana, there is growing intense resistance from certain segments such as women who are tougher than men ostensibly because of parenthood, from religious Americans and religious groups (white evangelicals and Hispanic Catholics) and from the "Silent Generation" i.e. those over 65 (Galston & Dionne, 2013). The Obama administration also angered many over his professed inability to stop the mass deportations even though he had promised to stop or defer the sending back of young people who entered the United States illegally as children (Nakamura, 2013). To be sure, one cannot expect a sitting president such as Obama to resolve intractable and complex issues such as immigration (MacGillis, 2016) and refugee policy, race relations or health care in just eight years, and neither should responsibility be attributed to him alone. The problems in 2016 are compounded from yesteryears, and responsibility needs to be shared between Obama and all his predecessors.

By the time Trump bulldozed through the Republican field, it became clear that his slate of issue-based positions on immigration, border security and economic rejuvenation of industries resonated with a large number of voters, particularly in the Rust Belt States. This resulted in a large surge of undecideds or swing voters in certain states. The reinforced mobilisation of the base through the party's messaging i.e. voter turnout, swing voters, particularly those who were not partisan or vote consistently appeared to be a big factor in the 2016 election (Cummings, 2016).

Trump's Hostile Takeover of the Republican Party

Against this socioeconomic background, the Republican Party has most happily seen her fortune reversed with the emergence of Trump (Guild & Rieger, 2021). This unconventional politician, a former member of the Democratic Party no less had completely energised the Republican base and incited one of the largest instances of swing votes in the Presidential elections. It would appear that the Republican Party had been completely hijacked (or hostile takeover) by Trump, as one commentator suggests, Trump presided over a movement, not a party (Azari, 2023). The Republican Party's and Trump's agenda at this point too provided a new lifeline to a host of parties with vested interests in his agenda, aside from Trump's popularity with the different groups that made up the Republican base. The first of course was all the former officials, bureaucrats and scholars who for some reason or other had been sidelined from the traditional Washington establishment. The second segment is those interest groups that would benefit directly from Trump's policies in office such as the military-industrial complex and energy companies (Nesbit, 2016).

Even though Trump had won the Republican primaries, but in the lead up to the 2016 election, there was every sign that the election was just going to be another run-of-the-mill election. Hillary Clinton looked every bit the front-runner who was going to win. The Democratic Party had in fact revelled in the fact that Trump had been nominated as the earlier assessment that he hardly posed a threat to their favoured nominee. The problem was that the Democrats had underestimated Trump's Republican Party and the anger on the ground (Peters, 2019). Trump was however extremely savvy about how the political machinations in Washington operate and how his Democratic opponent had the upper hand in influencing the institutions, organisations and people that mattered in traditional electoral politics.

Trump was not only fixated on his primary opponent, Hillary Clinton and by extension the institutions that he considered were under her obit of influence and the entire Democratic Party apparatus that was Washington D.C. Therefore, his narratives focused on attacking not only Hilary Clinton but also the general regular Washington D.C. governmental establishment which he labelled "the swamp". Most Presidential candidates would refrain from criticising the sitting President, especially in foreign policy. Trump not only attacked his main opponent Clinton but also singled out the then-sitting President Obama in his political rhetoric.

For the entire duration of the campaign, Trump's rhetoric of calling out Clinton, the Democratic Party, the "establishment" comprising of the traditional Washington political elites and the President dominated the airwaves, social and corporate media in the United States and the world. The greater his attacks, the more controversial he became and the more attention he attracted. The Republican Party has never had anyone since Ronald Reagan who was able to galvanised the party and give them the support they needed to win the election. The party was energised by the kind of attention its nominee was attracting, and soon enough there were many others who built a coalition and pandered to the agenda of the then Republican nominee. This strategy worked as there was a surge of support for the Republican Party's agenda that has never been seen before in US electoral politics.

A significant portion of Americans actually agreed with Trump's foreign policy agenda which included amongst other things: building a wall along the Southern borders and have the Mexicans pay for it; move all the factories back from China to bring back jobs and reduce America's deficit; have the Saudis and Iranians reconcile or for that matter adopt a better relations with Russia. These ideas sounded so absurd to the establishment and to the Democrats that no one would take them seriously. Once it became clear that Trump was a Republican Nominee, the reality of these foreign policy themes should have created a sense of urgency except it did not. Even though the national security establishment as well as the military-industrial complex and their supporters became extremely worried, the blanket negative portrayal of Trump and hyping of a Clinton victory provided a sense of false security.

Clinton's own campaign rhetoric and political posturing did not help her campaign either. At a fundraiser in New York City, Hillary Clinton had said that half of Donald Trump's supporters belong in a "basket of deplorables" characterised by "racist, sexist, homophobic, xenophobic, Islamaphobic views …. Unfortunately there are people like that. And he has lifted them up" (Reilly, 2016). While there could be an element of truth in Clinton's remarks, her words also speak of the contempt she had for what the Trump camp called "everyday Americans" (Reilly, 2016). The reality of course that Clinton was a true-blue East Coast Elite who attended Wellesley College and Yale Law School. A former First Lady, the Senator from New York for eight years before being appointed Obama's Secretary of State, Clinton was as close to the archetypical Washington insider one can get to. The Republicans and Trump ridiculed Clinton for a number of things: (1) ties to Wall Street, with the Big Banks allegedly "owning" her; (2) Corruption and Conflict of interest as the Clinton Foundation accepted donations in exchange for access to the State Department; (3) endangering servicemen abroad, specifically in the Benghazi where US Ambassador and three others were killed. The entire campaign was unprecedented in the sense that America was probably never more divided than before. The division was not just between the Democrats and the Republicans, but more importantly also between the Republicans themselves.

Using Foreign Policy to Fight Domestic Political Battles: The Role of Russia and China in the 2016 Presidential Elections

The Republicans and the Trump campaign also fixated on the idea that all the economic problems associated with the Red States were the result of long-time Democratic policies, mostly associated with Hillary Clinton's husband, Bill Clinton. The linking of "China" with the Democrats and economic decline is an important and effective strategy as it thoroughly galvanised the Republican base. Additionally, Trump's campaign strategy of utilising Clinton's email leaks through her use of private email servers became a consistent theme during the campaign. He tweeted "Crooked H destroyed phones w/ hammer, 'bleached' emails, & had husband meet w/AG days before she was cleared- & they talk about obstruction?" (Trump, 2017a). Trump also complained about how he had been unfairly treated given the Clintons too had dealings with Russia but no one had looked into them. The nature of Trump's complaints points to a central but understated issue of how candidates as well as the relevant political party's favoured "foreign enemy" plays out in domestic politics.

In defence, the Clinton campaign and the Democrats retort a narrative of how Moscow infiltrated the US political process and was in fact helping Donald Trump win the elections. The narratives also suggested that the personal animosity between Vladimir Putin and Hilary Clinton has driven Putin to have a single-minded determination to ensure that Democratic nominee do not win the election out of a personal vendetta. Putin had inserted himself unceremoniously into the American electoral process by placing a pro-Moscow President into the White House through direct convert action on his principal opponent Hilary Clinton who appeared to have developed quite a personal animosity with Putin when she served as Secretary of State and he, as the Prime Minister of Russia. In 2012, the US government approved the Magnitsky Act that sanctioned Russian entities that were involved in the death of Sergei Magnitsky who had exposed the corruption involving Russian State entities that were essentially stealing from American companies. There were suggestions that Russian officials, at the very highest levels, including Putin were involved. Naturally, as Secretary of State, Clinton stood at the very forefront of American tussles with Russia. She commented that Putin "doesn't have a soul", called him a "tough guy with a thin skin" and compared his annexation of Crimea to Hitler's actions in the 1930s (Bevan, 2018). Both Clinton and Putin seemed to have an antagonistic but mutually "useful" relationship: the tougher they were on the other, the more popular they became at home. It was therefore no surprise that Putin whether out of personal considerations or national interest acted to ensure that Clinton did not become President in 2016.

US officials from the FBI and the intelligence community were convinced that the Russian Military Intelligence (GRU) had carried out cyber security operations against the United States by hacking the Democratic National Congress email servers and furnishing the Clinton emails to Wikileaks, thereby providing the Republicans with a tactical advantage in the campaign against the Democrats (Euglund, 2016). The Russians had also allegedly targeted the Republican National Committee, particularly at State level organisations and campaigns, probing voter databases as well as spreading false and malicious information to sway the electorate. They drove divisive content on topics such as Black Lives Matter, immigration and gun control and pumped out content using hashtags like #hilary4prison to their followers (Abrams, 2019).

Regardless of what one might think of Trump or his methods and his agenda, his political messaging were tailored to a tee to suit the demographics he was appealing to. His ardent supporters of course completely agreed with him. However for the most part, his foreign policy agenda was made a mockery by the press, political opponents from both sides, beltway think tanks and just about anyone in the foreign policy and national security establishment. Their disdain and contempt for Trump's ideas ironically kept him constantly on the front pages and cable news, taking away airtime and exposure from his opponents and normalising his ideas in national discourse and mainstreaming them in the Republican agenda. The Trump campaign of course denied this vehemently, arguing that this was another one of Democrat's tactics of smearing him.

The Trump Doctrine: Operationalising the Global Right's Agenda

Trump's victory shocked most of the world since everyone had their information from the broadsheets like the New York Times, Wall Street Journal and Financial Times—all of which were predicting a comfortable victory for the Democratic Party (Murray, 2017). The 2016 election also allowed the Republicans control over the Senate and the House (Stepan, 2016). The results had left the country more divided than ever and to a large extent even though Trump had won the Presidency, his administration was crippled even before he started. Trump's (rather than the Republican) attack on the "swamp" in Washington, on the deep state and on the "dishonest press" meant that his campaign and the Republican Party were at war with some very powerful actors in the establishment. The deep state, in Trump's opinion, is a group of unnamed usually powerful officials that would stop at nothing to prevent an elected President from implementing his agenda if the agenda did not fit their interests. This was an unusual time for career bureaucrats as well as those in the national security and foreign policy establishment, for America had for the first time in history elected a President and a Commander in Chief that appeared to deeply disrespect their work. This was also a problematic situation for those involved in the military-industrial complex since this appeared to be a President who exhibited tendencies of an isolationist, who disparaged allies and who wanted to scale back America's global presence. Trump of course has his reasons made clear in his campaign, but naturally, those stood to lose (whether its prestige, importance or resources) would be unhappy. The Trump campaign had in fact had so much bad press surrounding his transition days that most of the country believed that Trump had trouble filling cabinet positions. Trump and his campaign's team composition and lack of experience created many uncertainties in the "establishment" Washington, the national security apparatus and the military-industrial complex. The transition however did go as planned, with much credit to the Obama's administration piety to the US Constitution, even though the Democrats and Republicans were still very much at war after the election.

Although his closest advisors Reince Priebus, Steve Bannon and Jared Kushner had minimal input, the Cabinet appointments were largely decided by Trump in a matter-of-fact top-down manner (Bearak, 2017). To everyone's relief, Trump appointed Rex Tillerson a former Exon Mobil Executive as Secretary of State over Former Massachusetts Governor and Senator Mitt Romney, former NYC Mayor Rudy Giuliani and Retired General David Petraeus. Trump had apparently like Tillerson's "strength" and the "outsized, Texan, can-do swagger" (Goldmacher et al., 2016). Likewise, Trump's selection of General James Mattis as Secretary of Defence went down well with both the Republicans and Democrats in reassuring that the Trump White House actually knew what they were doing. In hindsight, although both Tillerson and Mattis (Versoulis, 2018) had their disagreement with the President over his decisions, their appointment had helped Trump manoeuvre his way with what he calls the "deep-state" and the "establishment" and negate the commonly heard rumours that he would start World War III and would boost the legitimacy of his Cabinet. Having heavy weight cabinet members endorsed by former government officials such as Condoleezza Rice also provided a reassurance that the new President was still receptive to advice (contrary to popular opinion). This also made for good politics as this brought together the Republican Party which was necessary for governing in the aftermath. The bonus of course was that even Democrats were assured that the President was being "handled" (whether real or otherwise). For Trump personally, these appointments brought much credibility to his team and allowed him to have an easier time appointing his economic team with an eye to his foreign policy goals vis-à-vis China. This therefore paved the way for a series of unconventional appointments such as an anti-China non-mainstream economist Peter Navarro to the position of Director of Trade and Manufacturing Policy and the national Defense Production Act policy coordinator and long-time China sceptic Robert Lighthizer as the US Trade Representative (Phillips, 2016).

The biggest problem for Trump throughout his Presidency is the incredible antagonistic relationship the administration has with the Press. Trump had called the press " a disgrace, … false, horrible, fake reporting", "out of control", with reporters being "very dishonest people", with the coverage of "an outrage", with the New York Times as a "failing" newspaper, and CNN "terrible" (Trump, 2017; Kalb, 2017). In a tweet on 18 Feb 2017, he had outright pointed out that "The Fake News Media (failing @nytimes, @NBCNews, @ABC, @CBS, @CNN) is not my enemy, it is the enemy of the American People! (Trump, 2017). Even though the press was forced largely to become more respectful towards the newly inaugurated President, most of the press had leaned into the administration every day of Trump's Presidency. This of course is not to suggest that the Press has always been purposely deceitful, but rather the Trump White House has often not bothered to contain information that would become fodder for the Press. Whether it is the President's style of decision-making or disagreements between the President and his advisors or Trump's purported clashes with the government departments, the President has always been portrayed very unsympathetically by the Press.

It is therefore no exaggeration to say that the Trump White House faced one of the most hostile and confrontational media environment that any American presidency has seen. The narratives in the everyday reports present the Trump White House as being dysfunctional (Davis, 2020), nepotistic (CREW, 2017; ABC News, 2017; Harwell, 2016), and often not acting in the best interests of the United States (Sargent, 2018). The Democrats as well as the majority of the press asserted (rightly or wrongly) that the Republicans, led by Trump are in cahoots with the Russians (Nesbit 2016a; Crowley, 2017) or are actually a Russian Oligarch in reality (Applebaum, 2016). Even if Trump was not, he has certainly way too many ties to Russia. A report in New York Magazine, widely replicated even suggested that Trump has been a Russian asset since 1987 (Chait, 2021), while there are others who considered him a "useful idiot" rather than Putin's agent (Cunliffe, 2021). This sort of attack became the central and pervasive character of US domestic politics in the aftermath of Trump. The idea that Russia (or more accurately Vladimir Putin, in his disdain for Hilary Clinton and in his efforts to destroy the United States from within, had meddled in the democratic process and interfered in America's elections had become a central idea in

Democratic politics and discourse. There is no question that this narrative continues even after Trump steps down. As an observer notes, Even if he was not in reality (a Russian asset), Trump as President was everything that Putin had hoped for (Unger, 2022).

It was also evident that Trump was determined to implement his campaign promises unto policy, and he was eager for high-profile domestic political success as much as for foreign policy ones. For much of his policymaking, Trump was very concerned with ensuring that the "right" appointees were made to implement his campaign promises to "Make America Great Again". Whether acting on his own impulses or the advice of his staff, Trump's decision to showcase the Tech and Trade War on China was made in part on his desire to get re-elected for his second term. In the eyes of his constituents, China was the dominant threat and needed to be acted upon, not Russia. Therefore, for the better part of his Presidency, China became central to his political thinking, methodology and discourse. In his own words, he is the "chosen one" to take on China (Breuninger, 2019).

From the perspective of career diplomats, the military-industrial complex and national security apparatus, many of Trump's foreign policy ideas might look horrifying. Trump was labelled as an "isolationist", as someone who was "abandoning" their allies and appeaser during the campaign as he had promised to revisit security arrangements of allies who do not meet their obligations. Trump had demanded NATO as well as Asian allies stop taking advantage of United States and do more for their own defence, such as increasing the payment of their share of burden sharing. Germany did indicate she will contribute more to NATO's running cost as long as other allies also took similar steps (Siebold & Emmott, 2019), as did Japan (Sieg & Brunnstrom, 2017) and Canada (Wright, 2018). Likewise, the Republicans under the leadership of the Trump White House also pulled off the Abraham Accords on 28 January 2020, normalising peace between Israel, Bahrain and United Arab Emirates (UAE) a first since 1994 relations between Israel and Jordan. It was not before long that US allies were all coughing out more funding to buy US weaponry, goods and services to the delight of the President. Trump alarmed the world with his Twitter exchanges with Kim Jong-un and enchanted the world (some more than others) with his summits with Kim Jong-un.

Domestically, the biggest domestic achievement of the Republicans during the Trump administration was to bring about the biggest bipartisan consensus in becoming "tough" in the United States' dealings with China. Once Trump announced that he was going to confront the unfair trade practices and undertake a whole-of-government approach towards confronting China, there was a quiet but powerful shift behind the establishment constituents (military-industrial and national security apparatus) he had always attacked during his campaign to make America Great Again. The Trade and Tech War that ensued would remain an important turning point in American politics and foreign policy. The Republican Party had clearly leveraged what was happening in other places to redefine the Conservative moment into a populist one tapping into the frustrations of the electorate. Taking a leaf from his Japanese counterpart Shinzo Abe, China is framed to be the quintessential problem for the United States in the American political discourse. Beijing was a country that stole American intellectual property, robbed Americans of their job, traded unfairly, infringed environmental regulations, used exploitative labour to manufacture cheap products for export that is responsible for wiping out whole industries in the United States. In doing so, China has become rich on the backs of hardworking Americans and is now using her newfound wealth and power to dominate the world. Just like what happened in Japan, the daily discussions in the media (corporate and social) as well as in policy circles gained traction as public opinion of China plunged. Politicians from both parties saw how adopting a "tougher" posture towards Beijing became somewhat of a sure-fire political methodology that could advance their political careers while those that were pro-China had to disavow their thinking. The narratives of China that had been dominant in the United States in the yesteryears were completely destroyed as the Trump White House made mainstream the political philosophy and ideas of the Global Right, which in this case much of which was inspired by Shinzo Abe's thinking. Trump however was not blindly just duplicating Japan or just adopting blindly what the "Trump whisperer" (Abe) had in mind. In reality, what Trump was implementing was his own conceptualisation of his own ideas about politics and foreign policy into reality. Abe's ideas were interesting, but most importantly it fitted Trump's purposes.

The Trump Doctrine apparently is termed as "principled realism" by his own administration, but in reality, the doctrine can be understood as "America First" (O'Brien 2020). In openly stating this, the US President showed that there is nothing to be shameful about ensuring that

America's interests get taken care of first. In some way, he is a refreshing and less hypocritical politician than most others given he says what he thinks without political varnish and diplomatic niceties. Trump's language is straightforward, provocative and often difficult for many to accept by the foreign policy establishment, the academic and intellectual elite and the opinion-making class (Anton, 2019). While controversial, Trump's four years of foreign policy certainly reflected a leader who had actively attempted to steer US policy in a direction he saw fit (CFR, 2024). The problem with Trump's agenda is not necessary in the best interest of his constituents, particular of how his trade and tech war might actually backfire on US development in the years ahead (Austin, 2020).

The Rightwards Shift of US Politics and Its Impact on the Biden Administration

An important legacy of the Trump administration is no doubt the redefinition of what passes for traditional mainstream Conservative ideology in the United States. The President's foreign policy thinking cannot be pigeonholed squarely. He was neither a hawk (he criticised all the Wars before) nor a dove (he ordered a Syrian Airstrike before dinner with Xi and told Kim Jong-un that he had a "nuclear button that works" over Twitter). He is neither a liberal internationalist and certainly not a realist (after all he wanted to be friends with Putin and Kim). What he was most certainly was also not a conservative.

Today, Ronald Reagan is considered to be the main standards bearer for Conservatism in the United States. Reagan was also a President that Trump himself had professed to love even though he had also publicly criticised Reagan several times openly. Trump was unhappy about how Reagan had allowed the United States to be "taken advantage" of by various countries ranging (from Japan to Kuwait) (Trump, 1987) or misled into pointless military ventures in the Middle East (Trump, 2016). While Trump himself or his Republican colleagues such as Tom Cotton (Kruse, 2022) would prefer to see him (Trump) as being the twenty-first-century ideological pillar of the Republican Party, there were many others, including prominent Republicans that regard Trump poorly. These Republicans include the 41st President George H.W. Bush and his son, the 43rd President George W Bush, former Vice President Dick Cheney, his daughters Representative Liz Cheney and

Mary Cheney, Senator Mitt Romney, Mitch McConnell-all of whom have openly declared their disdain for Trump and his politics.

The New Yorker has suggested that today, the Republican Party faces a never before "identity crisis" (Lemann, 2020). Even though there actually isn't a standard textbook definition of what Conservatism as an ideology in America should be like, Reagan's definition of what his brand of Conservatism stood for is the advocation of individual liberty through the minimalisation of government. For him, the key was to minimise the intervention of government so that the economy would become more efficient, and the success of Reagan was in his conviction as much as was his pragmatism of wanting to work with everyone, including his detractors (Witcher, 2019). As Reagan puts it, "As government expands, liberty contracts" (Reagan, 1989), focused on reducing taxation, increasing defence spending to protect liberty and secure the United States and limiting the growth of the government. The inspiration behind the Trumpian agenda of cutting taxes was certainly drawn from Reagan, even though it appeared that the tax cuts benefitted the rich more than they did anyone else during the Trump era (MacGillis, 2016), as economists calculated that the richest 400 families in the United States paid an average tax rate of 23% while the bottom half of households paid a rate of 24.2% (Rushe, 2019). To be sure, Trump's advocation of the "deep state" sounded like Republican (or Reagan's) ideal of limiting the expansion of government and reducing inept bureaucracy, but the 45th President's idea of the deep state points to clandestine network of past and present career civil servants (usually at the Federal level) that would stop at nothing to grow their power and advance their own interests, even if it meant defying or working against the wishes of democratically elected President. The image of a shadowy illuminati of solders, diplomats and bureaucrats determined to sabotage the Presidency was what Trump had in mind, rather than redundant bureaucracy. The negative narratives surrounding his presidential bid, particularly the "Russia" connections were widely seen by the more radical segment of the Republican Party that the deep state was working against him.

Bureaucracies are naturally protective of their turf, budget and power and to that extent would naturally resist any attempt to downsize them. Trump is not the first to have that problem and won't be the last to struggle with the administrative state. The Republican support for Trump's agenda necessarily impacted the Administration's ability to run the country probably, particularly in terms of choosing the correct people with the relevant expertise, respecting the organisational mission (Moynihan, 2021). From the many testimonies and memoirs of senior staffers, it is clear that this impacted Trump's choice of advisors where he prized loyalty and fealty more than competence. In this respect, it impacted the kind of advice, may it be on the economic, defence, science and the environment the President received. This also influenced his very personal style of making political appointments (such as getting his son-in-law to helm Middle East policy) to important positions, given his reluctance or inability to fill some critical roles or have his appointees confirmed. For instance, the EPA administrator was vacant for 237 days between Scott Pruitt and Andrew Wheeler; the UN Ambassador was vacant for eight months between Nikki Haley and her successor, Kelly Knight Craft, a Republican donor and wife of coal magnate. The Republican Party also seemed to have internalised Trump's list of transgressions: (1) intimidating witness, bullying career civil servants, using his platform to spread lies, misinformation, conspiracy theories and attacking political opponents; (2) politicising the FBI and the Justice Department; (3)obstructing the Mueller investigation, making high profile pardons without consulting the justice department (e.g. Steve Bannon from fraud), (4) encouraging aides not to cooperate with investigations by dangling pardons, (6) withheld funds approved for Ukraine in order to blackmail Kiev into launching and investigation into the Bidens; (7) personalisation of government by demanding personal loyalty from government officials and (9) firing whistle blowers and truth-tellers and (10) profiting off the presidency by not divesting from his international business empire but rather turning control over to his adult sons (Cohen, 2021). While many of these behaviours are of course observed in Washington politicians, no President has ever transgressed so openly and blatantly as Trump. That being said, the only reason that Trump was able to do this was because of his perceived immense popularity and his general rhetoric that his political enemies, aided by the hostile press and the deep state were (and still are) out to get him.

By accommodating Trump and embracing his politics and agenda, the Republican Party has since moved away from "pure" ideals towards populism (Dallas & Wyoming, 2022). A segment of the party has aligned its new leader showing very little respect for the Constitution, Rule of Law and the ideals that Reagan held dear. Mitt Romney, in an interview, said " A very large portion of my party ... really doesn't believe in the Constitution", openly questioning if the radical element of the

GOP had always been in existence only to be activated by Trump, and if mainstream Republicans like himself had just sat there and allowed it (the authoritarianism) to happen (Coppins, 2013). The question of how the Capital riots could have been allowed to happen (Ball, 2022) and in its aftermath the inquiry being blocked by the GOP only goes to show that the Republican Party very much pledges loyalty to Trump, rather than ideals (Jalonick & Mascaro, 2021). Members of the GOP had during the Capitol Riots decided that electoral victory and holding office was a perfectly reasonable excuse to support Trump's authoritarian tendencies including the violation of the spirit of the US Constitution, and his assaults on the electoral process and the ideals of the American system. Today, there appears to be a significant segment within that supports the browbeating of members that refuse to toe the Party line set up by Trump in the GOP. There are an increased number of mainstream Republicans such as Romney (Obama's Presidential Opponent) and Liz Cheney who have found themselves a pariah within the Party when they spoke against Trump (Hudak, 2021; Heer, 2023).

Such an environment has created ample conditions that have turned Congress into dysfunctional echo chamber that indulges a deeply opinionated Commander-in-Chief who was determined to implement his agenda with little compromise. Whether it's advice, feedback or concerns, they are deflected from the consideration of the White House. What this also means is that the Global Right populist agenda that has now become mainstream US political thinking is being translated into US foreign policy. Despite the negative and combative relationship between the press and the White House, the Republican White House did have bipartisan support it came to foreign policy. As soon as the administration undertook decision action against her enemies, whether it was bombing Syria or confronting China, the President was able to swiftly rally a bipartisan consensus with very little confrontation. While the aims and the effects of Trump's policies were debatable, one of the key effects that Trump achieved during his administration was to completely and utterly destroy the understanding, constraints and guardrails that the United States had built in her relations with China since 1972. This shift towards populism has somewhat derailed the way Americans discuss not only domestic politics but also foreign policy. It has also created a significant difficulty for the Democrats when discuss about any China-related issues. The radicalness behind the wave of "anti-China" sentiments shocked everyone, particularly the Chinese themselves who joked that the United States was undergoing their own Cultural Revolution. Even at the height of the Covid pandemic, the political onslaught against China continued. Washington's China policy had become "poll-driven" with certain special interest groups (such as military-industrial complex) emerging as the ultimate winners over others (such as those with business interests in China). This rightwards shift continues to constrain the United States even after Trump's departure.

Democratic Hedging and Biden's Doubling Down on Trump's Policies

The upheaval following Trump's electoral loss and the advent of Biden's presidency straddled global efforts to find a vaccine to defeat the Covid virus. Trump's defeat and the subsequent 6 January attack on the US Capitol building in Washington D.C. by pro-Trump and far-right groups such as Oath Keepers and Proud Boys in an attempt to keep Trump in power by preventing the joint session of US Congress from formalising the victory of Biden (Mascaro et al. 2021; Reuters, 2022, Davis, 2021; Ryan, 2023). Trump has in actual fact commented that he would pardon the leaders of the far right groups that were jailed for their involvement in the Jan 6 Capital assault that he would pardon them as long as they came into power. Even though Biden won the election, there is no question that Trump still had substantial support on the ground. This was a problem for Biden as the Republicans remained a big threat to him since he too would want what every first term President wants—a second term. For both domestic and realpolitik reasons, Biden had to ensure that he appeared as "tough" as Trump on China domestically even though at the same time, his party's political focus and agenda also ensured that the Biden White House took a strong posture against Vladimir Putin's Russia.

The dynamics of the Clinton–Putin feud has by the 2016 election permeated US domestic politics that has escalated into a sustained "proxy" political war between the Republicans and the Democrats into the Biden era. Unlike the Republicans, Democratic adminstrations traditionally have had a better relationship with China. The Obama administration even with all the inherent tensions they have with Beijing in East and Southeast Asia, had never contemplated the Trumpian idea of decoupling economically with China. The Republican therefore relished on Trump's campaign as it undermined the credibility of the Democrats' traditional political and foreign policy agenda as it capitalised on the sentiments on the ground. A 2018 Pew survey has shown a great deal of bipartisan polarisation, where there appeared to be significant differences in how Democrats and Republicans viewed the goals for US foreign policy. Protecting the United States from terrorism and protecting jobs of American workers all appeared to be the top two items with bipartisan consensus. Confronting China was at this point much lower down the list. Trump's platform had linked "decoupling" with China to national security and job creation and therefore managed to rally the nation behind this theme. After Trump, no Presidential candidate could afford to be accused of "shipping" American jobs off to China again.

It is important to note that today (at the time of publication) this domestic political struggle between the Republican and Democrats continues to affect the dynamics of American foreign policy. Rather than reversing or relaxing Trump's tough policies on the Democratic Party's favoured "enemy" China, the Biden White House has in fact retained and double-downed on Trump policies. Clearly, for both political and strategic reasons, the Biden White House recognises that the Republicans and Trump were not clearly all wrong about China being the United States' peer competitor. At the same time, Biden has continued its tough posture towards Moscow, ostensibly because the Democrats are convinced of Russia's complicity in the interference of the United States electoral process. While this is not discussed very widely in the United States, the ramifications of how Trump-Biden (or Republican-Democrat) struggle using US foreign policy to target Russia and China to fight domestic political battles cannot be ignored.

Even as the Biden administration was trying to organise its economy and coordinate an international response against Beijing's vaccine diplomacy and orchestrate an international economic response to "secure" the supply chain for the United States and her allies, the United States increased pressure against Russia. While there is no question that it was Putin who gave the marching orders for Russian troops to seize Crimea and march into Ukraine, the question of who was exactly "responsible" for the War is still being discussed and debated. There are of course contrarian views. Owning to NATO's eastward expansion over the years, and the way Biden has cultivated Zelinsky and baited Putin, there is a school of thought that argues that the Biden White House has successfully "manuevered" the Russians into attacking Ukraine. This view of course is not widely accepted the official version is that Moscow had attacked Ukraine "unprovoked", there are however many prominent scholars and analysts such as John Mearsheimer and Jeffrey Sachs who pointed out that it was really US-encouraged NATO expansion over the last three decades that finally pushed Putin to act. Regardless of how one feels about this, the fact is that now a Democratic President that is now engaged in a proxy war with the Russians, and confronting a significantly more powerful China. This dynamic is unhealthy and has resulted in competitive demonisation of the two important states in US political discourse and debates, with the paradoxical results of "locking" a muscular foreign policy posture towards both Moscow and Beijing at the same time. The disagreement between the Republicans and Democrats over Russia and China has therefore resulted in the most significant alignment between the two strategic giants that esteemed American strategists and diplomats such as Henry Kissinger and Zbigniew Brzezinski have over the decades forcefully tried to prevent. At the time of writing, it would appear that despite the denials of the White House, the dominant narratives in Washington is that an emboldened Russia has emerged out of the Ukraine War standing shoulder to shoulder with a rejuvenated and determined China that would take on the United States. In the short eight years since Obama left office, the United States' conservative turn in domestic politics and global affairs have helped create a very different world indeed—a world that is more impoverished, divided and dangerous than ever before.

Level III: International System

The United States and the Asia–Pacific in the Pre-Trump Era

To appreciate the circumstances for the rise of the United States as a member of the Global Right fraternity using the third image of the Waltzian model, it is imperative to examine the changing strategic circumstances faced by the United States in the Asia–Pacific in the decades preceding the arrival of Trump. At the systemic level, China's growing power is threatening to displace the United States as the global hegemon, and the arrival of Trump in essence intensified the struggle to preserve US hegemony in global affairs, particularly after an exhausting two-decade-long war on Terror. Even though all of Trump's predecessors tried to address the question of the closing disparity between the United States and China, none had the audacity (and the recklessness) that Trump had in enacting policies to confront China. This of course was not entirely the fault of the previous Administrations, but rather a natural consequence of the rapid development of China that the US foreign policy establishment had not really seriously thought about in the preceding three decades, at least not until Obama.

Five months after the US Navy Seals killed Osama Bin Laden, US Secretary of State Hilary Clinton announced the reorientation of the Obama administration through an article published in Foreign Policy (Clinton, 2011) that the United States would "pivot" to Asia. Acknowledging that the United States had neglected the Asia–Pacific region, Washington would refocus their attention to areas of the world where the United States would be able to sustain its leadership, secure interests and advance values. The United States can thus secure the best return for her investment in the Asia–pacific region (Clinton, 2011). Obama conducted a whirlwind tour to Asia in the following month, visiting Australia where he addressed the Australian parliament and celebrated the establishment of a US Marines presence there before going to attend the East Asia summit in Indonesia (White House, 2011). Clinton clearly suggested that the United States during the Bush Administration had made a strategic mistake of overtly focusing on Iraq and Afghanistan in its pursuit of the War on Terror (Clinton, 2011), and squandered precious resources and political focus that could have been put to better use. The message of the Obama's pivot was threefold. First, for the administration's domestic opponents, the United States was not turning isolationist and thus would not be bringing its troops back. For the Asia–Pacific region and in particular her allies, the United States will be back in the leadership position in the region. Then for America's adversaries, North Korea, Russia and particularly China, the United States would do what it can henceforth to ensure the interests of the United States and her allies are protected and enhanced, even if these adversaries thought that the power balance situation in the region had tilted in their favour.

The Obama administration had a clear agenda of what it wanted to achieve. The United States sought to assert a sustained commitment to "forward-deployed" diplomacy through six important lines of actions: strengthening bilateral security alliances; deepening our working relationships with emerging powers, including with China; engaging with regional multilateral institutions; expanding trade and investment; forging a broad-based military presence; and advancing democracy and human rights (Clinton, 2011). The Obama administration appears to be picking up the tone where President George W. Bush had left off for US–China relations after the EP-3 Incident over Hainan Island in April 2001 when a

US Navy EP-3 reconnaissance plan and a People's Liberation Army (PLA) naval F-8 fighter collided and the EP-3 forced to land (Kan et al., 2001). Until September 11 when Al-Qaeda operatives crashed the planes into New York's Twin Towers, it did look like US–China relations were headed for a period of heightened confrontation. American officials have pointed out that since Obama came to office in 2009, China's behaviour in the region, particularly in the handling of its disputes with her neighbours such as Japan and the Southeast Asian nations, has reached a new peak in its assertiveness. This of course is a direct result of Beijing's increased confidence stemming from its increased economic power and military capability, and reflects a Chinese government that is now less encumbered by its strategic restraints, and more emboldened by its sense of irredentism and hegemonic aspirations. Viewed from Washington, China has since 2009 sought to challenge the United States as Beijing has always sought to undertake a clear and pre-mediated harassment campaign as part of a traditional practice as they did in 2001 with the Bush White House over the EP-3 incident (US News, 2009; Green et al., 2017). Even as Beijing tried to build better relations with the United States with the Chinese President's State visit in January 2011, the Obama White House came under attack by the commentators, who highlighted that the administration had allowed the PRC to humiliate the Presidency by testing their new stealth aircraft J20 just before the State visit of Hu Jintao to the United States (Blumenthal, 2011). This sort of commentary however is not unusual given the nature of American politics. Notwithstanding this, China had always viewed Sino-US relations as of critical importance, if not the most important to the People's Republic. As a country that had fought alongside the Allies in the Second World War (since the emphasis on Communist historiography of China's global leadership starts here), Beijing's evaluation of the role the United States played in supporting China in the latter part of the Cold War and her modernisation is overall a positive one. Hu's 2011 trip was therefore a successful one with all the pomp and pleasantry required of a state visit.

Obama's pivot back to Asia was warmly welcomed by the traditional allies in the region particularly Japan, South Korea and Southeast Asian countries such as Singapore and the Philippines. From the perspective of these traditional US allies, the security situation in the Asia–Pacific had deteriorated substantially due to the increased antagonism that China seems to be having with regional countries, particularly Japan. Under the leadership of Junichiro Koizumi (2001–2006), the charismatic nationalistic LDP politician, Japan adopted a very tough posture towards China over what Tokyo perceives as increased Chinese aggression in the East and South China Seas. Japan and China had high-profile confrontations over "incursions" to Senkaku islands, anti-Japanese protests over history, revised Japanese defence posture, dispute over East China Sea gas explorations, marine boundaries demarcation and the fishing trawler incident (2010) amongst others.

The United States (along with Japan) regarded that China was exploiting these incidents to pressure Tokyo and Washington for strategic gains. They are also indicative of the emergence of a more confident and assertive China seeking to expand her influence and revive an irredentist agenda that sought to integrate a more consistent approach towards her regional interests. In doing this, Beijing is perceived to be pursuing these "challenges" to test the political resolve, reactive policies and international public opinion of her adversaries. What is most worrying for the United States however is that there is a spreading concern amongst the Asian countries that the security architecture in place after the Second World War is being eroded, and that its viability and efficacy are being questioned by the regional countries.

The security dilemma in reality is being accentuated by the respective agendas of the nations involved. Japan governed by the Conservative LDP politician Junichiro Koizumi rallied around the "normalisation" agenda that saw Tokyo seeking to adopt a more muscular foreign policy against a China threat. Conversely, Beijing regarded Japan as becoming more militaristic, hell-bent on using China to foster a populist consensus to overcome the constitutional constraints, pacifist norms and structural reliance on the United States to become a strategically independent power. This competition was reinforced by the fact that peace and security in the region have traditionally been regulated or governed by balance-of-power alliance politics rather than any form of supranational conflict regulation mechanisms. America's involvement in the War on Terror meant that Japan had stepped into her shoes to play the role of the region's policeman of sorts, but any expectations of China remaining "checked" by either Tokyo or Washington with regard to her security goals would be a grave misjudgement or an illusion. By the time the Obama administration pivoted to the region, many in Washington realised that it might be a situation of too little, too late. China had by this time emerged stronger as a global manufacturing hub, an important trading power that was quickly accumulating substantial financial resources and most important translating their hard-earned currency into military modernisation.

The Obama Whitehouse was facing challenges in its Japanese policy. After Koizumi stepped down, Japan underwent a period of revolving Prime Ministerships—Abe, Fukuda, Aso, Hatoyama, Noda, Kan before Shinzo Abe returned to power in 2012. The domestic battles that were being fought in Japan meant that the Prime Minister was often not equipped with the appropriate political circumstances and political attention that was able to formulate policies that were able to push Japan in the correct direction. Obama in his memoirs had particular frustration with Japan, described the leader of the first DPJ Prime Minister Hatoyama as "awkward", and his rise is symptomatic of the "sclerotic, aimless politics that had plagued Japan for much of the decade (Obama cited in Japan Times, 2000). While the LDP politicians (Abe and Aso) were seen as historical revisionists that utilised populist rhetoric to advance their domestic political goals (Fukushima 2015), the DPJ Prime Minister, particularly Hatoyama was detrimental to US interests in the region seeing how he wanted to rebalance Japan's relations with the United States and her Asian neighbours (read: move away from the United States, cultivate better relations with her neighbours China and South Korea). During the Bush (not just Obama) years, there were also Japanese voices that felt that the United States was being weak on China in the sense that Washington did not back Tokyo fully when it confronted the Chinese. From the vantage point of Washington, although not everything was Beijing's fault, there was clear recognition that the LDP's conservatism and revisionist history could not help sell its narrative that China was a threat, given Tokyo's own record in the Second World War.

The anxiety in Washington however was whether the Obama administration was able to fulfil its promise to rebalance to Asia. In the region itself, the anxiety was instead about the staying power of the United States as it underwent a challenging geostrategic shift (Smith, 2014). The United States at that point was clear about playing a vital role in balancing and "stablishing" Sino-Japan tensions but was abundantly unclear if it was willing to sacrifice its political relations with Japan in the event that Tokyo and Beijing broke into a military confrontation. Political promises after all are easy to make, but the question if such promises can and will be followed through is an entirely different question. The Obama

Whitehouse of course was cautious about an outright confrontation with Beijing, as the United States policy in Asia–Pacific is calibrated to ensure the advancement of American national interests first above everything. Beijing was the largest holder of US treasury debt from 2008 ($1.01 trillion) to 2015 ($1054 trillion), with Japan coming in a close second. In 2009 when Obama came to power, China was consistently the second largest trading partner of the United States, coming in only after Canada but by the end of 2015, China had overtaken Canada to be the United States's top trading partner, accounting for 16% of total overall trade. Japan in the meantime consistently ranked 4th with a respectable 5.2% in 2015 (US Census, n.d.). Washington also realised that Beijing, rather than Tokyo is more often more suitable or better equipped to deal with security problems in and beyond the region that the United States would need help with (think Iran, North Korea or elsewhere in the Middle East). By 2015, the tensions over various issues between US and China became public (Webster, 2015).

With the restoration of Abe to the Japanese Prime Ministership in 2012, the US foreign policy establishment was naturally delighted with this (White House, 2013). Abe had highlighted he would work tirelessly to rejuvenate Japan's economy and repair her relations with the United States from the "damage" done during the DPJ years. From their perspective, a pro-US nationalist (Abe) after all would definitely be better than a balanced liberal who sought better relations with China and Korea (Hatoyama). At the same time, there were concerns with Abe's nationalism and revisionist take on history, as this was bound to create tensions in Japan-South Korea relations as well as Japan–China relations which might affect Obama's pivot to Asia. The United States after all wanted to engage China and draw South Korea closer so that the US bilateral relations could work properly.

Japan's domestic politics therefore provide a dilemma for the Obama administration insofar as long-cherished American values were concerned. Has Japan unwittingly manuevered the Obama administration into a situation where its support for US–Japan Security alliance also meant that Washington was also tacitly backing Abe's agenda of historical revisionism?

Just as alliances can help protect fellow allies from being chain-ganged them into an unnecessary war, would it also bind allies in terms of support for their domestic agenda? Unlike incidents linked to the denial of Holocaust and antisemitism, Washington policy elites have always

3 THE UNITED STATES' NEOCONSERVATIVE TURN: AMERICA ... 161

appeared to tacitly consent to historical revisionism in Japan in the name of security and national interests. This started with the Cold War, where Washington made the realpolitik masterstroke of course was the "rehabilitation" and promotion of Nobusuke Kishi, nicknamed the "Monster of the Showa era" as the Prime Minister of Japan to guide post-war Japan in a pro-American direction.[1] This perpetuated the power of pro-American politicians in Japan for generations, and Washington was always happy to accommodate them in the name of the struggle for freedom and democracy openly in every imaginable way as long as they were pro-American. The more loudly they advocated against the containment of Communists regimes (or their successor), the more their revisionist tendencies would be brushed aside all in the name of strategic convenience. Repeated enough times, revisionist transgressions would become the norm to be subsumed as perceptual differences in explaining the war and markers embedded in national identity. The problem however for many observers, Abe's and the ultraconservatives' attitudes are at least in part responsible for some of the tensions in the region.

For the United States to advance its pivot without looking like they are supporting the revisionists in Japan, it was necessary to rehabilitate Abe's reputation, at least in the United States) as well as the image of the US–Japan alliance globally. Washington cannot be seen to be supporting a pro-revisionist Prime Minister striving to push anti-China policy to advance its political goals in the region. For the US–Japan alliance to receive pan-Asian support, it needed a Japan focused on repairing her economy, rallying Asian allies and supporting the United States in a forward-looking manner. Thanks to the careerists that manage the alliance in Washington and Tokyo, mutual visits were arranged to ensure Abe's visit to the United States constituted visits to Arlington

---

[1] Kishi known for his rule over Manchukuo in Northeast China in the 1930s served in Wartime Cabinet as Minister of Commerce and Vice Minister of Munitions, was imprisoned as a Class A War criminal in the aftermath of war. He however was neither charged or put on trial but was made Prime Minister and became the key player in the consolidation of conservative parties in Japan and a key architect of the 1955 system which saw the Conservatives dominate Japanese politics since. He was instrumental in pushing for the revised US-Japan Security Treaty in order to secure Japan's interests until Japan is able to reclaim its Great Power status in the world. He was instrumental in pushing through the unpopular amidst widespread protests in 1960. Kishi is known for the rehabilitation of more War criminals, for the linkages to ultra-conservative factions and for supporting historical revisionist views of the War. Abe Shinzo is the grandson of Kishi who claimed that he intended to realise his grandfather's visions.

National Cemetery and Pearl Harbor, and Obama's reciprocal visit constituted visits to the Hiroshima Peace Memorial (White House, 2015; White House, 2016b; White House 2016c; Hu, 2016; Associated Press, 2016). For Japanese, Asian and American audiences, it would seem as though Abe had effected reconciliation and demonstrated remorse for Japan's World War II atrocities (Reuters, 2016a). This might have been enough for the domestic audiences in United States and Japan, this was however never quite well received by China and Korea. For the Japanese audience, Obama's visit might suggest the closing of wounds of something that was done seven decades ago. Settling the past aside would help boost the efficacy and efficiency of the US–Japan alliance. This is on top of the range of other issues that plagued US-Japan relations, such as the rape incident by US Marines in Okinawa (White House, 2016a). By 2016, it would therefore "appeared" that Obama and Abe had effected reconciliation on historical matters, and US–Japan relations had stablised in order to meet the challenges ahead. Obama's handling of Abe had an added bonus: it looked to China that the United States was able to rein in the very nationalistic Abe, as there was fear in Beijing that under the neglect of the Bush Administration, Japan had gone militaristic with the rise of Koizumi and Abe.

> History is harsh. What is done cannot be undone. With deep repentance in my heart, I stood there in silent prayers for some time. My dear friends, on behalf of Japan and the Japanese people, I offer with profound respect my eternal condolences to the souls of all American people that were lost during World War II (Abe to US Congress 2015) …

The Obama White House also realised that the situation over the Korean Peninsula and South China Sea had continued to deteriorate, as both North Korea and China continue to ratchet up pressure in these areas that creating significant tension that her regional deputy, Japan was unable to deal with, much less quell effectively. North Korea's third-generation leader, Kim Jong-un officially took the reins of the country in December 2011 after his father died. Kim Jong-il succeeded in conducting the first nuclear test in 2006 and a second test in 2009, and conducted a series of missile tests (2009) with the breakdown of the Six-Party Talks in the same year. In 2010 when Kim Jong-un was appointed as heir apparent and appointed to the National Defense Commission as daejang (4-star general), the DPRK was suspected to be the mastermind behind the sinking of the South Korean Warship Cheonan in March 2010 killing 46 sailors (Kim & Macfie, 2010), and the shelling of the Yeonpyeong Island in November 2010 where 4 South Koreans were killed and 5 civilians wounded (Kim & Lee, 2010). Kim had his uncle, Jang Song-Thaek (along with his extended family) who was appointed by his father to act as Regent to assist Kim executed in December 2013 for treachery, amidst other numerous reports of purges and human rights abuses to consolidate his rule and control the border with China. If anything, 2016 proved to be the year that many doubted whether the United States would be able to grapple with the strategic developments on two fronts. The first was North Korea. This year was a relatively sucessful year for the young Marshal. North Korea tested a miniaturised hydrogen bomb in February and in September, a 5th nuclear exploded a device powerful than the one dropped on Hiroshima (Choe, 2017). In the same year, despite a spate of US and UN sanctions and resolutions, Pyongyang test-fired a range of missiles from February to October: Taepodong-2 ICBM (February), SCUD-C Short range (March, July), Nodong Medium Range (March, July, August), Submarine-launched Pukguksong-1 (April, July, August), new Musudan Intermediate-range (April, May, June, October) (Choe, 2017; EveryCRSReport, 2020).

The South China Sea in the meanwhile has seen China (including Taiwan) embroiled in various disputes with her Southeast Asian neighbours. There have been much that has been written about these disputes but a short survey can be surmised as follows. The first is the dispute between China and Vietnam over the Paracel Islands (they had naval skirmishes in 1974, 1988). The second set of dispute is the Spratly Islands dispute with six parties involved: China, Taiwan, Vietnam, Malaysia, Philippines, Brunei (claiming only waterways). Related to the second, the third set of disputes revolves around overlapping maritime territorial claims because of the way states draw their maritime borders. This overlaps with their claims (disputes) to the Spratly Islands in many cases but also involves bilateral disagreements in the Spratly Island chain (e.g. Natuna Islands between China and Indonesia). It is important to remember that their disputes are not only with China but also between different members of the Southeast Asian states. To that end, the most serious of this involves the People's Republic of China because of her infamous 9-dash lines (now 10-dash lines) claims over the South China Sea which sees her in contention with one or more of the following entities: Brunei, Indonesia, Malaysia, the Philippines, Taiwan and Vietnam.

All states stake their maritime territories naturally also claim the following category of "assets" in their jurisdictions: (1) the hydrocarbon, gas and oil deposits that lie within the areas they claim and the right to exploit them; (2) ownership of reefs and islets; (3) sea lanes of communication and (4) marine resources and fishing rights.

The history of these disputes is complicated and convoluted. Suffice it is to say that the most contentious of these disputes involves China, the Philippines and Vietnam. Even though these disputes have existed for decades, the claimants have been relatively restrained and careful to ensure that they do not affect the bilateral and multilateral relations they have with each other. China had passed the Law on the Territorial Sea and the Contiguous Zone in 1992, creating a legal precedent for Beijing to act and secure its interests in the maritime sphere particularly vis-à-vis the United States and to hedge against its obligations that might be required otherwise under the 1982 UNCLOS (Kim, 1994). By this time, Beijing became increasingly wary of the United States after the Tiananmen Square incident, convinced that Washington was utilising the strategy of peaceful evolution to enact regime change in China.

China had by then also become increasingly prickly in its foreign policy, particularly if it involved territorial issues, continental or maritime even as it eventually sought to try and resolve its outstanding land border issues with most of its neighbours. The Third Taiwan Crisis (that occurred from July 1995 to March 1996 involving Taiwanese President Lee Teng Hui visit to Cornell University in June 1995 had created much embarrassment after the Clinton Administration walked back their promise not to issue Lee with a visa. The result was a series of military exercises over the summer of 1995 to reflect its anger and stern warning. The Clinton administration then staged the biggest display of military might in Asia since the Vietnam War in response that summer but this did not deter the Chinese who in March of 1996 implemented a quasi-blockade of Taiwan with similar missile exercises to the Keelung and Kaoshiung ports of Taiwan. The Clinton Administration once again announced the Independence Carrier group would deploy to international waters near Taiwan. It is this episode that arguably set China on an accelerated course of military modernisation. This gunboat diplomacy was able to stabilise the situation in the Taiwan Straits much like the previous occasions. It began during the 1950s when the US Congress passed the Formosa Resolution authorising Truman to send the US 7th fleet to "neutralise" the Taiwan Straits. This episode, unfortunately, infringed on the Chinese sensitivity, adding to their sensitivities in relation to their "hundred years of humiliation" and the realisation that they were just as helpless as they were fifty or a hundred years ago. After the 1995–1996 Taiwan Straits crisis, the Chinese leadership under Jiang was determined that China should not be again "humiliated" by American gunboat diplomacy just off its shores and accelerated its military modernisation program—reaching out to the Russians in acquire amongst other things advance fighter jets, Naval frigates and destroyers as well as missiles systems to counter the US carrier groups in future. The 1996 reaffirmation of the US Security alliance and the subsequent promulgation of various logistical and legal instruments to better prepare Japan to play its part in supporting the alliance were seen as important and necessary steps for the alliance to become more relevant in the face of the Chinese challenge. The Clinton administration however reached a Military Maritime Consultative agreement with Beijing but this instrument did not prove to be particularly useful when Beijing and Washington clashed over the Hainan island EP-3 incident in 2001.

The Southeast Asian waters, particularly the stretch that transverses the Spratly Islands are crucial for China's considerations of her survival as the northern waterways are dominated by US and Japanese naval assets. Even with a blue water fleet, China doubts her security and military's survival if she does not have the ability to deter or impede American naval access into the South China or East China Sea or for that matter, ensure nuclear parity of sorts with Washington if the PLAN submarines are not able to sail beyond the first island chain. If the situation were to be reversed and if instance, China has a massive military based in Cuba, the United States would find it equally unacceptable. Therefore, it should come as no surprise that in January 1996, wooden structures on stilts were "discovered" to have been built by the Chinese on Mischief Reef (which was claimed by China, Taiwan, Vietnam and the Philippines). Chinese security concerns, of course, are never the priority of Southeast Asian nations, especially from Vietnam's or Philippines vantage point. In fact, the opposite would be true, especially if these Southeast Asian states feel that it is necessary to restrain China.

In 2002, the ASEAN countries and China therefore reached an agreement to negotiate the ASEAN-China Declaration on the Conduct of Parties in the South China Sea, with China signalling that it would accept negotiations on a multilateral rather than on the bilateral basis that it has always insisted on. China, Philippines and Vietnam had discussed the prospects of joint development, both in terms of bilateral economic projects as well as in the development of hydrocarbon resources in the South China Sea through a mechanism named Joint Maritime Seismic Understanding (JMSU). During the tenure of Philippines President Gloria Arroyo (2001–2010), Manila exhibited a positive predisposition with China on bilateral cooperation in terms of jointly developing hydrocarbons in the South China Sea. This deal was later scuttled on the Philippine's side because of domestic political infighting and patronage politics amidst accusations of treason and corruption (Bower, 2010). There was massive unhappiness in Manila that actors involved (the President and the Speaker) in the deal had marginalised the Cabinet, the national security agency and the foreign service in Philippines to endorse policy recommendations from informal advisors, interest groups and cronies that stood to gain millions from this deal (Baviera, 2012). While China might have preferred quiet and behind the scene lobbying, the rambunctious nature of Philippines domestic politics would have made such a deal impossible for Beijing to reconcile and work with Hanoi and Manila. The underlying challenge in a region where domestic politics often forces the nation to adopt short-term interest-based positions as opposed to long-term cooperation. The narrative from Washington's perspective was that this was another example of corruptive Chinese influence in the domestic politics of third-world countries to reach agreements contrary to national interests (Bower, 2010; Hillman, 2019). Arroyo's successor, Benigno Aquino III who had campaigned hard about Arroyo's actions in the South China Sea too started out wanting to have positive relations with Beijing but eventually took on a hard-nosed attitude towards Beijing. China's diplomatic snub refused to grant clemency to three Filipinos on death row for drug smuggling offences had cost him greatly in domestic politics. From 2012 onwards, the Philippines became one of the most vocal challengers of China in the region working a tacit campaign with Japan which was challenging Beijing in the East China Sea. Aquino in an unusually high profile manner internationalised Manila's standoff, alleging China was an aggressor who was involved in unlawful annexation actions in the South China Sea (renamed as West Philippines Sea). In 2013, he authorised the filing of a complaint against China that questioned the validity of Beijing's claims in the South China Sea with the international arbitration tribunal which China refused to recognise or participate. By drawing in backing from Japan, Australia and eventually the United States, he completely moved away from ASEAN (which had been reluctant to back him) to challenge China openly. In a 2014 interview with the New York Times and again in another speech in Japan in 2015, he compared China to Nazi Germany in a speech, suggesting that the world cannot appease Beijing in its territorial claims (Phillips, 2014; Stout, 2015). Beijing refused to recognise the 2016 Tribunal ruling that was in favour of the Philippines. The Obama White House was actually very reluctant about getting into a direct confrontation with Beijing was it had just extracted itself out of the War on Terror that had drained much-needed resources from the United States in the previous decade. The Philippines move to take the dispute to arbitration was not supported by the United States because it would position the territorial dispute as one between the United States and China when in reality it is not (Glaser cited in VOA, 2012). Washington is wary of attempts by the Philippines asking for military upgrades and confirming that the South China Sea would come under the mutual Defense Treaty (Kurlantzick in VOA, 2012).

Vietnam too has disputes with China over maritime territory, fishing rights and oil prospecting in the South China Sea. There has been a history of Chinese police action at sea that has seen Chinese naval vessels fire at Vietnamese fishing boats or detaining their crews which in turn have led to anti-China protests in Vietnam such as those in 2007 or the summer of 2011 (Hoang, 2019). In June 2012, Vietnam passed a "Law of the Sea" that reaffirms the sovereignty of Vietnam over the Spratly and Paracel Islands. In response, China announced the creation of Sansha City, an administrative city based on the Paracel Islands that would have jurisdiction over Paracel Islands, Spratly Islands and Macclesfield Bank. In 2013, Hanoi accused the Chinese Naval craft of firing and causing their boats to catch fire off the disputed Paracel Islands in a police action (Associated Press, 2013). This saw once again an anti-China march in Hanoi that was clearly curbed by the government (NYT, 2013). In 2014, Hanoi again accused Beijing of ramming and sinking another Vietnamese fishing boat (Branigan, 2014), and a flare up over a Chinese oil rig that was seen prospecting oil in waters claimed by Vietnamese too (Reuters, 2014). Consequently, there appears to be an established pattern of Chinese Naval and paramilitary vessels in the region that have constantly fired upon and detained Vietnamese fishing boats (Nguyen, 2020).

Hanoi adopts a very different tack from the Philippines, largely because of the historical memories from the Third Indochina War and the proclivities of the Communist system that frowns on free speech and open politicking that is associated with democratic systems. Even though there are a lot of angry anti-China sentiments, most of these expressions are censored, controlled and shaped (Dien, 2020). It must however be noted that just like in China, nationalistic protests in the form of marches are often orchestrated or tacitly endorsed by the state often for the sole purpose of enabling the public to vent off steam and starve off domestic dissatisfaction, mobilise support for and justify a tougher foreign posture and often as a diplomatic bargaining chip. Since 2014, Vietnam has sought to increase her own capabilities to balance against China, adopt greater international integration with outside partners (such as the United States and Japan), and engage in "cooperation and struggle" with China at the same time (International Crisis Group, 2021).

From the United States' and her allies' perspective, Washington's pivot to Asia is something that is welcomed by nations in the region. China had by now in Manila's eyes become more assertive in her territorial disputes with Japan, Vietnam, the Philippines and other claimants. Chinese territorial claims in the South China Sea are particularly worrying as if they are left to stand they would: (1) reward Chinese irredentism and advance Chinese sovereignty claims over the ASEAN countries and Japan; (2) impede and erode the freedom of navigation for the United States and other regional states in maritime commons and (3) provide the PLAN with a strategic advantage over the United States Navy (4) erode the credibility of the United States in the eyes of the regional countries and (5) undermine the security architecture that the United States needs to preserve. Obama is keenly aware that the dynamics of what was going on was not just aggravated alone by China. The domestic politics of Japan and the Philippines as well as the leaders' nationalistic narratives played an important part i.e. there were indeed no "innocent" bystanders in reality as Japan and the Southeast claimant states had agency, and their perspective agenda too. Japan's new Prime Minister Shinzo Abe was also working very hard to shore up support against China by assiduously courting Philippines Aquino, India's Modi and the Vietnamese government in the pursuit of their respective claims against China. The regional tensions in Southeast Asia offered the perfect opportunity for Washington to announce its new doctrine (pivot) and to implement changes to shore up its position in Asia.

From Beijing's perspective, the interpretation of the situation is different of course. Chinese actions in the South China Seas are considered to be "reactive" to provocations by Southeast Asian claimant states, which are in turn done at the behest of the United States and her principal ally Japan. The ruling by the International Court of Arbitration was regarded as illegitimate by Beijing, as China did not agree or participate in the arbitration. Beijing thus perceived the multilateralism as another exercise in a long history of collective diplomatic bullying spearheaded by the United States to contain China's legitimate rise. China's rhetoric is not surprising of course to Washington, the problem was in her actions, particularly in her reclamation of the disputed reefs and islands. For the first time, Beijing's regional assertive behaviour created a legitimacy problem for the White House. With all the Asian region watching, how the United States reacted to Beijing's response was critical to her own credibility. After all, there was a steady stream of commentary that the United States did nothing to stop China's growing assertiveness. Chinese preference to use force and intimidation, its reclamation projects and its strident ignorance of calls to negotiate a mediated settlement all suggest a "hardening" of the posture of China's new president Xi Jinping bent on regional domination. This assertiveness however if left unchecked, might reinforce Chinese irredentist aspirations and behaviour. US intervention is also necessary to prevent the collective manoeuvres of the regional actors from further stoking their respective disputes into a larger "combined" regional one that would force Washington's hands should the Chinese intervene. By 2015, with a year left in the White House, the Obama White House thus became bolder, louder and more assertive with China as well.

The Belt and Road Initiative: Chinese Style "Marshall Plan" and "Fukuda Doctrine"

China's Belt Road Initiative (BRI, and formerly known as One Belt One Road Strategy) was based on ideas proposed in the 2000s in order to solve political-economic problems that Beijing was facing: widening disparity between inner provinces versus the coastal region, declining domestic demand, overcapacity in manufacturing and a staggering build-up of foreign reserves. Wang Jisi, a professor at Peking University, published a paper in July 2012 entitled "Marching West", argued that China should shift its attention from confronting the United States and her Asian allies to and instead focus more on Central Asia and the Middle East (Bradsher, 2023). The idea of reviving the ancient trade route to connect China's landlocked region was also attributed to the Communist Party School where Xi was President prior before he became the Secretary General of China. The idea of the Silk Road Economic Belt (as presented in Kazakhstan in September 2013) was first announced by Xi with great fanfare, and in the following month after Southeast Asian countries asked to be involved, China launched a maritime Silk Road to link Southeast Asia to South Asia, the Middle East and Africa. These two routes were then combined to form the One Belt One Road strategy. The announcement was met with confusion, scepticism and doubt by Washington and her allies as there was very little clarity as to why this was launched, what the objectives were and who was going to fund what and as well as the timelines, evaluative criteria and results were expected. Even within China itself, there were different explanations of what the BRI was about: an extension of Hu Jintao's Go West policy; a Chinese version of the Marshall Plan or Bretton Woods institutionalisation; a plan to meet the need to export China's industrial excess capacity; a manifestation of periphery diplomacy and upgrading an alternative way to Europe and the Middle East to avoid maritime chokepoints by the US Navy and finally a safer way to expend China's burgeoning US dollar reserves (Gabuev, 2017; Teo, personal communication with Chinese scholars; OECD, 2018). However, like all things in China, once it is launched it is everywhere in official narratives, and both in China and as well as countries involved. Even though officials in Washington and Tokyo were keen to find out specifics, it was very difficult. Over the course of the rest of the Obama administration, China began to work on the language and the narrative of the BRI to link it to Xi's articulation of the China Dream that suggests a rejuvenated nation that could achieve global status and influence commensurate with her economic power. For the most part, at the initial stage there was a sense that this would amount to nothing more than a propaganda drive to boost the popularity of Xi Jinping himself. There was even glee in some quarters that expected these projects to flop as the commercial viability and profitability prospects of building large-scale projects in these areas were relatively negative (at least from the United States and her allies' point of view). The published information at the onset was heavy on visions and grandeur but always short on specifics.

The Obama administration however did pay careful attention to the development as these large-scale projects are often not driven just by economics, but by other motives, and can serve as important conduits to understand China's national interests and ambitions. Even though American officials were not entirely sure of the details involved, what they were certain of is that by now China would have enough economic clout to actualise this conception into reality (in part at least) even if it involved significant challenges. This mega infrastructure push would grow the infrastructure market by 8 per cent annually over the next ten years, rising to 60 per cent of the global total in a region where the infrastructure needs estimates to exceed US$1 trillion annually (Hillman, 2016).

The BRI would help project and build regional influence as it creates visual statements of economic progress; helps address sustainable infrastructure to advance economic integration and increase reliance on China, and facilitates trade linkages as well as export Chinese standards to lock in further preferences for Chinese exports, especially in light of RCEP agreement (Meltzer, 2017). Other views of the BRI have ranged from being "an entirely mercantile endeavour", "aimed at establishing Chinese hegemony", "laying the foundations for a Sino-centric world order" to "hubris that would exacerbate Chinese economic slowdown" to the re-establishment of Eurasia as the largest market in the world to a "shift away from the dollar-based global financial system" along with more benign interpretations of course (Chance, 2016: 9–10). In the words of an American official, the normal reaction would be denial (it can't work), fear (it might work and the Chinese will take over) to "what is in it for us"; consequently the United States should be constructive and helpful rather than obstructive as this opportunity would allow the United States a stake to shape how Eurasia integrates (Freeman, 2016). The Obama White House however was assured by the fact that given that the Trans Pacific Partnership (TPP) would be able to ameliorate the impact of how BRI projects were introduced into the host countries and regulate the behaviour of China-related and BRI related entities in accordance to trade law as well as principles of trade liberalisation (Meltzer, 2017; Chow, 2016).

The BRI also meant that the United States and Japan would be excluded in the massive Chinese expansion of its sphere of influence across the world. Western and Japanese strategists feared that Beijing would potentially reap significant commercial and monetary incentives, monopolise raw materials and resources at rock-bottom prices, establish strategic outposts in terms of ports, airstrips and strategic waterways and buy up strategic assets around the world while corrupting local politics and edging out US influence. Naturally, Chinese narratives about this being all about win–win trade and development were dismissed. Initially, the BRI was not much of an issue largely because the United States and Japan were ambivalent that it was a vision that could not be realised in full since many of the places China was "investing" in were no-go zones for Western capital they were usually politically unstable, geostrategically insignificant or the projects were too costly. The problem however is that as the BRI developed, Beijing was seen to have an increasing number of wins in Southeast and Southeast Asia, Pacific Islands, the Middle East and even the Americas. This situation therefore became increasingly problematic as China was building and developing in the spheres of influence of Japan, India, Australia and the United States. Yet with increasingly difficult economic circumstances and limited capacity, it was the United States had limited options due to its competing priorities and agenda of its domestic constituents and external actors. As the Chinese economy grew from year to year, and its economic clout expanded, Beijing's global influence grew particularly in the global South.

The Trump Doctrine: The Indo-Pacific Strategy and Preservation of US Hegemony

Trump's ascension to the White House can be regarded as a watershed event as he single-handedly instituted policies that had far-reaching ramifications across the geopolitical landscape of the world. While his critics may regard that his Presidency had no great achievements, in reality, Trump's America might have just reignited and intensified a great power rivalry disguised as a renewed Cold War. This began with the announcement of his Indo-Pacific strategy that in a large way is still continued by the Biden White House at the time of writing.

From 2017 onwards, the United States was able to radically reorientate its foreign policy because of Trump's unorthodox methodology. The Trump White House had often attempted to conduct foreign and defence policy out of the Oval Office, often on a personal basis (such as Presidential Son-in-law Jared Kushner's working on a "Middle East Peace Plan"), and sidestepping "seasoned" career State and Defense officials. Needless to say there were outcries of corruption and nepotism, but these comments did not mattered to the administration (Citizen For Ethics, 2017; Bearak 2017). This is in part due to the President's style, in part because of the manifestation of Trump's desire not to be "handled" by the careerists officials he proverbially referred to as the "deep state" or "the swamp" in his campaign. Trump's official pronouncements are often announced by Presidential tweets, often bypassing or contradicting what his Secretaries of State and Defense had intended or proposed. The Trump White House was characterised as a place where there was constant loud and vehement disagreement daily as much as there was treachery and deceit between officials and staff there. There were numerous instances where his staff or his Secretaries had to "walk back" the President's controversial and/or polarising remarks, and conversely many would either be replaced or resigned because of their differences with the President. The high turnover of staff ultimately meant that increasingly the administration was staffed by individuals whose views squared with the President's agenda and outlook. Despite all the differences and disagreements, Trump found an issue that had overwhelming support in domestic politics and international relations—China. US and allied officials began amending the United States' foreign policy narratives in earnest.

The phrase "Asia–Pacific" was completely replaced by "Indo-Pacific" suggesting a doctrinal change in the US grand strategy. The White House signalled its intention to expand the way it conceived of the region by including into the framing as well as policy discussions of the other significant Asian power–India. In doing so, it ropes in a valuable partner at the behest of Japan's Shinzo Abe and in effect legitimises Abe's conceptualisation of the Quad into official US strategy (O'Brien, 2021). The idea of an "Indo-Pacific" strategy is not just semantic (in the sense the concept "dilutes" the importance of China as opposed to Asia–Pacific), but acknowledges the creation of the Quad that is focused on containing China. In 2017, the Trump White House implemented the President's 2017 National Security Strategy (NSS) and in February 2018, approved the Strategic Framework for the Indo-Pacific. According to Robert O'Brien, this Framework guided the development of various subordinate policy frameworks such as the *U.S. Strategic Approach to the People's Republic of China*, the *U.S. Strategic Framework for Countering China's Economic Aggression*, the *U.S. Campaign Plan for Countering China's Malign Influence in International Organizations*, and others. Together with its subordinate documents, the *Framework* has guided US whole-of-government actions to advance regional prosperity and stability, including sovereignty, freedom of navigation and overflight, reciprocity in trade and investment and respect for individual rights, rule of law and transparency to counter Beijing's vision to subordinate to a "common destiny" envisioned by the Chinese Communist Party (O'Brien, 2021). The Indo-Pacific strategy also stipulates that it is incumbent on the United States to exercise leadership to fight back against repressive regimes on behalf of those who value freedom and openness and hinges in a large part on the US–Japan alliance (Rich, 2016). In essence, the Trump Administration has in effect implemented an across-the-board change in US strategic and foreign policy to target China's growing economic influence and strategic power by instituting a mobilisation within and outside the United States to confront China.

The language used in the various instruments of the doctrine to justify the policies were reminiscent of the kind used by Cold War warriors such as George Kennan (to "contain" Chinese expansionism) and John Foster Dulles (to "roll" back Communism). At the heart of US concern was that China's development if left unchecked would lose its pole position to Beijing in a matter of time in the short term (DOD, 2018). The realpolitik calculus in the Beltway put forward by the Trump Administration was simple—China had to be stopped if Washington was to preserve its pre-eminence. Such doctrine cannot be justified based on a narrative that stresses the importance of power maintenance and realpolitik (Cronin, 2017), but rather on the provision of a (semi-) public good that the United States wants to offer her traditional allies and other neutral states—that of helping rid the world of an expansionist and tyrannical power.

Promoting Human Rights, Democracy and Freedom: Xinjiang, Taiwan and Hong Kong

The Administration therefore sought to ensure that its policy documents and official pronouncements summarised and reinforced the popular narratives generated by Japanese and beltway think tanks and news media on China, the Chinese Communist Party and its negative impact on the United States and the world. The general narrative goes as follows: China under the new leader President Xi Jinping has become increasingly authoritarian domestically and expanding aggressively in her foreign policy. The Communist Party in its bid to tighten its grip on the nation is increasing its political persecution of domestic political opponents, democracy and human rights activists as well as entrepreneurs at home, often under the guise of anti-corruption efforts. In reality, all the State efforts and propaganda not only reinforce the cultivation of the personality cult of Xi Jinping but also help consolidate his power and entrench his political longevity. The Chinese leader's personality and left-wing politics are the root causes of the political intrigue and palace politics at home.

It has also created unprecedented global tensions as China seeks to challenge the global international order based on the rule of law and a threat to democracy and freedom-loving people everywhere. In its realisation of the China Dream, Beijing is now aggressively pursuing an expansionist agenda through an accelerated and opaque military modernisation programme, building artificial islands in the South China Sea and has little consideration for her neighbour's sovereignty and interests. Beijing has little qualms about clashing with her neighbours such as Japan or India over territorial disputes as her growing strength is now feeding her aggressiveness and irredentism. While the Communist Party is committing atrocious human rights abuses at home and overwhelming popular opinion with propaganda, her foreign policy is hell-bent on pushing the United States out of the Western Pacific. Globally, the Belt and Road Initiative is a long-term political strategy to enslave Third World countries by offering a debt trap, and consequently advancing Chinese political-economic sway over the large swathe of territories in the Middle East, Latin America and Africa. China's growing political, economic and military power and influence is underpinned by its economic progress made possible because of the benign and magnanimous attitude that previous US administrations have shown by helping them cultivate their economic modernisation. China had in fact stolen technology from the United States through intellectual property violations, engaged in unfair trade through various manipulations, and robbed Americans of their future by taking their jobs and opportunities.

This portrayal of China in US official discourse, repeatedly propagated in corporate and social media narratives from 2017 onwards has had an important rallying effect in turning public opinion against China both domestically and internationally. The vehement denial and angry retorts from the PRC establishment itself were taken as further confirmation of Chinese ambition, aggressiveness, and irredentism as both nations continually engaged in a war of words. The essence of the discussion falls mainly on the character of China and Chinese people and the Chinese leaders themselves compared to the United States, US leaders and the Americans. The discussion focuses on the defence of good old American freedoms and values, and the preservation of values of the ideals and values of the United States and her allies. The language took on a Cold War dimension of the evil empire, except this time the main character in the portrayal was China, the Chinese Communist Party and Xi Jiping himself. The portrayal collectively informs Americans of human rights abuses over its dissidents home and abroad; of State-sponsored camps where Uighurs in Xinjiang are detained indefinitely and of slave labour in important Xinjiang industries such as the cotton industry. This of course comes on top of the accusations of the Falungong dissidents, and other run-of-the-mill human rights defenders such as the blind legal scholar Chen Guangcheng and artist Ai Weiwei. These dissidents became powerful forces of "information" warfare against the Chinese regime. Amongst the many formerly powerful and rich Chinese who were fallen former friends and associates of the senior members of the Communist Party, was a billionaire Miles Guo. He was wanted for fraud and other economic crimes but had escaped to the United States and then became a celebrity of sorts on YouTube and other social media channels attacking and revealing embarrassing details elites in Beijing. Guo was in fact very friendly with one of the key figures in the New Conservative moment in the United States and Trump's advisor Steve Bannon. Additionally, the Trump administration also began a high profile engagement with Tsai Ying-wen's government in Taiwan and upset Beijing since the Chinese decided that the United States had overturned decades of established diplomatic understanding. Additionally, the Trump Administration began to support the anti-extradition Treaty movement in Hong Kong and helped tacitly fan the brewing protests into a sustained revolt in Hong Kong that saw Hong Kongers coordinating international "protestors" and organisations to mount a sustained campaign against Beijing. What came after the Hong Kong episode was the outbreak of the Covid pandemic. Again, there was a substantial and explicit political and diplomatic attack on China as being "responsible" for the global outbreak.

This sustained rhetorical campaign helped to solidify the major theme of Trumpian doctrine. Challenging China became an important theme not only in fulfilling Trump's campaign promises, for the revival of the Republican Party, and for the preservation of US hegemony. It conjured "bipartisan" support in the very contested landscape of US domestic politics to a common challenge—China. Both the Republicans and the Democrats in the US Congress saw ample opportunities in coming to terms with this aspect of Trump's agenda, as did most of the Conservative politicians in allied countries such as the United Kingdom, Australia, Japan, Europe and even India. As with most of the international development in the post-1945 world, once the United States sets the tone for the strategic directions and language, most of her allies would follow. This rallying provides the United States with the language of righteousness and cementing the US role in stopping Chinese "aggression", protecting human rights and fighting for freedom and democracy with "like-minded" friends. Such simple characterisation had worked in Trump's domestic campaign, and to that effect it appears to be providing a boost to Conservative regimes elsewhere as these governments began in earnest to coordinate the reorientation of the United States. In their own ways, Australia, India and Japan accelerated efforts to replicate narratives on their supposed "like-mindedness" in protecting against foreign interference, and securitising all aspects of their countries interactions with China susceptible to national security considerations (Economist, 2023). The United States began to rally her allies against China by helping and promote these issues to fit the agendas of the conservative regimes in India, Japan and Australia boosting their legitimacy and righteousness for the global audience. There was considerable effort put into the United States and her allies' public diplomacy on corporate and social media to convince everyone that China's progress was unjust and needed to be stopped. The case was that China was a threat to the: rules based" order or the international system.

The Kim-Trump Summit: Pre-emptory Neutralisation of a Possible Chinese Proxy

Even though Obama's relations with the Trump campaign were testy at best, the Obama administration did highlight his administration's major concerns to Trump during the transition regarding the DPRK threat. Trump's Secretary of State Rex Tillerson as well as Secretary of Defense James Matis too shared the Obama Administration's views that the overwhelming problem for the United States in Asia was North Korea's nuclear proliferation (State Department 26 April 2017). Ironically, the North Korean regime was actually hopeful that Trump would reconsider the US position with regard to two important issues that the North Koreans were concerned about: ending the Korean war officially and resumption of US–DPRK relations so that economic sanctions could be lifted. The US State Department's policy has always been a consistent demand that DPRK undertake complete and verifiable denuclearisation before any sort of negotiations could take place. Even as Kim Jong-un had hoped that a Trump reconsideration of the situation would lead to a Kissinger-like reconciliation (i.e. Sino-US normalisation in 1972) between DPRK and United States, the North's hope was dashed when Donald

Trump and Kim Jung-un began a war of words on Twitter as DPRK's leader undertook a series of provocations from the sinking of Cheonan, the shelling of Yeongpyong island alongside the series of nuclear and missile tests for domestic political reasons. Given Trump's reputation for disregarding his advisors, and Kim's for ruthlessness and unpredictability, their exchange had the world very amused and very worried at the same time. Trump had sought to apply maximum pressure on the DPRK by increasing and enforcing multiple sanctions points on North Korea, including on its fuel sources. The United States also lobbied China to help tighten the screws on North Korea. Washington also sought to impose 3rd-party sanctions for the first time in US history against the DPRK, and this proved to be very effective i.e. The United States will sanction any entity caught working or trading with DPRK, principally targeting European and Chinese institutions or companies that has so far escaped unscathed before. In September 2017, Trump also sought to stop US citizens from going to North Korea in order to prevent a repeat of the Otto Warmbier incident. The sanctions hit the North particularly hard, as Beijing too sought to tighten the noose in order to bring pressure on Kim's regime whom they regard as becoming too rogue even for their taste. Contextualised against deteriorating US–China tensions, the White House had little choice but to prioritise the DPRK issue. Trump's advisors were adamant that North Korea needs to be handled. Trump himself was clearly obsessed with the idea of meeting Kim and making a "deal" with Kim as the issue had confounded many of his predecessors, on top of the personal prestige, political capital and the possibility of a Nobel Peace prize. The most important reason however was that a nuclear DPRK needed to be "neutralised" or "removed" as a possible China proxy on the strategic chessboard given the United States' looming conflict with China.

The initial interaction of Trump with North Korea's leader on Twitter was highly entertaining for the world but perhaps less so for his advisors. Trump had asked Kim on Twitter if the DPRK leader "had anything better to do" Pyongyang test fired a missile on the 3 July 2017. The Director of CIA then, Mike Pompeo raised the prospects of "separating DPRK Leader Kim from DPRK Nuclear program" (hinting at a regime change). On 26 July, DPRK threatened the United States with pre-emptive strikes. A little more than a week later, the UNSC passed sanctions enacted new sanctions against North Korea, and Kim Jong-un threatened the United States openly again, promising to payback a "thousand-fold". In response, Trump twittered he would unleash "fire and fury" in response to DPRK threats. On 11 August, Trump tweeted again that the United States is "locked and loaded" for a military response. In September 2017, the DPRK Ambassador to the United Nations warned of "forthcoming measures" in response to the unlawful sanctions. On the 17th of September, Trump labelled DRPK leader Kim "rocketman" via twitter and at the UN General Assembly vowed to "totally destroy North Korea" and "defeat the rocket man" on a "suicide mission". The North Korean Foreign Minister duly referred to the US President as a "dog barking", with a corresponding statement issued by DPRK leader that he will "tame the mentally deranged dotard with fire". Trump responded via twitter on 22 September that Kim was "obviously a madman who doesn't mind starving or killing his people, [and] will be tested like never before!". Trump officially embarked on an Asian trip which North Koreans denounced as a "warmonger's visit". Trump tweeted back "Why would Kim Jong-un insult me by calling me old when I will NEVER call him "short and fat?". Oh well, I try so hard to be his friend—and maybe someday that will happen". On 2 Jan 2018, Trump again tweeted that "North Korean leader Kim Jong Un just stated that the nuclear button is on is desk at all times ... Will someone from his depleted and food starved regime please inform his that I too have a Nuclear button, but it is a much bigger and more powerful one than his, and my button works!". As a show of strength, the United States dispatched three aircraft carriers to Pacific in a show of strength. As this war of words escalated, most governments were alarmed by these escalating tensions, making worse case assumptions regarding Trump's and Kim's mutual and escalating challenges. Insofar as China was concerned, the DPRK leader had too acted in defiance of Beijing's call for them to bring an end to the nuclear and missile tests with little effect. The North's sabre rattling and nuclear tests in the eyes of the Chinese were giving the United States and the Republic of Korea to introduce the Theatre Missile Defence (TMD) and over advance weaponry on the Korean Peninsula which was concerning much concern to Beijing. Seoul, during the 2018 Pyeongchang Winter Olympics managed to have officials from DPRK agree to a denuclearisation that eventually paved the way for US Secretary of State Mike Pompeo visit Pyongyang which secured the release of three Americans as a gesture that eventually led to the Kim-Trump Summit in Singapore in June 2018.

Trump had agreed to cease US and South Korean military exercises in exchange for a promise from Kim Jong Un to destroy a missile testing site. Despite the agreement, the United States still accused North Korea had still not dismantled its missiles and denuclearise, and proposed sanctions not be lifted. North Korea and the United States held another summit in Vietnam in February 2019. It did not achieve anything as Kim Jong Un wanted to negotiate for all sanctions to be lifted while Donald Trump had not felt that the time was not right. In addition, the North Koreans had apparently not agreed to denuclearise only partial sanctions were lifted (Sen, 2019). DPRK and the United States had reached a détente and DPRK relations with her neighbours have resumed normality and everyone in Asia was relieved by this outcome. Even as Trump's decision to meet with Kim was criticised by his staff members, the press and externally by some of his allies for a range of transgressions for ignoring decades of diplomatic efforts and progress, for "giving away something for nothing", to supporting tyrannical behaviour of the North's leaders. This however was not for nothing for two important reasons. Trump had to actually "neutralise" a possible ally of the Chinese and avert an outright confrontation with the DPRK by giving the DPRK leader a couple of photo-ops, and more importantly gain a fair measure of credibility in the eyes of his supporters since he managed to achieve a détente of sorts with North Korea that he claimed none of his predecessors did. Most importantly he neutralised a possible proxy piece from the chessboard the Chinese could use.

On the Offensive: The United States' Trade and Tech War on China

Almost contemporaneous with the handling of the North Korea issue, the formulation of Trump' doctrine towards China began to take shape. Donald Trump promised to revamp Washington by wanting to drain the proverbial "swamp", but it was evident that his "draining" did not materialise even though he refused or was unable to fill many vacancies. His administration was immediately hamstrung by the difficulties in staffing the administration and struggled with consistently bad press and toxic narratives advocated by political opponents within and outside the beltway. Trump's by now constant war of words with the press, as well as his determination to "side-line" parties of the "deep state", of which the military-industrial complex and the national security establishment has created considerable anxiety in Washington and elsewhere. This has in effect eroded much confidence in his administration and created domestic difficulties for him to be able to implement his policy with focus, but still he was able to get his message out on China.

The Trump White House waged a concerted Trade War on China that revolved around important sets of "battles" that revolved around different issue areas and industries, labelled as "battles", each with its own set of US legal rationale. They are as follows: (1) Solar Panel and Washing Machines that injure US industries; (2) Steel and Aluminium as National Security Threats; (3) Unfair Trade Practices for Technology, and Intellectual Property (IP); (4) Automotives as National Security Threat item; (5) Safeguarding US Semiconductor Supremacy (Bown & Kolb, 2023). While US Trade War targets a variety of nations (such as European Union, Canada, Turkey, Korea) for steel and aluminium, the majority of the focus is on China. The Trump White House was adamant that they wanted to fix the "deficit" the United States was suffering from, along with a host of other problems such as job losses, technological "thefts" through forced transfers, intellectual property thefts, anti-dumping, unfair trading terms through state subsidies and protectionist tendencies which Trump attributes blame to both his predecessors for not doing their "duty" to defend US interests, and to trading partners for "taking advantage" of United States.

The problem for Washington was that both her allies as well as the broader international community were sceptical about Trump's trade war as it was clearly protectionist in nature and in the case of certain countries such as China downright punitive. The Trump White House did not appear to have concrete objectives of what it was they wanted to achieve with the trade war other than it makes for good political theatre domestically. The reception was not uniform, and many respected economists as well as from the business community with large interests in China were shocked by Trump's proposals. There were additional concerns if the if the White House had a road map or more importantly clear end goals in mind when the trade war was launched. Did the United States expect target countries concerned to absorb the tariffs without a fight, or was this a ploy to goad nations concerned to renegotiate terms of trade that would ultimately benefit Washington?

From the viewpoint of allies such as South Korea or Japan, the US's moves were concerning to say the least. For other countries such as India and Turkey that too have a working relationship with the United States,

Trump's declaration introduced even more uncertainties into their respective relationships with the United States. Yet, in reality the main target of Trump's trade war battle cries was China. From Beijing's point of view, the totality of the trade war looked like a concerted effort by the United States to outright stunt and stop if not roll back China's economic growth and development. It was nothing short of an attempt by the US to stoke a renewed Cold War (Huang, 2021). Washington gave China a choice either to cave in to Trump's high-profile attacks openly, accept the tariffs and lose both economically and reputationally, or retaliate with the risk of ever-escalating counter-measures. There was no good way out as Beijing realises that it was a lose-lose proposition. The only option was choosing the least "worse-off" option. The Trump administration's calculations was that China would be forced to either accept the "rebalanced" terms of trade or retaliate and risk losing even more—either way which will benefit US industries even more and reaffirmed the validity of his policies.

The idea of a US–China trade war did excite members of the Global Right's national security establishment. Insofar as the Quad countries' military establishment were concerned, the idea of curtailing China's economic prowess did appear attractive as it represented a break from the pattern of the United States fuelling China's economic growth that in turn translated into China's military strength. Even though the three Quad members had different trade profiles with China, their key assumption was that Uncle Sam was principally responsible for helping China to become the economic behemoth that it is today. Reducing or "rebalancing" trade with China certainly means a reassessment and possibly an erosion of China's ability to continue to develop on its current trajectory.

For Tokyo, Trump's Trade War cries brought back memories of the US–Japan trade war during the Reagan era, as Washington forced the Plaza Accord on Japan in 1985, in the process devaluing the Dollar against Yen, and in 1987, levied 100% tariffs on many Japanese products blocking their access to the American market. This compounded problems for Japan, leading to the beginning of Japan's economic slowdown in the following decades. Trump himself was railing against Japan during that time, declaring during an interview on TV that "Japan had "systematically sucked the blood out of America … and "it's a huge problem, and it's a problem that's going to get worse… and [Japan] is laughing at us" (Griffiths, 2019). The Japanese establishment under the guidance of Abe of course was delighted that the news, with many assuming that the United States would be able to replicate with China what they did with

Japan. As the original proposer of a tough containment policy towards China, Shinzo Abe was of also delighted at the news of this growing rift between Washington and Beijing. Friction between the US and China was almost always good news for the former Prime Minister, as it meant greater political and diplomatic wriggling room for Tokyo insofar as her bilateral relations with Washington and Beijing is concerned. Increasingly, Japan looked like she is able to pivot from Obama to Trump with its agenda against China intact and worries alleviated (Hunt, 2016).

As discussed, Japan's worst nightmare is not only that China's capabilities far outstrip hers, but the possibility that her principal patron, the United States would eventually become either enamoured with China's growing power or worse, sacrifice her interests by reaching a "G2" deal where Japan's interests is ignored. The more problematic aspect of Trump's Trade War for Japan however was that Tokyo was too not spared even as an ally. As Trump went on a rampage by slapping tariffs on countries that were key US agricultural markets (China, Mexico, Canada and Europe), the farmers in these countries bore the full brunt of their retaliation. By 2019, Japan had made important concessions on agriculture through the US–Japan Trade Agreement, eliminating over 90 per cent of American food and agricultural products imported into Japan, but had gained relatively little in return. Tokyo's gestures was not met by same level of reciprocity, but characterised by omissions and one-sidedness, attributed to Japan's desire to want to avoid sanctions (EAF Editorial Board, 2019). A further reason was that Abe had personally wanted Trump to win, as Trump's policies benefitted his personal political vision and his party's neoconservative agenda more than the Democrats. Trump was his man in Washington.

The idea of curtailing China's economic growth and prowess appealed to the national security teams in this country. Disrupting Beijing's aggressive economic growth would help slow down Beijing's ability to fund her military modernisation, and reduce her asymmetric influence that she has with many economies around the world. Denting China's ability to push forward with the BRI and create political problems for the Chinese Communist Party at home as unemployment increases. The problem is that this Trade War was a costly endeavour in hindsight. It did disrupt China's economic growth; it did create a sense of "victory" in certain quarters as the Global Right countries did their best to assert and undermine China, but in the end, it had real cost for all the countries involved, particularly the United States that would eventually show (Hass & Denmark, 2020).

For Australia, there were both opportunities and risks in the Trade War. Writing in 2016, a Brookings analyst predicted that there will like be expectations that the long-term interest rates would rise as the markets try to cope with the increase in debt, and that the Federal Reserves would allow for substantial fiscal stimulus to raise demand, which would in turn cause hyperinflation. This would probably cause the US dollar to strengthen as foreign capital will flow in to finance the ever-rising US fiscal deficit (Mckibbin, 2016). The same analysis predicted a deep recession for the United States if countries retaliated, and that China would withdraw the financing of US debt. This would have grim implications for the global economy. In theory, the US–China trade war might create more demand for Australia's products, even as US–China tensions would put pressure on the Australia to "choose" sides. In reality, during Morrison's tenure, Australia–China relations plunged to a new low. Beijing was already angry with Australia and was considerably outraged by Morrison's remarks and policies. China felt targeted particularly over his government's insinuations that China was the origin of the Covid, and for Canberra full on support for Trump's anti-China policies as a member of the Quad.

China thus imposed curbs on shipments of virtually everything she imports from Australia: such as coal, timber, barley and wine under the pretence of health and safety concerns. This amount to 5.5% of its total annual exports, worth somewhat US$16 billion dollars in total. Even as there was a fair amount of public anger in Australia, there was also a sense of disappointment that set in when American and Canadian exporters began to fill the vacuum left open by Australia in the wine, cotton, timber, coal and even seafood industries (Tan, 2021; Mizen, 2021). Australia had been caught and was actually "paying the price" in the tussle between the two geopolitical powers as China accounts for nearly 40% of Australia's total exports according to the Australian Bureau of Statistics (Dobson, 2021). The realisation that the United States will prioritise her own economic needs ahead of her allies to an extent jolted the Australian public into reorienting their support towards the Labour Party. Writing In hindsight, an Economist editorial suggested that Australia has "survived and emerged stronger" from Chinese bullying, even though in reality the current reproachment between Australia and China in 2023 could be interpreted as a case where Australians had elected a more sensible and more balanced Prime Minister that sought to build a more forward looking bilateral relationship that befits Australian national interests.

New Delhi was one of Trump's Trade War targets. India was hit with a globally applied set of tariffs on steel and aluminium in March 2018 (Presidential Proclamation, 2018). The United States was unhappy with a slew of measures that the Indian government had instituted and regarded them as protectionist policies to help achieve Modi's plan of expanding domestic manufacturing. They included amongst other things increased custom duties, expanded local manufacturing mandates, price controls and enhanced testing regimes in particular industries that slowed imports (Rossow, 2022). By May 2019, Washington sought to clash with New Delhi over India's protectionism for its market. The Trump Administration argued that India had not given the United States "equitable and reasonable access to its markets", instituted tariffs on solar panels and washers, textiles, jewellery, auto parts and agricultural products (Swanson & Goel, 2019). It also imposed duties on steel and aluminium imports steel and aluminium imports using Section 232 of the 1962 Trade Expansion Act. Notwithstanding this, bilateral US–India commercial relations actually grew in the years preceding the pandemic and after (from July 20) onwards. By June 2023, the US–India trade war was finally resolved at the World Trade Organisation after India agreed to remove retaliatory tariffs on certain US products, including chickpeas, lentils, almonds, walnuts, apples, boric acid and diagnostic reagents (Palmer, 2023).

Of the three Quad partners, India appeared to be the country that could benefit the most from Trump's trade war with China. India's trade with China is actually miniscule compared to the US, Japan or Australia. To that extent a disruption in trade actually does not affect India or for that matter too much. For New Delhi, the prospects of having China's global trade disrupted offers much opportunity for her own manufacturing sector. This was probably what Shinzo Abe and Donald Trump had in mind too when they encouraged industries to relocate from China. Singapore DBS bank had reported that India could possibly benefit to the tune of $11billion as manufacturers shift their production to the country, even as the report acknowledged the challenges they might face in land acquisition and labour reforms (Soon, 2019). The reality was quite different. Discounting the pandemic period, it would appear that the diversion "gains" in manufacturing from 2017 to 2019 was only

$1.2 billion, while Vietnam's gain was a larger $8.5 billion (Kathuria & Srinivasan, 2022).

Washington's determination to wage the Trade War therefore translated into real policies for her many of her allies, including the United Kingdom, the European Union and also the QUAD members—Australia, India and Japan. Trump's trade war provided the national security establishment to gain an important edge over their commerce-related officials, businessmen and generally domestic constituents with ties to China. It also created an environment where National Security Hawks have a natural advantage in the domestic debates with those in diplomacy, trade and cultural work. Naturally, since the Trump Administration suggested an across the nation effort in "resisting" China, all these other dimensions are therefore reconnected.

A second key aspect of the Trump administration concerns about China becoming a high-tech power. Beijing was closing the gap in its technological prowess vis-à-vis the United States. The rapid modernisation of China over the last four decades meant that PRC's overall manufacturing and industrial capacity has grown to a level that the United States and her allies find discomforting. China has also caught up in many high-tech industries and is close to challenging US, European and Japanese technological superiority in these areas. From her achievements in Space technology to material sciences to telecommunications, the norm is now for US and Japanese policymakers to ascertain if China has caught up with them. The Trump administration attributed that China was largely responsible for the economic malaise that America finds herself: the burgeoning deficit, the mass unemployment, un-chair economic politics and most importantly the general inability of US enterprises to command an overwhelming level of technological superiority. To prevent China's domination in high-tech, Washington announced a tech war alongside the trade war. In addition to tariffs, sanctions were also used to either threaten or actually put a stop to the commercial activities of Chinese companies and entities that Washington targeted (Kawakami & Hoyama, 2019). The Trump White House initiated a strategy to put a stranglehold to prevent China's access to high-tech products as well as to prevent China from acquiring the know-how to further these high-tech industries at home. This of course was substantiated on the grounds of national security, preventing Chinese "ripping-off" American companies and the lack of reciprocal economic policies.

Washington targeted specific Chinese companies, but the most intense attacks were on emerging tech companies such as Huawei, ZTE, Baidu and TikTok. These high-tech companies were alleged to be (or will be) involved with China's national security apparatus to be used for espionage purposes. Washington therefore has the potential and capability to penetrate, cripple and American's (and their allies') communication infrastructure. Beyond that, Chinese companies could do great damage to the dominance of both US tech companies worldwide and consequently, the intelligence capability of the United States if various nations employed Chinese hardware infrastructure instead. This has repercussions for future Tech companies and the United States from intelligence gathering and military operations to continual funding of US R&D.

What probably appeared most outrageous was that the United States as a nation therefore targeted Huawei, a Chinese telecommunications company. It was actually very rare for any country to go after a company (rather than the government). The United States lobbied her European and Quad allies to undertake measures to ensure that Huawei is excluded from the development of 5G networks. The US Department of Commerce listed Huawei on its Entity List, effectively banning American companies from doing business with Huawei without prior approval from the US government. It also sanctioned Huawei and restricted its ability to purchase components and technology from United States corporations. Amongst other things, Huawei was prevented access to key technologies that her supply chain relied on, principally semiconductors (5G chips) as well as software (Google's Android system). Through diplomatic and political pressures, the United States undertook their initiatives to undertake similar measures with the end goal of excluding Huawei from participating in their country's telecommunications sectors and network. This included members of the Five Eyes Intelligence alliance (US, UK, Canada, Australia and New Zealand), with additional members such as Japan, South Korea and India. The attack on Huawei was multipronged— it was a coordinated attack on a growing tech company not only by attacking its mobile telephony businesses by thwarting critical components in its supply chain, but also ensuring that its products cannot be sold in its various export markets. Washington also attempted to disrupt the Chinese company by arranging for Canada to detain and arrest Meng Wanzhou, deputy Chair of the Board and Chief Financial Officer (CFO) of Huawei, when she was travelling in transit via Canada to Beijing on the request of the United States under the indictment of bank and wire fraud in violation of US sanctions against Iran by a Huawei subsidiary. This episode lasted for three years from the day she was placed under house arrest on the 1 December 2018 to 1 December 2022 when the charges were dropped. Conspicuously, two Canadians (now famously known as "The Two Michaels" in the Western world) were arrested shortly in China for espionage. Beijing vehemently denied that there was any connection to the Meng case. This created tremendous pressure on the Canadian government and provided tremendous leverage for the Chinese government.[2]

The United States took a broader industry approach towards crippling the rise of Chinese IT companies. The Trump administration issued an Executive Order on Securing the Information and Communications Technology and Services Supply Chain that mandated the US government and private entities to combat a threat posed by foreign adversaries in the IT Sector (White House, 2019). They involved amongst other things the construction of an Entity List as well as a Denied Persons List which is a far stricter version of the former with the latter banning all exports without exception. The first company to be on the receiving end of Trump's ban was ZTE, a Shenzhen company that was an international technology supplier with a revenue of US17 billion a year was blocked by the US Department of Commerce to American-made components for "failing to punish employees who violated trade controls against Iran and North Korea" (Zhong, 2018). ZTE was placed on the Denied Persons List in April 2028, forcing the company to the brink of bankruptcy until July 2018 when ZTE paid a US$1 billion penalty and put $400 million in escrow with an American bank, overhauled its leadership and allowed compliance monitors to be installed inside the company for 10 years. Being a small company, ZTE's executives were actually trying to survive by developing alternative untapped markets.

By October 2019, more than 200 Chinese companies and organisations appeared on the US Commerce Department's Entity List. In addition to telecommunications companies such as ZTE, Huawei, the United States also targeted companies ranging from supercomputers

---

[2] At the time of writing, the Two Michaels were in a lawsuit against the Canadian government for their imprisonment by China. Meng's and the two Michaels' arrest added an additional dimension of using the law and proxies in the US–China tech and trade war struggle.

(Xiamen Meiya Pico Information), Surveillance (Hikvision, Dahua Technology to Artificial Intelligence (e.g. facial recognition start-ups (IFlytek, SenseTime, Megvii and Yitu) to nuclear in China (Kawakami & Hoyama, 2019). The United States however did not use the most stringent Denied Persons List liberally, however, as Washington recognises outright ban creates problems for the US economy as much it does for Chinese companies. The Trump Administration also began to leverage pressure on other manufacturers to stop exporting machinery that could help China achieve self-sufficiency in critical items such as semiconductors.[3]

The COVID-19 Pandemic and the Quad's Quest to Secure the Supply Chain

The COVID-19 pandemic outbreak dampened Trump's Trade and Tech War and threw US–China relations into greater disorder. The pandemic straddled both Trump's and Biden's time in office, effectively taking the steam out of Trump's policies in his last year in office. The pandemic also affected the first twenty-six months of Biden's administration. On 11 March 2023, three years and hundred days after Trump's national COVID-19 global health emergency in 2019, the United States allowed the declaration of emergency to expire. The first Covid case was detected in the United States when a man arrived from Wuhan to Seattle on the 15 January and was confirmed after five days on the 20 January 2020. Three weeks earlier, a cluster of cases was reported by China on 31 December 2019 (Holshue et al., 2020). By March 2020, the United States entered into full panic broke as the virus spread. Trump had initially suggested that China was responsible for the outbreak, but that the virus was not manmade or genetically modified (Mangan & Berkeley, 2020). Nonetheless, that has not stopped the President from labelling the coronavirus is a "China virus" (Cillizza, 2020). US officials are adamant that the outbreak started in Wuhan due to the Chinese perchance for using exotic wildlife in their culinary practices (Rogers et al., 2021). The narratives promoted by the leading United States and replicated by global media

---

[3] At the time of the book going to press in 2024, the Trade and Tech War is still ongoing. The PRC has made much progress in several industries such as Electric Vehicles, Solar Energy and even semi-Conductors for computing, and have gained steady economic growth. What is not apparent is the gains that the United States have made continuing the Trade and Tech War.

outlets in particular pinpoint the Huanan Seafood Wholesale Market as the source of the outbreak (Doucleff, 2022). Trump in a speech in the Rose Garden pointed out that the world suffered as a result of "the malfeasance of the Chinese government … countless lives have been taken, and profound economic hardship has been inflicted all around the globe", without taking responsibility for the death of 100,000 Americans from the COVID-19 virus (McNeil & Jacobs, 2020). The Trump White House also announced that due to the incompetence of the WHO in their inability to stop the Chinese from spreading the disease, the United States would be withdrawing from its membership of the WHO, a decision that did not go down well with public health specialists as well as opponents domestically as well as with allies abroad (Rogers & Mandavilli, 2020).

Even as both China and United States entered into a period of prolonged lockdown, US–China tensions still continue to escalate over the dispute and subsequent debate over the origins of the outbreak. The Chinese reaction was fast and furious, with the foreign ministry coming out strongly to condemn this statement, outlining that the first place of detection should not be equated with the origin of the outbreak. Due to the outbreak of the SARs virus in China in 2002, the Chinese and the Hong Kong governments have put in place advanced measures to detect and deal with coronavirus outbreaks, and therefore being the first destination to discover the presence of such diseases is normal. In reality, the Chinese national response was considered by the WHO-China joint national working group as one that is "ambitious, agile and aggressive disease containment in history" against a new infectious disease, after nine days of meetings and site visits in China from 16 to 24 February (Nature Editorial, 2020). This of course is strongly contested in the narratives in the United States and globally.

Beijing viewed Trump's personal comments as well as the Administration reports and narratives as being an overt attempt aimed to discredit China as well as the Chinese leadership in an international blame game (Salcedo, 2021). Beijing did not want to be seen to be ultimately responsible of this global outbreak. Beijing's reaction to any such suggestion was swift and aggressive, fearing that she had lost the right to assert any sort of posture with regard to this outbreak since it provided the United States with a moral high ground. This defensive posture highlighted the intense insecurities in China, either because Beijing felt that it either had nothing to hide or worse that they actually knew what happened and were trying to cover up. The crux of the allegations is that misinformation and the lack of transparency meant that China was concealing the real "truth" of the event, hinting at a bioweapons lab leak or accident that had resulted in the global pandemic. The American perception and presentation of what was happening in China and the accusations and innuendos floated were actually creating a fog that was unhelpful in enabling the root cause of the virus and establishing diagnostic tools (Gupta, 2020) necessary to move forward.

As the pandemic unfolded, there were three key challenges that emerged globally: (i) developing a vaccine and fighting the Covid virus; (ii) sustaining supplies globally for daily necessities from energy to food to medical supplies; (iii) sustaining national economies to economic collapse. Insofar as global governance and cooperation were concerned, the pandemic proved to be a time when the much-needed leadership that was traditionally expected from the United States did not appear forthcoming. The first glimmer of hope came from the global pharmaceutical companies when they announced that vaccine trials had been relatively successful. The Biden administration which came into power in 2021 inherited Trump's difficult legacies (including the ongoing Tech and Trade War).

Biden's policies were in essence a continuation of Trump's policies. The White House saw a political need to pre-empt and dull a potential Trump bid (or a Republican using Trump methodology) in 2024. Biden cannot be seen to be "soft" on China and had to adopt the pseudo-conservative elements of Trump's policies. In other words, the politics of the Biden Administration were policies with Trumpian "spirit" (America First) with the traditional Democrat packaging and spin. Biden not only "doubled down" on confronting China, but ironically also increased pressure on Russia as well. If one expected the antagonism between the United States and China to intensify rather than subside as Biden took reigns of the presidency, then he would be sorely disappointed.

"America First" Biden Style

One of the "new" fronts that emerged during the Covid pandemic was the vaccine diplomacy that saw Washington D.C. and her allies versus China trying to persuade nations across the world over the efficacy and efficiency of Covid vaccines that companies associated with them that were being put forth (Lin 2021). In the history of vaccine development, the making COVID-19 vaccine can be considered miraculous in terms of its development trajectory. COVID-19 was first identified in early 2020 (Lee, 2023). The very first two vaccines (Pfizer-BioNTech and Moderna) were announced and given emergency approval by the US FDA in December 2020, followed by Jansen. Johnson & Johnson in 2021. Eventually, a plurality of Covid vaccines were being put forth based on different technologies from different countries: MRNA technology vaccines such as America's Moderna/Spikevax and Pfizer-Biotech; inactivated whole virus vaccines such as China's Sinovac and Sinopharm and Viral Vector Vaccines such as United Kingdom's Oxford AstraZeneca and Russia's Sputnik V. Even though the United States had made it abundantly clear that vaccines were to be acquired for domestic consumption after the companies fulfilled their commercial obligations to initial investors (such as UK, Israel and Singapore for instance), there were little signs that the American government intended to expand the availability of these vaccines to nations that could not afford to pay. In April 2021, China announced that the results of the phase three trials conducted by the health workers in Brazil yielded an efficacy rate of just 50.7% just barely about the 50% set by WHO. The results were discouraging but nonetheless, the Chinese government continued to press on to offer the vaccine to various countries under its diplomatic efforts. Like many other industries in China (e.g. the semiconductor industry), Beijing has always been reliant on the global MNCs to pave the way for product innovations and service provision even though its domestic capacity was improving. Despite the tremendous size, China did not have any domestic drug companies that were at the forefront of cutting-edge R&D even though it had identified that this was a critical weakness in its infrastructure. Due to the tensions in US-China relations, Beijing realised that it had to go it alone in seeking its own vaccines, and beyond that share her developments as an international public good to ameliorate the difficulties.

The United States and her allies, particularly the Quad countries began collectively lobbying against China's vaccine, arguing that it was vital that "like-minded" countries could band together to protect their supply chain resilience, including that of the Covid Vaccine and medical supplies. Western and Japanese narratives in conventional and social media had strongly promoted doubts about the efficacy and effectiveness of Chinese-made vaccines. This created a lot of doubt and confidence in Chinese Vaccines and resulted in even developing countries like North Korea, who could not afford or access Moderna or Pfizer vaccines, dismissing the Chinese-made vaccines (UNICEF, 2021). The narratives around the inferiority of Chinese vaccines discredited Beijing's attempts to donate or sell her vaccines, which had a detrimental impact on countries that could not afford or access COVID-19 vaccines, prolonging the vulnerability of their people and the crisis. The economics of vaccine development meant that early state investors, such as Israel, the United States, the United Kingdom, and Singapore, were some of the states that had managed to obtain the vaccine first for their population. As the crisis prolonged, lower-income countries such as Thailand and Uruguay adopted the position that "some protection is better than no protection" and chose to administer the vaccine Sinovac.

The Covid pandemic hit China very badly. Although its government was more effective (or draconian) in terms of being able to lock down any city or province it wanted within hours, the economic, human, and ultimately political costs were extremely high. Additionally, the way quarantine was conducted was more akin to a wartime "captive" approach rather than a medical prevention approach, which further tarnished the international image of China, the Communist Party, and her leader Xi Jinping. Although China has argued that there is no evidence she was not responsible for the outbreak, Beijing was keen to ensure that her public diplomacy was stepped up to counter US accusations and to repair her image.

Beijing had initially harboured hope that Trump's posture and rhetoric was him just negotiating for a "better" deal, but later became convinced that Trump was determined to partake in a struggle to wage a new Cold War. While Trump's true intentions with regard to China's leadership are unclear, what was evident was that his plans involved derailing the continued and sustained development of the Chinese people and the ascendance of China. The Chinese leadership was convinced that the United States was in part responsible for the emergence of the virus outbreak in China for the simple reason that a pandemic was the best way to disrupt China's economic ascendance. This view of course was rejected by most of the Western government as Chinese propaganda and attempts to cover up the origins of the Covid outbreak. The Covid episode had brought severe repercussions for the Chinese government as for the first time since the Cultural Revolution China's economy was spiralling downwards because of the lockdown. The level of pressure brought upon China since Trump's ascendance as President drove US–China relations to a new low never seen before in the history of US–China relations. The also pandemic came in the aftermath of the US-led campaign against China on themes such as genocide in Xinjiang, the intimidation of Taiwan and the killing of democracy and rolling back of the "one country, two systems" in Hong Kong.

Even though some in Beijing had a glimmer of hope that this attack would desist with the ascendance of Biden, even though most reports in Beijing indicate that this would be otherwise. China recognises that this was not a "Trump" problem per se, but rather Sino-US tensions had to do with international realities and domestic structural constraints of the American political systems. By 2023, there were various versions and explanations of how Covid emerged through the official Chinese channels and social media, but all fingers on the PRC side pointed towards the United States' possible covert actions (The Standard, 2023) or imported by soldiers participating in the military games in Wuhan before the event (Rogin, 2021). China had hosted military games where members of the US military had been to the Huanan market in particular, and was in fact seeking medical attention in a hospital. Ironically, this theory was also investigated by the United States as a "super spreader" event (i.e. that the soldiers imported the virus from China). On the US side, there are other variant explanations such as the "lab leak" theories, which could be categorised into malicious or accidental on the Chinese part (Leahy & Cookson, 2023). In essence, it alleged that Chinese scientists who were experimenting with viruses were negligent in their biosecurity precautions (Barnes, 2023). Many Republican senators have gone further to suggest that the Biden Administration is hiding the fact that this could be a result of China's biological weapons program gone awry (USHRPSCI-Minority, 2022).

Insofar as the Quad countries are concerned, China's vaccine diplomacy is to be guarded against. Japan and Australia of course were able to procure their Covid vaccine relatively quickly from Pilzer and Moderna. Unfortunately, India with her escalating cases had turned down China's offer of assistance with the Covid situation, instead appealing to the West and other countries in Asia for assistance with the situation. All however remained committed to the narrative that China was responsible for the Covid outbreak.

From Unilateral Decoupling to Multi-lateral De-Risking: Prioritising Security Goals Before Economic Interests

An important aspect of Biden administration was to emphasise a shift away from Trump's unilateralism and reinvigorate US alliances to jointly confront China (MOFA, 2023). While the language is different from the Trump era, the substance of much of Biden's policies remain similar. Biden subsumed the ideas of the Tech and Trade War, and acknowledged that American security concerns must be placed ahead of economic interests. Trump's "decoupling" sought to convince nations to cut their economic interactions and reliance on China, and strengthen instead the connections with "like-minded" friends. Biden however appeared to have emphasise the reality that it was not possible to decouple from the Chinese economy in the short run. The narrative began to switch to one of "de-risking" and the securing of the supply chain of the United States and her allies. All economic activities, including the formation of regional trade associations and organisations, the routine investment activities of firms, innovation and financial transactions, as well as the acquisition of raw materials, labour, or markets for industrial operations, should take into account national security considerations. The United States and her European as well as Quad allies should not rely on China anymore but instead seek opportunities to relocate manufacturing away from China.

The only problem that often goes unstated is whether the replacement products or services from "like-minded" friends are accessible both in terms of availability and of pricing. The problem for the United States is not only did the trade deficit (which was the main reason for addressing Chinese "treachery" and "predatory" trade practices) not decrease, but in fact it had increased quickly over the Covid years. During the pandemic, not only was China the main supplier of affordable commodities, it was in fact very often the only source. The Biden administration changed the language to "de-risking" instead of "decoupling" to acknowledge the fact that the United States and her allies were unable to decouple from China in the short-run, and that the economic realities exposed the short-sightedness of American policymakers and their rhetoric. This language also helped reassure the business communities as well as more moderate elements within the government as well as from China herself. An additional problem is that in response to the Covid, as well as the tech and trade war, the United States had created an inflation that was creating a problem for the living standards in the United States.

The Chinese COVID-19 lockdown did provide an opportunity for the United States to rally her allies, both within and outside the Quad settings to come together to discuss enhancing their cooperation in several fields, beginning with vaccine diplomacy to counter the perceived growing influence of China to securing the supply chain and increase the resilience of trade amongst member states. The Quad went from a security dialogue to a mechanism where the allies tried to help and shore up each other's "supply chain", but this presented tremendous challenges still as it was just not possible to exclude China. This became apparent as Beijing went into "lockdown" mode from 23 January 2020 (starting from Wuhan, Hubei province) spreading across different provinces until August 2022, with lockdowns of two weeks to twenty-one weeks (Shanghai). The inability of the Quad countries and the rest of the world to wean themselves off trade with China speaks volumes as to how the Quad "de-risking" strategy might play out eventually. This however does not mean that China is "winning" for a fact as the Quad has largely succeeded in ensuring that economic and commercial decisions in their countries would increasingly become subjected to political and security considerations henceforth. China has therefore every reason to increase and intensify trade linkages with other areas of the world to compensate for its troubled trade relationship with the United States, Japan, India and Australia.

Biden's Doubling Down and Trump's Return: Great Power Hegemonic Struggle and Cold War Redux

The invasion of Ukraine occurred just as the Biden administration was rallying her allies in Asia to reorient the Quad with an eye on China. At the beginning of the Ukraine invasion, there was considerable unity in Europe and the United States this was a policy failure to stop Russia from seizing Crimea earlier had embolden Russia. Domestically within the United States, there was a dissenting view that it was the United States that had disregarded Russia's repeated warnings in her relentless pursuit of NATO expansion of Russia that had stoked the crisis. In fact, the Biden administration had repeatedly warned Ukraine of the impending invasion even as Ukraine's leaders had purportedly tried to dismiss this while trying his utmost to calm the situation. Despite Ukraine's protests, Russia had decided to undertake its military operations to safeguard the rights of Russian speakers in the Eastern part of Ukraine. Europe, the

US and her other allies of course maintained it was Russia's greed and expansionist ambitions rather than anything else that was responsible for this tragedy. The seizure of Crimea was the most obvious evidence of this. As of 2024, it is clear that the greatest losers in this conflict turning out to be Russians, Ukrainians and the Europeans, whereas the countries that gained the most are the US government, energy, military-industrial complex and asset management companies that could be involved in reconstruction work as well as countries like India that have made a tidy profit from the oil trade involving Russia and Europe. Ukrainian President Zelinsky and his close associates are also private beneficiaries of this conflict. The Ukraine conflict has enabled the United States and NATO countries to clear of its obsolete weaponry, and ensured that billions have been pumped into the industrial complex that would ready the next generation of weapons. The same can be said of Russia and her allies such as Iran and North Korea. The United States has reaped tremendous profit for its gas and energy sales to Europe in the aftermath of the blowing up of the Nordstream pipeline, whereas US companies are now in talks with Kiev about agricultural, mining and reconstruction projects in the aftermath of the conflict. Apart from the high Russian casualty numbers, Moscow has not fared too badly either. Its economy has grown respectfully, with Western sanctions barely affecting Russia after a year into its conflict. The most ironic achievement is that the United States through the Ukraine conflict and the "containment" of China forced Beijing and Moscow to become closer. Domestically, the Biden White House has hedged the Republican's prospects of being able to "get into bed" with the Russians easily. The Ukraine conflict has in effect forced public opinion to turn against Russia, just as Trump has forced public opinion to turn against China. This "doubling down" has in fact forced the Cold War that has the effect of getting both European and Asian allies to reinvest and reinvigorate NATO and the bilateral alliance, respectively.

The constraints of this book do not allow for much extended discussion of the developments in Ukraine and the Middle East. The Biden administration in their infinite wisdom has elected to continue Trump's policies against China. At the same time, acting on intra-party politics as well as realpolitik considerations, the Biden administration has also steered the United States into a proxy War with Russia in Ukraine. Trump's Great Power rivalry with China has now morphed into an actual confrontation resulting in Russia and China coming together to face the United States strategically. The doubling down of American policy has reinvoked

Cold War tensions. Like the Korean and Vietnam War, the proxy wars are often fought at the behest of Great Powers who have ingratiated themselves into regional disputes, Ukraine, Taiwan and Korea are now new fronts for the US, Russia and China rivalry. These tensions are rooted in geopolitics, but the domestic developments within the US, Russia and China have exacerbated these tensions. In all countries concerned, variants of nationalism and conservatism have been fused in prevailing ideology and political discourse. For the United States, the Democratic Party has shifted rightwards to counter Republican attacks. For its foreign policy, the Global Right has chosen to sustain Trump's Indo-Pacific strategy and reinvigorate the Quad as an institution. While the Quad might have fared well politically from 2016 onwards, such a mechanism is still difficult for the United States have complete control over. India had "switched" sides to work with Russia, especially in buying and reselling oil from Moscow to New Delhi's benefit, and Australia has restored some normality in trading ties with China. Australia has largely mended ties with China. With the death of Abe, Japan's right-wing faction seemed to have lost its influence even though by and large the LDP is still committed to Abe's vision. By and large, the Global Right has still a very strong presence in international relations largely because in many countries, the disparity has seen a swelling in support for parties espousing right-wing politics. Even though China appears to face huge economic challenges today, Beijing is hardly the only country to have massive economic challenges. The United States, Japan, Europe and many other countries too have equally if not more trying economic problems. China seems to have put the worse behind them in terms of dealing with the Global right— that is, until the recent re-election of Trump. With the ongoing war in Ukraine, the Middle East and confrontation in Taiwan and South China Sea, Trump's impending return to the White House would only escalate US-China tensions. Within the United States, the narratives emanating from mainstream media and Beltway think tanks are that Russia and China are in such bad shape that a victory over China (and Russia) is almost a certainty, the only question is how and when this would happen. Viewed from outside the United States, the view is not all that optimistic and uniform. Many regard US policies today (such as the Trade and Tech War) as hardly reassuring; after all, how does anyone actually believe that an additional 60% tariff on imports from China would actually benefit the American people suffering from the high inflation within the country? Or for that matter, how could any good be done in Ukraine and Gaza by continued weapon sales and escalating rhetoric. The problem is many of the narratives from the mainstream media and some of the US think tanks are the same actors that have continually dismissed Trump as a political force within the United States, a country where most of them live in. One therefore could wonder how they might actually have a clue as to what is going on in other parts of the world. The second Trump Administration faces a more ready and a more formidable China. Beijing has since 2017 committed time, resources and energy to accelerate its military modernisation program and made economic reforms to prepare for a looming US-China conflict ahead. The United States did not prevail in the last two wars fought in Asia—the Korean War and the Vietnam War. It is unlikely that the United States would have the "decisive" victory it wants if a conflict breaks out with Beijing. Today, even if institutions such as Quad has meetings now and again with narratives and initiatives to "counter" China, this institution would have to subsumed under the dynamics of the larger framework of the US-China Great Power rivalry that is currently morphing into renewed Cold War. With Trump's grand ambition to ensure that the United States remains the world's dominant power, and Beijing's refusal to give up its continued development and ascendance, we are likely staring at the edge of a strategic precipice in the near future.

References

(USHRPSCI-Minority) United States House of Representatives Permanent Select Committee on Intelligence (Minority/Republicans), Unclassified Summary of the Second Interim Report on the Origins of the Covid-19 Pandemic, Washington D.C. December 2022, https://intelligence.house.gov/uploadedfiles/final_unclass_summary_-_covid_origins_report_-_dec._2022.pdf

ABC News, "10 Times Trump Attacked China and Its Trade Relations with the US", 9 November, 2017, https://abcnews.go.com/Politics/10-times-trump-attacked-china-trade-relations-us/story?id=46572567

ABC News, "Nepotism Laws Don't Apply to Jared Kushner Appointment, DOJ Says", ABC News, 22 January 2017, https://abcnews.go.com/Politics/nepotism-laws-apply-jared-kushner-appointment-doj/story?id=44951811

Abrams, Abigail, "Here's What We Know So Far About Russia's 2016 Meddling", Time Magazine, 18 April 2019, https://time.com/5565991/russia-influence-2016-election/

Alexander, Dan, "Here's How Much Donald Trump Is Worth", Forbes, 3 October 2023, https://www.forbes.com/sites/danalexander/article/the-def initive-networth-of-donaldtrump/?sh=2086495b2a8e

Austin, Greg, Can There Be Any Winners in the US–China 'Tech War'?, International Institute for Strategic Studies, IISS Online Analysis, 20 January 2020, https://www.iiss.org/online-analysis/online-analysis//2020/01/csfc-any-winners-in-the-us-china-tech-war

Anton, Michael, "The Trump Doctrine", Foreign Policy, 20 April 2019, https://foreignpolicy.com/2019/04/20/the-trump-doctrine-big-think-ame rica-first-nationalism/

Applebaum, Anne, "The Secret to Trump: He's Really a Russian Oligarch", The Washington Post, 19 August 2016, https://www.washingtonpost.com/opi nions/the-secret-to-trump-hes-really-a-russian-oligarch/2016/08/19/bc7 226a2-6623-11e6-be4e-23fc4d4d12b4_story.html

Associated Press, "China Denies Starting Fire on Vietnamese Fishing Boat", The Guardian, 27 March 2013, https://www.theguardian.com/world/2013/ mar/27/china-denies-fire-vietnamese-boat

Associated Press, "Shinzo Abe Visits Pearl Harbor in What Barack Obama Calls 'Historic Gesture'", The Guardian, 27 December 2016, https://www.thegua rdian.com/world/2016/dec/27/shinzo-abe-pearl-harbor-visit-obama-japan

Azari, Julia, "Trump's Dominance in the GOP Isn't What It Seems", Politico, 18 May 2023, https://www.politico.com/news/magazine/2023/05/18/ donald-trump-paradox-gop-00097458

Ball, Molly, "How Trump's Effort to Steal the Election Tore Apart the GOP—And the Country", Time, https://time.com/5927410/trump-electoral-col lege-republicans/

Bands, Henry, "You Are Remembering Reagan Wrong", Time Magazine, 16 May 2015, https://time.com/3858793/ronald-reagan-history/

Barakat, Matthew, "Analyst Igor Danchenko Acquitted AT Trial Over Discred-ited Trump Dossier", Huff Post, 18 October 2022, https://www.huffpost. com/entry/igor-danchenko-trump-russia-probe_n_634f120ee4b03e8038d 905e4

Barnes, Julian E., "Lab Leak Most Likely Caused Pandemic, Energy Dept. Says", The New York Times, 26 February 2023, https://www.nytimes.com/2023/ 02/26/us/politics/china-lab-leak-coronavirus-pandemic.html

Baviera, Aileen S. P., "The Influence of Domestic Politics on Philippine Foreign Policy: The Case of Philippines-China Relations Since 2004", S. Rajaratnam School of International Studies, Singapore, 5 June 2012, https://www.rsis. edu.sg/wp-content/uploads/rsis-pubs/WP241.pdf

BBC, "Donald Trump's Life Story: From Hotel Developer to President", BBC News US Election Feature, 1 March 2021, https://www.bbc.com/news/ world-us-canada-35318432

Bearak, Max, "Trump Would Join Motley Crew of Nepotists with Appointment of Son-in-law", The Washington Post, 10 January 2017, https://www.washingtonpost.com/news/worldviews/wp/2017/01/10/trump-would-join-motley-crew-of-nepotists-with-appointment-of-son-in-law/

Bennett, Brian, "How Donald Trump's Control Over the GOP Became a Hostage Situation", Time Magazine, Time, 15 November 2022, https://time.com/6233840/donald-trump-gop-hostage-announcement/

Bevan, Matt, "Why does Vladimir Putin hate Hillary Clinton?", ABC News, 22 May 2018, https://www.abc.net.au/news/2018-05-22/vladimir-putin-and-hillary-clinton-hatred-explained/9783076

Blumenthal, Dan, "China Humiliates Gates, Obama", The Weekly Standard, 12 January 2011, https://www.aei.org/articles/china-humiliates-gates-obama/

Bolton, John, The Room Where It Happened: A White House Memoir, Simon & Schuster: New York 2020.

Borger, Julian, "Rex Tillerson: A Rocky Road With Trump That Ended With a Surprise Firing", The Guardian, 13 March 2018, https://www.theguardian.com/us-news/2018/mar/13/rex-tillerson-fired-what-happened-trump-secretary-state

Bown, Chad, and Kolb, Melina, "Trump's Trade War Timeline: An Up-to-Date Guide", Petersen Institute for International Economics, 31 December 2023, https://www.piie.com/blogs/trade-and-investment-policy-watch/2018/trumps-trade-war-timeline-date-guide

Bower, Ernest, "The JMSU: A Tale of Bilateralism and Secrecy in the South China Sea", Center for Strategic and International Studies Commentary, 27 July 2010, https://www.csis.org/analysis/jmsu-tale-bilateralism-and-secrecy-south-china-sea

Bradsher, Keith, "China Invested $1 Trillion to Gain Global Influence. Can That Go On?", New York Times, 16 October 2023, https://www.nytimes.com/2023/10/16/business/chinas-belt-and-road-initiative-bri.html

Branigan, Tania, "Vietnam and China trade accusations over sinking of Vietnamese fishing boat", The Guardian, 27 May 2014, https://www.theguardian.com/world/2014/may/27/vietnam-china-accusations-sinking-fishing-boat

Breuninger, Kevin, "'I Am the Chosen One,' Trump Proclaims as He Defends Trade War with China", CNBC, 21 August 2019, https://www.cnbc.com/2019/08/21/i-am-the-chosen-one-trump-proclaims-as-he-defends-china-trade-war.html

Burns, Alexander & Martin, Jonathan, "Trump's Takeover of the Republican Party Is Almost Complete", The New York Times, 3 April 2019, https://www.nytimes.com/2019/04/03/us/politics/trump-republican-party.html

Bush, Daniel, "Trump and Tillerson's Biggest Policy Disagreements", PBS The Nation, 13 March 2018, https://www.pbs.org/newshour/nation/trump-and-tillersons-biggest-policy-disagreements

CFR, "Trump's Foreign Policy Moments", Council on Foreign Relations, (2017–2020) Council For Foreign Relations 2024, https://www.cfr.org/timeline/trumps-foreign-policy-moments

Chait, Jonathan, "An Ex-KGB Agent Says Trump Was a Russian Asset Since 1987. Does It Matter?" New York Magazine, 20 February 2021, https://nymag.com/intelligencer/article/ex-kgb-agent-trump-russian-asset-mueller-putin-kompromat-unger-book.html

Chance, Alek, & Mafinezam, Alidad, American Perspectives on the Belt and Road Initiative: Sources of Concern and Possibilities for Cooperation, Institute for China-America Studies, 2016, https://chinaus-icas.org/wp-content/uploads/2017/02/American-Perspectives-on-the-Belt-and-Road-Initiative.pdf

Choe, Sang-Hun, "North Korea Claims to Have Developed a Missile-Ready Hydrogen Bomb", The New York Times, 2 September 2017, https://www.nytimes.com/2017/09/02/world/asia/north-korea-hydrogen-bomb-missile.html

Chow, Daniel C. K., "How the United states Uses the Trans-Pacific Partnership to Contain China in International Trade." *Chicago Journal of International Law* 17, no. 2, Article 2, https://cjil.uchicago.edu/print-archive/how-united-states-uses-trans-pacific-partnership-contain-china-international-trade

Cillizza, Chris, "Yes, of course Donald Trump is calling coronavirus the 'China virus' for political reasons", CNN The Point, 20 March 2020, https://edition.cnn.com/2020/03/20/politics/donald-trump-china-virus-coronavirus/index.html

Citizens for Ethics, "Nepotism and Conflicts of Interest—Jared Kushner and Ivanka Trump, 25 April 2017, https://www.citizensforethics.org/reports-investigations/crew-reports/nepotism-and-conflicts-of-interest-jared-kushner-and-ivanka-trump/

Clinton, Hillary, America's Pacific Century, Foreign Policy, 11 October 2011, https://foreignpolicy.com/2011/10/11/americas-pacific-century/

Cohen, Marshall, "Chronicling Trump's 10 Worst Abuses of Power", CNN, 24 January 2021, https://edition.cnn.com/2021/01/24/politics/trump-worst-abuses-of-power/index.html

Collinson, Stephen, "How Donald Trump Took the Republican Party by Storm", CNN, 15 December 2015, https://edition.cnn.com/2015/12/14/politics/donald-trump-republican-party-history/index.html

Collinson, Stephen, "Republicans Seize Senate, Gaining Full Control of Congress", CNN, 5 November 2014, https://edition.cnn.com/2014/11/04/politics/election-day-story/index.html

Coppins, McKay, "What Mitt Romney Saw in the Senate", The Atlantic, 13 September 2013, https://www.theatlantic.com/magazine/archive/2023/11/mitt-romney-retiring-senate-trump-mcconnell/675306/

CREW, "Neopotism and Conflicts of Interest—Jared Kushner and Ivanka Trump", Citizens for Responsibility and Ethnics in Washington, 25 April 2017, https://www.citizensforethics.org/reports-investigations/crew-reports/nepotism-and-conflicts-of-interest-jared-kushner-and-ivanka-trump/

Cronin, Patrick, How to Asymmetrically Outcompete Xi Jinping's One Belt One Road Initiative, War On the Rocks Commentary, 2 March 2017, https://warontherocks.com/2021/03/how-to-asymmetrically-out-compete-xi-jinpings-one-belt-one-road-initiative/

Crowley, Michael, "All of Trump's Russia Ties, in 7 Charts", Politico, March/April 2017, https://www.politico.com/magazine/story/2017/03/connections-trump-putin-russia-ties-chart-flynn-page-manafort-sessions-214868/

Cummings, Mike, "Swing Vote 'Trumped' Turnout in 2016 Election", Yale News, 21 April 2021, https://news.yale.edu/2021/04/21/swing-vote-trumped-turnout-2016-election

Cunliffe, Kyle, "Donald Trump Spying Allegations: More Likely Useful Idiot Than Putin's Agent", The Conversation, 5 February 2021, https://theconversation.com/donald-trump-spying-allegations-more-likely-useful-idiot-than-putins-agent-154300

Dallas, Phoenix, & Wyoming, Jackson, "Donald Trump's Hold on the Republican Party is Unquestionable", The Economist, 18 August 2022, https://www.economist.com/briefing/2022/08/18/donald-trumps-hold-on-the-republican-party-is-unquestionable

Davis, Aaron, "Timeline: How Law Enforcement and Government Officials Failed to Head Off the US Capitol Attack", The Washington Post, 18 January 2021, https://www.washingtonpost.com/graphics/2021/national/national-security/capitol-response-timeline/

Davis, Dave, 'Stable Genius' Authors Describe Trump Presidency As A 'Den Of Dysfunction', NPR Author Interviews, 22 January 2020, https://www.npr.org/2020/01/22/798498535/stable-genius-authors-describe-trump-presidency-as-a-den-of-dysfunction

Dien, Nguyen An Luong, How Hanoi is Leveraging Anti-China Sentiments Online, ISEAS Yosof Ishak Institute, Perspective, 13 October 2020, https://www.iseas.edu.sg/wp-content/uploads/2020/09/ISEAS_Perspective_2020_115.pdf

Dimock, Michael, "How America Changed During Barack Obama's Presidency", Pew Research Center, 10 January 2017, https://www.pewresearch.org/2017/01/10/how-america-changed-during-barack-obamas-presidency/

Dobson, Mahalia, "Australia Embraces U.S. and Pays Price With China as Trade War Hits Bottom Line", NBC News, 20 June 2021, https://www.nbcnews.com/news/world/australia-embraces-u-s-pays-price-china-trade-war-hits-n1270458

DOD (United States Department of Defense), "Assessment on US Defense Implications of China's Expanding Global Access", US Department of Defense, 20 December 2018, https://media.defense.gov/2019/Jan/14/2002079292/-1/-1/1/EXPANDING-GLOBAL-ACCESS-REPORT-FINAL.PDF

Dominic Rushe, "Trump's Tax Cuts Helped Billionaires Pay Less Than the Working Class for First Time", The Guardian, 9 October 2019, https://www.theguardian.com/business/2019/oct/09/trump-tax-cuts-helped-billionaires-pay-less#:~:text=But%20Trump%27s%20tax%20cuts%20-%20his,lower%2050%25%20of%20US%20earners

Douclef, Michaeleen, "Newly Published Evidence Points to Wuhan Seafood Market as Pandemic Origin Point", NPR, 27 July 2022, https://www.npr.org/sections/goatsandsoda/2022/03/03/1083751272/striking-new-evidence-points-to-seafood-market-in-wuhan-as-pandemic-origin-point

EAF (East Asian Forum Editorial Board), US–Japan Trade and Trump's Political Trophy, Australia National University, ANU, 14 October 2019, https://www.eastasiaforum.org/2019/10/14/us-japan-trade-and-trumps-political-trophy/

Economist, "Australia Has Faced Down China's Trade Bans and Emerged Stronger, Asia Editorial, The Economist", 23 May 2023, https://www.economist.com/asia/2023/05/23/australia-has-faced-down-chinas-trade-bans-and-emerged-stronger

Ekins, Emily, The Five Types of Trump Voters: Who They Are and What They Believe, Democracy Fund Voter Study Group, June 2017, https://www.voterstudygroup.org/publication/the-five-types-trump-voters

Euglund, Will, "The Roots of the Hostility Between Putin and Clinton", The Washington Post, 28 July 2016, https://www.washingtonpost.com/world/europe/the-roots-of-the-hostility-between-putin-and-clinton/2016/07/28/85ca74ca-5402-11e6-b652-315ae5d4d4dd_story.html

EveryCRSReport, North Korea: A Chronology of Events from 2016 to 2020, 5 May 2020, https://www.everycrsreport.com/reports/R46349.html#_Toc39838318

Fahrenthold, David, "Trump Recorded Having Extremely Lewd Conversation About Women in 2005", The Washington Post, 8 October 2016, https://www.washingtonpost.com/politics/trump-recorded-having-extremely-lewd-conversation-about-women-in-2005/2016/10/07/3b9ce776-8cb4-11e6-bf8a-3d26847eeed4_story.html

Finnegan, Connor, "Tillerson Calls Trump 'Pretty Undisciplined,' Trump Calls Him 'Dumb as a Rock'", ABC News, 8 December 2018, https://abcnews.go.com/Politics/tillerson-calls-trump-pretty-undisciplined-president-frustrated-told/story?id=59679249

Freeman, Chas W., "One Belt, One Road: What's in it for Us?", Remarks to the Workshop on Reconnecting Asia at China Maritime Studies, Institute, 7 November 2016, https://reconasia.csis.org/one-belt-one-road-whats-it-us/

FT, "Trump Labels China a Strategic 'Competitor'", Financial Times, 19 December 2017, https://www.ft.com/content/215cf8fa-e3cb-11e7-8b99-0191e45377ec

Fukushima, Glen S., "US-Japan Relations Under Abe Shinzo", 5 February 2015, https://theasanforum.org/us-japan-relations-under-abe-shinzo/

Gabuev, Alexander, "Belt and Road to Where? Council for Security and Cooperation in the Asia-Pacific", 8 December 2017, Carnegie Endowment for International Peace, https://carnegieendowment.org/2017/12/08/belt-and-road-to-where-pub-74957

Galston, William & Dionne, Eugene Josepeh, The New Politics of Marijuana Legalization: Why Opinion is Changing, Brookings Institute, Brookings Governance Studies, May 2013, https://www.brookings.edu/wp-content/uploads/2016/06/Dionne-Galston_NewPoliticsofMJLeg_Final.pdf

Galston, William, President Barack Obama's First Two Years: Policy Accomplishments, Political Difficulties, Brookings, Akron Beacon Staff Writer, When Obama Had "Total Control of Congress", *Akron Beacon Journal*, 9 September 2012, https://www.beaconjournal.com/story/news/2012/09/09/when-obama-had-total-control/985146007/

Galston, William, Trump's Character Problem, Brookings Institute, 5 March 2020, https://www.brookings.edu/articles/trumps-character-problem/

Gass, Nick, "The 15 Most Offensive Things That Have Come Out of Trump's Mouth", Politico, 8 December 2015, https://www.politico.eu/article/15-most-offensive-things-trump-campaign-feminism-migration-racism/

Goldmacher, Shane, Dawsey, Josh, and Nussbaum, Matthew, "Why Trump picked Rex Tillerson", Politico, 13 December 2016, https://www.politico.com/story/2016/12/rex-tillerson-donald-trump-secretary-of-state-232581#:~:text=He%20liked%20his%20strength.",long%20process%20to%20get%20there

Gonyea, Don & Montanaro, Domenico, "Donald Trump's Been Saying The Same Thing For 30 Years", National Public Radio (NPR), 20 January 2017, https://www.npr.org/2017/01/20/510680463/donald-trumps-been-saying-the-same-thing-for-30-years

Graham, David, Green, Adrienne, Murphy, Cullen, & Richards, Parker, "An Oral History of Trump's Bigotry", The Atlantic, June 2019, https://www.theatlantic.com/magazine/archive/2019/06/trump-racism-comments/588067/

Green, Lloyd, March of the Trump Memoirs: Mark Meadows and other Republican Reads, The Guardian, 12 December 2021, https://www.theguardian.com/books/2021/dec/12/trump-memoirs-mark-meadows-kayleigh-mcenany-peter-navarro-scott-atlas

Green, Michael, Hicks, Katheleen, Cooper, Zack, Schaus, John, Douglas, Jake, Countering Coercion in Maritime Asia: The Theory and Pratice of Gray Zone Detterence, CSIS Washington D.C, Rowman and Littlefield Publishers, 2017, https://csis-website-prod.s3.amazonaws.com/s3fs-public/publication/170505_GreenM_CounteringCoercionAsia_Web.pdf

Griffiths, James, "The US Won a Trade War Against Japan. But China is a Whole New Ball Game", CNN News, 24 May 2019, https://edition.cnn.com/2019/05/24/business/us-china-trade-war-japan-intl/index.html

Guild, Blair, & Rieger, J. M., "How the Republican Party Became the Party of Trump", The Washington Post, 11 June 2021, https://www.washingtonpost.com/politics/2021/06/11/how-republican-party-became-party-trump/

Gupta, Sourabh, Viral Mistruths: Separating Fact and Fiction Regarding China's Early Covid-19 Response in Hong et al., US-China Relations in the Age of Covid-19: Politics, Polemics and Pandemic Response Measures, Institute for China-America Studies, Washington D.C. September 2020, https://chinaus-icas.org/wp-content/uploads/2021/03/US-China-Relations-in-the-Age-of-COVID19-ICAS-Report-2020-FINAL.pdf

Hadar, Leon, "The Limits of Trump's Transactional Foreign Policy", The National Interest, 2 January 2017, https://nationalinterest.org/feature/the-limits-trumps-transactional-foreign-policy-18898

Harwell, Drew, "Trump's Conflicts of Interest are without Precedent in American Presidential History", The Washington Post, 9 November 2016, https://www.washingtonpost.com/news/wonk/wp/2016/11/09/trumps-conflicts-of-interest-are-without-precedent-in-american-presidential-history/

Hass, Ryan & Denmark, Abraham, "How, More Pain than Gain: How the US-China Trade War Hurt America", Brookings Commentary, 7 August 2020, https://www.brookings.edu/articles/more-pain-than-gain-how-the-us-china-trade-war-hurt-america/

Heer, Jeet, "Mitt Romney's Lonely Exit", The Nation, 15 September 2023, https://www.thenation.com/article/politics/mitt-romney-gop-trump/

Hillman, Jonathan E., "Corruption Flows Along China's Belt and Road", Center for Strategic and International Studies CSIS Commentary, 18 January 2019, https://www.csis.org/analysis/corruption-flows-along-chinas-belt-and-road

Hillman, Jonathan E., "OBOR on the Ground: Evaluating China's "One Belt, One Road" Initiative at the Project Level", Center for Strategic and International Studies, CSIS Commentary, 30 November 2016, https://www.csis.org/analysis/obor-ground-evaluating-chinas-one-belt-one-road-initiative-project-level

Hoang, Phuong, "Domestic Protests and Foreign Policy: An Examination of Anti-China Protests in Vietnam and Vietnamese Policy Towards China

Regarding the South China Sea." *Journal of Asian Security and International Affairs* 6, no. 1 (2019): 1–29, https://doi.org/10.1177/234779701 9826747

Holshue, Michelle. L., DeBolt, Chas., Lindquist, Scott., Lofy, Kathy H., Wiesman, John., Bruce, Hollanne., Spitters, Christopher., Ericson, K Keith., Wilkerson, Sara., Tural, Ahmet., Diaz, George., Cohn, Amanda., Fox, L LeAnne., Patel, Anita., Gerber, Susan. I., Kim, Lindsay., Tong, Suxiang., Lu, Xiaoyan., Lindstrom, Steve., Pallansch, Mark. A. Pallansch, Weldon, William C., Biggs, Holly M., Uyeki, Timothy, Pillai, Satish, Washington State 2019-nCoV Case Investigation Team, "First Case of 2019 Novel Coronavirus in the United States." *The New England Journal of Medicine* 382, no. 10 (2020): 929–936, https://doi.org/10.1056/NEJMoa2001191

Horowitz, Juliana, Menasce, Igielnik, Ruth & Kochhar, Rakesh, "Trends in Income and Wealth Inequality", Pew Research Center, 9 January 2020, https://www.pewresearch.org/social-trends/2020/01/09/trends-in-income-and-wealth-inequality/s

How America Changed During Barack Obama's Presidency, https://www.pew research.org/2017/01/10/how-america-changed-during-barack-obamas-pre sidency/

Howell, Ron, "Sale of Hotel Items Marks Condo Switch, Newsday", (Newspaper) New York, 21 December 1985, https://web.archive.org/web/202 10811230722/https://www.newspapers.com/clip/83261418/sale-of-hotel-items-marks-condo-switch/

Hu, Elise, "Domonosokem Camila, Obama Makes Historic Visit To Hiroshima Memorial Peace Park", NPR 2016, https://www.npr.org/sections/thetwo-way/2016/05/27/479691439/president-obama-arrives-in-hiroshima-the-first-sitting-commander-in-chief-to-vis

Huang, Yukon, "The US-China Trade War has Become a Cold War, Carnegie Endowment for International Peace", Commentary, 21 September 2021, https://carnegieendowment.org/2021/09/16/u.s.-china-trade-war-has-become-cold-war-pub-85352

Hudak, John, "Liz Cheney's Excommunication from the Church of Trump", Brookings Commentary, 11 May 2021, https://www.brookings.edu/art icles/liz-cheneys-excommunication-from-the-church-of-trump/

Hunt, Joshua, "Japan's Pivot from Obama to Trump", The New Yorker, 9 December 2016, https://www.newyorker.com/news/news-desk/japans-pivot-from-obama-to-trump

International Crisis Group, "Vietnam Tacks Between Cooperation and Struggle in the South China Sea", ICG Report 318, 7 December 2021, https://www.crisisgroup.org/asia/north-east-asia/china/318-vietnam-tacks-between-cooperation-and-struggle-south-china-sea

Jalonick, Mary Clare & Mascaro, Lisa, "GOP Blocks Capitol Riot Probe Displaying Loyalty to Trump", Associate Press, 29 May 2021, https://apnews.com/article/michael-pence-donald-trump-capitol-siege-government-and-politics-4798a8617bacf27bbb576a4b805b85d9

Japan Times, Obama Recalls with Frustration Japan's 'Revolving-Door' Leadership, https://www.japantimes.co.jp/news/2020/11/18/national/obama-japans-revolving-door/

Jilani, Zaid, "Neoconservatives Declare War on Donald Trump", The Intercept, 29 February 2016, https://theintercept.com/2016/02/29/neoconservatives-declare-war-on-donald-trump/

Johnson, Eliana, Stephenson, Emily & Lippman, Daniel, "'Too Inconvenient': Trump Goes Rogue on Phone Security", Politico, 21 May 2018, https://www.politico.com/story/2018/05/21/trump-phone-security-risk-hackers-601903

Kalb, Marvin, "Trump's Troubling Relationship with the Press", Brookings Commentary, 21 February 2017, https://www.brookings.edu/articles/trumps-troubling-relationship-with-the-press/

Kamarck, Elaine, The Fragile Legacy of Barack Obama, Brookings Institute, 31 May 2024, https://www.brookings.edu/articles/the-fragile-legacy-of-barack-obama/

Kan, Shirley, Best, Richard, Bolkcom, Christopher, Chapman, Robert, Cronin, Richard, Dumbaugh, Kerry, Goldman, Stuart, Manyin, Mark, Morrison, Wayne, O'Rourke, Ronald, Ackerman, David, "China-U.S. Aircraft Collision Incident of April 2001: Assessments and Policy Implications",CRS Report for Congress, Congressional Research Service 10 October 2001, https://sgp.fas.org/crs/row/RL30946.pdf

Kathuria, Sanjay and Srinivasan, T.G, "How India and its South Asian Neighbours Fared During the US-China Trade War 2022, https://thewire.in/economy/how-india-and-its-south-asian-neighbours-fared-during-the-us-china-trade-war

Kawakami, Takashi & Hoyama, Taisei, "Trump's Blacklist Squeezes 200 Chinese Companies as Net Widens", Nikkei Asia, 19 November 2019, https://asia.nikkei.com/Economy/Trade-war/Trump-s-blacklist-squeezes-200-Chinese-companies-as-net-widens

Kim, Hyun-Soo. "The 1992 Chinese Territorial Sea Law in the Light of the UN Convention." *The International and Comparative Law Quarterly* 43, no. 4 (1994): 894–904, http://www.jstor.org/stable/761006

Kim, Jack & Lee, Jae-won, "North Korea Shells South in Fiercest Attack in Decades", Reuters, 23 November 2010, https://www.reuters.com/article/us-korea-north-artillery-idUSTRE6AM0YS20101123

Kim, Jack & Macfie, "South Korea Urges World to Rein in Reclusive North", Reuters, 4 June 2010, https://www.reuters.com/article/idININdia-490387 20100604

Kruse, Kelvin, "Tom Cotton: Yes, Trump and Reagan Were a Lot Alike. That's Not a Good Thing", MSNBC Opinion, 10 March 2022, https://www.msnbc.com/opinion/msnbc-opinion/trump-reagan-were-more-alike-you-think-n1291315

Leahy, Joe & Cookson, Clive, "China Investigated Covid Lab Leak Claims, Says Top Scientist", Financial Times, 30 May 2023, https://www.ft.com/content/cd633f52-c2d2-4ee4-b940-d1bef6a5d910

Lee, Seow Ting, "Vaccine Diplomacy: Nation Branding and China's COVID-19 Soft Power Play". *Place Branding and Public Diplomacy* 19 (2023): 64–78. https://doi.org/10.1057/s41254-021-00224-4

Lemann, Nicholas, "The Republican Identity Crisis After Trump", The New Yorker, 23 October 2020, https://www.newyorker.com/magazine/2020/11/02/the-republican-identity-crisis-after-trump

Lewis, Renee, "Opponents React to SCOTUS Decision on Same-Sex Marriage", Aljazeera America, 26, http://america.aljazeera.com/articles/2015/6/26/right-wing-conservatives-react-to-scotus-decision.html

Lin, Bonny, Funaiole, Matthew P., Hart, Brian & Price, Hannah, "China Is Exploiting the Pandemic to Advance Its Interests, with Mixed Results", Center for Strategic and International Studies, 30 September 2021, https://www.csis.org/analysis/china-exploiting-pandemic-advance-its-interests-mixed-results

Lweis, Tanya, "The 'Shared Psychosis' of Donald Trump and His Loyalists", Scientific American, 11 January 2021, https://www.scientificamerican.com/article/the-shared-psychosis-of-donald-trump-and-his-loyalists/

MacAskill, Ewen & Goldenburg, Suzanne, "US Elections: Barack Obama wins Democratic Nomination for President", The Guardian, 4 June 2008, https://www.theguardian.com/world/2008/jun/04/barackobama.hillaryclinton

MacGillis, Alec, How Washington Blew Its Best Chance to Fix Immigration, 15 September 2016, https://www.propublica.org/article/washington-congress-immigration-reform-failure

Mahdawi, Arwa, "Why Are There So Many Trump Staff Memoirs? The Authors Need to Whitewash Their Reputations", The Guardian, 25 September 2021, https://www.theguardian.com/commentisfree/2021/sep/15/why-are-there-so-many-trump-staff-memoirs-the-authors-need-to-whitewash-their-reputations

Mahler, Jonathan, "Tenants Thwarted Donald Trump's Central Park Real Estate Ambitions", The New York Times, Feature on "Trump Investigations", 18 April 2016 https://www.nytimes.com/2016/04/19/us/politics/donald-trump-central-park-south.html

Mangan, Dan, "Read How Much Trump Paid—Or Didn't Pay—In Taxes Each Year", CNBC, 20 December 2022, https://www.cnbc.com/2022/12/21/trump-income-tax-returns-detailed-in-new-report-.html

Mangan, Don, & Berkeley, Lovelace, "Trump Suspects Coronavirus Outbreak Came From China Lab, Doesn't Cite Evidence", CNBC News, 30 April 2020, https://www.cnbc.com/2020/04/30/coronavirus-trump-suspects-covid-19-came-from-china-lab.html

Mascaro, Lisa, Tucker, Eric, Jalonick, Mary C and Taylor, Andrew, "Pro-Trump mob storms US Capitol in bid to overturn election", Associate Press, 6 Jan 2021, https://apnews.com/article/congress-confirm-joe-biden-78104aea082995bbd7412a6e6cd13818

McAdams, Dan, "The Mind of Donald Trump", The Atlantic, June 2016, https://www.theatlantic.com/magazine/archive/2016/06/the-mind-of-donald-trump/480771/

McKibbin, Warwick, "What would a Donald Trump trade war cost the Australian economy?", Brookings Commentary, 28 November 2016, https://www.brookings.edu/articles/what-would-a-donald-trump-trade-war-cost-the-australian-economy/

McNeil, Donald G., & Jacobs, Andrew, "Blaming China for Pandemic, Trump Says U.S. Will Leave the W.H.O.", The New York Times, 29 May 2020, https://www.nytimes.com/2020/05/29/health/virus-who.html

Meltzer, Joshua P., China's One Belt One Road Initiative: A View from the United States, Brookings, 19 June 2017, ASAN Forum National Commentaries, https://www.brookings.edu/articles/chinas-one-belt-one-road-initiative-a-view-from-the-united-states/

Miller, Laura, "I Read (Almost) Every Memoir by a Former Trump Official", Slate, 29 June 2020, https://slate.com/culture/2020/06/best-trump-books-memoirs-bolton-room-where-it-happened.html

Mizen, Ronald, "Australia's Allies Are Profiting From China Trade Bans", Australian Financial Review, 17 September 2021, https://www.afr.com/politics/federal/australia-s-allies-are-profiting-from-china-trade-bans-20210913-p58rar

MOFA (Ministry of Foreign Affairs Japan), "Japan-United States of America, Relations", Index on Japan-US Security Consultative Committee (2+2) Meetings, 11 January 2023, https://www.mofa.go.jp/region/n-america/us/security/scc/index.html

Moynihan, Donald, Populism and the Deep State: The Attack on Public Service Under Trump in Bauer, Michael, Peters, Guy, Pierre, Jon, Yesilagit,Kutsal, and Becker, Stefan, Democratic Backsliding and Public Administration How Populists in Government Transform State Bureaucracies, Cambridge, Cambridge University Press, 2021, pp. 151–177. https://doi.org/10.1017/9781009023504.008

Murray, Mark, "12 Days That Stunned a Nation: How Hillary Clinton Lost", NBC News, 23 August 2017, https://www.nbcnews.com/politics/elections/12-days-stunned-nation-how-hillary-clinton-lost-n794131

Nakamura, David, "Obama Comment on Immigration Draws Anger, Frustration", The Washington Post, 18 September 2013, https://www.washingtonpost.com/politics/obama-comment-on-immigration-draws-anger-frustration/2013/09/18/0a6b4da6-2082-11e3-8459-657e0c72fec8_story.html

Nature Editorial, "Coronavirus: The First Three Months as it Happened", Nature, News Article, 22 April 2020, https://www.nature.com/articles/d41586-020-00154-w

Nesbit, Jeff, "Donald Trump's Many, Many, Many, Many Ties to Russia", Time, 15 August 2016a, https://time.com/4433880/donald-trump-ties-to-russia/

Nestbit, Jeff, "The Secret Origins of the Tea Party: How Big Oil and Big Tobacco Partnered with the Koch Brothers and Take Over the GOP", Time Magazine, 2016 Editorial, https://time.com/secret-origins-of-the-tea-party/

New York Times, "Rare Protest in Vietnam Raises a Call to Curb China", The New York Times, 3 June 2013, https://www.nytimes.com/2013/06/03/world/asia/rare-protest-in-vietnam-raises-call-to-curb-china.html

Nguyen, Thanh Trung, "The Cauldron Boils Over: Vietnam Versus China", Asia Maritime Transparency Initiative, 20 April 2020, https://amti.csis.org/the-cauldron-boils-over-vietnam-vs-china/

Nye, Joesph, "Trump's Transactional Myopia", Project Syndicate Commentary, 4 February 2020, https://www.project-syndicate.org/commentary/trump-renounces-key-ingredients-of-american-global-leadership-by-joseph-s-nye-2020-02?barrier=accesspaylog

O'Brien, Robert, (ed) Trump on China: Putting America First, White House, 2 November 2020, Archives Publication, https://trumpwhitehouse.archives.gov/wp-content/uploads/2020/11/Trump-on-China-Putting-America-First.pdf

O'Brien, Robert, "A Free and Open Indo-Pacific" (Declassified Framework), White House Released Statement, 5 January 2021, https://trumpwhitehouse.archives.gov/wp-content/uploads/2021/01/OBrien-Expanded-Statement.pdf

OECD, China's Belt and Road Initiative in the Global Trade, Investment and Finance Landscape, OECD Business and Finance Outlook 2018, OECD Publishing Paris, https://doi.org/10.1787/bus_fin_out-2018-6-en

Palmer, Doug, "U.S., India Resolve Trade Disputes, Launch 'New Beginning'", Politicopro, 22 June 2023, https://subscriber.politicopro.com/article/2023/06/u-s-india-resolve-trade-disputes-launch-new-beginning-00103269

Peters, Jeremy W. "The Tea Party Didn't Get What It Wanted, but It Did Unleash the Politics of Anger", The New York Times, 30 August 2019, https://www.nytimes.com/2019/08/28/us/politics/tea-party-trump.html

Pew Survey, "Conflicting Partisan Priorities for U.S. Foreign Policy", Pew Research Center, 29 November 2018, https://www.pewresearch.org/politics/2018/11/29/conflicting-partisan-priorities-for-u-s-foreign-policy/

Phillips, Tom, China Says Trump's Pick of Hostile Trade Adviser is 'No Laughing Matter', 23 December 2016, https://www.theguardian.com/world/2016/dec/23/china-says-trumps-pick-of-hostile-trade-adviser-is-no-laughing-matter

Phillips, Tom, "Philippine President Compares China's Expansion to Nazi Germany", The Telegraph, 5 February 2014, https://www.telegraph.co.uk/news/worldnews/asia/china/10618722/Philippine-president-compares-Chinas-expansion-to-Nazi-Germany.html

Raymond Zhong, "Chinese Tech Giant on Brink of Collapse in New U.S. Cold War", The New York Times, 9 May 2018, https://www.nytimes.com/2018/05/09/technology/zte-china-us-trade-war.html

Reagan Library, The Reagan Presidency, National Archives Write Up, n.d. https://www.reaganlibrary.gov/reagans/reagan-administration/reagan-presidency

Reagan, Ronald, Farewell Address to the Nation 11 January 1989, https://www.reaganlibrary.gov/archives/speech/farewell-address-nation

Reilly, Katie, "Read Hillary Clinton's 'Basket of Deplorables' Remarks About Donald Trump Supporters", Time, 10 September 2016, https://time.com/4486502/hillary-clinton-basket-of-deplorables-transcript/

Remnick, David, "Obama Reckons With a Trump Presidency", The New Yorker, 18 November 2016, https://www.newyorker.com/magazine/2016/11/28/obama-reckons-with-a-trump-presidency

Reuters, "Obama says Japanese Leader's Pearl Harbor Visit Shows Power of Reconciliation", Reuters, 28 December 2016a, https://www.reuters.com/article/us-usa-japan-pearlharbor-obama-idUSKBN14G1TA

Reuters, "'A Bloody and Desperate Fight:' U.S. Prosecutors Release Oath Keepers' Communications", Reuters News, 14 January 2022a, https://www.reuters.com/world/us/a-bloody-desperate-fight-us-prosecutors-release-oath-keepers-communications-2022-01-13/

Reuters, Russia's Prigozhin Admits Interfering in U.S. Elections, 8 November 2022, https://www.reuters.com/world/us/russias-prigozhin-admits-interfering-us-elections-2022-11-07/

Reuters, "Top China Diplomat to Visit Vietnam Amid Oil Rig Row", Reuters World News, 17 June 2014, https://www.reuters.com/article/china-vietnam-idINKBN0ES0NG20140617

Rich, Motoko, "Approach to US-Japan Ties Maybe Tested", The New York Times, 27 December 2016, https://www.nytimes.com/2016/12/27/world/asia/shinzo-abe-barack-obama-alliance.html

Rogers, Katie, & Mandavilli, Apoorva, "Trump Administration Signals Formal Withdrawal From W.H.O.", The New York Times, 7 July 2020, https://www.nytimes.com/2020/07/07/us/politics/coronavirus-trump-who.html

Rogers, Katie, Jakes, Lara, & Swanson, Ana, "Trump Defends Using 'Chinese Virus' Label, Ignoring Growing Criticism", The New York Times, 18 March 2021, https://www.nytimes.com/2020/03/18/us/politics/china-virus.html

Rogin, Josh, "Congress is investigating whether the 2019 Military World Games in Wuhan was a covid-19 superspreader event", The Washington Post, 23 June 2021 https://www.washingtonpost.com/opinions/2021/06/23/congress-wuhan-military-games-2019-covid/

Rossow, Richard, "U.S.-India Trade Turbulence: Quieter, Not Gone", CSIS Newsletter, 28 September 2022, https://www.csis.org/analysis/us-india-trade-turbulence-quieter-not-gone

Ryan, MacKenzie, "Proud Boys and Oath Keepers: What Is Their Future With Top Leaders Jailed?" The Guardian, 13 May 2023, https://www.theguardian.com/us-news/2023/may/13/proud-boys-oath-keepers-future-arrest-of-leaders

Salcedo, Andrea, "Racist Anti-Asian Hashtags Spiked After Trump First Tweeted 'Chinese Virus,' Study Finds", The Washington Post, 19 March 2021, https://www.washingtonpost.com/nation/2021/03/19/trump-tweets-chinese-virus-racist/

Sargent, Greg, "Trump Doesn't Have America's Best Interests At Heart", The Washington Post, 6 March 2018, https://www.washingtonpost.com/blogs/plum-line/wp/2018/03/06/trump-doesnt-have-americas-best-interests-at-heart/

Schupmann, Bejamin, Why is Former US President Donald Trump Still So Influential? https://www.channelnewsasia.com/commentary/donald-trump-popular-america-republican-party-us-election-biden-2314381

Sen, Ashish Kumar, "Trump's reversal of North Korea sanctions sends a dangerous signal", Atlantic Council, 22 March 2019, https://www.atlanticcouncil.org/blogs/new-atlanticist/trump-s-reversal-of-north-korea-sanctions-sends-a-dangerous-signal/

Siebold, Sabine, Emmott, Robin, "Pressed by Trump Over Defense, Germany Says Can Pay More for NATO Running Costs", Reuters, 11 October 2019, https://www.reuters.com/article/us-germany-nato-usa/pressed-by-trump-over-defense-germany-says-can-pay-more-for-nato-running-costs-idUSKBN1WQ1YR/

Sieg, Linda, and Brunnstrom, David, "Japan's Abe Hopes Promises on Jobs, Defence Will Temper Trump's Tone on Trade", Reuters, 8 February 2017. https://www.reuters.com/article/idUSKBN15N0PO/

Sisak, Michael, "Donald Trump Was a Fraud for Years as He Built a Real-estate Empire Off Loans From Wall Street, Judge Rules:

'That is a Fantasy World, Not the Real World'", Fortune, 22 September 2023, https://fortune.com/2023/09/26/donald-trump-fraud-banks-insurers-real-estate-judge-new-york/

Smith, David, "Mattis Details Differences With Trump Over NATO Allies and Torture in New Book", The Guardian, 28 August 2019, https://www.theguardian.com/us-news/2019/aug/28/james-mattis-call-sign-chaos-trump-memoir-book

Smith, Sheila, Our Anxiety as the President Heads to Asia, Council for Foreign Relations, 18 April 2014, https://www.cfr.org/blog/our-anxiety-president-heads-asia

Soon, Stella, "India Could be a Winner in the US-China Trade War", CNBC, 18 September2019, https://www.cnbc.com/2019/09/19/india-could-be-a-winner-in-the-us-china-trade-war.html

Stepan, Alfred, "Unchecked Trump", The Atlantic, 12 November 2016, https://www.project-syndicate.org/commentary/trump-election-checks-and-balances-by-alfred-stepan-2016-11

Stiglitz, Jospeh, The Price of Inequality: How Today's Divided Society Endangers Our Future, W.W. Norton & Company, 2012

Stout, David, "Philippine President Slams Beijing for Acting like Nazis in the South China Sea", Time, 3 June 2015, https://time.com/3906811/philippines-china-nazi-germany/

Straits Times Editorial, Trump Tech War With China Changes the Game for US Business, https://www.straitstimes.com/world/united-states/trump-tech-war-with-china-changes-the-game-for-us-business

Sullivan, Eileen, "Five Policy Clashes Between John Bolton and President Trump", New York Times, 10 September 2019a, https://www.nytimes.com/2019/09/10/us/politics/trump-bolton.html#:~:text=at%20her%20funeral.-,Mr.,of%20the%20negotiations%20blamed%20Mr

Sullivan, Kate, "The Trump Decision that Pushed James Mattis to His Breaking Point", CNN Politics, 1 September 2019b, https://edition.cnn.com/2019/09/01/politics/james-mattis-trump-breaking-point-syria/index.html

Sullivan, Laura & Schuknecht, Cat, "Inside The White House's Bitter Fight Over China", NPR, 7 May 2019, https://www.npr.org/2019/05/07/719947020/inside-the-white-houses-bitter-fight-over-china

Swanson, Ana & Goel, Vindu, "Trump Administration Strips India of Special Trade Status", The New York Times, 31 May 2019, https://www.nytimes.com/2019/05/31/business/trump-india-trade.html

Tan, Su-Lin, "US Exports to China Grow at 'Expense' of Australia After Beijing's Trade Ban", The South China Morning Post, 19 May 2021, https://www.scmp.com/economy/global-economy/article/3133952/us-exports-china-grow-expense-australia-after-beijings-trade

Taniguchi, Tomohiko, President Obama's Hiroshima Visit: How It Happened and Why No Apology Was Expected in Japan, Sasakawa USA, https://spfusa.org/publications/president-obamas-hiroshima-visit-happened-no-apology-expected-japan/

Taylor, Scott, "Donald Trump: Just How Good a Businessman Is He?" The Conversation, 28 January 2016, https://theconversation.com/donald-trump-just-how-good-a-businessman-is-he-53713

The Guardian, 12 December 2021, https://www.theguardian.com/books/2021/dec/12/trump-memoirs-mark-meadows-kayleigh-mcenany-peter-navarro-scott-atlas

The Koch Foundation is Trying To Reshape Foreign Policy, https://www.nytimes.com/interactive/2019/09/10/magazine/charles-koch-foundation-education.html

The Standard, "US "Intentionally Released the Covid Virus in Wuhan" EU Summit Told". The Standard (HK) News, 22 May 2023, https://www.thestandard.com.hk/section-news/section/11/252653/US-%27intentionally-released-Covid-virus-in-Wuhan%27-EU-summit-told

The White House, "Economic Report of the President", Final Economic Report of the Obama Administration (2017 Council of Economic Advisers Annual Report), January 2017, https://www.gpo.gov/fdsys/pkg/ERP-2017/pdf/ERP-2017.pdf

Thoma, Mark, "How much impact can a president have on the economy?", CBS, 31 August 2016, https://www.cbsnews.com/news/how-much-impact-can-a-president-have-on-the-economy/

Trump, Donald, "1987 Interview Larry King Live", Youtube Video, 19 February 2016, https://www.youtube.com/watch?v=A8wJc7vHcTs

Trump, Donald, "Does Trump Think George W. Bush Lied About Iraq?" CNN, 2 September 1987, https://www.youtube.com/watch?v=iiw0ILaXJf0

Trump, Donald, "The Fake News Media", Twitter, 18 February 2017, https://twitter.com/realDonaldTrump/status/832708293516632065

Trump, Donald, Tweet "Crooked H Destroyed Phones", 16 June 2017a https://twitter.com/realDonaldTrump/status/875441788110110727?ref_src=twsrc%5Etfw%7Ctwcamp%5Etweetembed%7Ctwterm%5E87544178811 0110727%7Ctwgr%5E00f542afc907de60f51ed188e9ee5e5620260b05%7Ctwcon%5Es1_&ref_url=https%3A%2F%2Ftime.com%2F4820708%2Fdonald-trump-russia-investigation-hillary-clinton-obstruction%2F

Trump, Donald, Tweet "Just Remember, the Birther Movement was Started by Hillary Clinton in 2008. She Was All In!" 23 September 2015, https://twitter.com/realDonaldTrump/status/646508464085311488?ref_src=twsrc%5Etfw%7Ctwcamp%5Etweetembed%7Ctwterm%5E646508464085311488%7Ctwgr%5E8324dbb8b1a124aa3d71ae5517c74c3b8e75636c%7Ctwcon%5Es1_&ref_url=https%3A%2F%2Fabcnews.go.com%2FPolitics%2F67-times-donald-trump-tweeted-birther-movement%2Fstory%3Fid%3D42145590

Turnbull, Malcolm, "Former Australian PM Malcolm Turnbull on Donald Trump: 'You don't suck up to bullies'", The Guardian, 20 May 2020, https://www.theguardian.com/australia-news/2020/apr/20/malcolm-turnbull-on-donald-trump-you-dont-suck-up-to-bullies

Unger, Craig, "Donald Trump Was Everything Vladimir Putin Could Have Wished for", The New Republic, 3 March 2022, https://newrepublic.com/article/165553/donald-trump-everything-vladimir-putin-wished-russian-asset

UNICEF, "North Korea Rejects Offer of Nearly 3 Million Sinovac COVID-19 Shots", Cited in Reuters, 1 September 2021, https://www.reuters.com/world/asia-pacific/north-korea-turns-down-sinovac-covid-19-vaccine-doses-wsj-2021-09-01/

US Census, Top Trading Partner, United States Government Census Service. n.d. https://www.census.gov/foreign-trade/statistics/highlights/top/index.html#2009

USNews, Is China Testing the Obama Administration? 11 March 2009, https://www.usnews.com/opinion/articles/2009/03/11/is-china-testing-the-obama-administration

Versoulis, Abby, "Mattis Quit After Trump's Syria Pullout. Here Are All the Times He Publicly Split With the President", Time, 20 December 2018, https://time.com/5486300/james-mattis-disagree-donald-trump/

VOA (Voice of America) "Challenging Beijing in the South China Sea", Voice of American News Blog, 31 July 2012, https://blogs.voanews.com/state-department-news/2012/07/31/challenging-beijing-in-the-south-china-sea/

Walker, Chris, "Trump Ranks Last in "Moral Authority" in Survey of Presidents", The Truthout, 30 June 2021, https://truthout.org/articles/trump-ranks-last-in-moral-authority-in-survey-of-presidents/

Webster, Graham, "2015: The Year US-China Relations Went Public", The Diplomat, 23 December 2015, https://thediplomat.com/2015/12/2015-the-year-us-china-relations-went-public/

White House, "Executive Order on Securing the Information and Communications Technology and Services Supply Chain", Executive Order, 15 May 2019, https://trumpwhitehouse.archives.gov/presidential-actions/executive-order-securing-information-communications-technology-services-supply-chain/

White House, "President Obama Meets with Prime Minister Abe of Japan", Obama White House Archives, 22 February 2013, https://obamawhiteho use.archives.gov/blog/2013/02/22/president-obama-meets-prime-minister-abe-japan

White House, "Remarks by President Obama and Prime Minister Abe after Bilateral Meeting", Obama White House Archives, 25 May 2016a (Before G7 Meeting/Okinawa Rape Case), https://obamawhitehouse.archives.gov/the-press-office/2016/05/25/remarks-president-obama-and-prime-minister-abe-after-bilateral-meeting

White House, "Remarks by President Obama and Prime Minister Abe of Japan in Joint Press Conference", Obama White House Archives, 28 April 2015 (Arlington Memorial Visit), https://obamawhitehouse.archives.gov/the-press-office/2015/04/28/remarks-president-obama-and-prime-minister-abe-japan-joint-press-confere

White House, "Remarks by President Obama and Prime Minister Abe of Japan at Hiroshima Peace Memorial", Obama White House Archives, 27 May 2016b (Hiroshima Peace Memorial), https://obamawhitehouse.archives.gov/the-press-office/2016/05/27/remarks-president-obama-and-prime-minister-abe-japan-hiroshima-peace

White House, "Remarks by President Obama and Prime Minister Abe of Japan at Pearl Harbor", Obama White House Archives, 27 December 2016c (Pearl Harbour), https://obamawhitehouse.archives.gov/the-press-office/2016/12/28/remarks-president-obama-and-prime-minister-abe-japan-pearl-harbor

White, Martha, "Eight Years Later: The Economy and President Obama's Legacy", NBC News, 6 January 2017, https://www.nbcnews.com/storyl ine/president-obama-the-legacy/eight-years-later-economy-president-obama-s-legacy-n703616

Whitehouse, "President's 2011 Asia Pacific Trip", The Whitehouse Obama Archive, 19 November 2011, https://obamawhitehouse.archives.gov/issues/australia-and-indonesia-2011

Witcher, Marcus, Getting Right With Reagan: The Struggle for True Conservatism, 1980–2016, Kansas, University of Kansas, 2019, https://www.jstor.org/stable/j.ctvx8b7f4

Wright, Teresa, "PM Trudeau Bills 10-year Defence Spending Plan as Answer to Trump's Persistent Demand", CTV News, 12 July 2018, https://www.ctv news.ca/politics/pm-trudeau-bills-10-year-defence-spending-plan-as-answer-to-trump-s-persistent-demand-1.4010355

Zelizer, Julian,The Presidency of Barack Obama, New Jersey: Princeton University Press, 2018

CHAPTER 4

The Era of the Conservatives and Australia's Relations with China and the United States

With a population of 21 million people scattered in cities mostly along coastal cities, Australia's mainland occupies itself on a continent that is separated away from its nearest neighbours by significant distances - New Zealand (1500 km), Papua New Guinea (2368 km), Indonesia (3457 km) and China (7448 km). Australia's isolated geographical location and size, as well as its natural oceanic barrier, means that it is almost impossible for any nation to mount an invasion of Australia's mainland. The Japanese Wartime Prime Minister Hideki Tojo had actually considered the idea of doing so but eventually dismissed it as unfeasible.

The coming of age of Australia as a political and strategical independent entity did not come easy. After all, London rather than Canberra had been calling the shots in Australia until October 1942. It was only with the passage of the 1942 Statute of Westminster Adoption Act where Australia achieved full legislative independence. The Australia Act of 1986 in the United Kingdom removed the right of the UK Parliament to make laws, ended the role of the British government in the governance of Australia and removed the right of appeal from Australia courts to the Privy Council in London. After Australia's experience of fighting Japan during the Second World War, the Labor Prime Minister Ben Chifley accelerated Australia's immigration program from Europe to ensure that Australia would have the demographic mass to fight any future menace from the North. His successor Liberal Party

© The Author(s), under exclusive license to Springer Nature Singapore Pte Ltd. 2024
V. Teo, *Cold War Redux Amidst Great Power Rivalry*, https://doi.org/10.1007/978-981-97-3733-8_4

219

Prime Minister Robert Menzies aligned Australia with the United States, partaking with Australia's Second World War ally in the Cold War. For much of Australia's modern existence, Australia has been deeply integrated as a member of the West—particularly with the United Kingdom and the United States. Australia's experience in fighting the Japanese during the Second World War, the North Koreans and the Chinese during the Korean War, and the Vietnamese during the Indo-China War shaped early Australian outlook towards the Asian region.

Australia's foreign relations after the Second War were guided by two important Treaties: the 1951 ANZUS Treaty with the United States and New Zealand (against Japanese rearmament) and the 1954 SEATO agreement with Southeast Asia to counter the spread of Communism (ended 1977). In both the Korean War and the Indochinese War, Australia supported the United States against Communist China and Vietnam. From a foreign policy standpoint, it would not be an exaggeration to suggest that even though Australia is physically stuck in the Asia–Pacific, her heart and soul will always be with Washington and London. Indeed, as one scholar puts it, much of Australia's anxiety today is driven by the fact that it is "an isolated European outpost on the edge of Asia" (Curran, 2022).

Australia's self-identification with Asia was never easy or natural. During the First World War, even Chinese Australians were not regarded as "European" enough to die for their country (Young, 2019). The legacy of the White Australia policy has left a residual legacy that many in Australia are reluctant to admit. Consequently, there has always been a degree of pattern of uncertainty with regard to how she should behave and who she should be allied with in the aftermath of the Vietnam War. Australia's first real attempt at connecting with Asia came only in the 1970s. Whitlam had created a foreign policy change based on a new domestic consensus based on the elimination of fear, racism and prejudice that worked well for East Asia (Woodard, 2005). Australia also reconciled with Japan in 1952 with the establishment of diplomatic relations and exchange of ambassadors and signed a Basic Treaty of Friendship and Cooperation in 1976. The Indochinese Wars highlighted the importance of human rights in Australia's foreign policy and the multiple pressures it faces as a modern nation-state that needed to be more in tune with changes in its democratic impulses, geopolitical realities and larger strategic environment.

Canberra, therefore, faces a certain conflict in being able to reconcile the orientation and maintenance of relations with her Asian neighbours, some of whom are amongst the most egregious human rights violators, with her desire to build close economic ties, versus the maintenance and allegiance to the United States. The importance of Asia to Australia's future economically and strategically and the desire to adhere to her "true" Western allies have put increased pressure on how Canberra acts in her foreign relations. At the heart of this dilemma is Canberra's self-identity as a member of the advance Western democratic fraternity and its location in the Asia–Pacific. The importance of the Asian region is not lost to Australia, particularly with the lessons learnt from the Japanese invasion, the threat posed by the spread of Communism and the experience of the Cold War, contextualised against the promise of rapidly rising regional economies.

LEVEL ONE: THE POLITICAL LEADERSHIP

The Rise of Conservatives

As a mature democracy, Australia's politics is significantly different from Quad countries such as Japan, India or the United States particularly when it comes to the emergence of charismatic populist leaders. Unlike Japan, India and the United States where populist leaders such as Abe, Modi and Trump emerged, Australia's system saw the rise of three right-of-centre leaders from 2013 onwards. Even though Australian politics has to a large extent shifted rightwards from the 1990s onwards with the election of John Howard, Australians have never seen themselves as having the kind of security challenges that Japanese or Indians faced in recent years. How Australians have interpreted their relationship with China and the United States is therefore more "balanced" in this respect as most understand the importance of China to Australia's national growth. It is this sentiment that most politicians, even those from the Liberal Party are able to accurately premise their China policy on. John Howard for instance was just as fixated on growing Australia's trade with China just as he was in supporting the United States. The kind of "trade off" that the Prime Ministers of the last decade saw was never something the Howard administration did try to implement even though Canberra at that time was interested in security hedging against Beijing and Moscow. In order to understand what transpired changes in Australian politics, and particularly Australia's reorientation towards China from 2013 onwards, it is essential that we examine the rise of Tony Abbott, Macolm Turnbull and Scott Morrison and understand their personality and politics vis-à-vis their agenda and thinking on China. There are important preliminaries to point out if one needs to understand why Australia is unable to produce charismatic right-wing leaders in the likes of Abe or Modi or even Trump. While not impossible, it would be unlikely for such personalities to emerge in Australia for a few reasons as follows.

First, unlike the United States, Australia's parliamentary system means that the Prime Minister is not nationally elected, as the leader of the largest bloc of lawmakers after the election is named Prime Minister and forms the government. There is no need to wait for four years before an unpopular leader can be deposed. Lawmakers can actually revolt by calling a leadership spill (leadership contest) and pick a new leader if they did not like the existing leader with no feedback from the voters and little repercussions. Such a system creates great political pressure and paranoia for incumbents, while fermenting conditions for infighting if no dominant leaders exist. Australia has been known in some quarters as the "coup capital of the Pacific" (Perrigo, 2018).

Second, Australia's history of mature bipartisan politics meant that there was little room for any one party to dominate in national politics. Although there have been historical instances of very well like leaders who have been in office for three or more terms, there is still a healthy tendency of turnover of power in Australia's recent history between parties. Unlike Japan, Australia has never been dominated by a single party almost over the duration of its entire post-war history. The dynamics of Australia's democracy is much healthier. Neither the Labor nor Liberal party has domineering control or influence over the country's corporate or social media or other important institutions central to the smooth functioning of a democracy.

Third, Australia's factional politics are often alliances based on loose partnerships or groups predicated on political outlook and expediency, implicitly paying less attention to seniority or hierarchy. Unlike Japan, it would be difficult to think of any politicians that can emerge and have a stranglehold on Australian politics, no matter how well-credentialed, articulate or persuasive the person is. While factions exist, they cannot be likened to the dynamics we see in Japanese politics. In short, it is rather difficult for dominant charismatic personalities such as Abe or Modi to emerge in Australian politics.

Fourth, a strong and vibrant healthy voter culture means that there is little room for personality cults and worship in contemporary Australian politics. Even though there have been some very dominant political leaders in the course of post-War Australia, recent history have shown that Australian Prime Ministers are now finding it very difficult to hold onto power. Voters are sceptical, discerning and less apathetic than their counterparts—a direct result of the greater liberalism, varied media discourse and democratic culture in the country. In today's Australia, Prime Ministers are more at risk of losing their job than their counterparts in Japan, in India or in the United States. It is not just that politics have become more treacherous nor opponents formidable, it is because we now live in a hyper-information age where no one has a monopoly on the flow of information, finance and discursive power. In an advanced democracy, corporate and social media are just as easily used against an incumbent Prime Minister just as the existing government attempts to control and manipulate them for their own ends. The key here is that it cuts both ways, as popular Prime Ministers who have come on the back of popular support riding on social and corporate media often find themselves on the receiving end of endless criticisms and attacks on social media too.

Fifth, due to the history of Australia and the multiculturalist orientation of the nation, the articulation of nationalism has limited functionality in Australian parliamentary politics in the decades after the 1970s. Australians have never had the likes of an "external" enemy like India has in Pakistan nor Japan in China or North Korea. Australian politicians have traditionally find it extremely difficult to champion the kind of nationalism articulated in India's majoritarian politics or Shinzo Abe's cultural-statist nationalism. The "imagined" other comes therefore not from politicians pointing their fingers at a close neighbour infringing on their territory or one who had fought historical battles, but more from threats to Australia's heritage or historical legacy. In Australia's contemporary nationalism, the only battles that right-wing conservatives can harken to are the battles that Australia fought during the most recent wars in the nation's history, and the more contemporary ones where Australia's way of life is being "threatened" by immigration.

In May 2011, nearly ten years after 9/11, President Obama announced that an American Special Operations Force had killed Osama bin Laden in Pakistan, putting a de facto end to the War on Terror. Australia had by then already committed approximately 1550 soldiers to the NATO-led International Security Assistance Force (ISAF) in Afghanistan, with the hope that Australia would be able to transfer control of the operations to the Afghanistan government by 2014 (Watt, 2010). Julia Gillard, the Labor Prime Minister who had succeeded in replacing Kevin Rudd in June 2010 was in her own words, "uncomfortable with the handling of foreign relations". Even as the Rudd–Gillard rivalry played out into the open, Australia under Labor was moving to align her position much more closely with the United States even as Gillard was also trying hard to restore Beijing's relationship with Canberra (ACCIW 2015b). The intense rivalry between Rudd–Gillard however hurt the Labor's political capital and paved the way for the election of Tony Abbott. With the political pendulum swinging sharply to the right, Abbott's ascendance coincided with the rise of a global right-wing populism.

What this essentially means is that this broad momentum brought to the fore the rise of populist politicians who pandered to right-wing agendas as the world saw a broad rightward shift in mainstream politics. Whether it is centre-of-left or conservative, most politicians have changed the rhetoric if not substance to embrace right-wing policies. This global movement has not eluded the Australian public nor the politicians, and by 2013, we see the rise of three political personalities that bore a strong imprint on Australian politics. Unlike in the case of India, Japan and the United States, there isn't one particular Prime Minister we can attribute Australia's worsening relations with China with but to at least four of them. Even though they all have broadly different backgrounds and personalities, their worldview and outlook are essentially the same, particularly with regard to Australia's China policy (Laurenceson 2016). Over the course of a decade, they completely altered the course of Australia's relations with China that the Whitlam government had managed to put in place since the 1970s.

Unlike the case in Japan or India, the outlook of Australian Prime Ministers did not play an extraordinary role in the determination of Australia's China policy. This is to say that in Canberra's case, we do not see someone as invested in wrecking Australia's friendship or singling out Beijing as the "enemy" in such a fundamental way as Japan's Shinzo Abe or India's Narendra Modi. This of course is relative—as all the Prime Ministers during the period of study had in effect articulated a brand of nationalism that broadly emphasises the essence of Australian "tradition" heavily premised on their cultural and identity ties with the United States and United Kingdom.

The events of September 2001 have compelled the Howard government to broaden its horizons and to interpret global events as having an important impact not only on Australia's foreign policy but also on domestic politics. The blurring of lines between what is "foreign" and "domestic" was not lost on the Prime Minister nor his cabinet colleagues, as the Howard Administration began to advocate for a foreign policy that closely associated with the United States, even to the extent of joining the Iraq War that was waged on false evidence (APMD, 2001). This urge to closely associate with the United States is of course not new, and arguably has been the central tendency of Australian foreign relations since its independence from the United Kingdom. Even though Howard was one of the most successful Prime Ministers in post-war Australia with four successive terms, Kevin Rudd a former diplomat and a "China hand" managed to defeat Howard's run as Prime Minister by campaigning on generational change, fiscal prudence and the modification of Australia's stance on the War in Iraq. Rudd had argued that Howard's policy of supporting US-led attacks had not been able to be able to prevent terrorist attacks such as those in the Madrid Train attacks; that there was no link between Weapons of Mass Destruction and the Iraqi regime; that foreign policy of states considered "rogue" have not been modified and that there has been little humanitarian assistance in Iraq (France24, 2008). Ultimately it was the domestic opposition to Australia's commitment to the unpopular war in Iraq and public fatigue with Howard that led to the downfall of the liberals. The attack on Howard and Australia's participation in the Iraqi War saw Labor winning the election. Once again the tensions of how Australia is aligning itself with its traditional ally have come under question. Kevin Rudd, the leader of the opposition with little Federal government experience replaced Howard as the Prime Minister of Australia. As a student of Chinese history and language and a diplomat, Rudd's knowledge of foreign relations was appreciated by the Australian electorate, but at the same time, he too must have appreciated the gravity of attacking the incumbent Prime Minister's alliance with the United States, given Washington's propensity to frown upon such acts of leaders in allied countries (Matovinovic 2022). As someone who had studied Chinese history and language in Taiwan during his student days, Rudd tried to capitalise on himself as a Beijing "whisperer" by showing what he could win over and influence the Chinese. As leader of the opposition, he managed to "upstaged" John Howard at the Sydney APEC summit by addressing Chinese President Hu Jintao in Chinese (Dubecki 2007; Sydney Morning Herald, 2007), with his election he was hailed by the Chinese media (Reuters, 2007). While the Chinese media boost was no doubt appreciated, anyone in Beijing who thought that Rudd would change Australia policy radically was sorely mistaken. Any such thinking would be wishful thinking on the part of the Chinese officials (or more accurately the Chinese media). Rudd did not make a major shift on Australia's foreign policy but chose to keep Howard's foreign policy intact through maintaining excellent trilateral ties with Japan and the United States. Rudd, who was supposed to have excellent China expertise kept Australia on relatively good terms with Beijing (Marr 2010). During a four-day visit to China in 2008, where he called for Beijing to adopt a synthesis of "harmonious world" and "responsible stakeholder" by working to "maintain and develop the global and regional rules-based order", emphasing China and Australia could become true friends where both countries could go "beyond immediate interests" to become a partner predicated on "broader and firm basis for continuing, profound and sincere friendship" (Rudd, 2008). In the same speech, he rejected calls for boycotts of the Beijing Olympics even though Australia too had concerns about human rights in Tibet. However, by 2009, Rudd's administration had brought Australia's relations with China to a new low with a series of incidents. First, Beijing reacted angrily to the release of Australia's Defense Whitepaper in 2009 where Canberra highlighted China's military modernisation to be an item of concern. There was a controversy over China's arrest of Australian Rio Tinto executive Stern Hu on bribery and espionage charges and over Australia's granting of a visa to Ughyur World Congress President Rebiya Kadeer. Despite Rudd's proclamation of his "expertise", it was clear that Australia–China relations dove to a low point during his tenure as Prime Minister. During the climate conference in Copenhagen in 2009 which the likes of Barrack Obama, and Gordon Brown were attending. Rudd believing that the Chinese were trying to sabotage any deal that involved binding obligations and international monitoring, was alleged to have said "Those Chinese fuckers are trying to rat-fuck us" in the West's negotiations with China. For better or for worse, it might be just as what Rudd had wanted. His successor Julia Gillard ironically managed to build better relations with China, even has she retained Rudd as Foreign Minister (September 2010 to February

2012). Owing to her own symbiotic and yet competitive political relationship with Rudd, Gillard has never had any disagreement with her predecessor over foreign policy while she was the Deputy Prime Minister. Gillard managed to bring Australia–China back on track agreeing with Beijing to annual leadership talks and provided Canberra with greater access than any other Western powers (Kenny, 2013). She was however happy to leave the planning of specific initiatives to Rudd, knowing that political longevity hinges on domestic rather than foreign policy performance, and thus has located herself in the mainstream of Australia's diplomatic tradition playing a pragmatic role instead(Fullilove, 2010). There is no question that because of Gillard's conservative approach to foreign relations enabled Beijing to take her more cautiously and more seriously than Rudd. After all, Gillard had declared that Australia could maintain a close strategic alliance with the United States while also enhancing its friendship with China (Buckley, 2011). This policy essentially continued through Rudd's second term of three months as Prime Minister.

Australia's approach towards China since the Howard Administration has therefore been one of "engage and hedge". This is true for all the different administrations from Howard to Rudd to Gillard to Rudd (2nd) to Abbott: each of these administrations did not see the need to give up Australia's expanding relations with China even as they sought closer relations with the United States. Whether it is Liberal or Labor, making money with China is almost as important as obtaining security from the United States—the only real difference is how they spoke about and discuss China—but the underlying substance is not all that different. This of course does not mean that Beijing would interpret or receive their approaches all the same as evidenced by the development of Australia-China relations in the decade under study.

The Liberal-National Prime Ministers

The ascendance of Tony Abbott in 2013 as Australia's Prime Minister is a story that mirrored what happened six years before when Kevin Rudd managed to depose popular Conservative Prime Minister John Howard. Abbott had basically inherited the Gillard–Rudd foreign policy structure and made very little adjustments to it. Gillard had helped coordinate and adjust Australia's posture to match Barack Obama's "pivot to Asia" when he visited Australia and announced the stationing of marines in Darwin. By 2012, Gillard had already banned Huawei from participation in Australia's National Broadband Network on national security grounds—even though at the same time, Australia was looking to cultivate and bring her economic relations with China onto a higher plane. Gillard conducted a successful visit to China and actually orchestrated Beijing to participate in a high-level dialogue. She had also effectively softened Australia's tone on China's military buildup and Canberra's concerns on issues such as developments in Beijing's South China Sea manoeuvres and human rights transgressions. Rudd who deposed Gillard three months later too sought to build on the achievements of Gillard's government by continuing to improve Australia's relations with China and at the same time deepening security collaboration with the Americans. In the three months he was in power, Rudd effectively endorsed Gillard's Australia in the Asian Century White Paper, and while trying to accelerate the Free Trade Agreement negotiations with the United States.

Tony Abbott

Tony Abbott became Prime Minister by defeating Rudd in an election. Abbott was a British national, being born to a British father and an Australian mother in Lambeth London, United Kingdom in 1957. At the age of three, he moved to Australia where his father set up an orthodontics practice. Abbott read Economics and Law at the University of Sydney. While a student in Sydney, Abbott had trouble with the law involving the bending of a street sign, false allegations of fathering an illegitimate child as well as an incident where Abbott was accused of indecent assault that was later dropped (The Age, 2004). He was a right-wing student activist who vehemently opposed left-wing politics and supported Australia's Governor-General John Kerr who dismissed the Whitlam government in 1975 (Rundle, 2020), a true blue right-wing politician in the making. According to Abbott's biographer, David Marr, the Prime Minister is a profoundly Catholic Man, and had faith in absolution, where the slate can be wiped clean. Given that most of the panel for the Rhodes Scholarship were from the Conservative establishment, Abbott was selected for Oxford despite his reputation in Sydney, where he transited from a "campus hothead to conventional politician" and where he "deepened his Catholicism and conservatism". He attended Queen's College, Oxford as a Rhodes Scholar where he read Politics, Philosophy and Economics (PPE), and he considered his days at Oxford the golden period in his life. Abbott networked with many fellow Australian political elites and travelled to the Soviet Union and Africa after Oxford, before trying to become a Priest and later a journalist before joining the Liberal Party (Beckett, 2013).

Abbott became an Australian citizen in 1981 so that he could qualify for a Rhodes scholarly and in 1993, he renounced his British citizenship whilst confirming that he does not have Netherlands or New Zealand citizenship in order to run for Australian parliament (APH, 2019). There should therefore be no surprise that Abbott's outlook and worldview are strongly influenced by his upbringing, outlook and politics. Abbott was described as someone who was "heir to British notions of class and race that arrived with the First Fleet", and had in a conversation with Angela Merkel described Australia's attitude towards China as one of "fear and greed without acknowledgement of their humanity" (Macklin, 392).

Tony Abbott's political agenda was mostly domestic. He had campaigned on stopping the flow of refugees into Australia (where Peter Dutton the leader of right-wing coalition member National Party was appointed as his immigration minister), promised to "fix the budget" while wanting to improve productivity and job creation, as well as to remove the carbon tax (at the expense of addressing climate change) (Badham, 2013). He came across as being brash, unsympathetic and disdainful, creating an image of a Prime Minister who is in dissonance with the general expectations of the Australian public. In a Pacific Forum in Papua New Guinea, Abbott was caught on the hot mike laughing at Dutton's joke at the meeting running late: "Time doesn't mean anything when you're about to have water lapping at your door", incurring the wrath of environmentalists and Pacific island leaders (Grimson, 2015). Abbott also angered women when he remarked that women had benefitted from the scraping of the carbon tax as being particularly focused on the household budget, echoing his remarks as Opposition Leader that such a move would help women as it helped reduce the cost of electricity used in ironing (BBC, 2014).

Under Abbott, Australia sought to build a more muscular foreign policy by moving closer to the United States strategically by lashing out at Russia over the downing of Malaysian Airlines over eastern Ukraine in September 2014, and by suggesting that Australia was "simply doing what [she] can as a good international citizen to try and keep people safe" (Abbott cited in Siegel, 2014). This comes in the aftermath of an extremely unpopular budget that eventually cost him his Prime Ministership (Murphy, 2017). Whether Abbott was acting to shore up his popularity or out of his predisposition to stand in line with the United States (more likely both), this was the beginning of Australia's divergence from the long-standing policy to accommodate China. Abbott's worldview of the importance of the Monarchy as well as the shared heritage between Australia and the West predisposes Abbott to hold a staunchly pro-US worldview that underlays an unconditional attitude towards Australia–US relations. As he suggests in a speech in the United States, Abbott regards that the United States and Australia are

> more than allies. We're family. Around the world we seek no privileges, ask no favors, crave no territory. Our objectives are to promote trade, prevent aggression, and, where possible, to foster democracy based on the rule of law. (Abbott, 2012)

Abbott's embrace of identity politics suggests that he has gone further than most of his predecessors in wholeheartedly electing to serve the US alliance unconditionally to further Australian interests, rather than to see the alliance as a particular instrument (out of many) that Canberra has in its disposal in foreign policy making. On the surface at least during the initial months, Abbott's policy did not look too different from Gillard's or Rudd's, but in reality, it marked a departure of Australia's foreign policy in a direction that was reminiscent of a previous era. Even though Gillard had said that foreign policy was "not her passion", her government had drafted the white paper on Australia and the Asian Century in response to the United States' "pivot to Asia" in 2010 (Flitton, 2018). Although this document had the political effect to help burnish Gillard's foreign policy credentials in order to stave off challenges from her leadership rival Rudd, both Gillard and Rudd had still actively sought to ensure that Beijing was still respected and courted. Although by December 2014, Abbott had established Free Trade Agreement with the three East Asian countries, Japan, Korea and China, he had taken the first steps to shift Australia away from the balanced foreign policy line taken by his predecessors, Gillard, Rudd and even Howard before. Ironically, Abbott was often criticised for his FTA with China (Qiddah, 2014). Abbott sought to further reorientate Australia's foreign and security policy towards the United States, while looking to increasingly scrutinise Australia's economic relations with China in the name of security. His decision was by no means accepted across Australia's think tanks and Universities, but in highlighting how certain economic interactions had security implications, Abbott undertook the first official attempt to politicise economic and commercial that Australians had built with China. This of course was widely endorsed by segments of the defence and intelligence community, and by many within the Liberal party. Abbott also did not hide his affection for Japan's Prime Minister Shinzo Abe, whom he said he had admired for a long while. By signalling his affection for Abe, and insisting that Australia's submarine acquisition be filled by Tokyo, Abbott sent strong signals that Abbott was standing shoulder to shoulder with Japan in their disputes against China. Abbott's lack of sensitivity towards the Chinese with regard to choosing to align wholly with the Japanese Prime Minister who had spent the better part of his career propagating a revisionist history of the Pacific War and Japan's atrocities in Asia where victims included Australian servicemen and women.Further, Australia's decision to increase her intervention in the Middle East while antagonising China further in siding with United States and Japan actually distracts Canberra from the possible consequences in her own backyard (Siegal, 2014). Abbott's ascension had all but brought back the dynamic of Australia–China relationship unseen since the Menzies' era. Despite this, Abbott still saw fit to invite Chinese President Xi Jinping to address Australia's parliament when Xi arrived to attend the G20 Summit in Brisbane in 2014. Not withstanding this, Abbott, without question was the Prime Minister that had openly set the tone for the decline of Australia's relations with China in the decade ahead (ACCIW 2015a).

Malcolm Turnbull

Malcolm Turnbull succeeded Tony Abbott as Prime Minister after defeating Abbott in a leadership (Frew 2015). There was hope that his ascension would bring the "revolving door" Prime Ministers to a halt, much like what Japan went through after Koizumi Junichiro stepped down. Turnbull was born in Sydney Australia, with his paternal ancestry tracing back to Scotland and the United Kingdom. In his early days, his parents divorced and Turnbull was brought up by his businessman father in Australia. Turnbull excelled in humanities and languages in school, finally attending the University of Sydney with degrees in Political Science and Law. He subsequently worked as a journalist before winning a Rhodes Scholarship to read law at Brasenose College at Oxford in 1978. Upon returning to Australia, he practised law where he was involved in several high-profile trials such as the defence of Australian media tycoon

Kerry Pack's murder trial, the Spycatcher trial where MI5 tried to stop the publication of book written by a formal spy Peter Wright, before joining Goldman Sachs Australia in 1997 after stints in the logging and the telecommunications industry. In many ways, Turnbull became an important political rival of Abbott.

Turnbull is a staunch Republican, which sets him apart from many of the other Conservatives (such as Abbott) who are religious and/or pro-monarchy, as they see the indomitable linkage between the Christian heritage, western cultural affinity and the divine right of the Royals to rule. Even though Turnbull understands the importance of Australia's English heritage and its influence on Australia politics, his Republicanism meant that he has always been adamant that Australia's interests rather than identity politics play a more central role in government and politics.

Turnbull's political philosophy thus reflects his leaning as a true liberal conservative and reflects his upbringing, education and working experience as a lawyer and an entrepreneur. For Turnbull, what distinguishes the Liberals and the Labor is their view on the government's role in Australian society. For Liberals, the key is to get government to cultivate an environment that enables "the citizen to do his or her best" whereas in the case of Labor, it is a deep belief that the "government's role is to determine what is best" for the people (Turnbull cited in Mane, 2012). Turnbull favors "strong" but not "big" government and is extremely suspicious of the welfare state. He also regards "big government" to be responsible for many of the ills facing contemporary capitalistic societies (such as the role of state-endorsed firms behind the subprime crisis in the United States). For that same reason, Turnbull's views on how State-owned enterprises can actually ruin societies extend too to China. He is therefore fundamentally opposed to the Labor's agenda on the critical and central government can play an important role in an economy, especially during a crisis. Turnbull's beliefs in classical neoliberal ideals of economic freedom as well as civil libertarianism sets him apart from other politicians such as Abbott in the Liberal party (Knobloch, 2020; Manne, 2012).

Turnbull had expressed his interest in working for the workers union and had been courted by Labor but he expressed that he never sought ALP membership (Turnbull, 2009). However, Turnbull's centralist views influenced his thinking on race relations, multiculturalism and Australia's role in the world. Turnbull can be regarded as the bastion of the true liberal wing of the Conservative Party in Australia. His ideas of multiculturalism come across as being very progressive as compared to his predecessor. Within the Conservative establishment, there is always a residual current of resistance against acknowledging the difficulty Australia's history had for minorities, particularly indigenous people as well as the central role that multiculturalism should play in Australian society. The reluctance of Conservative politicians who pander to "traditional" white nationalism raises questions regarding the Liberal party's real attitudes towards race and ethnicity that so infect their platform and discourse towards issues such as immigration, minority loyalty and racial reconciliation. The resurgence of social conservatism and a more insular Australia under the Howard years was of course enforced by the developments of Sep 11 events. Even though the last Liberal government (under the Howard administration) was careful in the control of new arrivals from further ashore like the Keating administration, the difference between them was in their outreach to Indigenous reconciliation. Keating was strong in constructing both symbolic and substantive outreach, while the Howard government had much difficulty in saying sorry. In the recent debate on the national referendum on the Albanese government's backing for "Voice to Parliament" for indigenous reconciliation (i.e. giving this population a voice on policies that impact them) there was considerable controversy. What is most revealing was former Prime Minister Howard's argument that colonisation was "the luckiest thing that happened to [Australia]" when he doubled down on his support for the No vote. Howard argued that he "holds the view that the luckiest thing that happened to {Australia} was being colonised by the British", acknowledging that "not that they were perfect by any means, but [the British] were infinitely more successful and beneficent colonisers than other European countries" (Lane, 2023).

If the ideals of multiculturalism are something more than just recognition of the ethnic diversity and the success of post-war migration program, but rather a celebration of the ways in which Australia has been enriched by the fact that citizens of non-British or Irish ancestry do not have to shed ethnic identities and assimilate to become fully Australian (Manne, 2012), then it might have regressed during the tenure of the Liberal Prime Ministers. Turnbull had indeed argued that while no government can guarantee the absolute absence of terrorism, Australia is very well placed to deal with the threat because of the "strength of [Australia's] intelligence agencies, secure borders and successful multicultural society; one that manages to be both secure and free" (Taylor, 2016). Even though Turnbull's outlook on multiculturalism appears to be more positive than his predecessor, he was reluctant to support the case for indigenous reconciliation, arguing the "mood" of the country, and the possible negative consequences that the failure of such a gesture might have on the country. This of course was interpreted as a complete disinterest on the part of Turnbull by the opposition in the country (Rudd 2018). This however might be more a reflection of the fragility of Turnbull's grip on power than his personal political philosophy. Abbott had actually defeated Turnbull as Leader of the Opposition by a single vote in December 2009, to find himself eventually losing majority support to Turnbull as his popularity ran its course. Throughout Turnbull's tenure as Prime Minister, Abbott continued to undermine and snipe against his successor contextualized against a larger media campaign against him (Brissenden & Anderson, 2018). The problem with lacking majority support for any Prime Minister is that the individual is often held hostage to backdoor deals and intra-party backstabbing. The dynamics faced by Turnbull in fending off his attacks from his resentful predecessor was just as bad as the politicking that went on in Rudd–Gillard dynamic.

From 1993 to 1995, Labor's Labor Paul Keating had actually collaborated with Malcolm Turnbull who was head of Australia's Republican Movement to reshape Australia into a truly independent nation by severing ties with British Monarchy (Davis, 2017). Turnbull was thus a clear advocate of Australia's full autonomy in her role in the world. It should also come as no surprise that Turnbull would appeared to be very supportive of the United States and the alliance even though he personally holds a very clear eye view with regard to the US–Australia alliance relationship. While in opposition, Turnbull had mocked Gillard's "American-worship" trip to Washington and had indicated that he was worried about the dysfunctional nature of American politics, the rise of Republican extremism and the corrupting influence of power (Manne, 2012). There is also evidence that Turnbull while concerned with issues associated with China's rise, does not see eye to eye with many of Australia's political elites and public intellectuals, particularly against those who just want to "demonise China" or "demonise anyone who does not demonise China" (Manne, 2012). Turnbull's attitude towards China was far more positive than Abbott, not because Turnbull had a particular affinity for the Chinese, but more likely because of the Prime Minister's experience in dealing with China and the Chinese, as well as his more forward-looking views of Australia–Asia relations. Malcolm Turnbull actually has a family connection to China as his daughter-in-law is

4 THE ERA OF THE CONSERVATIVES AND AUSTRALIA'S ...   235

scion of a Chinese scholar (Grigg, 2015). Nonetheless, Turnbull's political weakness meant that his government was often held hostage to the politics of his coalition partner. Should Turnbull's faction take a stand against the xenophobic, protectionist ultra-right One Nation or should it seek to woo the supporters of the ultra-right? In the former, would the Nation Party, its coalition cooperation? (Abjorensen, 2017).

Even as Australia–China economic relations surged under Turnbull, there was actually little that can be done to slow down the accelerating growth since there was so much actual profit to be made on all sides. Turnbull however did see the importance of Asia, China and not just the United States to Australia: Asia is economically crucial to Australia, and Australia's standing in Asia enables Australia to play an even more important role in the US bilateral alliance system. Australia however is realistic in terms of how much China can change or modify her behaviour, and that Canberra's exhortations or lobbying should not diminish her pursuit of national interests. Australia–China trade relations continued unabated until 2020 after Liberal Party's Scott Morrison took over. Despite this, Turnbull too has shown his nationalistic streak against anyone, including the Chinese attempting to take control of Australia's resources. He most famously said that China was a "Frenemy", which aptly sums up the attitude of this Prime Minister toward China. In response, former prime minister Kevin Rudd has accused Malcolm Turnbull of running an "anti-China jihad" in response to the government's tough talk against Beijing over the introduction of laws designed to stop foreign interference and espionage, suggesting Turnbull had embraced "neo-McCarthyism" (Tillet, 2018).

Scott Morrison
Scott Morrison who succeeded Malcolm Turnbull was somewhat of a surprise to many observers of Australian politics. As a career politician, Morrison lacks both the illustrious profile and conviction of his more well-known colleagues. He descended from William Roberts, a convict who was accused of stealing yams and sent to Australia on the First Fleet in 1788. Morrison grew up as a child actor, and attended the University of New South Wales, majoring in economic geography where he wrote a thesis on Christian Brethren assemblies in Sydney (Hardaker, 2021). Morrison then worked in the New Zealand's Office of Tourism and Sport before becoming the Managing Director of Tourism Australia from 2004

to 2006. There were allegations that this appointment was highly political, and his work there was equally controversial. Indeed, a newspaper investigation suggested that Morrison had run afoul of procurement guidelines in the award of contracts for the Board's work (Middleton, 2019). In the following year, he was elected as a Member of Parliament for the division of Cook in New South Wales, and appointed into the shadow government. Upon the Liberal-National coalition's victory in the 2013 polls, Morrison was appointed the Minister for Immigration and Border Protection where he was responsible for implementing Operation Sovereign Borders. In the following year, Scott was named as Social Services Minister who oversaw the controversial automated debt assessment and recovery scheme named the Robodebt Scheme which has since been ruled illegal. In fact, he was advised in 2015 that the scheme was illegal since it carried a reverse burden of proof but went ahead anyway to implement (SBS, 2022). By the time Turnbull replaced Abbott, Morrison had clearly managed to charm Turnbull into giving him a promotion. Morrison was appointed Treasurer in the Turnbull cabinet in September 2015. Almost three years later, Morrison was chosen as the replacement candidate after the resignation of Turnbull in a leadership challenge that saw hardcore nationalist politician Peter Dutton, Deputy Prime Minister Julie Bishop and Scott Morrison competing as candidates.

Scott Morrison hails from the Centre Right Faction of the Liberal Party, whereas the previous two Prime Ministers were from the Moderate/Center Left (Turnbull) and National Right (Abbott). Unlike the moderates who are economically conservative but socially progressive, Morrison and his faction are considered "pragmatic" i.e. in other words not confined to a particular ideology but would capitalize on opportunities to showcase their conservatism when such chances arise. As a keen observer notes, Morrison's "beating heart is a focus group", as he is so "unencumbered by belief", "eschews transparency and accountability", and "totally focused on winning, ruthless, transactional, controlling" and focus "tactics" (Grattan, 2022). Morrison is also observed to maintain a "deep animosity towards the NSW Independent Commission Against Corruption" and has been allegedly described by French President Emmanuel Macron, Banaby Joyce and Malcolm Turnbull as someone is not trustworthy (Grattan, 2022). Turnbull in fact had reminisced that Morrison was definitely in part one of the parties working silently with Abbott and others that led to the demise of his premiership.

Even though it is not very well known, Morrison is apparently also very religious, as he has openly spoken about how he believed that he and his wife, Jenny have been called upon to do God's work as Prime Minister (Martin, 2021). Morrison's religious expressions did not escape eagle-eyed journalists who were paying attention: he has had photos taken during his campaign worshipping in Horizon Church's Easter service while campaigning in 2019; there are leaked videos of him in an online prayer group; trying to procure access to the White House for Head of Religious collective, Hillsong and his comments where is calls the misuse of social media the work of the devil (Poulos, 2022). There is every indication that Morrison is a fan of the Tea Party movement premised on evangelical faith in the United States (Hardaker, 2022a, 2022b) at least insofar as he likes to see the divisions between religion and politics blur (Reuters, 2019). Morrison's religious conservatism therefore has influenced his views on immigration, multiculturalism, Australian identity and national security. This in turn had a definitive influence on his politics, public policy and foreign relations. Morrison's brand of politics was a lot closer to Tony Abbott than he was to Malcolm Turnbull even though he appeared careful in managing his relations with other Conservatives as long as they were politically useful.

As Shadow Immigration minister, Morrison demonstrated his willingness to challenge the Gillard government's extension of funding for relatives of the asylum seekers who had died in the Christmas Island disaster, arguing that there is no reason why the funeral cannot be done on Christmas Island itself (Millar, 2011). He defended that the timing of his remarks was insensitive but was unrepentant as he was right to be angry with such fiscal imprudence but the government suggested that Morrison was pandering to the right-wing populist rhetoric for political gain. During his time as immigration Minister, Morrison came across as exceedingly unsympathetic, displaying a hardline position towards asylum seekers, much to the delight of the right-wing conservative elements of the Party. He incurred both praise and condemnation for this but ultimately pleased the right-wing faction of the Conservatives and garnered much support from a broad spectrum of Australians who had grown tired of numerous boatloads of asylum seekers arriving in Australia. Morrison in retrospect spoke very proudly of this achievement. In the course of his duties, he had clashed numerous times with various domestic constituents and even New Zealand Prime Minister Jacinda Ardern (Ferguson, 2020) but clearly from his biography he did not seem to mind these encounters as he regarded himself as being responsible to his office and leader.

During Morrison's tenure as Prime Minister, Morrison saw a quiet resurgence of the Christian right in Australian politics. Most conspicuously, this is felt in the debate on religious freedom (i.e. the Religious Discrimination Bill 2021). This bill was seen to have the most negative impact on the LGBTIQ+ community and was shelved in 2022 on the objections of the Christian right that it did not go far enough. What was most controversial in this bill was the "statement of belief" clause that would have allowed people to make discriminatory statements under the guise of freedom of religion on issues/people they disagree with, in effect allowing for bigotry to be justified under the name of religious freedom (Lixinski, 2022; Martin & Karp, 2023). Critics argue that Morrison, through this bill empowered both culture warriors (both the religious and the not religious sort) to openly discriminate against transgender people. This division no doubt galvanized the religious right but also stirred up anger in the Community against the Prime Minister.

It is however not only Morrison's views on religion that irked Australians. Like many in the United States' Republican Party and his colleagues in the Australia Liberal-National Coalition, Morrison's views on climate change are controversial. Morrison had consistently downplayed and even rejected the science of climate change. In Jan 2020, his public image suffered immensely when he was caught taking a vacation to Hawaii as wildfires raged killed 26 people and destroyed over 2000 homes. Many Australians regarded his government made an inadequate response to the disaster, comparing it to the 2005 Bush response to Hurricane Katherina. They naturally linked it to the Morrison and his party' unrelenting position on climate change (McGuirk, 2020). The anger was immense as Morrison was cursed and called out online as an "idiot" and a "moron" both at home and abroad. In the aftermath of this, Morrison did pay much attention to his plunging popularity and redeemed his public image slightly during the Covid pandemic when he decisively shut down travel between China and Australia and followed the advice of the country's top health official to the letter. However, his fortunes did not last with political scandals that followed - Morrison was criticised for backing his attorney general Christian Porter who was accused of rape in his teenage years and the cover-up of the rape of a junior staffer in Australian Parliament House (Cave, 2021).

Morrison has been regarded by domestic political observers as a shape-shifter as a Prime Minister (Murphy, 2020) as this is a politician who appears to endorse everything but actually supports nothing (Murphy, 2021). In a biography, Morrison is portrayed as a politician who does not appear to stand for anything in particular. It comes across as no surprise of course, as his positions, words and policies all appeared to be poll-driven rather than centred on issues. He is seen as a leader who frequently lies about the economy and someone who uses public policy for the enrichment of himself and his friends (Pini, 2021; Denniss, 2022). In March 2022, an Australian senator, Concetta Fierravanti-Wells from Morrison's party denounced Morrison as a ruthless autocrat and a bully with no moral compass with Morrison brushing her off as a bitter politician who has blamed him for her own career failings (BBC, 2022). Polls have consistently shown that he is one of the least trusted Prime Ministers in the history of Australia, with one such poll showing that Morrison is even more distrusted than Vladimir Putin in Australia, ranking above right-wing politician Peter Dutton (Murray, 2022).

However, if there is one area where Morrison truly left a mark, it is on Australia–China relations. Under his watch, Australia–China decline to its lowest point since the establishment of Australia–China relations. While it is understandable that as a Conservative leader, Morrison would likely continue the policies put in place by his predecessors like Abbott or Turnbull with regard to China, Morrison seemed to have doubled down on throwing Australia's weight behind the Trump Administration unconditionally. Unlike his predecessors, Morrison seems to have very little interest in ensuring that the domestic constituents' interests are not "hurt" by Australia's foreign policy and therefore saw no necessity to calibrate a balance in Australia's China policy. Was the Prime Minister influenced by identity politics and a misguided sense of zero-sum understanding of US–China relations and Australia role in it; alternatively was he concerned by what he perceived as China's asymmetrical influence in Australia's domestic politics or was he concerned by his fledging popularity and that adopting a tough stance towards China was a way out?

Morrison's decisive action in closing down flights from China and putting in the Covid measures won him much-needed reprieve from the public criticism he faced. He went further leading the global rhetorical charge, jumping into a debate between the United States and China on the origins of the Covid pandemic. While both domestically and internationally there are many angry people who would have agreed with the idea that the origins of the pandemic should have been investigated, and therefore ensuring that there will not be a repeat of these events, Morrison's rhetoric further inflamed the tensions between Canberra and Beijing. The perception of the Chinese was that Morrison was acting in no uncertain terms acting in concert with Washington and parroting Trump's and Pompeo's accusations that Beijing should be held to account for the spread of the pandemic (Karp and Davidson, 2020).

This incident of course is not isolated, given the Australian leader's prominent role and high-profile accusations in calling out China over the past decade or so in all manners of issues: human rights abuses in Tibet, Xinjiang, South China Sea dispute, Hong Kong democracy movement to Taiwanese intimidation. In pursuing the narrative of China's responsibility for the COVID-19 outbreak, Morrison thoroughly angered the Chinese government. There is however no expectation on the part of anyone, the Australians, the Chinese or for that matter, any other observers that Morrison should speak for anyone other than Australians. Morrison had actually asked questions that many people agreed upon, but by this point the Chinese were convinced that Australia had gone so far down the line in siding with the Trump administration that they were not behaving "rationally" or "reasonably".

This hardline attitude of course did not dissipate with Morrison stepping down. Most of Morrison's political contemporaries (such as Mike Pompeo or Liz Truss) ended up running high-profile trips for exorbitant fees to either Taiwan or Tokyo after stepping down. In a speech in Tokyo, Morrison in fact had claimed credit for urging others to speak out against China's "bullying", and compared the West of accommodation to the "appeasement of Hitler with the Munich agreement" during a speech at the Inter-Parliamentary Alliance on China's Tokyo Symposium (Hurst, 2023b). Given the audience of global conservatives at a time when Sino-Japanese relations was at their lowest, Morrison's message of course must be taken with a pinch of salt. Despite the anger felt against the Chinese in Australia [(rightly or wrongly) for the range of transgressions, Australians do also have a sense that bipartisan politics and the politicians' personal politics have more to do with this as much as if not more than geopolitics.

This had both global and domestic repercussions, further eroding Beijing's narrative that the spread of the pandemic might not have originated from China alone. Domestically, there is no doubt that there is much anger directed towards China amongst ordinary Australians. There is also a consensus that the questions Morrison raised are hardly trustworthy especially when it comes to China. By 2023, the electorate had clearly become disappointed with Australian politics under Morrison.

Collectively, Tony Abbott, Malcolm Turnbull and Scott Morrison have kept the Liberal Party in power from 2013 to 2022. Abbott became Prime Minister when his party defeated the Labor Party in the 2013 Federal elections leading the centre-right Liberal-National Coalition to victory, while Turnbull defeated Abbott in a leadership spill and Morrison assumed Prime Ministership after Turnbull resigned. Malcolm Turnbull led the Liberal-National fought the 2016 Elections successfully but had their seats in Parliament reduced by 14 seats, and Scott Morrison won a third term for the Liberal-National led government in the 2019 elections with a marginal improvement of two seats. Within the coalition, the Liberals have traditionally had a close relationship with its partner the National Party. Their traditional outlook and political philosophy is relatively close, but they draw their support base from different areas of the country as the Liberals serve the urban-metropolitan areas whereas the National Party draws its supporters from the rural agricultural areas. Even though their politics are similar, Liberal politicians often find themselves circumscribed by their more right-wing counterparts in the advocation of their policy. Peter Dutton, the Shadow Opposition Leader who had served as Immigration and Home Affairs under the Abbott and Turnbull governments and Defence Minister under Morrison had often taken a vocal anti-immigrant and anti-China stance (Flitton, 2018; Bolger, 2018; Davis, 2022a, 2022b). Dutton features prominently as a tough in Australian and American media as someone very tough on China (hence implicitly a potential Australian leader (Babones, 2021; Wang 2021a, b; Galloway, 2022). This creates an environment where politicians compete to demonise the PRC. Even as these Prime Ministers appeared to use different narratives and rhetoric, their position on domestic security, migration and economic security has been relatively consistent. The appointment of politicians such as Dutton enables the government to get someone with policing experience to help the security services to ensure that the political tough decisions are implemented right, appease the right-wing of the party and enable the Prime Ministers to look at least reasonably moderate.

All three Prime Ministers might not have had a particular dislike or distaste for China and the Chinese in particular. They are however certainly of the same political mould in their conservative counterparts in Japan, India and the United States when it came to China. They appreciated the power of populist politics and nationalism and how its articulation could help boost their popularity at home, their standing with their main security partners (the Japanese, Europeans and British) and patron the United States and their global image as defenders of freedom and democracy. They also assume that their political quarrels Beijing is unlikely to undertake massive unilateral actions against them in particular as economic interdependency would certainly mean hurt China as well. Abbott had praised Japan openly and embrace Abe as one of his best friends, while Turnbull became very critical of human rights in Xinjiang (Associated Press 2013). Despite these antagonisms, both Prime Ministers sought to cultivate and ensure that the economic relationship remained on track. Beijing was unhappy but chose to plod along until Morrison's tenure. Morrison stood out as the only Prime Minister who appeared to have done Australia a great disservice by derailing almost five decades of economic cooperation with China. Naturally one can counter accuse that it was the Chinese who had decided to wreck the economic cooperation, but the key variable is why the Chinese chose to do this during Morrison's tenure rather than in Abbott or Turnbull's tenure. One can never be too sure why Morrison chose to conduct his policy towards China the way he did, but one can be sure that he had way more interest and expertise in image maintenance, and party politics than in foreign relations. After all, there is nothing more powerful in these times than to rely on the good old nationalist argument that it was more vital than ever to stand up to the Chinese bully and safeguard national sovereignty, democratic freedoms and liberal values. Beyond this, it is always easier to tear things apart than it is to build bridges and overcome adversity.

LEVEL TWO: CHINA IN AUSTRALIA'S DOMESTIC POLITICS

The impact of political leaders on foreign policy varies from system to system. In autocracies, political leaders are traditionally far more influential on foreign policy than their democratic counterparts. Likewise in most countries regardless of whether democracies or autocracies, daily bread-and-butter issues such as unemployment and healthcare often matter far more to voters than do foreign policy issues. Foreign policy issues often only become important in electoral contexts when they are politicised and linked (either perceptually or in real terms) to domestic politics.

This of course can happen in a variety of contexts: when a particular leader chooses to scapegoat a foreign country or nation for a downturn of events within her own country; or when a political party embarks on an insidious covert programme to bring about political change or across a broad spectrum of innocuous but often extreme activities that lend to creating notions of enmity amongst the electorate such as stereotyping, social media controversies over trivial matters and constant negative press coverage. For that matter, a nation can also regroup and react to externally inspired or stimulated internal challenges (real or perceived) but take more assertive steps towards the challenge.

By 2013 when Tony Abbott assumed the Prime Ministership, Australia's relations with both the United States and China had become significant in a way Australia had never experienced before. The role by which China plays in Rudd's or Abbott's Australia far exceeds the role China played in Whitlam's Australia. By this time, China has become Australia's largest trading partner, the most important export market for a number of commodities and primary sector products as well as one of the most important sources of consumer product imports, student revenue and migration. Unlike other Quad countries such as the US, India and Japan, Australia actually maintains a huge trade surplus with China. The quality and intensity of Australia's interactions simply cannot be compared to those five decades or so earlier. If a comparison is made to the United States or Great Britain, the contrast cannot be clearer. Other than Australia's security partnership in the US–Australia alliance under the ANZUS Treaty, and its recent decade-long partnership in the War on Terror, Australia's actual linkages with Europe and US appeared to rather "insubstantial" to China's if economics is factored in. The critical question is how Australia could cope with having a strong security relations with the United States while maintaining very vibrant economic relationship with China at a time when US–China strategic competition was intensifying.

Australia's Cultural Heritage and its Strategic Affinity for the United States

Australia is a vibrant democracy with a population of 25 million people that officially defines Australia as a multicultural nation. As a constitutional monarchy, Canberra has strong historical linkages, cultural similarities and political affinity with the United States and United Kingdom.

One should therefore not be surprised if Canberra's strategic impulses and political narratives mirrors those of Washington and London. One British legacy that had deeply affected Australia was the 1901 Immigration Restriction Act passed by the British in the Federal Parliament, essentially an encapsulating set of racist policies that aimed to forbid people of non-European ethnic origin, especially of Asian origins, but also Pacific islanders to migrating to Australia. This officially ended by the Holt government in 1966, but Australian politics continue to be plagued by an undertone of racial politics (Tavan, 2016) even as most politicians would deny this.

Australia's domestic politics is marked by the dominance of struggle between two main political parties, the Labour Party and the Liberal Party, along with its small partner the National Party. Traditionally the Australian Left, dominated by the Labor Party has portrayed itself as a democratic socialist Party that is sympathetic to the working class concerns and global poor. Therefore from a broad political survey, the Labor Party appears to be more accommodating towards non-democracies abroad, more so than the Liberal Party. This is not to say that the Labor approves of these political systems or what they stand for, but rather it is a recognition on the part of Labor of the existence of other political systems apart from democracies, and that Australia has to find ways to coexist and work with them. The dynamics of Labor versus Liberal-National coalition divide in this respect could be interpreted as quite similar to those between the Republican Party and the Democratic Party in the United States for a better part of the post-war period. While the parties have vied over a variety of political and economic issues, one key political differentiation between the Labor and Liberals is their orientation towards Asia and China. The Labor Party had actually advocated for the recognition of the PRC as early as 1954 by Gough Whitlam when he was a Member of the Australian Parliament. In 1971, Whitlam's trip to PRC preceded Henry Kissinger's secret preparatory trip for Nixon's reproachment 1972 visit to China. Prime Minister William McMahon, from the Liberal Party had accused Zhou Enlai had "played Whitlam like a trout" (Middleton, 2021), of acting as a pawn for the Communist power and a spokesperson for the enemy being fought in Vietnam, and that any recognition of China was not possible.

The Liberals on the other hand had a staunch worldview of Australia standing shoulder to shoulder with the United States and had the proverbial rug pulled out from under his feet by the Americans. McMahon's accusations of Whitlam as a pawn of Communist power and a spokesman for the enemy being fought in Vietnam meant that his ruling coalition was severely embarrassed and "betrayed" by the United States when news of Kissinger's visit broke out. Whitlam became the first Australian Prime Minister to visit China in 1973, and signed the Trade Agreement between the Government of Australia and the Government of the People's Republic of China that provided the foundation for basis for future Australia–China relationship, exchanges and dialogues. This episode had three important implications for Australia's domestic politics and consequently foreign policy.

First, both the Australian Labor Party and the Liberal Party learnt from this episode that by hitching Australia's security posture to that of the United States, it could have adverse political consequences at home. Vietnam was essentially the first "televised war", and the political mood in Australia followed those of the United States closely. Both the Labor and the Liberal parties learnt that public mood swings can change political fortunes very quickly since transnational media reports have made social movements "transmissible" and are capable of influencing public narratives and political agenda. Any Australian political party that slavishly follows the positions of their traditional patrons or colonial masters might not necessarily work in their favour, both in terms of party interests, as well as national interests.

Second, the Indochinese War affected how racial relations and migration are discussed in Australia. The overall approach undertaken by Whitlam-led Labor government was to renounce the White Australia policy in favour of a multiculturalist approach to Australian immigration policy. This was aimed at removing the vestiges of openly racist approach towards the growth of Australian nation. Through the ratification of the Convention on the Elimination of Racial Discrimination and combating racial prejudice within Australia, Labor's approach puts it as the more "forward-looking" party in terms of race relations as Labor began to champion cultural diversity and the construct of Australia as a multicultural nation. This paves the way for Australia's outreach to her neighbours in Asia, as well as welcoming more migrants from Asia, rather than just the United Kingdom or the United States to Australia. The vocabulary of multiracialism had officially entered the political discourse and identity of Australia then. The big question is how fast, wide and quick can this notion be internalised and put into practice by all Australians.

Third, this episode also changed the way how political parties and politicians come about to discuss economic linkages and relations with their neighbours in Asia. Australia's plan to expand and extend its economic linkages to China and Asia enabled Australia to see beyond trade with the Old World as an alternate means to prosperity. Labor's building of Australia–China relations that led to the resumption of trade modified how Australians perceived China and Asia, and how they thought of the world and Australia's place in it. This historicity of how Labor had used race, multiculturalism and diversity in domestic and foreign political discourse had entrenched it as the more "forward-looking" party in Australian politics and for most part had guided the country in a more progressive direction, at least in the eyes of her neighbours and the world, although not necessary of Australian people themselves. In some ways, this has mirrored the situation in the United States. Australia's tenacity to grapple with her colonial linkages and her nascent ties with China and Asia however does not the tendency for most Australians to see themselves as part of the Western world or part of their global democratic fraternity has dissipated. Even as Australians search for ways to shore up relations with her neighbours and to establish new linkages with other parts of the world, Australians have continually viewed themselves through the prism of a democratic society. For ordinary Australians, the importance of advancing human rights, of religious and other civic freedoms and the rule of law are paramount values that set Australia apart from other countries.

Australian National Identity and Nationalism: Human Rights, Freedom and Values

The debate of whether Australia should lean towards her traditional allies, the United Kingdom and the United States or find her future in Asia, particularly in seeking out new partners such as China has been an intense one over the decades.

Over the years, Australians have often frowned upon certain aspects of China that they find troubling. The most obvious aspect is the political system and perceived differences over rights and values in China and Chinese society. Australians are concerned about China and Chinese migrants not only because of their unfamiliarity with Chinese ethnicity and culture, but more so because of the perceived indifference to the respect for human rights. As a Constitutional Monarchy founded on the rule of law, Australia perceives itself to have a strong tradition of upholding and cherishing human rights. In particular, the protection of Human Rights are enshrined in both the Constitution and the Common Law at the Federal and State levels. Within Australia as with all other democracies, how the protection is envisaged, implemented and enforced is often a work in progress. Nonetheless, the Australian people have often prided themselves as members of the global community that is invested in the enhancement of human rights as a cherished value of the nation with much commonality as with the United States, Britain and Western Europe. This is probably one of the key drivers that Australians perceive as their key similarities to the Western democracies, but has often been challenged in recent times.

For instance, Human rights were the key issue that angered an entire generation of Australians during and after the Indochina Wars. Many regarded that it was important for Australia to take a somewhat independent path in world affairs. Whether it is the US, China, Vietnam or the Pol Pot regime, the Indochina Wars had a huge impact on how Australians saw the world subsequently. Even though Vietnam became a central security concern, Australians were also driven by the sympathy they had for the Khmer (Cambodian) people due to the murderous activities of the Pol Pot regime whose "ruthlessness and disregard for democratic rules and human rights are virtually unrivalled" (APS, 1981). From the 1970s through to the 1980s, domestic debates in Australia compelled the Federal government to become more accepting of migrants from Indochina and elsewhere. By 1982, Prime Minister Malcolm Fraser's government had accepted approximately 60,000–70,000 Vietnamese refugees for resettlement in Australia without much fanfare. Australians are therefore very critical of countries that violate human rights. The Indochinese wars have made ordinary Australians more acutely aware of how both Western as well as Asian regimes are capable of human rights abuses. This also shapes the early attitudes towards migration.

In the aftermath of the Tiananmen Square incident, Prime Minister Hawke lamented at the awful human cost of the decision of the Chinese Communist Party as "(Chinese troops) had orders that nobody in the square be spared, and children … young girls were slaughtered as mercilessly as the many wounded soldiers from other units there" (Hawke cited by Seccombe, 2019). Accordingly, Hawke made a unilateral decision to let 27,000 Chinese students stay in Australia and cumulatively granted

42,000 permanent visas for Chinese students he was tremendously disappointed with the Chinese leadership as he had emphasized greatly on his friendship with the PRC as well as his deep belief in Australia as a compassionate society (Walden, 2016). Hawke's account was supposedly a personal account but this did not go unchallenged. There are counter oral history and narratives from the Chinese communities, as well as evidence to suggest that Hawke's decision was not unilateral, as the decision had indeed been considered by the Cabinet and jointly announced by the Prime Minister and the Immigration minister. Then there are challenges about how much of what Hawke said was put into practice in terms of admission numbers. This runs in the face with the conception of Australia's unimpeachable generosity and benevolence then, as the Hawke government also at the same time began instituting policies that made immigration and asylum tougher (Wang, 2021a, b). The Cambodian refugees that arrived by boat in 1989 were then labelled as economic refugees by the Hawke government. From 1989 to the end of 1993 over 47% were granted refugee status or entry on humanitarian or other grounds. Since 1994 less than 10 per cent have been granted entry to reside permanently in Australia. If Sino-Vietnamese boat people are excluded the rate of acceptance of refugees since 1994 is around 10 per cent.

Even after the Vietnam War, Australia continues to have political tussles with China that their leader feels are important for instance on issues such as human rights and religious freedoms. Labor Prime Minister Paul Keating met Dalai Lama in 1992, as did Conservative Prime Minister John Howard in 2007. As an editorial captures what most Australians feel about Dalai Lama and Tibet:

> [China] will not attain the respect it craves as long as it continues to violate human rights, whether in Tibet or in China … Beijing must be aware that there is considerable world sympathy for the desire of the Tibetan people for independence. While Australia has long accepted the Chinese occupation of Tibet, that does not mean there should be no criticism of the regime there, nor that we should not support greater autonomy for the Tibetan people… The Dalai Lama holds enormous moral authority. For him to be snubbed by Australian politicians would not only demonstrate a timid subservience to Chinese demands but cause grave offence to the thousands of his Australian followers. (The Age, 2002)

Even as Australia–China economic ties intensify, there is clear bipartisan support on the part of Australian leaders to ensure that Australia's principles, worldview and values are upheld. This difference is one that Beijing probably understood, but nonetheless Australia saw fit to kick up a political fuss and diplomatic spat just to make a point. Even under Labor Prime Minister Kevin Rudd, Australia–China relations were not exactly smooth. Rudd, as someone who had studied Chinese history and is fluent in "Beijing" politics was initially seen as a chance by many in both Australia and China for better Australia-China relations. By 2009, the difficulties over how each country interpreted the freedom and rights of people including those arrested for offences. A naturalised Australian citizen, Stern Hu who was arrested and detained by Beijing for industrial espionage and bribery in Beijing created an uproar in Australian society. Kevin Rudd however had refused to intercede personally in the case.

For ordinary Australians, this concern over human rights and freedoms has underpinned their sense of nationhood and global outlook for generations. After all, during the Second World War, they stood hand in hand and fought alongside the British and the Americans to defend the world against the tyranny of Nazi Germany and Imperial Japan. It was the same concern for human rights that led them to distance from the Americans in the aftermath of the Vietnam War and compelled them to look beyond their traditional allies to Asia to build a new relationship. Even as Australia has grown from being a disinterested dominant "white" neighbour to Asia to a nation that embraces multiculturalism and regards herself as part of the Asian community, Australia's national identity is still strongly influenced by her heritage. In embracing her geographical future, Australia has never lost sight of her heritage. Ordinary Australians still for the most part regard themselves as members of the rich developed Western democracies, having more in common with the average American or British person than they do the average Indonesian or Vietnamese. Some Australian politicians "understand" the ASEAN way of non-interference, and appreciate the narrative of Asian values, but it would be wrong to assume that they would embrace or partake in this under the broad umbrella of diversity.

In the aftermath of September 11, the domestic political debate and strategic attention of Australia shows Canberra's fidelity to the Western worldview and values. This is not to suggest that the other Asian countries do not share the shock and horror at this terror attack, but Canberra's willingness to deploy troops to participate in America's War on Terror suggests that even as Australia sought to engage in Asia, her heart and soul wholeheartedly lie in her relations with the West. The 2002 Bali bombings reinforced the Australian public's support for the government's participation in the War on Terror as Australians recoiled in shock and horror. There were of course questions raised with regard to Australia's broad involvement with the United States again by members of the civil society particularly with regard to Iraq, but by and large Australia was committed to standing alongside the United States. Within Australian society, there was increased evidence to show that the political culture and ambience were increasingly securitised, and that the fear of terrorism manifested in the psychological responses of the larger society through an intensified search for meaning, as defined by heightened patriotic nation-alism rhetoric, the suppression of dissent and the acceptance of extreme measures all contributed to a prolonged state of insecurity amongst the public (Aly, 2014). For more than a decade until Obama's "pivot to Asia", Australia's strategic culture has advocated for a close with the United States to combat the scourge of terrorism, and later over China's intent and actions in Southeast China Sea.

The differing approach towards human rights, towards how political differences and dissent are tolerated (or not tolerated) invariably becomes condensed into distinctions that underpin the understanding of Australia's and China's global outlook and political thinking. There is no question that Canberra and Beijing do not see eye to eye in terms of systemic differences, values and consequently identity. Yet, in other to smoothen the differences both countries try their best to work with each other, using the economic and commercial interactions as "gel" to smoothen their working relationship and harmonise their interactions. Australia and China was for a period immensely successful at this. The United States and Britain too had adopted this practice since the 1980s. Like the Australians, they too had spent decades reaping immense benefits from their relation-ship with China, and therefore have not chastised Australians on any level about this.

Through the growing bilateral trade, China benefitted immensely from imports of minerals and agricultural products just as Australians enjoyed cheap consumer goods made in China. The impact of the increased presence of ethnic Chinese and China-related organisations in Australia however also has real, and often negative repercussions for the local community (as they do for Canadians, Hong Kongers, etc.). The nega-tive externalities were real in some instances (competition for school places to the lack of social integration) but at times could be exaggerated and imagined. The problem however is that they are never only socio-economic and would often become political. For instance, well-heeled Chinese businessmen or wealthy individuals who meet the requirements for investment-related migration would often invest and acquire large chunks of real estate investments, thereby generating upward pressure on prices, often creating conditions of a buoyant economy. Real estate agents and local businesses would often benefit from these investments as do owners of existing properties nearby, but the negative impact would often manifest in an upward pressure on rent, and the pricing out of locals from affordable housing. This would particularly hit people who work in essential services such as firemen, police, nurses and teachers and municipal workers. Social and corporate media would play up these allegations, never mind if they are true (i.e. if the Chinese community is actually behind this). This would put pressure on the ruling party, relevant portfolio Ministers, Members of Parliament and other groups with interest in the issue e.g. right-wing groups, etc.). From the 2000s onwards, China-related organisations and the Chinese community became an important factor in Australian domestic politics as there was a popular perception that they were involved in negative impact activities such as pricing locals out through massive real estate investment, wholesale acquisition of traditional local businesses and assets, and direct political influence by participating in the electoral process through lobbying or donations (Parton, 2020).

Foreign interference is not new in Australia. Australia's closest ally the United States has in fact played a leading role in the interference in Australian politics. The United States has never made it a secret that they frown upon politicians who advocate a more "balanced" approach against Washington in Japan (think Hatoyama Yukio), South Korea (think Moon Jae-in) or other places in Southeast Asia (think Malaysia's Mohd Mahathir or Indonesia's Sukarno). Every Australian politician knows the danger of what might happen should they become too vocal about the United States. Given the nature of Australian nationalism, the influence that the US and the Western corporate and social media have in Australia, not to mention the strength of US intelligence in the region, there is no question that Washington is in a far better position to influence opinions in mainstream society in Australia than any other country. This however does not mean that Washington is not concerned with Canberra's growing ties with

China. In fact China's influence in Washington's allied states is something that Washington is extremely worried about.

It is also important to note that there are also domestic constituents who were also worried about the growing Australia–China ties. Within the Chinese-speaking (or related) community, there are many opponents of the Chinese Communist Party. This would include former PRC residents with a variety of grudges against the Chinese government, absconded businessmen, dissidents, Hong Kong democrats, Taiwanese independence advocates and even Tibetan or Uighur refugees. The complexity of the community concerned with how Australia should orientate or treat China and Chinese necessary meant that China-related issues are linked to political capital and votes.

While it is certainly expected that all foreign powers will attempt to influence sovereign governments in power—the allegations of China's attempts to influence Australian politics, academia, media and businesses certainly sent shockwaves across the nation. While these might have occured in the past, what is new is that today, such activities have been weaponised in domestic politics not only between the Liberal-Coalition and Labor Parties but also between forces that are pro-Beijing and anti-Beijing. Unhappiness with China has never been an important issue in Australian domestic politics, since most Australians have always regarded China as a "foreign policy" matter, and something not so intractable that they would detail the fundamentals of Australia–China relations that both countries had built up over the last forty-five years. What was different this time is that debate in Australia has adopted the nexus of a foreign-domestic dimension previously not seen before. This of course was a result of issues being exaggerated and amplified selectively by Conservative politicians both as a political strategy as well as a goal (as it helped their poll numbers and their electoral platform and dent those of their opponents). The events of the last decade therefore thoroughly surprised Beijing as it is inconceivable in China that anyone would risk derailing so much economic gains for what Chinese Beijing considereds for so little

China's Economic Ascendance and Its Impact on Australian Domestic Politics

According to the Australian Embassy in China, two-way trade between China was valued at around A$113 million in 1973 after the establishment of diplomatic relations to A$78.2 billion in 2009 valued in total about A$85.1 billion. For better or worse, from the 1990s to the 2010s, Canberra did cultivate a mutually beneficial relationship with China. Both Labor and Liberal governments benefitted from Australia's robust trade ties with the rapidly expanding Chinese economy. The Australian and Chinese economy has enjoyed great complementarity for at least four decades. Merchandise trade has grown from around $100 million in 1972 to $114 billion in 2011, while services trade negligible in 1972—is now worth over $7 billion. China's share of Australia's total merchandise trade rose from 1 per cent in 1972 to almost 25 per cent in 2011–12, with statistics showing that one day's trade in 2011–2012 was worth more than one's years trade in the early 1970s (Au-Yeung et al., 2012).

In 2009, China surpassed Japan to become Australia's largest export market. By 2014, Australia upgraded their relations to a "comprehensive strategic partnership" even as Australia–China relations began to show signs of strain and backsliding. The rise of China as a trading powerhouse meant that for most countries, their dealings with China at all levels have correspondingly increased. This political and economic intercourse has seen a rise in interactions with China officially and at the same time with Chinese firms, businesses.

Australia's generous acceptance of refugees and migrants in the 1990s have made Australia appear very progressive and forward looking to the rest of the world. Insofar as China is concerned, Australia was beginning to see less of refugees and dissidents, and more of business persons and highly skill labour. From the perspective of well-heeled or highly skilled migrants from developed countries, Australia stands out as an outstanding destination for migration. In this respect, Australia's experience with the resurgence of China is not much different from the developed world, whether it is the United States, Canada or the United Kingdom. There are of course imperfections to the vision's implementation. Like every other country, immigration is a hot-button issue politically. From Spain to Canada to South Korea, receiving host nations often have segments of their population opposed to liberal migration policies.

Well-heeled Chinese migrants are increasingly establishing themselves as business owners and leaders while self-financing Chinese students have now become cash-cows for Australian universities and in turn, have become very much dependent on them. This sense of mutual dependency, which has become interpreted as one of reliance has struck a raw nerve in Australia society. Effectively, the appearance of clusters of newly rich migrants, the clout of Chinese enterprises and required adjustments of Australian society to the new rising China meant that effectively at both the political and societal level, China had become an important but controversial player in the domestic politics of Australia. This phenomenon is not unique to Australia but is experienced across the board by developed economies such as the US, UK, Canada and even Japan and South Korea (Ng, 2021; HKFP, 2019).

The effects of this free movement of Chinese investment and capital, of students, professionals and migrants provide not only material benefits for those working with them, but at the same time often create negative externalities from their behaviour. For many ordinary Australias who did not benefit from this exchange, this has become an emotional and often contentious issue. Just as Hong Kong and Singapore have often complained about the behaviour of new Chinese migrants from the PRC, communities in Canada, Britain and elsewhere have also complained of various issues with Chinese migrants. At the core of the unhappiness is usually associated with the behaviour (anti-social behaviour and/or non-integration), and with their consumption pattern (large-scale influx of Chinese money, often buying up traditional businesses or real estate). These practices are often regarded as "predatory" and incured the wrath of the communities that were affected. Very often, these incidents were a result of behaviour of Chinese migrants who usually did not have anything to do with the PRC government. At the same time, many Australians were also becoming increasingly unhappy about the possible future prospects of the country if Australia was to become increasingly reliant on the Chinese. The impact of over-reliance registered in the statistics, as in 2018–2019 alone, Australia–China trade was about A$240 billion, which was worth more than the next three largest partners combined (Japan, US and Korea). The United States is not even in the top ten of the list (Mao, 2020).

This sense of how China has become increasingly important could be seen in terms of China related issue became widely discussed throughout the 1990s in Australia's domestic debate. Australia's strategic community was at the forefront of this debate with their counterparts in the United States, Japan, Britain and Europe over the viability of the "China Threat" thesis as Beijing's economic clout increased. This debate was not just confined to the members of foreign and intelligence community, but was broadly a societal conversation. One might therefore expect that the new migrants mentioned above would be rallying in support of China. In reality, this cannot be further from the truth. Many of the Chinese migrants hail from overseas Chinese communities in Southeast Asia, Europe, Hong Kong and Taiwan, and in reality, they create a very diverse community of Chinese diaspora alongside those who had moved from China. There are also those who are themselves or with family members being persecuted by the Chinese Communist Party or wanted by the Chinese government for corruption, bribery or other crimes. Others could be protesting because they are united in their support for the Uighurs or Tibetans or against human rights abuses caused by government policy (Burgess et al., 2022). The reality is that there could be many in the Chinese community with an axe to grind against China. Of course, there are those who believed that the Australian government that partaking in a attempt to split and/or contain China and these views would likely be expressed politically through the support of China (Power, 2019).

China and the Chinese in Australia Domestic Politics: Scapegoating, Strategic Industries and Democratic Participation

According to Australia's Home Affairs Bureau, by the end of 2021, there will be 595,630 Chinese-born people living in Australia, 53.7 per cent more than the number (387,420) on 30 June 2011, making Chinese migrants the third largest migrant community in Australia after the United Kingdom and India. This is equivalent to 7.9 per cent of Australia's overseas-born population and 2.3 per cent of Australia's total population (Home Affairs Australia Website, N.D). Somewhat similar to the situation in California, the earliest Chinese immigration to Australia in the 1850s were driven by the gold rushes, but this was effectively curtailed by the British implementation of the White Australia Policy (1901–1973). In June 1966 less than 0.3% of Australia's population consisted of Chinese or half Chinese residents (Inglis, 1972). Since the 1980s, Chinese migration has upsurged, and of the Chinese migrants, almost one-third came from Hong Kong and Taiwan, and the other two-thirds from mainland China. There were naturally cultural and social tensions experienced by these migrants from these two particular areas. The first is the domination of ethnic Chinese students in Australia's Institutes of Higher Education and the second, the attribution of rising real estate prices because influx of Chinese migrants or migration.

While there is some truth to these assertions with regard to Chinese migration in general, it might actually not be completely true in the Australian case. There is evidence (Chung, N.D.) to suggest that a majority of Chinese migrants to Australia are purchasing real estate because for residential or business / investment purposes rather than ill intent purposes of, of sweeping up "everything". In addition, the Chinese migrants were not just buying up all the real estate in any one particular estate, and the price increases were not because of Chinese purchases or investment. The sensationalising or association of how "China" was driving up prices has to do with speculation on the part of many and often based on a racial undertone of the "White Australia" policy that has yet to dissipate (Chung, N.D., Zhou, 2021). What could have been at work was the perpetuation of a subversive form of politics that distorted the real truth: that it is the way the Australian housing system is constituted rather than a particular ethnic group that is creating the affordable housing issue (Rogers, 2014). Racism (through the Asian invasion myth) is often an easier answer to mask inadequate planning, policy failure and the influx of mobile and growing group of rich real estate investors, not only from China but also elsewhere around the world (including the United States who in 2012 were response for A$8.1 billion), double of what the Chinese investment of A$4.2 billion (Rogers, 2014). In reality, Chinese investment into the Australia real estate sector only amounts to 2% (Hendrischke, Li, 2015). In a similar debate in Canada, this outrage against Asians or Chinese was often led by newspaper columnists (who are no real estate experts) but bent on a new type of populism that induces politicians to quickly jump on the bandwagon to crack down on the so-called "toxic demand" from Asia and China (Ng, 2021). The challenge with affordable housing in Australia is currently still being debated, but there are views that the Australian government's ideas that deregulation and the market will somehow respond to low-income household's needs is hugely problematic as opposed to a more interventionist approach

(Pawson et al., 2022). These sentiments still persist today as international students from China risks being scapegoats as they return to China (Lehmann, 2023).

In a national survey conducted by Lowry Institute in 2020, 36% of Australians say they have the impression that there is 'a lot of discrimination against people of Chinese heritage', and the results showed a generational bias in response to this question: the majority of 18–29 year-old Australians (57%) say there is 'a lot of discrimination' against people of Chinese heritage—a view shared by only a quarter (25%) of Australians over 60 (Kassam & Hsu, 2021: 17). This raises an interesting question as to why the elderly thought there is less discrimination. The same report that many Australian Chinese are proud of both their adopted country as well as China, with a sizable minority suggesting that there they faced some sort of discrimination. Yet, ironically there is little consensus on the various issues of the day that are being reported by the media, from the questions on foreign interference, biased media reporting, and preferred types of government to "the Chinese dream". The authors attribute the differences to migration history, personal identity and leaning and other factors (Kassam & Hsu, 2021),

The key to the propagation of discrimination and racial stereotypes is often found in corporate and social media. Most of the discussions on issues on this platform are often reduced to headlines and talking points. The ideals of democratic freedom, free speech and media holding public officials accountable often promote and stoke social divisions, not heal them. Whether it is "foreign interference" or "pricing out the locals", the rampant competitive and often negative coverage of media reports often encourages racism and hostility towards the Chinese community. A survey conducted by the UTS suggested that 70% of respondents in the Chinese community felt that these media reports fuelled suspicious and unfriendly attitudes towards the community, particularly as the media uses phrases like "Chinese spy" or "Chinese threat" (Hurst, 2023b). The same study suggests while a significant portion of those interviewed that they do not have a problem with the media running negative stories on China, 51% distrusted the media, and 76% say they rarely or never feel they have a shape in shaping public discourse, especially when there is a "news-making agenda in Australian English-language media that frames PRC and Chinese-Australians as hostile entities" (Hurst, 2023b).

Contemporary Australian nationalism is still very much predicated on the reaffirmation of Australia's heritage and cultural connections with

Great Britain and the West. What underpins the Australian sense of nationhood stems from the social memories of their countries standing shoulder to shoulder with the Allies during the First and Second World War, but also other difficulties and tribulations that the nation has faced in her past. Even though Australians have by and large moved beyond the notion that Australia is a white nation to one that is premised on multiculturalism, the undercurrents of white Australian nationalism remain. This form of racial dynamics is not unique to Australia and is common in multicultural societies such as France, Britain and the United States. The welcoming of migrants, particularly from Asia to Australia to form a new multicultural nation has been one of the most forward and looking gestures contemporary Australia has made in the construct of the modern Australian nationhood.

When the Commercial Becomes Political: Stopping the Growth of Firms and Barring Purchase of Domestic Strategic Assets

One of the most prominent domestic debates during the period under study involved the participation of Chinese companies in Australia's economy and the sale of assets to China-linked companies. During this decade, how China participated in Australia's economy became increasingly politicised and securitised. China's economic linkages are no longer just associated to ideas of just "economic growth" but also related to loss of strategic autonomy, political interference, national security, human rights and geopolitics. This marked the beginning of a decade of a major departure from how cooperation with China was discussed about in Australia. Naturally from the perspective of the Abbott-Turnbull-Morrison governments these discussions were well justified, but from Beijing's perspective, these moves are seen to as geopolitical in nature, designed to hemmed in the growth of Chinese firms and the expansion of their legitimate interests overseas.

The earliest and most prominent of this was the telecommunications industry. In 2013, Abbott banned Huawei from taking part in bidding for Australia's National Broadband Infrastructure. It is interesting to note that Abbott did this while shutting out his own Communications Minister and political rival Malcolm Turnbull in the final review. Turnbull was a lawyer turned entrepreneur who supported Huawei's participation, saying that his Ministry had due careful due diligence and technical review on Huawei, and that the Ministry was satisfied that Huawei was a "credible business" with a great future in Australia (Ireland, 2013). Abbott however seemed to have made up his mind up even before hearing out Turnbull as the Australia Intelligence and Security Organisation (AISO) had indicated that Huawei had possible links to Chinese government. These allegations provoked a strong reaction on the part of the Chinese since it appeared at this juncture that Australia privileged their security and intelligence relationship with the United States more than their economic and trading partnership with Beijing. China was angry (but not all that shocked) that years of trade and engagement did not pay off in terms of getting the Australians to see things their way, after all, Rudd's publication of his defence White Paper outlining the China threat gave Beijing a preview into the minds of Australian leaders. The attempt to exclude Huawei continued and in 2018, the Australian government again blocked Huawei and ZTE from taking part in the rolling out of the 5G network just four months after the United States blocked ZTE from providing telecommunications equipment for seven years because it had sold technologies to Iran and North Korea defying a US Trade Embargo (VOA, 2018).

From China's perspective, the decision to ban Huawei was an anti-competitive move designed to stop Huawei's expansion into providing 5G infrastructure globally. Beyond that the allegations of cybersecurity concerns and building backdoor into critical infrastructure was vehemently denied by Huawei and other Chinese companies. Even though the Chinese had initially hoped that this was a short term political tactic on the part of the Trump administration, they eventually accepted that this was going to long term strategy of the United States to pre-empt further Chinese development, especially into high-tech industries, as well as further in-roads to block Chinese influence, especially in US allied countries such as Australia, Britain and Japan.

Ports, Utilities and Cattle Ranches

The second controversial issue that occurred during Abbott's term involved the 99-year lease of the Darwin Port. In 2015 when the Northern Territory government under the Liberals decided to privatise the facility in an open bid, with Chinese-owned company Landbridge was declared the successful bidder with a significant bid of $506 million for the long-term lease after rigorous assessment by both the Defence Department and the AISO. The Territory government indicated they hoped that this would open new trade routes for Darwin and its surrounding areas for cattle, mining and gas industries (Gibson, 2022). This proved to be very controversial to the extent that President Obama (who had in 2011 established an agreement to base Marines in the Barracks nearby) raised this later in a meeting with Turnbull who had succeeded Abbot, even though they did not request that the port lease deal be unwound (Correy & Tingle, 2015). The port deal however did attract a fair amount of debate and discussion, with some Australian lawmakers arguing that the government should scrutinise the inward investment of Chinese bids for strategic assets and services in the country.

In 2015, Tony Abbott announced the Australian Foreign Investment Review Board (FIRB) that examines proposals by foreign persons to invest in Australia, declaring that foreign investment had to be "properly policed" so that Australian home buyers won't be disadvantaged as he was "determined to crackdown on any illegal activity that could be putting upward pressure on property prices" (Gerber, 2015). Abbott also changed the rules to charge foreign investors a premium, increased fines and possible jail terms for investors or agents who breach the foreign ownership laws, claiming that it would "level the playing field" and give locals a "fair go" (Slater & Quinn, 2015). Abbott's Treasurer, Joe Hockey had asked the Head of Evergrande Real Estate Group, to sell a mansion he acquired illegally in 2014 for 39 million dollars (Gough, 2016). These moves appeared to show that his government was actually doing something against the popular perception that the Chinese were "buying up everything" particularly in the real estate market and making housing unaffordable. While the large influx of funds for real estate deals were indeed true, the buyers included amongst nationalities from a wide range of countries, including Europeans and Americans. In February 2017, the Government forced foreign nationals to sell over $100 m worth of illegally acquired Australian real estate, including 15 Australian residential properties, taking this to a total of 61 forced sales with a combined value of A$107 million. These 107 properties were owned by Chinese, Taiwanese, Philippines, Saudi, Indonesia, Singapore, UK, India, Malaysia, and German investors (ATM, 2017).

Ironically, the FIRB also lowered the threshold for reviewing agricultural land and agribusiness purchases by foreign investors, including those from China. This however did not prevent Morrison from blocking the sale of 2.5% of agricultural land (or 1.3% of Australia's land mass) for USD$288 million to Dakang Australia Holdings on the basis that it may be "contrary to national interest" (Chan & Taylor, 2016). The deal was eventually approved by Morrison when the Chinese company partnered with a local Australia Mining Magnate Gina Rinehart, and excluded the defence-sensitive Anna Creek Station from the purchase (Schwartz et al., 2016; Brown, et al., 2016; Brann, 2023).

This pattern of politicising commercial decisions and deals extended to other industries too. In 2016, the Turnbull government rejected USD$7.7 billion bid from competing Hong Kong and Chinese groups for 50.4% stake in a utility company, Ausgrid that supplies electricity to New South Wales, including Sydney. Ironically, this included mainland groups as well as Cheung Kong Holdings, the latter of which is owned by Lee Ka-Shing who had already divested most of his holdings away from mainland China, and is widely rumoured to be in Beijing's crosshairs. This of course did not mattered to politicians. Scott Morrison who was Treasurer then had suggested that these measures were not country-specific, and the decision was made strictly because of the nature of assets (Gough, 2016).

However, after revelations of ties between the Chinese company that bought the port, Landbridge Corporation, and the People's Liberation Army, the deal has sparked a new focus on Chinese investment in critical infrastructure as bids close on the $9 billion sale of the NSW electricity grid and an associated optical fibre network which is used by defence bases and data centres.

Political Interference and Party Politics

One of the biggest challenges that involves China is the extent of its influence operations in democratic societies. Prime Minister Turnbull defined behaviour that is "covert, coercive and corrupting" as the line that separates legitimate influence from unacceptable interference" (Parton, 2020). Designed specifically for China (Needlam, 2021), it is also clear that one of the key aims of this legislation was design to prevent Labor from soliciting any help from domestic sources that would try and stop the Liberals from doing the damages it intends to by curbing China's economic influence. In 2014 and 2020, there were two cases of high-profile political interferences cases that rocked Australia society. In both cases, Members of Parliament from the Labor Party were involved, allegedly fronting for China's interests in Australia. The first MP (Senator 2013–2018) Sam Dastyari, a naturalised Australian of Iranian descent declared that a Chinese company had provided him with funds to settle his legal and travel bills which he declared. Dastyari had also disagreed with the government's (hence the Conservative Party's) take on the South China issue, and Prime Minister Malcolm Turnbull wasted no time in attacking the Labor Party, asking if it's "foreign policy is for sale" (Murphy, 2016). Dastyari was also linked to a Chinese real estate developer and Australian Permanent Resident Huang Xiangmo who was suspected by Australian Intelligence of having ties to the Chinese Communist Party. Huang was stripped of his Australian permanent residency and barred from Australia despite having established a family in Australia all of whom are Australian citizens. Huang was allegedly being investigated for corruption in Guangdong before he left for Australia. This real estate tycoon behaved typically like most real estate moguls, seeking to cultivate goodwill in his new country by making a series of donations: A$1.8 million to University of Technology Sydney for a New China Institute led by former Pro-Beijing Foreign Minister Bob Carr; A$4.5 million to several universities, and most importantly to both political parties i.e. both Labor and Liberal party amount to A$3 million dollars from 2012 to 2015, but most problematically, his influence had gone beyond normal advocacy to the possible enticement of Labor Party to support the election of an ethnic Chinese as Member of Parliament (HKFP, 2019). After his eviction from Australia, Huang established himself in Hong Kong and became a member of the Committee to elect the next Chief Executive (Doherty, 2021). The funny thing about this is of course such a narrative of interference does not apply to their Liberal party. Peter Dutton who held the Immigration and subsequently Defence Minister Portfolio, was reportedly to have met the same Chinese billionaire seeking help with his Australian citizenship in 2016 (SBS, 2019).

Given that Foreign donations were permitted in Australia in most states, this incident paved the way for the passage of a new set of law that defines what constitute foreign interference and provide security agencies the powers to investigate and prosecute (Hutchens, 2018). In 2020, another Labor Member of Parliament was again accused by Scott Morrison of engaging in aiding and abetting China's agenda. Shaoquett Moselmane of Lebanese descent had praised Beijing's handling of the Covid pandemic, and that directly contravened Australia's official position after Scott Morrison angered Beijing by calling for an open investigation into the origins of the Covid virus. Moselmane was interrogated and searched by Australia Security Services and had his Labor membership suspended. He also had his Parliamentary privileges suspended but he was never charged or question and was eventually cleared. His lawyer was an ethnic Chinese Australian named John Zhang, and he was too investigated by Australia's Spy Agency ASIO, and this invited a tit-for-tat retaliation by which an Australian TV anchor was arrested in Beijing (Rubinsztein-Dunlop, 2020). This effectively became the first high-profile criminal investigation of Chinese influence peddling to be made public after the passage of the Foreign Interference Law. Moselmane was not charged after almost four months of investigation, and the Labor Party was forced to restore his status.

From the vantage point of most of Australian society, this probably constituted Beijing's attempt to influence Australian politics, interfere with civil society debate and most seriously, actively subvert and "plant" their own agents or preferred candidates in the Australian Parliament. While this is probably true, the fact of the matter is that lobbying, political donations and advocating for candidates to gain a seat in Parliament is actually what happens in a democracy. The real problem here is that the "agent" might or might not be acting in place for China, just as there are other actors and agents who are actively lobbying for other parties and possibly other countries amongst the mainstream political establishment as well. Collectively, these three Conservative Prime Ministers acted to take an increasingly tougher stance position against China during this decade.

Even as Abbott started to tackle the possible economic security aspects of Chinese foreign investment, it was Malcolm Turnbull who introduced legislation to counter foreign interference in Australian domestic society, politics and institutions. These measures were theoretically aimed at safeguarding Australian democracy and addressing the concerns of the China state-sponsored activities in Australia. When the legislation was implemented no countries were named, but everyone knew that it was clearly aimed at China. Morrison's government fixated on the question of national security like Abbott and foreign interference like Turnbull. Morrison introduced the Foreign Influence Transparency Act 2018 which is modelled on the American Foreign Agents Registration Act. This was in fact a continuation of the work that the Turnbull government had been working on and was in fact drafted in close consultation with the Trump Administration. The Act requires anyone who engages in lobbying or any kind of communications activity for the purpose of political influence" on behalf of a "foreign principal" to register with the Australian Federal government, and imposes criminal penalties for failure to do so. Turnbull himself admitted that the key purpose of the legislation (passed under Morrison's government) was to expose China's activities in Australia, particularly those with links to China Communist Party's United Front Work Department but the scheme had "failed" to do so because those with links did not "appear on the register" when they are supposed to have declared themselves with links and done so (Turnbull cited by Needham, 2023). Morrison's ascendance in Australia politics brought the anti-China sentiments in China to new heights, particularly so against the backdrop of global Covid pandemic. Although all three Prime Ministers had some continuity in their national security policies, their politics were never quite the same.

There are many schools of thoughts as to why Morrison was able to prevail or why Turnbull lost. One can look instinctively back to Turnbull's struggle with Abbott in the early days before Liberal took back power. The division in Liberal party's support for Abbott and Turnbull was quite balanced. Turnbull was ideologically committed and less "pragmatically" inclined; he was one of the leaders that wanted to move the Party towards true Liberalism, and that his climate change agenda had upset many in the Party who did not want to implement genuine action on climate change (Manne, 2012). Even though his policy orientation was not really of the Global Right persuasion, the political climate and day to day politics had him "boxed" in.

The Conservative Methodology: Cultural Nationalism, Racial Tarring and Identity Politics

Australian domestic developments cannot be divorced from the rise of conservatism across the world. While the support for far-right movements is not new, what is striking is that by the end of a decade of 2010s, conservative ideology and right-wing politics had become mainstream in many countries. To be sure, no one can certainly account for the origins of this phenomenon, but what is clear is that the popularity of this movement certainly appeared to be fuelled by organic grassroot reactions to the hyper-globalised world over the past four decades. Years of free trade, capital flow and free movement accentuated income inequalities and class disparity in almost any advanced capitalistic society, this is often triggered by a deepened desire for greater security. Economic troubles, often accentuated by these deep social divisions often propel primal sentiments of identity and security to the fore, and this often triggers deep soul-searching by those affected and dislocated by globalisation for alternative (or familiar) ways to organise and reorganise societies. Often, Conservatives offer appealing rhetoric and policy promises to improve the nation's political and cultural status and the socio-economic status of the average citizen (Howe et al., 2022). Nationalism necessitates an "other" often as scapegoats, and often such narratives create conditions for immigration, identity and security to be moved to the fore of societal debate. Conservative narratives often run counter to the narratives of left-leaning parties on the importance of open borders, free trade agreements or multiculturalism. What is evident is that the ideals of multiculturalism were not only being attacked from the far right but also by mainstream politicians in the United Kingdom, United States and Europe (Mudde, 2020). Naturally, the emergence of conservatism saw the rise of populist politicians capitalising on the prevailing sentiments. Whether it is the rise of the Tea Party movement in the United States or Boris Johnson's election as the Mayor of London, aspiring politicians are re-examining their overall approach in their political images, narratives and campaigns. In Asia, the rise of nationalist politicians such as Junichiro Koizumi and Shinzo Abe in 2012 certainly provided much inspiration for their peers elsewhere. If anything, the political longevity of Japanese Prime Minister Junichiro Koizumi as well as the successful second coming of Shinzo Abe in 2012 certainly demonstrated that their core strategy worked. Given that the Australian Labor Party politicians such as Kevin Rudd had successfully utilised his knowledge and his handling of China for Australia's benefit, the Conservative politicians needed a strategy to dislodge Labor's plans and messaging. This is important on a few levels. Labor's successful management of Chinese inward investment would put Labor candidates ahead of Liberal candidates if the economy does well. The central tenet is therefore to disrupt the momentum of their Labor opponents and seize the agenda on China. The Conservatives' strategy is to securitise the debate, and play up existing feelings against migrants as their strategy to protect Australians.

There is therefore an institutionalised form of bias that is being drummed out by the Conservative camp. The tendency to "tar" any China-related narratives, and explanations should be completely blocked out as "influence" operations. As a CSIS notes in a study:

one Australian politician was drummed out of parliament after it was revealed that he pandered to "Chinese language media on South China Sea policy and warned his CCP-linked patron about government survelliance", as well as growing questions about China's influence in Australian Universities and CCP-linked efforts to coopt Chinese language and civic groups in Chinese Australia Community. (Searight, 2020)

This sort of narrative has been very effective in blocking out any outreach, gestures or messages coming from China (legitimate or not), and has sought to mobilise "like-minded" countries against China and the Chinese in general. The major attack on "foreign interference" in and out of Parliament necessitates that anyone who speak out for China or Chinese is definitely "bought" by Beijing, and it tars arguments made to suggest that Australia could have taken a different and less hardline track with China as "working with the enemy" (Cave, 2017). This presents a problem in that the minority Chinese population (or just about anyone) who speaks out in a counter-narrative manner as being "pro-China/Chinese". At the same time, narratives supporting the Conservatives would always emphasize this line of thinking is not "racist" in nature, as when Australians think about China it is always more about the government than the people (Huang et al., 2022).

This kind of racist "tarring" therefore has become a staple in Australian politics, but often played out very prominent before elections, especially during Morrison's term. Just before the Federal elections, Morrison's Defence Minister and Leader of the National Party Peter Dutton was determined to keep up false claims that Labor had a back door deal with the Chinese Communist Party, suggesting that the CCP was keen to enact a change of government (Bergin, 2022). Ads before the Federal elections found on trucks across Australia read: "CCP says Vote Labor" (funded by Lobby Groups Advance Australia) implying a vote for opposition Labor meant supporting China; experts say this kind of messaging will lead to more prejudice against Asians, keeping them "othered" (Tan, SMCP, 9 May 2022). Morrison had also called Labor Party's Deputy leader, Richard Marles a Manchurian candidate, implying he was a puppet of Beijing with a strangely high number of meetings with Chinese diplomats (Guina, 2022). Ethnic Chinese candidates such as Jason Li have reported that they have been accused of maintaining ties with the Chinese Communist Party even when his parents arrived in Australia more than sixty years ago (Guina, 2022). It is however not just Conservative candidates that are attacked. Liberal Party Candidate Gladys Li who was born in Hong Kong was also tarred as having intimate ties with China in 2019, and had been accused of taking money from the Chinese government, and branded as a Chinese Spy by Labor Queensland Branch, suggesting that she is Xi Jinping's candidate for Chisholm (Bergin, 2022).

This sort of racial political manoeuvring is very effective. Beyond attracting public support and moving public narratives towards affirmations of cultural nationalism and identity politics, it also restricts the way citizens think about public policy. Such rhetorical manoeuvres put perimeters on rational discussions and reduces the vision (in a myopic way) of how one can conceive of options to public or foreign policy challenges. Most ethnic Chinese would refrain from public disagreement with such politics, given their minority status and the risk this puts them in. It also changed the way ethnic Chinese migrants live their day to day lives, and many were worried about going to "white areas" (Guina, 2022). Conservative politicians would go on the rhetorical offensive attacking China to maximise the political effect of their posture (Hurst, 2022). If China does not respond, it is a direct victory. If it elicits an angry reaction or retaliatory policy from China, it affirms everything that has been said about them and provides a platform to pontificate their righteousness, particularly over their tough stance on values or security (Bagshaw, 2020; Daizell, 2020; Davis, 2022a; Hurst, 2023a). Either way, it pleases their friends in the Quad countries. If the political opposition raises a ruckus, the standard response would be to question their loyalty. As Morrison claimed: "What I don't understand is that when something of this significance takes place, why would you take China's side?" in a debate on the China-Solomon island agreement (Hurst, 2020), suggesting their opponents are aiding and abetting the enemy. Either way, such a strategy lends credence to the dominant narrative created outside of China by the global right and reaffirms the Conservative camp's position at home. This effectively puts most people on the defence, even for exceptional well-credentialed individuals. Even if they offer contrarian views, the impact of their views remains limited. Such political attacks would only stop if the politicians realise that these tactics are costing them votes (Maiden, 2021).

Level III: The International System

Systemic Drivers and Australia's Conservative Turn

Australia's post-war strategic culture and worldview have been shaped by historical linkages and social memories with the US and UK since the Second World War. On 29 April 1952, the ANZUS Treaty the three countries signed in 1951 came into force. The signatories pledged to overcome and "meet the common danger" in the event of an armed attack on one of the members. This treaty comes a decade after both Australia and New Zealand saw how easily British defences fell in Singapore in February 1942, and their subsequent experience of fighting alongside the United States and the United Kingdom in the Asia–Pacific in the Second World War. As part of British and Commonwealth forces, Australia deployed forces to Europe in campaigns against Germany and Italy in Europe, the Mediterranean and North Africa and against Japan in Southeast Asia and Pacific islands. The horrors of the Holocaust and the shock of the Japanese attack on Pearl Harbour as well as the threat to the Australia mainland naturally reoriented Australian elites into entering an alliance with the United States. Not surprisingly, Australia became part of the San Francisco System in 1951 (along with Japan) by entering into a security agreement with the United States. With the ANZUS Treaty, Australia took on its role as a junior partner in the United States' anti-communist Cold War struggle against the USSR, fighting alongside with UN troops in Korea and later on in Indochina. Canberra reconciled with Japan in 1952, co-founded SEATO as a member, and became an important member of the US-led security system, and supporting Washington in her unpopular war in Vietnam. Australia's support of the United States went to the extent that there were discussions on how it could provide support for the United States' use of nuclear weapons against the Communists, even there was a concern about how its relations with Asia would be affected by (APMD, 1962). Canberra initiated an unpopular conscription policy and committed 8500 personnel, suffering losses of 3000 wounded and 521 dead, leading to street protests that mirrored those in the United States in the 1970s (ANIB, 1970). Australia had refused to accede to a US request to increase her deployment to Vietnam owing to these domestic difficulties.

These sentiments also helped the election of Labor opposition leader Gough Whitlam who had preferred Australia retain a certain amount of strategic autonomy from the United States. He was subsequently seen as the Prime Minister who implemented several measures that were seen as unfriendly to the United States. Whitlam had approached China even before Kissinger, and instituted measures to ensure that Australia's relations were not subservient to the United States. This probably was the most significant episode that created difficulties in US-Australian relations. Whitlam had later alleged that the CIA was involved in his removal, and that Carter had later promised Whitlam that the Americans would not involve themselves in Australia's democratic process. Whitlam's dismissal by the Governor-General was controversial as the CIA and the Americans were deemed to be part of the movement that saw him tossed out of office. After all, Whitlam was seen to have "ended colonial servility, abolished royal patronage, moved Australia towards Non-Aligned movement, supported zones of peace and opposed nuclear testing" but most importantly he was trying to ensure that CIA and Mi6 did not continue to operate without impediment in Australia. This ultimately cost him his career (Pilger, 2014). To this day, there is no politician who does not know of the dangers of not acceding to Americans and British interests and influence, especially those in the Australian Labor Party.

Even as Australia's relations were "normalised" during the Reagan Administration, Canberra understood the importance of maintaining her strategic ties with Washington. The United States after all was Australia's second-largest trading partner after Japan, and maintained deep and well-rounded ties with Australians across all spheres of her relations. There is however, a recognition as a Middle Power with nuclear weapons, Australia would have to diverge from United States policy in accordance with her own national interests, even as Canberra understood and appreciated the burden the United States bore as the leader of the Western alliance (AMFA, 1981). After the 9/11 incident, Australia joined the United States by invoking the ANZUS Treaty, thereby becoming one of the first members in the "coalition of the willing" to fight terrorism. Australia deployed her special forces to fight alongside the United States in Afghanistan against Taliban and al Qaeda, particularly in the mountainous regions near Kabul. The Bali Bombings in 2002 that killed 88 Australians reaffirmed Australia's resolve to participate in the War against Terror. The operations in Afghanistan were suspended until 2005 due to developments in Iraq. Canberra also deployed with the United States in the invasion of Iraq in 2003 but this raised considerable domestic opposition when no Weapons of Mass Destruction were found. This however did not affect Australia's resolve, and collectively Australia maintained a security presence to help the US-led coalition in helping mount counter-insurgency operations and participated in training detachments for local forces and protective details for diplomats and reconstruction forces until 2009. Australia also maintained her security forces as part of a NATO-led force in Afghanistan to target and fight terrorist insurgencies and help developed the Afghan local forces. Likewise, Australia also deployed against ISIS in Syria. For the most part, Australia's deployment demonstrated the importance and resolve of Australia's commitment to the US-led Western alliance. It is of course no surprise to find that when the United States announced her pivot to Asia in 2012, Canberra reinforced and double downed on her commitment to support the United States. For more than a decade from September 11, Australia has in effect worked closely and in tandem with the United States on its War of Terror, even has its trade with China grew from year to year. At the same time, Howard also sought to work up a viable and positive relationship with China, at least in public discourse. It had developed from an economic relationship (1996), to an economic relationship with strategic significance (1997), to a strategic economic relationship (2003), and finally to an explicit strategic relationship (2004) (McDowall, 2009).

It is not easy for Australia to label China as security threat. Historically the only country that had launched attacks on Australia's mainland was Japan when they bombed Darwin and Broome in 1942. The United States used Australia as a base to attack Japan and defend the allies' interests in the South Pacific, and Japanese nationals (along with Italians and Germans) during the War. While the Australians too had fought the Chinese People's Volunteers during their deployment in the Korean War, it was done under the Umbrella of the UN forces. Unlike India or Japan, Australia has no maritime or common land border issues or sovereignty disputes with China, but rather with Indonesia (Strating, 2021).

Australia–China relations have actually a history of five "ice ages": (1) 1949–1972 where Australia sided with the United States refusing to recognise the PRC until the US–China rapproachment; (2) 1989–1991 when Prime Minister Bob Hawke suspended visits, exchanges and military contacts with China after the Tiananmen Square incident, allowing the largest wave of Chinese migration to Australia; (3) 1996 when PRC and the Howard government clashed over PRC's intimidation of Taiwan elections; (4) 2008–2009 when China increased pressure on Australia because of Prime Minister Kelvin Rudd's calling out on Beijing over a host of contentious matter, from its exercise of power to human rights in Tibet (Dobell, 2018).

Australia's trade with China is not asymmetrical in the "traditional" sense like what most of other countries trading with China experiences (i.e. China exports more to Australia while importing little). Australia actually maintains a trade surplus with China most of the time, and both countries have in fact gained immensely from this relationship. Under such positive trading circumstances, only identity politics and nationalistic narratives could be used to justify the reframing of China in Australia's everyday discourse. There is very little possibility of dislodging China from the important role it plays in Australia's economy.

The Need for a Rejuvenated San Francisco System: Hard Pivot to the United States

The birth of the San Francisco system in 1951 is predicated on the series of bilateral alliances that the United States had reached with its principal allies to counter the Communist threat that was perceived to be sponsored by the USSR and China and spreading across Asia through North Korea and Vietnam in Indochina. Australia and New Zealand naturally became part of this asymmetric hub-and-spokes system that saw the United States offering military security and economic privileges to its partners. In joining the San Francisco system, Australia joined the ranks of Treaty allies such as Japan, Republic of Korea, Taiwan and Philippines in constructing a security system. While the People's Republic of China fought the United States in Korea and Vietnam, it wasn't until the 1972 US–China reproachment that saw China's relations with the United States and her allies change. Once China embarked on her reforms in 1978 under Deng Xiaoping's direction, China's role in the San Francisco System change. Even though China was not formally an ally, Beijing was instrumental in helping the United States put more pressure to counter the Soviet threat. China like most of American allies was allowed to have access to American technology, capital and assistance to reform and rebuild her economy. By the end of the Cold War, China's economy had become interlinked with the US and her allies' economies intimately. In this respect, China's economic growth had in many ways fuelled and powered the San Francisco System as she was an integral part of the US global capital system. Australia's growing ties with China (as well as the rest of Asia) must be viewed in this light.

The supposed end of the Cold War brought a sense of strategic anxiety as to whether the Americans would withdraw or retrench their presence in the Asia–Pacific. For much of the 1990s, this was the number one question that was on the minds of analysts from Tokyo to Canberra. A related debate is whether China's rise posits as a threat. Under the leadership of Paul Keating (1991–1996), Australia focused very intensely on building her relations with her neighbours based on the idea that Australians are very much part of the Asian community. The Howard administration seems to have taken a more aloof view on this, in part because the government is put on the defensive by ultra-right politicians such as Paula Hanson, in part because it was honestly difficult to top what Keating's had said and done with Asia without looking like they had given up the Liberal party's position and outlook. (White, 2003). In order to push the US–Australia alliance to greater heights, the Howard government can only try to incorporate a bilateral free trade agreement to reshape and strengthen the alliance (White, 2003). Australia then had wanted the United States to maintain its presence in the region, after all, Washington was widely viewed as a benign hegemon compared to the possible options. Australia's Prime Minister John Howard had adamantly supported the shoring up of the US presence in the Asia–Pacific region to prevent a possible strategic withdrawal. After all, Australia's most reliable alliance is with Washington.

By the end of the War on Terror, the strategic situation in Asia had changed radically. China had wisely focused her efforts on undertaking a variety of reforms and growing her economy consistently even though she faced increasingly challenging diplomatic conditions in Asia, particularly from Japan and Southeast Asia. Across the world, China has become the most important trading partner to many countries, often being able to build asymmetrical relations that would lend her significant political sway in those countries. Within the San Francisco system, China's economic linkages has grown so great that not only is she able to influence the actions of the United States bilaterally, but also exert significant pressure economically on the US allies such as Japan, South Korea and Australia. As much as neoliberals in the West in these countries love to expound on the beauty of economic interdependency, the narrative has now (or term) become "economic coercion" when it comes to China.

The relative waning of American and Japanese power vis-à-vis China in the region meant that the US security architecture needed to be adjusted and rejuvenated. From the standpoint of the United States, her allies need to reduce their economic interactions with China for three reasons: to reduce the ability of China to utilise trade to sway political influence over them, particularly in their decisions to support Washington in the event of a US–China conflict; to reduce the ability of China to hurt their supply chain and to curb the growing power of China as the United States and her allies have allowed Beijing to become the world's factory. China's growing clout manifests itself in a variety of ways from her military modernisation projects to her ability to fund and build strategic initiatives such as the Belt and Road Initiative. China's power simply cannot be curbed unless the United States and her allies embark on across the board to rid themselves of the Chinese ties they have built up since the 1980s. Australia's role in this struggle therefore became all the more important.

In 2000, George W. Bush criticised the Clinton White House for seeking a "strategic partnership" with China, suggesting that he would define China as a "strategic competitor". Tensions increased in Sino-US relations, and this was clearly evidenced by the EP3 Incident. A Chinese fighter had collided in mid-air and forced the US spyplane to land in Hainan, and provided Beijing with an intelligence windfall (Zetter, 2017). The events of September 11 effectively made Al Qaeda the number one enemy of the United States and the Bush Administration, giving China a respite. By the time the War on Terror was over, the United States once again decided that China represented one of the greatest threats to the United States' interest in the region. As one of the most important alliances in the Indo-Pacific region, Washington has required her allies to support the United States in her "pivot" to Asia.

Obama's "pivot" is not just empty talk. The United States needed to tighten and reinforce her alliance system in Asia urgently. It is important to note that the Prime Ministers who led Australia from 2010 onwards lived in very different times compared to their predecessors two decades ago. Apart from Kevin Rudd, a former diplomat and a student of Chinese history, language and politics, most of the other Prime Ministers have had no training in diplomacy nor interest in China or Asia. Gillard, Abbott and Turnbull were lawyers, and Scott Morrison had an interesting background in acting, marketing and tourism promotion. Despite the differences in their party affiliation and domestic politics posture, they all seemed to have taken rather similar lines in their foreign policy, particularly in crafting Australia's relations with the United States and China. All these leaders were born and grew up during the height of the Cold War where Australia was significantly under British and American influence and control. They also lived through the Vietnam War and the golden years of peace and prosperity that Australia enjoyed since the 1980s. To a large extent, it would not be inaccurate that these leaders had the same worldview as each other, and understood Australia's role in the San Francisco System, and appreciated the fact that the United States was Australia's principal security guarantor. It would only be natural that these politicians saw a need to express public support to back the US play, even if the initiatives came from Donald Trump.

This need to support American strategy however comes at a huge cost to Australia economically as Canberra had actually maintained a healthy trade surplus with China. The election of Liberal-National coalition Conservative politicians with wafer-thin margin of support in an environment where leaders can be overthrown via shifts in faction alliances created the perfect environment by which the country's politics and foreign policy can be moved. In little over a decade, developments both in and outside Australia caused the government to thoroughly bring down Australia's burgeoning trade with her number one trading partner China by five relatively short-lived Prime Ministers who were more than eager to perform and please the electorate through populist policies. Being poll-driven, they were often more concerned with maintaining great popularity to maintain a one-up over their political rival than to consider the longer-term repercussions of their policies. Naturally, their concern by which how their decisions were perceived by the electorate ratherthanthelong-term actual implications.

With the rise of the global conservative movement, these politicians were perhaps merely capitalising on the moment. In the words so often spoken by the Conservative leaders, Australia's rise to protect her national interests and preserve its values, freedoms and democracy against an increasingly assertive and militaristic China was necessary for Australia's destiny. Notwithstanding alliance politics, Australia however does have many concerns with regard to Chinese activities just like many of her Southeast Asian neighbours.

Securing Australia's National Interests and Addressing Security Concerns South China Sea and Australia's Defence

Australia's interest in the Indo-Pacific is not at all passive. In fact, Canberra like New Delhi and Tokyo has its own strategic calculus insofar as China is concerned. The only time when Australia has been attacked in recent history was during the Second World War. The Japanese Imperial Army invaded New Guinea in 1942 planning to use it as a base to move south to Papua, and eventually to attack the Australia mainland and shipping in the Pacific. From 1942 to 1943, the Japanese effectively stationed their aircraft carriers in the Timor Sea and bombed Darwin, and killed 243 people and wounded between 300 and 400 people (AIDR, n.d.). There were additional air raids on Horn Island, Broome, Exmouth Gulf, and Townsville. Japanese submarines carried out attacks on allied warships as well as hospital ships in Sydney, Queensland and in the Pacific. From a strategic standpoint, the countries and the waters to the North of Australia presents the greatest likelihood for any invading or attacking force to come from. Australia's strategic priority since the War has therefore to ensure that this does not happen again. Southeast Asia and by extension South China Sea has therefore become an extremely important security zone for Canberra.

Australia's decision to proactively partake in measures to counter China's claims in the South China Sea appeared to have been made sometime in the Abbott government. Setting aside the fact that Beijing does have legitimate claims in the South China Sea (even if most nations ridicule the 9 dotted lines), the very fact that she is reclaiming and militarising these reefs in the South China Sea created much concern for Australian planners. Granted, China is not the first to utilise this method, but the political arithmetic is simple: in siding with the United States and Southeast Asia, Australia gains an additional measure of security in solidarity with many more partners. The lessons of World War II suggest that in the event of any hostility between the United States and China, South China Sea would become vital to the conflict.

For Canberra, the turning point occurred when Chinese President Xi said they are not militarising the islands in the South China Sea. The South China Sea is vital for Australia's principal allies' (US's and Japan's) security interests. If the PRC was able to dominate and control this region, it would be able to threaten maritime lifelines to Japan, South Korea and Taiwan. Yet more importantly as China has greatly expanded on her aerial and naval power, the idea that the United States can achieve victory swiftly over China in a conflict in East or South China Sea is no longer a foregone conclusion. If the original interest in the Quad is to keep the United States engaged and lock in the region, then surely for Australia, participation in Quad 2.0 is an exercise to further the "insurance" in the event of a great power conflict. The premise of course for most of the United States and her allies is that the Americans would prevail in any *eventuality* of a conflict with China. It would be in Australia's interest to ensure that the Americans do not lose. As China is already Australia's number one trading partner, and if the Chinese end up dominating the region in the security realm as well, Canberra is concerned that her interests might not be preserved on such favourable terms.

South Pacific and Australia's Role as Regional Hegemon Cum Watchman

The Pacific Ocean is the largest and deepest Ocean, and extends from Artic in the North to Antarctica to the South. It occupies about 165.25 million square kilometres, and covers about 32% of the earth's surface with untold oceanic resources and minerals. The Western Pacific has connections to adjacent seas such as the South China Sea, East China Sea, the Philippines Sea, the Sea of Japan, the Coral Sea and Timor Sea. With a string of idyllic islands that stretches from Micronesia to Melanesia to Polynesia, the Pacific connects Asia and Australia to the United States. The vastness of the Ocean provides a natural barrier that accords much strategic solace and security to both the United States and Australia. To overcome this barrier, any country would need very capable blue ocean fleets and a presence on the bigger Pacific islands in order to project their power. For decades, only the United States have had this privilege (Meick 2018), and the allied countries have not forgotten how important the Pacific islands were during the Second World War. Given Australia's proximity to the Pacific, Canberra has always been keen to ensure her de facto front yard remains secure and free. Other than the brief interruption caused by heavy Japanese fighting in the Pacific, Australia has always exercised a certain amount of influence and control over this vast region.

China's strategic and diplomatic interests in the Pacific islands are driven by its desire to curb Taiwanese diplomatic space, expand its economic and humanitarian Belt Road Initiatives, obtain new sources of raw materials (fisheries, marine resources) and increase its political influence amongst Pacific Island Countries (PIC). There was considerable discomfort on the part of Australia and the United States when Australian media company Fairfax reported that Vanuatu (which is 2000 km away from Australia) was considering allowing China to build a military base (Torode & Wen, 2018). This however has been denied by both Beijing and Vanuatu. In 2021, another Australia Media company reportedly that

China is planning to build a multi-use port on Papua New Guinea's Manus Island, which has been regarded as pivotal because of its sweeping command of the Pacific Ocean and maritime approaches to Asia (Maley & Riordan, 2018). Papua New Guinea in the end turned to Australia and the United States to redevelop the port instead.

Beijing successfully persuaded the Solomon Islands to switch diplomatic recognition from Taipei to Beijing in 2019 and subsequently reached a security pact with the government which grants permission for the Chinese Navy to dock and replenish there. Additionally, the pact also allowed the Solomon Island leadership to seek assistance from Chinese security forces to maintain law and order, given that the leader Manasseh Sogavare had seen unrest there. Morrison had dispatched Australia's security forces to help quell the unrest, which was stirred up in part by opposing politicians who supported Taiwan strongly (Walden et al., 2021). Prime Minister Sogavare in turn had reassured the Pacific Island Forum in 2022 that he would not allow for a Chinese Naval Base in the area. In March 2022, the draft version of the security pact was leaked where the leader has agreed to allow Beijing to deploy forces to protect the safety of Chinese personnel and projects on the island (Tuilaepa-Taylor, 2022). The Morrison government was severely criticised for this as one of the worst foreign policy failures since 1945 as the Solomon Islands confirmed that the pact was indeed signed (Martin, 2022). This begs the point: why would Sogavare be reaching out to the Chinese instead of the Australians or Americans for his domestic security issues? Naturally, Australia has regarded him to be a corrupt leader that Beijing has managed to sway since the Morrison government had been in contact with the political opposition on the island since August 2021 (Martin, 2022). In 2023, China and the Solomon Islands officially upgraded their relations to a Comprehensive Strategic Partnership Featuring Mutual Respect and Common Development (PRC MFA, 2023). Beijing had also managed to persuade Kiribati to switch diplomatic recognition from Taipei in 2019 shortly after Solomon Islands did so. Taiwan had managed to persuade Kiribati to recognise her diplomatically in 2003, twenty-three years after she first established diplomatic relations with the PRC. In May 2020, the PRC opened its diplomatic mission on the island, and has stepped up cooperation in infrastructure development, fighting climate change, addressing the Covid pandemic and engaging in sustainable development. Kirabati, with its population of 110,000 had requested loans and a Boeing 737 aircraft from Beijing, and said that its decision to recognise Beijing was made after "following a long internal review and assessment of our international relations in accordance with the best national interest for our country and people" (Reuters, 2019). For Australia and the United States, however, the greatest concern is that Kiribati has requested China to refurbish a US-built World War II airstrip on Kanton Island to allow for commercial islands between the capital and other islands (Giannini, 2023). China has managed to tout this as an infrastructure project without military dimension to deflect criticisms, and this has left the United States and Australia with serious concerns. Kiribati, along with four other Micronesia states (Palau, Marshall Islands, Micronesia, Nauru) had in fact left the Pacific Islands Forum in 2022 after a leadership contest dispute but nonetheless was asked by Fiji to re-joined in 2023. In that year, Kiribati was able to improve on her negotiations with China. The Labor Foreign Minister had in 2023 scaled up security and development cooperation with Kiribati to counter what Canberra perceives as a Chinese attempt to gain a strategic foothold on the island. Australia in turn had promised that they would upgrade a Wharf and provide Kiribati with two patrol boats to pre-empt any attempt by China to build a naval base on the island. There were also allegations that China has been spying on the former President of the Federated States of Micronesia while he was in Fiji, and he has been lobbying for a diplomatic switch back to Taiwan after he lost his elections. Naturally, there are widespread allegations and counter-allegations of corruption and electoral intervention (Antony, 2023).

There is no question that from the perspective of Australia, the South Pacific is seen as a front yard and a sphere of influence. Beijing's attempt to reach out to the South Pacific countries has been seen by both Washington and Canberra as an extension of China's Great Power ambitions to mimic the US strategy of gaining footholds and bases around the world. It is also a first attempt to build a sea-path that can be potentially used against the US during times of war. In reaching out to these islands to offer economic and developmental assistance, Beijing's moves are interpreted as the first step to offer a sweetener to entice the local governments to accept and normalise a Chinese presence. Such an interpretation is causing much discomfort to Canberra. These islands have always been considered Australia's "Near Abroad" or for lack of a better word, Australia's front yard. In military terms, it would bring China's near-capable fleets one step closer to Hawaii, Guam and Australia, in line

4 THE ERA OF THE CONSERVATIVES AND AUSTRALIA'S ...   279

with China's strategy to project force to the Second Island Chain in the near future.

Australia, the Quad and AUKUS

When the Quad was first proposed by Shinzo Abe in his first term (2006–2007), the concept was met with lukewarm reception. Despite being a Liberal democracy, the historical revisionist proclivities of right-wing Conservative politicians are well known outside of Japan. In the golden years of the 1980s when contemporary Sino-Japanese relations were arguably at their best, the first quarrel between China and Japan surfaced over the Japanese history textbooks' interpretation of the invasion by the Japanese Imperial Army as "advancing" into China, as well as the fondness of Japanese politicians to worship at the Yasukuni Shrine where the War Criminals are enshrined. Even though a crop of issues surfaced in the 1990s in Sino-Japanese relations, both countries nudged the relationship along until the early 2000s when Junichiro Koizumi became Prime Minister. Koizumi was the first to employ a hardened posture against the Chinese, and aggressively use the media to amplify a tough image to rally domestic support. He succeeded admirably and became one of the longest serving Prime Ministers. His Chief Cabinet Secretary at that time Shinzo Abe was well aware of this political methodology and employed it so well that he became the longest serving Prime Minister in Japanese post-war history. Koizumi's and Abe's success in their domestic political methodology became important case studies for Conservative politicians worldwide. In theory, their revisionist message should upset all those countries who had fought the Second World War against the Nazis and Japanese Imperial Army, including the United States, Japan and Australia. The lessons offered by history however has been tempered overtime, and in their place replaced by more urgent strategic exigencies. In modern day geopolitical discourse, the dominant narrative now contextualised Japanese revisionism as a rightful reaction to the China threat.

In the early years, Australian Prime Minister John Howard first met US Vice President Dick Cheney, Japanese Prime Minister Shinzo Abe and Indian Prime Minister Manmohan Singh on the sidelines of ASEAN Regional Forum to discuss the concept of the Quad. This was followed by a large-scale naval exercise that involved 25 ships and 20,000 personnel code-name Exercise Malabar. When Beijing signalled its displeasure and by 2008, the then new Labor Prime Minister Kevin Rudd indicated that

Australia would no longer participate in the activities. While there have been criticisms Rudd had caved in to Chinese pressure or was "pro-Chinese", Rudd had in fact defended his decision as a rationale one. His main criticism was that both the concept and the objective of Quad were unclear; neither were the benefits to Australia. The concept died a natural death the following year once President Bush stepped down and Prime Minister Shinzo Abe lost power. Australia however did choose to deepen its defence relationship with the United States even as they tried to steer clear of the Quad for the time being. Rudd, however, began the process of evaluating the defence modernisation of Australia including the replacement of aged submarines. Rudd's successor Gillard published a White Paper (Australia in the Asian Century) arguing that Australia will:

> consider a strong and consistent presence by the United States in the region will continue to be as important in providing future confidence in Asia's rapidly changing strategic environment as it has in the past. We will support this through our alliance with the United States", but at the same time, Canberra would also "We welcome China's rise, not just because of the economic and social benefits it has brought China's people and the region (including Australia), but because it deepens and strengthens the entire international system … and (Australia) accepts that China's military growth is a natural, legitimate outcome of its growing economy and broadening interests. It is important that China and others in the region explain to their neighbours the pace and scope of their military modernisation, to build confidence and trust. (Australia Government, 2012: 228)

Under her tenure, Australia reached an agreement with the Obama administration that allows United States Marines to be stationed in Darwin. Gillard successor, Tony Abbott that took concrete steps that he felt would push Australia's cooperation further with the United States and Japan.

An avid fan and friend of Shinzo Abe's, Abbott wanted to ensure that Australia's new submarines would be built overseas wholly by Japan for reasons to do with both cost, speed as well as cementing Australia's relationship with like-minded partners in Asia such as Japan (Nicholson, 2023). The Labor government had leaned towards domestic production in favour of boosting employment, particularly in Southern Australia, but Abbott favoured efficiency (Carr, 2016). The Japanese conglomerate made up of Mitsubishi Heavy Industries and Kawasaki Industries unfortunately relied too heavily on the gentlemen's agreement between Abbott and Abe and not enough on domestic politics with regard to employment.

Abbott's main political rival, Malcolm Turnbull (who as Communications Minister had his decision to support Huawei overturned by) torpedoed and scuttled the deal with the Japanese in favour of the French. Turnbull's government concluded that the French design and technical specifications were better and more suited than the Japanese. As a major weapons seller, France has a vast and experienced military-industrial complex and an experienced Australian lobbyist who ensured that the French deal would include creating submarine-building jobs in Australia itself (Karp 2016). Australia's acquisition sought to replace a "Future Submarine" fleet of 12 Attack Submarines to replace six Collins class submarines that is expected to be withdrawn by 2036 (ANAO, 2019).

Across the Pacific, 2016 was an exceptional year in US political history as Donald Trump competed intensely with Hillary Clinton to be the US President. For the first time in US contemporary history, a non-establishment candidate ousted a member of the political royalty. During the run-up to the election, Barrack Obama assured Australian Prime Minister Turnbull in his visit to the White House by saying: "Don't worry, Malcolm. The American people will never elect a lunatic to sit in this office" (Turnbull, 2020). As it turns out, Obama was wrong. Not only did the lunatic win, he won handsomely. Australia stood out as one of the US allies that was not demonised by Trump during the campaign. When running for election, Trump had attacked European and Asian allies for a variety of transgressions, most often for not doing enough and "free-riding" on US efforts. There were of course other astonishing promises of course, including a high-profile campaign to build a wall between United States and Mexico to keep out refugees and asylum seekers.

Although Trump's rhetoric was alarming in the run-up to the election, Australia was not targeted by Trump for "freeriding" etc. The major US allies such as Germany and Japan were called out instead. Trump however did criticise the agreement the Turnbull government made with the Obama administration regarding the resettlement of about 2000 Muslim refugees held on Nauru and Papua New Guinea's Manus Island, even though he later grudgingly accepted this (Bell, 2017). The Turnbull government also changed Trump's mind on imposing tariffs on Australian steel and aluminium imports by attributing this to Australia's "fair and reciprocal military and trading relationship" with the United States (Turnbull, 2020).

After Trump's inauguration in 2017, Australia, as with other allies watched in dismay as the United States withdrew from the Trans-Pacific Partnership, reversed the US–South Korea Free trade agreement, asked NATO heads of State and governments to "contribute their fair share", withdrew from the Paris Agreement, order missile strikes on Russia while all the time conducting a very public tit-for-tat rhetorical brinksmanship with North Korea's Kim Jong-un. All these steps however are secondary, and in some cases (such as North Korea's engagement) is to prepare for the coming challenge with China. Thus from Turnbull's point of view then, Australia's principal challenge is that in Trump's haste to disentangle America from its engagement in the Middle East and Afghanistan, and withdraw from global institutions it had created, the United States might be less influential as it retrenches from its global responsibility even though it regains her strength. An American leadership respite might mean a vacuum that could be filled by others with values different from Australia's, and therefore it is in Australia's interests to keep America continually committed to the region (Turnbull, 2020). This is the clearest indication of identity politics at play. Ironically, one of Australia's goals then was, therefore, to steer clear of anything that the Americans (or more accurately Trump) might be unhappy about (Dobell, 2019), and ensure that US-Australian relations stayed strong and relevant.

Scott Morrison took office in August 2018 approximately four months after Donald Trump jettisoned his first Secretary of State Rex Tillerson in favour of CIA Director Mike Pompeo. Defense Secretary Jim Mattis was also replaced by Mark Esper in January 2019. The Trump Administration had by this time began to wage a very high profile trade war with China. Under Morrison, Australia began to align herself more tightly with the United States, paying little heed to China's sensitivities. Australia had joined in to condemn China for human rights abuses in Xinjiang (Karp, 2019), crackdown on human rights, democracy activism and the enacting of the national security legislation in Hong Kong from 2019 onwards (Lai, 2022). While the concerns about China might be valid from the viewpoint of the United States and her allies, the high profile and incessant rhetorical attacks on the press had created escalating conditions that disallowed for disengagement. Australia had joined in the global public opinion attack and roundly hyped up the China threat to a whole new level during the Covid pandemic.

Morrison took a high-profile media blitz by agreeing with Trump's comments that the virus originated from Wuhan, and insinuated that China should be held responsible for the deaths and economic destruction worldwide, to which Beijing angrily denied. On 3 April 2020, Morrison asserted on a radio program (Radio 2GB) that the virus started in China and spread throughout the world; and defended his Home Affairs Minister Peter Dutton's comments that the origin and spread of Covid was in China as they have seen US State Department cables on how Covid has spread (Doran & Henderson, 2020). There are additional reports carried in the Western media that the Covid virus started in a Bioweapon program lab in Wuhan, along reports that the Chinese eat bats and all other sorts of wildlife which perpetuated the Wuhan origin theory. In September 2020, Morrison in addressing the UN General Assembly, called for an inquiry into the roots of the pandemic as the "virus as inflicted a calamity on our world and its peoples", and that everyone must do what they "understand what happened for no other purpose than to prevent it from happening again" (Packham, 2020). He made the same call again at G20 meeting in October 2021 (Coorey, 2021) arguing that the WHO is too beholden to China and needs to be stronger, more independent and transparent. The end result of this of course is an increasingly angry, and defensive China that issued official rebuttals to the allegations made by Australian and US politicians (PRC MFA, 2020) both diplomatically and economically by throttling a range of Australian imports ranging from wine, barley, coal, Timber, etc., worth A$17 billion dollars.

The United States reaped many strategic benefits from this episode. Australia, a country that has immense trade was at the receiving end of Chinese economic sanctions, proving its narrative about the Chinese threat and coercion. Having Australia source and find alternative markets other than China disrupted the means of influence that China has on one of its most important allies. The discourse of "decoupling" and "securing supply chains" began to be popularise in Quad countries (this is now replaced by "derisking") of course. What both the Labor and the Liberal government however did not reveal to the Australia public is perhaps not so much about Communism and values, but more about capitalism and how the United States is losing out in the market competition to China (Marx, 2020).

Morrison had every reason to utilise this to push for his agenda of deepening cooperation with the United States, and to hedge against possible future "gains" the domestic political opposition might have in mending ties with China. The quarrel also helped abate some of the other political issues he had, notably in his handling of the wildfire episode before. However, most importantly, the escalating rhetorical (and later economic) dispute with China on all fronts provided the Morrison government to justify the deepening of their relationship with the United States in two aspects—the development pertaining to AUKUS and the revival of Quad 2.0.

Media reports have suggested that AUKUS episode first happened when Australia approached the United Kingdom to signal its interest in March 2021 acquire powered submarines (Bodkin, 2021). The Morrison government had sent its top intelligence official to Washington to talk about this in April 2021 (Gordon, 2023). In September 2021, Morrison informed France that Australia is negating Turnbull's US$2.4 billion agreement with France and instead opting to purchase nuclear-powered submarines from the United Kingdom and the United States. This deal of course enraged the French while the Japanese watched with quiet glee. President Macron's Ambassador to Australia had described this episode as "an unprecedented new low in terms of how to proceed and also in terms of truth and trust" (Thebault cited in Dziedzic and Hitch 2019). President Macron had accused Morrison of betrayal and lying but the Prime Minister defended the "not telling him (Macron) is not the same as lying to him" revealing that he had actually worked two years in secret (i.e. in 2019) with the United States and United Kingdom before the September 2021 announcement (Morrison cited in Camut, 2023). He indicated that it was necessary that "Chinese walls be built" in case the negotiations damaged the French deal. In another talk at the Hudson Institute, Mike Pompeo, Boris Johnson and Scott Morrison were regarded as 'architects of AUKUS" agreement. Domestic reactions were mixed of course, as former Prime Minister Abbott cheered Morrison on, given his political outlook on the United Kingdom and United States, while Turnbull and other former leaders were enraged (Butler, 2021). Keating had suggested Morrison government had unwisely "chained" Australia herself to the United States to "contain" China but that these efforts were unwise not only from a cost-effectiveness point of view, but would only accentuate great power competition and worsen the security of the Australia since the submarines won't be ready anytime soon (Worthington, 2023).

Given that Australia had actually began to negotiate the AUKUS agreement in 2019, it should therefore be no surprise that Morrison was pushing for the Quad 2.0 with full enthusiasm.

From 2019, Quad foreign ministers have met annually along with working group experts and senior officials. In part, this initiative was only possible with the climate achieved by Trump's open challenge of the Chinese, and the coming together of the conservative Quad leaders in the name of defending democracy and freedom. By 2023, Australia had already participated in Five Quad Leaders' Summit (March 2021, Virtual; September 2021 Washington; March 2022 Virtual, May 2022 Tokyo; May 2023 Hiroshima). While Australia was not the instigator of the revival of Quad, her active participation provided the country with an additional layer of security. Currently, Australia is working hard jointly with the other Quad countries to advance and integrate maritime security into the basis of the Quad activities as the maritime defence of the Pacific is now key to Australia's goals in the region. Beyond that, there is every indication that Australia is using the Quad to seek and open up new markets for its products (Maude, 2022). In other words, Canberra seeks a "durable strategic balance" in the Indo-Pacific to protect her interests in an Indo-Pacific that Morrison describes as "favourable to freedom" and where Australia need not defer to the dominant economic power against its wishes.

Course Adjustment in the Post-Conservative Era

The decision undertaken by the Liberal Leaders over the course of the last decade or so is a conscious choice to tighten and deepen Australia's alliance with the United States regardless of how the government of the day has decided to "frame" the shift. Australian corporate and social media, as well as conservative commentators have lost no time in attacking Paul Keating when he spoke up, arguing that Keating was "living in the past" when he denounced the AUKUS deal. The real problem is that the moves by Scott Morrison, Boris Johnson and Mike Pompeo has shifted Australia back to the days of the past where "White Australia" thinking and policy rules. As one author suggested, such a strategy echoed the "white men's defensive transnational identifications of more than 120 years ago when first faced with the rise of Asia". This moved Australia into a past world "in which transnational white Anglo-Saxon solidarities are reinvigorated to ensure the pre-eminence of the United States and the supremacy of the white man" (Lake, 2023). The challenges that Australia face in China—whether human rights concerns, Taiwan or South China seas all predate Xi Jinping's era. The last decade has seen an increasingly sharp tilt towards the right even as relations were managed relatively well. By the time Morrison took the reins of power, he adopted the kind of populist-led, reactionary policymaking (Clayton, 2021) that all but destroyed Australia's years of relations with China. The Conservatives would no doubt say it is entirely Beijing's fault, but the fact of the matter is that a lot of the domestic initiatives and rhetoric are undertaken to create conditions for a tighter bandwagon with the United States. The Liberal Governments of Abbott, Turnbull and Morrison has shifted from Rudd's emphasis on a common "strategic road map" in the US–Australia relationship to one that is moving from "shared interests to shared values" as US misadventures abroad (regardless of how ill-conceived they might look) are undertaken mostly with human rights or democracy in mind. (Dobell 2020; Hiscock, 2013). This sort of identity politics undertaken by Australian leaders has led Canberra to revise its determination of its national interests, priorities and strategies. Despite all the pretensions of multilateralism, Australia under Morrison has shown that it is prepared to cut ties with her largest and most important trading partner that has helped her prosper through the decades to bandwagon with her traditional strategic ally without little hesitation. The reaction from Beijing has provided the fuel, ammunition and imperative that inflamed Australian nationalism and hardened the Australian people's resolve and determination to show that "the Australian people have stood up" (Kassam, 2020).

The Labor government after Morrison in fact has kept on most Liberal's strategic and foreign policy posture despite using very reconciliatory language with the Chinese. All the elements are present: Quad, AUKUS and a very tight alliance with United States and Japan, known as "mini-laterals" (Collinson, 2023). Defence Minister Richard Marles has in fact said that the new government wants the alliance to move from "interoperability to interchangeability" (Collinson, 2023). Even as the relationship with Beijing seems to have improved, there is no question that tensions still run deep between China and Australia (Zelinsky, 2023), at least from Canberra's perspective. Australia is an outer-lier in the sense that the other Quad countries such as India, Japan and the US actually has a lot more concrete and intractable issues with China than Australia. Canberra under Labor has however chosen its diplomatic tone, language and approach towards Beijing wisely. However, not withstanding Labor's news approach; Morrison in moving from "conditional engagement" to "non-participation" with China, has cost Australia greatly in terms of trade and commerce (Laurenceson, 2021). There is still a long way for Australia and China going forward to restore its relations to "normality", but with the selection of Trump, this might not be possible,

It is therefore still a big challenge for Australia to continue to try and recalibrate her relationship with China as a major "work-in-progress". It should encompass efforts at both government as well as grassroots level. Notwithstanding Labour's gains, the right-wing political forces in the likes of Morrison are still working hard to ensure that their policy position remain a dominant force in Australian politics, particularly with regards to China (Harrison, 2023).

The AUKUS deal had in fact accentuated tensions without helping to improve Australia's security since the submarines will not come soon enough. The Quad still remains a "talk shop" even though it seems to be expanding cooperation across the fields, from vaccine provision to cybersecurity (Storey, 2022). Yet, the fact of the matter is that much of the cooperation takes place outside of the Quad too, so the impact beyond dialogue does not seem significant. Added to this is the question of having too many layers of network and organisation. There are benefits of course, one positive aspect is that such cooperation can entice an increasing number of countries to join without much cost, and in turn creating more strategic confusion for Beijing.

The Biden's administration decision not to show up at the 2023 Quad Summit that Australia was hosted also reflects the changing priorities that the Americans have. The meeting itself cost A$23 million to prepare, but this was not so much the problem. The greater issue is the excuse the United States provided (Hurst, 2023a; CNBC, 2023). Officially, apologies were given because the President needed to fly home to deal with a recalcitrant congress that had refused to lift the debt ceiling, but unofficially and most likely, the President had realised that the United States had disrupted Sino-US relations to the extent that the Chinese were determined to fight and confront the United States. The Chinese and in tandem with the Russians are now leading a global wave of de-dollarisation efforts and reduction of US debt at a time when Washington can ill afford it. So far, the Biden administration has avoided a direct confrontation with China, but the re-elected Trump administration might see things differently. Trump would like do his utmost to rid of his domestic political enemies, including members of the Deep State, and just about anyone who is not loyal to him or his agenda. He would also do his utmost to prepare the US and her allies for an external war with China.

There is no question that as US-China hegemonic struggle escalates, the world is starting down the abyss of a renewed Cold War. Penny Wong, the current Foreign Minister, had reminded Australians that it was the Labour Party that put China and Asia at the centre of Australia foreign policy where it should remain, and that Australians would need to recognise that they should find their security in Asia, not from Asia (Keating, 1996). Australia's search for her own identity and how she would position herself to her neighbours, her region and the world has thus far been a key struggle for how she relates herself to the United States vis-à-vis China going forward. Like many countries in the region who had come to rely on the US for security protection and China for economic growth, Canberra's strategic balancing would likely become more difficult in face of the impending Cold War.

REFERENCES

AIDR (Australia Institute for Disaster Resilience), Knowledge Hub Entry on "Wartime Bombing Darwin, 1942", n.d., https://knowledge.aidr.org.au/resources/other-disasters-wartime-bombing-raids-northern-territory-1942/#:~:text=Wartime%20bombing%2C%20Darwin%2C%201942&text=They%20were%20launched%20from%20four,lasted%20for%2020%2D25%20minutes

Abbott, Tony, "The Australia–U.S. Alliance and Leadership in the Asia–Pacific", Speech Delivered at Heritage Foundation, 2 November 2012, https://www.heritage.org/asia/report/the-australia-us-alliance-and-leadership-the-asia-pacific

Abjorensen, Norman, "Malcolm Turnbull and the Liberal Party's Identity Problem", Inside Story, 11 December 2017, https://insidestory.org.au/malcolm-turnbull-and-the-liberal-partys-identity-problem/

ACCIW (Australia Centre on China in the World), The Abbott Government and Australia-China Relations, Australia National University, 2015a, https://aus.thechinastory.org/archive/the-abbott-government-and-australia-china-relations/

ACCIW (Australia Centre on China in the World), The Gillard Government and Australia-China Relations, Australia National University, 2015b, https://aus.thechinastory.org/archive/the-gillard-government-and-australia-china-relations/

Aly, Anne, "A New Normal? Australian Responses to Terrorism and Their Impacts", in Samuel Justin Sinclair, and Daniel Antonius (eds), The Political Psychology of Terrorism Fears (New York, 2013; online edn, Oxford Academic, 23 January 2014), https://doi.org/10.1093/acprof:oso/9780199925926.003.0009, accessed 29 August 2023

AMFA (Australia Ministry of Foreign Affairs), "The Reagan Administration and its Implications for the Australia-United States Relations", News Release, 23 April 1981, https://parlinfo.aph.gov.au/parlInfo/search/display/display.w3p;query=Id:%22media/pressrel/HPR08009660%22

ANAO (Australia National Audit Office), Future Submarine Program—Transition to Design (Department of Defence), Auditor-General Report No. 22 2019–20, Performance Audit, (2019)https://www.anao.gov.au/sites/default/files/Auditor-General_Report_2019-2020_22.pdf

ANIB (Australia News and Information Bureau), "Protest Against the Vietnam War Outside Old Parliament House" A1200, L85635, 1970, https://www.naa.gov.au/students-and-teachers/learning-resources/learning-resource-themes/war/vietnam-war/protest-against-vietnam-war-outside-old-parliament-house

Antony, Kelvin, "'We Are Witnessing Political Warfare': Micronesia Leader Drops China Bombshell", Radio New Zealand, 14 March 2023, https://www.rnz.co.nz/international/pacific-news/485893/we-are-witnessing-political-warfare-micronesia-leader-drops-china-bombshell

APH (Australia Parliament House), Members Citizenship, 2019, https://www.aph.gov.au/~/media/03%20Senators%20and%20Members/32%20Members/Citizenship/45P/AbbottT_CTZ45P.pdf

APMD (Australia Prime Minister's Department), Transcript of Prime Minister John Howard's Speech to the Australian Defence Association, Melbourne, 2001, https://pmtranscripts.pmc.gov.au/release/transcript-12374

APMD (Australia Prime Minister's Department), "Australia-United States Talks About Vietnam War and Nuclear Weapons" Top Secret Papers, NAA: A1209, 1962/708, 1962, https://www.naa.gov.au/students-and-teachers/learning-resources/learning-resource-themes/war/vietnam-war/australia-usa-talks-about-vietnam-and-nuclear-weapons

APS (Australia Parliament Statement), "Australia and Indo-China", Parliamentary Statement Report of the Joint Committee on Foreign Affairs and Defence on "Power in Indochina Since 1975" (1981).

Associated Press, "Tony Abbott Invites Shinzo Abe, Saying Japan is Australia's 'Best Friend in Asia'", Associated Press Editorial, 20 October 2013, https://www.theguardian.com/world/2013/oct/10/aboott-invites-abe-japan-friend

ATM (Australia Treasury Media Release), "Government Forces Foreign Nationals to Sell Over $100m Worth of Illegally Acquired Australian Real Estate", 6 February 2017, https://ministers.treasury.gov.au/ministers/scott-morrison-2015/media-releases/government-forces-foreign-nationals-sell-over-100m

Australia Government, Australia in the Asian Century White Paper, 2012, https://www.murdoch.edu.au/ALTC-Fellowship/_document/Resources/australia-in-the-asian-century-white-paper.pdf

Au-Yeung, Wilson, Keys, Alison, & Fischer, Paul, "Australia-China: Not Just 40 Years", Australia Treasury Publication, 12 December 2012, https://treasury.gov.au/publication/economic-roundup-issue-4-2012/australia-china-not-just-40-years

Badham, Van, "100 Days Under Abbott: Is His Real Legacy What We're Not Being Told?", The Guardian, 16 December 2013, https://www.theguardian.com/commentisfree/2013/dec/16/100-days-under-abbott-is-his-real-leg acy-what-were-not-being-told

Bagshaw, Eryk, "Morrison Says Australia Won't Back Down to China Threats on Free Speech, Security", Sydney Morning Herald, 19 November 2020, https://www.smh.com.au/world/asia/morrison-says-australia-won-t-back-down-to-china-threats-on-free-speech-security-20201119-p56g10.html

Babones, Salvatore, "Will Australia's New Defense Minister Play Bad Cop to China?", Foreign Policy, 6 April 2021, https://foreignpolicy.com/2021/04/06/australia-new-defense-minister-peter-dutton-china/

BBC, "Australia PM Abbott: Cutting Household Bill Helped Women", BBC News, 22 December 2014, https://www.bbc.com/news/world-australia-305 72242

BBC, "Scott Morrison: Australian PM's Own Senator Calls Him Autocrat and Bully", BBC News, 30 March 2022, https://www.bbc.com/news/world-aus tralia-60909636

Beckett, Andy, "Tony Abbott at Oxford: Fighter, Networker, Thatcherite", The Guardian, 16 August 2013, https://www.theguardian.com/world/2013/aug/16/tony-abbott-at-oxford-university

Bell, Benjamin, Brown, Ely, Caplan, David, Dwyer, Devin, Phelps, Jordyn, & Thorbecke, Catherine, "What We Know About the Refugee Resettlement Deal Obama Forged With Australia", ABC News, 3 February 2017, https://abcnews.go.com/Politics/refugee-resettlement-deal-obama-forged-australia/story?id=45219111

Bergin, Julia, "Ratcheting UP a Red Line: How China Is Being Used in the Australian Election Campaign", First Draft, 11 May 2022, https://firstdraf tnews.org/articles/ratcheting-up-a-red-line-how-china-is-being-used-in-the-australian-election-campaign/

Bodkin, Henry, Samuel, Henry, & Crisp, James, "'Declaration of War': How UK's Secret Nuclear Pact Blindsided Europe's Elite", The Telegraph, 19 September 2021, https://www.telegraph.co.uk/politics/2021/09/18/fra nces-aukus-anger-reveals-stark-truth-place-world/

Bolger, Rosemary, "Peter Dutton: A Brief History of the Man Who Wants to be Prime Minister", SBS News Feature on Immigration, 21 August 2018, https://www.sbs.com.au/news/article/peter-dutton-a-brief-history-of-the-man-who-wants-to-be-prime-minister/iu83e09wu

Brann, Matt, "Gina Rinehart Sells Four More S. Kidman & Co. Cattle Stations in Queensland, NT", ABC News, 11 April 2023, https://www.abc.net.au/news/rural/2023-04-11/gina-rinehart-sells-more-kidman-cattle-stations/102205502

Brissenden, Michael, & Andersen, Brigid, "Liberal Party Elders Lash Tony Abbott for Acts of Revenge on Turnbull's Government", ABC News, 27 August 2018, https://www.abc.net.au/news/2018-08-27/liberal-party-elders-lash-tony-abbott-for-acts-of-revenge-on-tu/10166590

Brown, Carmen, Fowler, Courtney and O'Callaghan, Deb, "South Australian family prepares to take over world's largest cattle station", ABC News (Australia), 12 December 2016, https://www.abc.net.au/news/rural/2016-12-12/anna-creek-williams-family-kidman-cattle-empire/8112370

Buckley, Chris, "Australia's Gillard to woo China, press on human rights", Reuters, 26 April 2011, https://www.reuters.com/article/china-australia/australias-gillard-to-woo-china-press-on-human-rights-idINL3E7FP10A20110426/

Burgess, Annika, Cheng, Joyce, & Xing, Dong, "Pro-democracy Movement Unites Chinese Australians as Community Speaks Out Against Zero-COVID Policy", ABC News, 1 December 2022, https://www.abc.net.au/news/2022-12-01/chinese-community-australia-unite-at-pro-democracy-protest/101707312

Butler, Josh, "Appalling: Former PMs blast submarines deal, question AUKUS", The New Daily (Australia) 29 September 2021, https://www.thenewdaily.com.au/news/2021/09/29/former-pms-subs-aukus

Camut, Nicolas, "Ex-Aussie PM admits he hid submarine plot from Macron", Politico, 21 June 2023, https://www.politico.eu/article/ex-australia-pm-scott-morrison-submarine-emmanuel-macron/

Carr, Andrew, "Submarines Decision Ultimately Shows the Merits of partisan Debate on Defence", The Conversation, 26 April 2016, https://theconversation.com/submarines-decision-ultimately-shows-the-merits-of-partisan-debate-on-defence-57796

Cave, Damien, "Espionage Bills in Australia Stir Fears of Anti-Chinese Backlash", The New York Times, 19 December 2017, https://www.nytimes.com/2017/12/19/world/australia/australia-china-backlash-influence.html

Cave, Damien, "It 'Just Didn't Happen': Australia's Attorney General Denies Rape Claim", The New York Times, 3 March 2021, https://www.nytimes.com/2021/03/03/world/australia/christian-porter-rape-case.html

Chan, Gabrielle, & Taylor, Lenore, "Australian Treasurer Overrules Sale of 1.3% of Country to Chinese Firm", The Guardian 29 April 2016, https://www.theguardian.com/australia-news/2016/apr/29/australian-treasurer-overru les-sale-of-13-of-country-to-chinese-firm

Chung, Mona, "Why we shouldn't blame Chinese buyers for rising house prices", Deakin University "This" Public Website write up, N.D., https://this.deakin.edu.au/society/why-we-shouldnt-blame-chinese-buyers-for-rising-house-prices

Clayton, Kate, "The Influence of Domestic Politics on Australia's China Policy", 9Dashline, 25 June 2021, https://www.9dashline.com/article/the-influence-of-domestic-politics-on-australias-china-policy

CNBC, "Australia Cancels Quad Meeting in Sydney After Biden Postponement", CNBC News, 18 May 2023, https://www.cnbc.com/2023/05/17/austra lia-pm-says-quad-meeting-will-not-go-ahead-in-sydney-next-week.html

Collinson, Elena, "Review of Australia's China Odyssey: From Euphoria to Fear", Council for Foreign Relations Blog Post Book Review, 30 May 2023, https://www.cfr.org/blog/review-australias-china-odyssey-euphoria-fear

Coorey, Phillip, & Tingle, Laura, "'Let us Know Next Time': How Obama Chided Turnbull Over Darwin Port Sale", Australian Financial Review, 19 November 2015, https://www.afr.com/politics/let-us-know-next-time-how-obama-chided-turnbull-over-darwin-port-sale-20151118-gl1qkg

Coorey, Phillip, "PM Repeats Call for Pandemic Origin to be Investigated", Australia Financial Review, 30 October 2021, https://www.afr.com/pol itics/federal/g20-pm-repeats-call-for-pandemic-origin-to-be-investigated-202 11030-p594m4

Curran, James, "Australia-China relations: Understanding how we arrived at this point", The Interpreter, Lowry Institute, 27 July 2022, https://www.lowyin stitute.org/the-interpreter/australia-china-relations-understanding-how-we-arrived-point

Daizell, "Scott Morrison Says Australia Won't Respond to Chinese 'Coercion' Over Warning About Universities", ABC News 11 June 2020, https://www.abc.net.au/news/2020-06-11/australia-morrison-china-respond-coercion-on-universities/12342924

Davis, Anne, "Republic Model Bound Destiny of Keating and Turnbull, Cabinet Papers Show", The Guardian, 31 December 2017, https://www.thegua rdian.com/australia-news/2018/jan/01/republic-model-paul-keating-mal colm-turnbull-1995-cabinet-papers

Davis, Miriah, "Defence Minister Richard Marles No Better Than His 'Extremely Anti-china' Predecessor Peter Dutton, Says Beijing", Skynews Australia, 18

July 2022a, https://www.skynews.com.au/australia-news/politics/defence-minister-richard-marles-no-better-than-his-extremely-antichina-predecessor-peter-dutton-says-beijing/news-story/b98d803970728649dbe03ae7af7 4c897

Davis, Miriah, "Opposition Leader Peter Dutton Told to Scale Back Attacks on Beijing to Win Back Chinese-Australian Voters", Skynews Australia News, 10 August 2022b, https://www.skynews.com.au/australia-news/opposition-lea der-peter-dutton-told-to-scale-back-attacks-on-beijing-to-win-back-chineseau stralian-voters/news-story/366be2c8dfa9049646e85691e0886a5d

Denniss, Richard, "Morrison's Economic Lies", The Australian Institute Opinion (Published in The Saturday Paper), 19 March 2022, https://australiainstitute. org.au/post/morrisons-economic-lies/

Dobell, Graeme, "Australia-US/East Asia Relations: Turnbull Tumbles, Trump Mateship, China Frost" Comparative Connections, Vol. 20, No. 2, 2018 pp. 121–131, https://cc.pacforum.org/2018/09/turnbull-tumbles-trump-mateship-china-frost/

Dobell, Grame, Scott Morrison, Donald Trump, and the Indo-Pacific, Comparative Connections, Vol. 21, No. 2, September 2019, pp. 122–134, https://cc. pacforum.org/2019/09/scott-morrison-donald-trump-and-the-indo-pacific/

Dobell, Graeme, "Turnbull Memoir Lays Out Australia's Shift on China", The Strategist, Australia Strategic Policy Institute, 11 May 2020, https://www.asp istrategist.org.au/turnbull-memoir-lays-out-australias-shift-on-china/

Doherty, Ben, "Huang Xiangmo: Alleged Agent of Chinese Influence Exiled from Australia Now on Hong Kong Electoral Body", The Guardian, 20 October 2021, https://www.theguardian.com/australia-news/2021/oct/ 20/huang-xiangmo-alleged-agent-of-chinese-influence-exiled-from-australia-now-on-hong-kong-electoral-body

Doran, Matthew, & Henderson, Anna, "Scott Morrison Defends Peter Dutton's CALLS for Transparency From China Over the Origins of Coronavirus", ABC News, 23 April 2020, https://www.abc.net.au/news/2020-04-23/cor onavirus-morrison-defends-dutton-criticism-of-china/12177510

Dubecki, Larrisa, "Rudd's Mandarin Skills Aired in China", The Age 6 November 2007, https://www.theage.com.au/politics/federal/rudds-man darin-skills-aired-in-china-20071106-ge68eo.html

Dziedzic, Stephen, & Hitch, Georgia, "French ambassador says leaking of text messages between Scott Morrison and Emmanuel Macron 'unprecedented new low' ", ABC News (Australia) 3 November 2021, https://www.abc.net.au/news/2021-11-03/french-ambassador-jean-pierre-thebault-submarines/100590382

Ferguson, Kathleen, "Scott Morrison, Jacinda Ardern Clash Over Policy to Deport Convicted New Zealand Nationals", ABC News, 28 February 2020, https://www.abc.net.au/news/2020-02-28/morrison-ardern-clash-over-deportation-policy/12012052

France24, "Australian PM Rebuffs Arguments for Iraq War", France24 News, 2 June 2008, https://www.france24.com/en/20080602-australian-pm-rebuffs-us-arguments-iraq-war-australia-iraq-war

Flitton, Daniel, "How Peter Dutton Changes Australian Foreign Policy", The Interpreter, Lowy Institute, 23 August 2018, https://www.lowyinstitute.org/the-interpreter/how-peter-dutton-changes-australian-foreign-policy

Frew, Wendy, "How It All Went Wrong for Australian PM Tony Abbott", BBC News, 14 December 2015, https://www.bbc.com/news/world-australia-34241486

Fullilove, Michael, "In Australia, Prime Minister Gillard has a different Global View", Brookings Commentary 1 July 2010, https://www.brookings.edu/articles/in-australia-prime-minister-gillard-has-different-global-view/

Galloway, Anthony, "Australia Will 'Lose Next Decade' Unless it Stands Up to China: Dutton", Sydney Morning Herald, 7 February 2022, https://www.smh.com.au/politics/federal/australia-will-lose-next-decade-unless-it-stands-up-to-china-dutton-20220112-p59ntk.html

Gerber, Jacob, "Foreigners Face Big Fines and Jail for Illegal Home Buying", Australian Financial Review, 2 May 2015, https://www.afr.com/property/foreigners-face-big-fines-and-jail-for-illegal-home-buying-20150501-1mxysp

Giannini, Dominic, "Fresh Concern Over Chinese Interest in Pacific Airstrip", The West Australian, 22 March 2023, https://thewest.com.au/politics/fresh-concern-over-chinese-interest-in-pacific-airstrip-c-10123842

Gibson, Jano, "Why did the Northern Territory lease Darwin Port to Chinese-owned company Landbridge?", ABC News, 7 May 2022, https://www.abc.net.au/news/2022-05-07/darwin-port-lease-china/101040810

Grattan, Michelle, "His beating heart is a focus group': what makes Scott Morrison tick?", The Conversation, 15 May 2022, https://theconversation.com/his-beating-heart-is-a-focus-group-what-makes-scott-morrison-tick-182940

Grigg, Angus, "Liberal Leadership: Malcolm Turnbull's China Links", Financial Review, 15 September 2015, https://www.afr.com/world/liberal-leadership-malcolm-turnbulls-china-links-20150915-gjn6uv

Grimson, Matthew, "Australia PM Abbott Caught Laughing About Rising Sea Levels in Pacific", NBC News, 11 September 2015, https://www.nbcnews.com/news/world/australian-prime-minister-tony-abbott-caught-laughing-about-climate-change-n425741

Gordon, Michael, "How the U.S. Agreed to Provide Nuclear Sub Technology to Australia", The Wall Street Journal, 13 March 2023, https://www.wsj.com/articles/how-the-u-s-agreed-to-provide-nuclear-sub-technology-to-australia-2b631d8f

Gough, Neil, "Australia Rejects Bids From Chinese Investors for Electricity Provider", The New York Times, 11 August 2016, https://www.nytimes.com/2016/08/12/business/dealbook/australia-china-ausgrid-nsw-sydney.html

Guina, Amy, "Racism Against Chinese Australians Is Being Made Worse by Anti-China Election Rhetoric", Time Magazine, 20 May 2022, https://time.com/6176970/australia-election-china/

Hardaker, David, "Revealed: Scott Morrison's Little-Known Work on the Christian Brethren Church", Crikey, 14 April 2021, https://www.crikey.com.au/2021/04/14/scott-morrison-thesis-christian-bretheren/

Hardaker, David, "Morrison had evangelical Christian Mike Pompeo on speed dial for two years. Who knew?" Crinkey News (Australia) 7 Feb 2022a, https://www.crikey.com.au/2022/02/07/scott-morrison-mike-pompeo-speed-dial/

Hardaker, David, "Morrison and Pompeo: an off-the-books foreign policy bond that needs probing", Crikey News (Australia), 16 August 2022b, https://www.crikey.com.au/2022/08/16/morrison-and-pompeo-secret-foreign-policy-bond-needs-probing/

Harrison, Melissa, "Five Eyes sabotage of Albanese's China trip", Australia Citizens Party, 16 October 2023, https://citizensparty.org.au/five-eyes-sabotage-albaneses-china-trip

Hendrischke, Hans, & Li, Wei, "Chinese investment in residential real estate amounts to just 2%", The Conversation, 13 September 2015, https://theconversation.com/chinese-investment-in-residential-real-estate-amounts-to-just-2-47404

Hiscock, Geoff, "How Australian Political Rivals View China", CNN Special, 5 August 2013, https://edition.cnn.com/2013/08/04/opinion/australia-election-rudd-abbott/index.html

HKFP (Hong Kong Free Press), "Explainer: Why Australia Revoked Chinese Tycoon's Citizenship Citing 'Political Interference'," Hong Kong Free Press Voices, 17 February 2019, https://hongkongfp.com/2019/02/17/explainer-australia-revoked-chinese-tycoons-citizenship-citing-political-interference/

Howe, Philip, Szöcsik, Edina, & Zuber, Christina, "Nationalism, Class, and Status: How Nationalists Use Policy Offers and Group Appeals to Attract a New Electorate." *Comparative Political Studies* 55, no. 5 (2022): 832–868. https://doi.org/10.1177/00104140211036033

Huang, Christine, Clancy, Laura, & Gubbala, Sneha, "When Asked About China, Australians Tend to Think of Its Government, Not Its People", Pew Research Center, 26 September 2022, https://www.pewresearch.org/short-reads/2022/09/26/when-asked-about-china-australians-tend-to-think-of-its-government-not-its-people/

Hurst, Daniel, "Factcheck: the Coalition Says Labor always 'Takes China's Side', But Are the Parties' Positions so Different?" The Guardian, 21 April 2020, https://www.theguardian.com/australia-news/2022/apr/22/factcheck-the-coalition-says-labor-always-takes-chinas-side-but-are-the-parties-positions-so-different

Hurst, Daniel, "Factcheck: the Coalition says Labor always 'takes China's side', but are the parties' positions so different?", The Guardian 21 April 2022, https://www.theguardian.com/australia-news/2022/apr/22/factcheck-the-coalition-says-labor-always-takes-chinas-side-but-are-the-parties-positions-so-different

Hurst, Daniel, "Kevin Rudd Attacks 'idiot' Peter Dutton Over 'Hairy-Chested' Comments on China", The Guardian, 12 May 2022, https://www.theguardian.com/world/2022/may/12/kevin-rudd-attacks-idiot-peter-dutton-over-hairy-chested-comments-on-china

Hurst, Daniel, "The Cancelled Quad Summit is a Win for China and a Self-Inflicted Blow to the US's Pacific Standing", The Guardian, 2023a, https://www.theguardian.com/australia-news/2023/may/17/cancelled-quad-summit-meeting-china-us-pacific-standing

Hurst, Daniel, "Chinese Migrants Believe Australian Media Fuels Hostility Towards Them, Study Shows", The Guardian, 23 August 2023b, https://www.theguardian.com/australia-news/2023/aug/30/chinese-migrants-believe-australian-media-fuels-hostility-towards-them-study-shows

Hutchens, "Gareth, Sweeping Foreign Interference and Spying Laws Pass Senate", The Guardian 28 June 2018, https://www.theguardian.com/australia-news/2018/jun/29/sweeping-foreign-interference-and-spying-laws-pass-senate

Inglis, Christine. "Chinese in Australia." *The International Migration Review* 6, no. 3 (1972): 266–81. https://doi.org/10.2307/3002459

Ireland, Judith, "Tony Abbott Rules Out Change to Huawei ban", The Canberra Times, 1 November 2013, https://www.canberratimes.com.au/story/6150027/tony-abbott-rules-out-change-to-huawei-ban/

Karp, Paul, "France to build Australia's new submarine fleet as $50bn contract awarded", The Guardian, 26 April 2016, https://www.theguardian.com/australia-news/2016/apr/26/france-to-build-australias-new-submarine-fleet-as-50bn-contract-awarded

Karp, Paul, "Australia 'Deeply Concerned' About China's Treatment of Uighur People", The Guardian, 15 Jul 2019, https://www.theguardian.com/world/2019/jul/15/australia-deeply-concerned-about-chinas-treatment-of-uighur-people

Karp, Paul, & Davidson, Helen, "China Bristles at Australia's Call for Investigation into Coronavirus Origin", The Guardian, 29 April 2020, https://www.theguardian.com/world/2020/apr/29/australia-defends-plan-to-investigate-china-over-covid-19-outbreak-as-row-deepens

Kassam, Natasha, & Hsu, Jennifer, "Being Chinese in Australia: Public opinion in Chinese Communities", Lowry Institute Public Opinion Survey, 2021, https://interactives.lowyinstitute.org/features/chinese-communities/reports/2021%20Being%20Chinese%20in%20Australia%20Poll%20-%20Lowy%20Institute.pdf

Kassam, Natasha, "Great Expectations: The Unraveling of Australia-China Relationship", Brookings Commentary, 20 July 2020, https://www.brookings.edu/articles/great-expectations-the-unraveling-of-the-australia-china-relationship/

Keating, Paul, "Australia, Asia and the New Regionalism", Singapore 17 January 1996, Prime Ministers of Australia Transcripts, https://pmtranscripts.pmc.gov.au/release/transcript-9905

Kelly, Tim, Altmeyer, Cyril, & Packham, Colin, "How France Sank Japan's $40 Billion Australian Submarine Dream", Reuters, 29 April 2016, https://www.reuters.com/article/us-australia-submarines-japan-defence-in-idUSKCN0XQ1FC

Kenny, Mark, "Gillard Scores Coup With China Agreement", The Sydney Morning Herald, 10 April 2013, https://www.smh.com.au/politics/federal/gillard-scores-coup-with-china-agreement-20130409-2hjin.html

Knobloch, Bruce, "How Australia's Labor Movement Helped Build Neoliberalism", The Jacobin, 18 October 2020, https://jacobin.com/2020/10/australia-labor-party-neoliberalism-accord

Lai, Bernie, "Australia's Response to the Hong Kong Democracy and Human Rights Crisis", Australia Parliament House Research Papers, 13 September 2022, https://www.aph.gov.au/About_Parliament/Parliamentary_departments/Parliamentary_Library/pubs/rp/rp2223/AustraliasResponseHongKongCrisis

Lake, Marilyn, "The "China Threat": Can We Escape the Historical Legacy of Anti-Chinese Racism?", Arena Quarterly, 29 June 2023, https://arena.org.au/the-china-threat-racism/

Lane, Isabelle, "From 'Lucky' Colonisation to Misinformation Fears: Former PMs Weigh in on Voice Debate", SBS News 27 July 2023, https://www.sbs.com.au/news/article/from-lucky-colonisation-to-mis information-fears-former-pms-weigh-in-on-voice-debate/pemowjsrp

Laurenceson, James, "Costly Choices: Establishing the Facts of Australia's China Policy Since 2016", Australian Centre on China in the World, Australian National University, 29 March 2021, https://www.thechinastory.org/costly-choices-establishing-the-facts-of-australias-china-policy-since-2016/

Laurenceson, James, "Costly Choices: Establishing the Facts of Australia's China Policy Since 2016", The China Story, 29 March 2021, https://www.the chinastory.org/costly-choices-establishing-the-facts-of-australias-china-policy-since-2016/

Lehmann, Angela, "Commentary: International Students From China Risk Being Scapegoats for Australia's Housing Crisis", Channel News Asia, 2 March 2023, https://www.channelnewsasia.com/commentary/australia-int ernational-student-china-housing-crisis-accommodation-rent-degree-study-online-campus-3314986

Lixinski, Lucas, Explainer: What Happened to the Religious Discrimina-tion Bill? https://www.humanrights.unsw.edu.au/research/commentary/exp lainer-what-happened-religious-discrimination-bill

Maiden, Samantha, "Peter Dutton's Blunt Warning Over Prospect of War With China", News Australia 17 September 2021, https://www.news.com.au/tec hnology/innovation/military/peter-duttons-blunt-warning-over-prospect-of-war-with-china/news-story/15d47f2f5b3d48ca2f43a4648a8b5531

Maley, Paul & Riordan, Primrose, PNG Port Plan Stokes Fears of China Military Build-Up, The Australian, 26 August 2018, https://www.theaustralian.com.au/subscribe/news/1/?sourceCode=TAWEB_WRE170_a_TWT&dest=https%3A%2F%2Fwww.theaustralian.com.au%2Fnational-affairs%2Fpng-port-plan-stokes-fears-of-china-military-buildup%2Fnews-story%2Ff0fa6fc36a1db fc8d8acfe2bb4ea2907&memtype=anonymous&mode=premium&v21=dyn amic-high-test-score&V21spcbehaviour=appendend

Manne, Robert, "One Morning with Malcolm Turnbull", The Monthly, April 2012 Edition, https://www.themonthly.com.au/issue/2012/april/133774 4204/robert-manne/one-morning-malcolm#mtr

Mao, Frances, "How Reliant is Australia on China?" BBC News, 17 June 2020, https://www.bbc.com/news/world-australia-52915879

Marr, David, "Power Trip: The Political Journey of Kevin Rudd", Quarterly Essay No. 38, June 2010, https://www.quarterlyessay.com.au/essay/2010/06/power-trip/extract

Martin, Sarah, "Scott Morrison Fends Off Claim Solomon Islands-China Pact is Worst Foreign Policy Failure Since 1945", The Guardian, 20 April 2022, https://www.theguardian.com/australia-news/2022/apr/20/scott-morrison-fends-off-claim-solomon-islands-china-pact-is-worst-foreign-policy-failure-since-1945

Martin, Sarah, "Scott Morrison Tells Christian Conference he was Called to Do God's Work as Prime Minister", The Guardian, 26 April 2021, https://www.theguardian.com/australia-news/2021/apr/26/scott-morrison-tells-christian-conference-he-was-called-to-do-gods-work-as-prime-minister

Martin, Sarah, & Karp, Paul, "Coalition Shelves Religious Discrimination Bill After Christian lobby Says Changes Do 'More Harm Than Good'", The Guardian, 14 September 2023, https://www.theguardian.com/world/2022/feb/10/coalition-shelves-religious-discrimination-bill-after-christian-lobby-says-changes-do-more-harm-than-good

Marx, Paris, "Scott Morrison's Grudge Against China Is About Capitalist Competition", The Jacobin, 16 June 2020, https://jacobin.com/2020/09/scott-morrisons-grudge-against-china-is-about-capitalist-competition

Matovinovic, Lukas, "Australian PM Kevin Rudd Was Toppled by Labor Notables Who Snitched for the US", The Jacobin, 4 October 2022, https://jacobin.com/2022/04/kevin-rudd-cia-us-embassy-julia-gillard-alp-coup

Maude, Richard, "How to Understand the Quad: A Short Guide for Australian Business", Asia Society Australia Feature, 9 February 2022, https://asiasociety.org/australia/how-understand-quad-short-guide-australian-business

McGuirk, Rod, "Australian PM's Leadership Criticized During Wildfire Crisis", Associated Press, 8 January 2020, https://apnews.com/article/294379d425934cb44fcd1f7e5ebf482a

McDowall, Roy Campbell, Howard's Long March: The Strategic Depiction of China in Howard Government Policy, 1996–2006. Vol. 172. ANU Press, 2009, http://www.jstor.org/stable/j.ctt24h3pb

Meick, Ethan, Ker, Michelle, & Chan, Han May, China's Engagement in the Pacific Islands: Implications for the United States, US-China Economic and Security Review Commission, Staff Research Report, 14 June 2018, https://www.uscc.gov/sites/default/files/Research/China-Pacific%20Islands%20Staff%20Report.pdf

Middleton, Jim, "How aSecret China trip crippled an Australian Prime Minister", The Sydney Morning Herald, 15 July 2021, https://www.smh.com.au/world/asia/how-a-secret-china-trip-crippled-an-australian-prime-minister-20210715-p589wk.html

Middleton, Karen, "Fresh Documents in Morrison's Sacking", 8 June 2019, https://www.thesaturdaypaper.com.au/news/politics/2019/06/08/fresh-documents-morrisons-sacking/15599160008252#hrd

Millar, Barbara, "Controversy over shipwreck funerals", ABC News, 15 Feb 2011, https://www.abc.net.au/news/2011-02-15/controversy-over-shipwreck-funerals/1943634

Murphy, Katherine, "Sam's Expenses Scandal A 'Cash for Comment' Moment, Says Turnbull", The Guardian, 2 September 2016, https://www.theguardian.com/australia-news/2016/sep/02/sam-dastyaris-expenses-scandal-a-cash-for-comment-moment-says-turnbull

Murphy, Katherine, "Abbott Defends 2014 Budget: 'We Would Be Living Within Our Means'", The Guardian, 7 April 2017, https://www.theguardian.com/australia-news/2017/apr/07/abbott-defends-2014-budget-we-would-be-living-within-our-means

Murphy, Katherine, "Scott Morrison: How He Went From Artful Dodger to Political Shapeshifter", The Guardian, 4 September 2020, https://www.theguardian.com/australia-news/2020/sep/05/scott-morrison-how-he-went-from-artful-dodger-to-political-shapeshifter

Murphy, Katherine, "Scott Morrison, Aerodynamic Populism and the Art of Never Choosing a Side", The Guardian, 29 January 2021, https://www.theguardian.com/australia-news/2021/jan/30/scott-morrison-aerodynamic-populism-and-the-art-of-never-choosing-a-side

Murray, Duncan, "Survey Reveals Australia's Least Trusted Politicians", NCA News Wire, 23 March 2022, https://www.news.com.au/national/politics/survey-reveals-australias-least-trusted-politicians/news-story/61ad9239532b255dc4d75eb4eb5c0d07

Needlam, Kirsty, "Australia's Foreign Interference Laws Designed for China—Former PM Turnbull", Reuters, 21 February 2021, https://www.reuters.com/world/asia-pacific/australias-foreign-interference-laws-designed-china-former-pm-turnbull-2023-02-21/

Needham, Kristy, "Australia's foreign interference laws designed for China - former PM Turnbull", Reuters, 21 Feb 2023, https://www.reuters.com/world/asia-pacific/australias-foreign-interference-laws-designed-china-former-pm-turnbull-2023-02-21/

Nicholson, Brendan, "Former Defence Minister Recalls Turning Point in Australia–China Relations", The Strategist, Australia Strategic Policy Institute Paper, 4 August 2023, https://www.aspistrategist.org.au/former-defence-minister-recalls-turning-point-in-australia-china-relations/

Ng, Weng Hoong, "What 'Blame Chinese' Crowd Missed About Vancouver Home Prices", Asia Times, 25 March 2021, https://asiatimes.com/2021/03/what-blame-chinese-crowd-missed-about-vancouver-home-prices/

Packham, Colin, "Australia Says World Needs to Know Origins of COVID-19", Reuters, 26 September 2020, https://www.reuters.com/article/us-health-coronavirus-australia-china-idUSKCN26H00T

Parton, Charles. "Revealing China's 'Hidden Hand'". *Journal of Democracy* 31, no. 4 October 2020, pp 182–85

Pawson, Hal, Randolph, Bill, Leishman, Chris, Gurran, Nicole, Mares, Peter, Phibbs, Peter, & Miligan, Vivienne, "The Market Has Failed to Give Australians Affordable Housing, So Don't Expect It To Solve the Crisis", The Conversation, 14 October 2022, https://theconversation.com/the-market-has-failed-to-give-australians-affordable-housing-so-dont-expect-it-to-solve-the-crisis-192177

Perrigo, Billy, "Why Does Australia Keep Getting Rid of Its Prime Ministers?" Time Magazine, 24 August 2018, https://time.com/5377190/why-austra lia-changes-prime-ministers/

Pilger, John, "The British-American Coup that Ended Australian Independence", The Guardian, Commentary, 23 October 2014, https://www.theguardian. com/commentisfree/2014/oct/23/gough-whitlam-1975-coup-ended-austra lian-independence

PRC MFA (Ministry of Foreign Affairs, Consulate of the People's Republic of China Sydney), Reality Check of Australian Allegations Against China, 14 July 2020, http://sydney.china-consulate.gov.cn/eng/zlgdt/202208/t20 220825_10752788.htm

PRC MFA, (Ministry of Foreign Affairs, People's Republic of China) Joint Statement on Establishing a Comprehensive Strategic Partnership Featuring Mutual Respect and Common Development For a New Era Between the People's Republic of China And Solomon Islands, Communiques, 11 July 2023, https://www.fmprc.gov.cn/mfa_eng/wjdt_665385/2649_6 65393/202307/t20230711_11111191.html#:~:text=The%20two%20sides% 20agreed%20that,support%20and%20mutual%20benefit%20between

Pini, Michelle, "Morrison's Top 10 Bare-Facd Lies", Independent Australia, 25 November 2021, https://independentaustralia.net/politics/politics-display/ morrisons-top-10-bare-faced-lies,15787

Poulos, Elenie, "Did the Morrison Government Change the Relationship Between Religion and Politics in Australia?" The Conversation, 25 September 2022, https://theconversation.com/did-the-morrison-government-change-the-relationship-between-religion-and-politics-in-australia-190650

Power, John, "Chinese-Australian Group to Rally Against Hong Kong Protests", South China Morning Post, 16 August 2019, https://www.scmp.com/ news/asia/australasia/article/3022977/chinese-australian-group-rally-aga inst-hong-kong-protests

Qiddah, "Alan Jones Gives Tony Arbott An Earbashing Over China Trade Agreement", Radio Recording of Conversation, Youtube 18 November 2014, 1:54 https://www.youtube.com/watch?v=iNo5PXniDog

Reuters, "China and Indonesia Welcome Rudd Win in Australia", 25 November 2007, https://www.reuters.com/article/us-australia-election-rea ction-idUSSP15565420071125

Reuters, "Kiribati Says National Interest Behind Cutting Taiwan Ties in Favor of China", 21 September 2019, https://www.reuters.com/article/us-taiwan-diplomacy-kiribati-idUSKBN1W609C

Rogers, Dallas, "Racism hides true culprit of housing discrimination", ABC News (Australia), 25 Feb 2014, https://www.abc.net.au/news/2014-02-25/rogers-chinese-investors-myth-vs-reality/5281538

Rubinsztein-Dunlop, Sean, "Former Labor Staffer John Zhang Investigated for Money Laundering After Chinese Foreign Interference Taskforce Finds Bundles of Cash at Sydney Home", ABC News, 17 November 2020, https://www.abc.net.au/news/2020-11-18/investigation-finds-bundles-of-cash-at-ex-labor-staffers-home/12890806

Rudd, Kevin, A Conversation With China's Youth on the Future (Peking University), 9 April 2008, https://pmtranscripts.pmc.gov.au/release/transc ript-15854

Rudd, Kevin, "Turnbull No Longer Cares About Reconciliation with Indigenous Australians", The Guardian, 26 February 2018, https://www.theguardian.com/commentisfree/2018/feb/26/turnbull-no-longer-cares-about-reconcili ation-with-indigenous-australians

Rundle, Guy, "In the 1970s, a Soft Coup Removed Australia's Left-Wing Prime Minister", The Jacobin, 16 July 2020, https://jacobin.com/2020/07/gough-whitlam-dismissal-letters-john-kerr-australia

SBS, "Peter Dutton Had Private Lunch With Chinese Billionaire Seeking Australian Citizenship", SBS News Feature, 9 April 2019, https://www.sbs.com.au/language/dari/en/article/peter-dutton-had-private-lunch-with-chi nese-billionaire-seeking-australian-citizenship/f68wsomob

SBS, "Scott Morrison Warned Robodebt Scheme Would be Illegal Without Changes, Inquiry Hears", SBS Australia, 7 December 2022, https://www.sbs.com.au/news/article/scott-morrison-warned-robodebt-scheme-would-be-illegal-without-changes-inquiry-hears/4plop5a8e

Schwartz, Dominique, Vidot, Anna and Jasper, Klint, "S Kidman and Co: Scott Morrison approves sale of cattle empire to Gina Rinehart, Chinese company", ABC News (Australia), 9 December 2016, https://www.abc.net.au/news/2016-12-09/s-kidman-and-co-sale-to-rinehart-approved/8106694

Searight, "Amy Countering China's Influence Operations: Lessons from Australia", CSIS Commentary, 8 May 2020, https://www.csis.org/analysis/countering-chinas-influence-operations-lessons-australia

Seccombe, Mike, "From the Archives: Hawke Weeps as He Tells of Massacre", Sydney Morning Herald, 17 May 2019, https://www.smh.com.au/national/from-the-archives-hawke-weeps-as-he-tells-of-massacre-20190517-p51ofm.html

Siegel, Matt, "For Australian PM Abbott, Crises Lead to Strident Foreign Policy", Reuters, 5 September 2014, https://www.reuters.com/article/us-australia-crisis-policy/for-australian-pm-abbott-crises-lead-to-strident-foreign-policy-idUSKBN0H00M820140905

Slater, May, & Quinn, Liam, "Australia to Crack Down on Foreign Investors Buying Up Property… as It's Revealed Chinese Owner has Found a Buyer after Being Forced to Sell One of Australia's Most Expensive Mansions", The Daily Mail UK, 2 May 2015, https://www.dailymail.co.uk/news/article-3064941/Australia-crack-foreign-investors-buying-property-revealed-Chinese-owner-buyer-forced-sell-one-Australias-expensive-mansions.html

Slater, May & Quinn, Liam, "Australia to crack down on foreign investors buying up property", Daily Mail, 2 May 2015, https://www.dailymail.co.uk/news/article-3064941/Australia-crack-foreign-investors-buying-property-revealed-Chinese-owner-buyer-forced-sell-one-Australias-expensive-mansions.html

Strating, Bec, "Troubled Waters? Australia-Indonesia Maritime Boundary in the News", The Interpreter, Lowy Institute, 2 June 2021, https://www.lowyinstitute.org/the-interpreter/troubled-waters-australia-indonesia-maritime-boundary-news

Storey, Henry, "Why Australia Shouldn't Put All Its Eggs in the Quad Basket", The Interpreter, Lowy Institute, 27 June 2022, https://www.lowyinstitute.org/the-interpreter/why-australia-shouldn-t-put-all-its-eggs-quad-basket

Tan, Su-Lin, "China-Australia Relations: Threat of War, Race-Baiting Feature in Campaigning Ahead of May 21 Election", South China Morning Post, 9 May 2022, https://www.scmp.com/week-asia/politics/article/3176819/china-australia-relations-threat-war-race-baiting-feature

Tavan, Gwenda, "The Beginning of the End of the White Australia Policy", Inside Story, 1 July 2016, https://insidestory.org.au/the-beginning-of-the-end-of-the-white-australia-policy/

Taylor, Lenore, "Malcolm Turnbull: Multiculturalism and Tolerance Will Combat Terrorism", The Guardian, 23 March 2016, https://www.theguardian.com/australia-news/2016/mar/23/malcolm-turnbull-multiculturalism-and-tolerance-will-combat-terrorism

The Age, "Mr Howard, meet the Dalai Lama", The Age Opinion, 21 May 2002, https://www.theage.com.au/opinion/mr-howard-meet-the-dalai-lama-20020521-gdu809.html

Torode, Greg, & Wen, Phillip, "Explainer: Possible Chinese Military Base in S.Pacific Fills Gap, Sends Strong Message to U.S. and Allies", Reuters 10 April 2018, https://www.reuters.com/article/us-china-defence-vanuatu-base-explainer-idUSKBN1HH1B4

Turnbull, Malcolm, "I've Never Sought ALP Membership: Turnbull", The Sydney Morning Herald, 23 August 2009, https://www.smh.com.au/national/ive-never-sought-alp-membership-turnbull-20090823-euu4.html

Turnbull, Malcolm, "Former Australian PM Malcolm Turnbull on Donald Trump: 'You Don't Suck up to Bullies'", The Guardian, 20 April 2020, https://www.theguardian.com/australia-news/2020/apr/20/malcolm-turnbull-on-donald-trump-you-dont-suck-up-to-bullies

The Age, "I Faced Assault Charge, Admits Abbott", 18 July 2004, https://www.theage.com.au/national/i-faced-assault-charge-admits-abbott-20040718-gdya1v.html

The Sydney Morning Herald, Rudd Outshines PM with Language Skills, 7 September 2007, https://www.smh.com.au/national/rudd-outshines-pm-with-language-skills-20070907-gdr1t8.html

Tillett, Andrew, "Kevin Rudd Accuses Malcolm Turnbull of Running Anti-China Jihad", Australia Financial Review, 12 February 2018, https://www.afr.com/politics/kevin-rudd-accuses-malcolm-turnbull-of-running-antichina-jihad-20180212-h0vybe

Tuilaepa-Taylor, Moera, "China-Solomon Islands Security Agreement Leaked on Social Media", Radio New Zealand News Report, 25 March 2022, https://www.rnz.co.nz/international/pacific-news/463957/china-solomon-islands-security-agreement-leaked-on-social-media

VOA, "Australia Bans 2 Chinese Telecom Giants from New Broadband Network", VOA News, 23 August 2018, https://www.voanews.com/a/australia-bans-2-chinese-telecom-giants-from-new-broadband-network/4540776.html

Watt, David, Australian Defence Force in Afghanistan (2010) Australian Parliamentary Briefbook Entry, https://www.aph.gov.au/About_Parliament/Parliamentary_Departments/Parliamentary_Library/pubs/BriefingBook43p/adfafghanistan

Walden, Max, Dziedzic, Stephen, & Wasuka, Evan, "Here's What's Behind the Violent Protests in the Solomon Islands Capital, Honiara", ABC News, 25 November 2021, https://www.abc.net.au/news/2021-11-25/solomon-islands-protests-explainer-china-taiwan/100648086

Wang, Amber, "Beijing Tells Australian Defence Minister Peter Dutton to Abide by One-China Principle After Taiwan Warning", South China Morning Post, 26 April 2021, https://www.scmp.com/news/china/diplomacy/article/3131147/beijing-tells-australian-defence-minister-peter-dutton-abide

Wang, Tandee, "Beyond Hawke's Tiananmen Tears", Australian Centre on China in the World ANU, 3 June 2021, https://www.thechinastory.org/beyond-hawkes-tiananmen-tears/

Walden, Max, "Australia's 'Boat People': Then and Now", The Diplomat, 21 June 2016, https://thediplomat.com/2016/06/australias-boat-people-then-and-now/

White, Hugh, Mr. Howard Goes to Washington: The U.S. and Australia in the Age of Terror, Comparative Connections, Vol. 5 Issue 2, 2003, https://cc.pacforum.org/2003/07/mr-howard-goes-washington-u-s-australia-age-terror/

Woodard, Garry, "Whitlam Turned Focus Onto Asia", The Age, 11 November 2005, https://www.theage.com.au/national/whitlam-turned-focus-on-to-asia-20051111-ge17vk.html

Worthington, Brett, "Paul Keating savages AUKUS nuclear submarine deal as Labor's worst since conscription", ABC News (Australia) 15 March 2023, https://www.abc.net.au/news/2023-03-15/paul-keating-anthony-albanese-penny-wong-aukus-nuclear-china/102098142

Young, Ian, "'Not Substantially European': The Chinese Anzacs Who Fought for Australia in First World War Had to Fight Racism First", South China Morning Post, 25 April 2019, https://www.scmp.com/news/asia/australasia/article/3007399/not-substantially-european-chinese-anzacs-who-fought

Zelinsky, Misha, "The China-Australia Relationship Is Still Close to the Rocks", Foreign Policy, 6 July 2023, https://foreignpolicy.com/2023/07/06/china-australia-diplomacy-sanctions/

Zetter, Kim, "Burn After Reading: Snowden Documents Reveal Scope of Secrets Exposed to China in 2001 Spy Plane Incident", The Intercept, 10 April 2017, https://theintercept.com/2017/04/10/snowden-documents-reveal-scope-of-secrets-exposed-to-china-in-2001-spy-plane-incident/

Zhou, Naaman, "More than 80% of Australians mistakenly believe Chinese investors are driving up house prices", The Guardian, 8 July 2021, https://www.theguardian.com/australia-news/2021/jul/08/more-than-80-of-australians-mistakenly-believe-chinese-investors-are-driving-up-house-prices

CHAPTER 5

India's Global Right Moment and Its Grand Strategy

India has for most part of her post-independence existence maintained a politically neutral stance in its global outlook. Under the leadership of Jawaharlal Nehru, India was a founding member of Non-Aligned Movement (NAM) that emphasised important values with other Third World leaders such as peaceful coexistence, decolonisation and development. New Delhi played a critical role in the 1955 Bandung conference with other Third World countries like Indonesia, Egypt, North Korea Yugoslavia and China that emphasise the importance of Asian and African nations behind this movement. While Indo-China relations got off to a good start as both countries adopted the spirit of Bandung Conference, it was not long before both Asian giants clashed over territorial demarcation and the granting of an asylum visa to Dalai Lama. Indo-China relations deteriorated to a new low with the 1962 War in the Himalayas resulting in New Delhi leaning towards USSR for support against China. Henceforth, India-China relations remained tense and difficult throughout the Cold War until Rajiv Gandhi became Prime Minister.

Today, India–China relations remain difficult and challenged. Unlike the United States and Japan, China does not feature prominently in Indian domestic political discourse. These two nations have relatively very little interaction throughout the Cold War and have largely remained relatively indifferent to each other. Until the ascendance of the BJP and the arrival of Narendra Modi, India's foreign relations direction has remained

© The Author(s), under exclusive license to Springer Nature Singapore Pte Ltd. 2024
V. Teo, *Cold War Redux Amidst Great Power Rivalry*,
https://doi.org/10.1007/978-981-97-3733-8_5

307

relatively unchanged in the sense that India emphasised strategic independence, development and improving relations with various countries in Asia, the Middle East and the United States. Ever so the maverick politician, Narendra Modi brought seismic changes to India's domestic politics and orientation to the world since 2014. The changes in the political landscape in New Delhi provided the impetus for a sea change in the orientation of India in terms of how it dealt with the external world.

As in previous chapters, the chapter will examine the role of Indian leader during the period under study, the changes in its domestic political system and finally India's evolving role in global politics to make sense of how India became an enthusiastic member of the Global Right, an ally of the United States and her efforts to participate in the Quad to help contain a rapidly rising China.

Level I: The Political Leadership

The Rise of Narendra Modi

Like the other leaders focused on in the book, Narendra Modi belonged to the post-war generation. He was born on September 17, 1950, in Vadnagar, a small town in the Mehsana district of Gujarat, India. Modi's early life experiences were marked by poverty. Modi's family is from the "Ghanchi" community which is one of the 146 communities classified as "Socially and Economically Backward Castes" (SEBC) or also known as OBCs, under Schedule 25-A of the Government of India (BJP Statement in Times of India, 2014). The Ghanchi (oil pressers) caste, produces and sells cooking oil, and Modi's father too was an oil trader before becoming a businessman. In his youth, Modi helped out at his family tea beverage business at the railway station where he served customers. This narrative however is also being challenged by his political opponent, former Gujarat Assembly leader Shaktisinh Gohil, who has alleged that the Prime Minister was a "Mohd Vanik" a prosperous business community (Mohd Ghanchis) of the Vaishya caste, and not of "Teli" caste like the Muslim Ghanchis of Gujarat who enjoy OBC status (DNAindia, 2014). The official narrative stipulates that that the Prime Minister completed his schooling in Vadnagar, and worked for his master's at the University of Gujarat after having completed his bachelor's degree by correspondence at the University of Delhi. The BJP had confirmed that he obtained his BA from Delhi University and MA from Gujarat University by showing his certificates on twitter in response to questions raised (BJP, 2016). This aspect of the Prime Minister's credentials however continues to be controversial today, as there are questions surrounding whether he has been truthful and ultimately whether his fitness to govern is in question (The Tribune, 2023; Chowdhury, 2023). For many Indians however, the image of the Prime Minister is that he is one of their own, representing a modern-day story of a boy from a humble background made good, whose ascendance to high office represents their voice at the highest echelons in government.

What is most noteworthy about the Prime Minister's career however is his linkages to grassroots organisation where his political skills are honed. Modi started his early career moves with his membership of the right-wing Hindu Nationalist organisation, the Rashtriya Swayamsevak Sangh (RSS) in the 1960s. A member of the RSS at eight years old, Modi is known to have remarked: "I went to the Vivekananda Ashram in Almora. I loitered a lot in the Himalayas. I had some influences of spiritualism at that time along with the sentiment of patriotism—it was all mixed. It is not possible to delineate the two ideas" (Jaffrelot, 2021). He also joined the Navnirman protest movement against corruption in Gujarat, but by 1975, he went underground to escape the Emergency declared by Indira Gandhi (Jaffrelot, 2021). In his Gujarati book "Sangarshma Gujarat" published in 2018, Modi described how he evaded attack after many pracharaks (organiser) for the RSS were imprisoned and his work by changing his name and donning disguises and worked with other RSS of the underground movement to distribute literature, spread the organisation's ideology and recruit new members (Anand, 2021). He also looked after families of RSS prisoners and solicited aid from Gujaratis who had emigrated abroad, and subsequently had the responsibility of writing a book from the accounts of those imprisoned under the Emergency, enabling him to travel through India to meet Jana Sangh politicians who were targeted (Jaffrelot, 2021). Modi subsequently rose steadily from branch to division head organiser to RSS to become the architect of demonstrations in the form of processions (*yatra*) such as the Nyay Yatra to demand justice for the Hindu victims of the Hindu–Muslim riots (Jaffrelot, 2021b: 36). Modi's skills as a grassroots mobiliser, political fixer and effective opponent to the Congress Party did not go unnoticed. By the 1980s, Modi was invited by L.K. Advani to work for the BJP, and by 1987 became the organisation secretary for the Gujarat Branch of the BJP. With a penchant for dealing with the masses, and the skills of an political fixer, Modi was able to hone his skills in mobilising grass-roots organisations such as village councils and municipal corporations to power and growing his influence in both rural and urban areas. Modi became the Secretary General of the BJP in 1998, and Chief Minister of Gujarat in 2001. Modi's growth as a politician is overshadowed by his role in Communal politics and the tensions between Hindus and Muslims as manifested by the Communal riots in India (1947–1986) (Galonnier, 2013).

As a politician, Narendra Modi's key to political power stems from three important personal visions or outlooks that provided him with a broad appeal to the Indian electorate. Modi has deep personal conviction that his political journey as an anti-corruption fighter, a reformer and development advocate and a leader of a nationalist movement that aspires to Indian statehood is premised on Hindu nationalism. Due to his humble background and savvy demeanour, Modi appeals to the lower caste. He was also able to portray himself as a defender of the rights of the working class very well. The Prime Minister's previous training as a political organiser and campaign fixer meant that he has over-the-top ability to rally, cajole and persuade the man-in-street to political action by his humble background, savvy demeanour and fiery political speeches.

Anti-Corruption Fighter, Development Advocate and the "Hindu First" Doctrine

An important aspiration deeply cherished by the modern Indian nation is that greater reform should be undertaken so that India can deviate from the old ways of the Indian political aristocrats so that the nation move forward. Modi comes across as a pragmatic servant of the people when in place would allow him to ameliorate the excess of India's traditional political establishment. As such Modi commands the support across different castes and regions to support his political outlook and goals, particularly drawing support from the broad spectrum of Indian society that had grown wary of old-style Indian politics. Modi thus often comes across somewhat as an anti-establishment figure with a penchant for helping the "little" guy, the average man (or woman) in the street as he too was once oppressed and intimidated by the establishment. In that sense, Modi is not only the literal and figurative anti-establishment guy for domestic politics, he is also the new father figure for going against the "established" hierarchical relations in India's foreign relations.

The Prime Minister also regards himself as a reformer and developmental advocate, as opposed to the anglicised elites from the Indian Congress Party who were more interested in maintaining power and advancing their own interests. Modi's appeal to a large swath of the Indian electorate is therefore historically unrivalled. He was also able to tap also on the frustrations of the middle-income urban dwellers as well as farmers from rural areas with regard to bureaucratism and corruption. As a politician, he appears to genuinely share the people's concerns regarding how previous Congress governments were phenomenally incapable of governing effectively and efficiently. By promising governmental reform and anti-corruption, Modi essentially promised the electorate new and improved services. These are essentially what urban middle-class Indians want to hear, particularly as they see their taxes are put to good use. As he succinctly puts it, "Congress owns corruption, and the BJP owns "Armit Kaal" (development), indicating that during the tenure of the Congress Party, it was all about nepotism and corruption. His message was that the Old Regime was detrimental to the Dalits, the tribals and the people of backward society which the BJP was working for (Roushan, 2023). While this might or might not actually be true in terms of the rhetoric on poverty eradication (Sandefur, 2022) and development, Modi's government has indeed performed admirably well judging by how people had welcome the improvements to the basic services they need in their daily lives, ranging from the provision of clean water, sanitation and access to basic banking services.

Modi regards himself as a unifying nationalist bent on creating an Indian nation premised on Hinduism, as opposed to the country's professed secular state instituted by Gandhi and Nehru. Modi's views on this echo the strong sentiment that the Indian middle class felt about how the Anglicised elites had failed to secure and protect the essence of the Indian nation. Hindu nationalism (Hindutva) has its roots in the early twentieth century that arose as a response to the imposition of inclusive secularism that began with the modern project of constructing a modern Indian nation. Like most other movements in the twentieth century, it is an avowal of the inimitable sociocultural–religious nexus of the Hindu identity against the overwhelming harmonising force exerted by the nation-state project of the government. To that extent, the Bharatiya Janata Party (BJP) had its roots in the 1980s rose to prominence as a party that promised to protect the identity and rights of the Hindu community, particularly against the encroachment of the Muslims. Modi's association with this popular movement began in his earlier days as a member of the Rashtriya Swayamsevak Sangh (RSS), a right-wing Hindu nationalist organisation that defined this movement. He rose through the ranks as a grassroots political organiser and political fixer and assumed the all-important post of the Chief Minister of Gujarat in 2001. If compared to the political figures in Japan, Modi is someone who had the nationalist rallying power of Shinzo Abe with the grassroots political skills of his Chief of Staff and subsequent successor Suga Yoshihide. As Gujarat's Chief Minister, Modi was instrumental in the promotion of policy items that would broaden his popularity and energise his base such as the construction and inauguration of the revamped Hindu Makakali temple that was destroyed by the fifteenth-century Gujarat leader Mahmud Begda (Langa, 2022).

This embrace and message of "Hindu First" resonated with a broad spectrum of Indians both within and outside of India. Modi's appeal to Hindu culture and identity by emphasising the use of culture-dominant language, rituals and symbols and practices in his public engagements. For instance, in implementing the BJP's infrastructure building plans since 2014, Modi's BJP has renamed roads that were originally named after historic Muslim leaders, erected massive statues depicting Hindu gods and leaders, and inaugurated a parliament filled with Hindu symbols and rituals (Schultz et al., 2023). Another example is the Central Vista (named Path of Duty to replace Rajpath "Kings Way") redevelopment project in New Delhi worth 1.7 billion US dollars (Harris & Gordon, 2023). In the 2024 election, Modi has appealed directly to the Indian people by claiming he is someone that God has asked him to serve. As with most good politicians, Modi's charm and persuasiveness convey a personal connection with the masses distinct from other rarefied elitist politicians that ordinary Indians are familiar with. For many, Modi is one and the same with them, and in the words of one interlocutor, when Modi speaks, there is great ethnic pride amongst the Hindu masses.

The affinity for Modi also comes from the warm reception to his economic and developmental agenda that promises to enhance the peoples' daily lives. His strengths as a politician not only rest on his pontification of broad abstract visions of the future, but rather, the key to Modi's popularity lies in his vision and policy agenda that often rests on different grassroots initiatives that could make a concrete difference for the people. They might not be as grand when compared to his foreign counterparts' political promises but Modi's projects often have important implications for the daily lives of his constituents. To that extent, his programs have received a popular level of acceptance particularly those in infrastructure development, job creation and material improvement in essential services for the daily lives of the people. This combination of embracing grassroots ethnic-religious nationalism and appealing to the Hindu identity along with a promise to defend the interests of the Hindu community against the alleged (imagined or real) threats unabashedly from Muslims and secular political elites proved to be sure win populist electoral strategy.

The Pragmatic Nationalist

There is no question that amongst the world leaders that have emerged in this decade, Prime Minister Modi stands out as one of the most charismatic and skilled politician and foresighted thinker. His years of training and working in one of the world's toughest political environments as a grassroots leader, campaign strategist and political fixer meant that he has far more skills than any of his contemporaries do at the global level. As a politician, Modi comes across as having the elements and traits of his global right contemporaries. Like the late Shinzo Abe, Modi appears to be leading a revival (or renaissance) of pride and affection for the cultural renaissance of the nation's largest and most influential group through the emphasis of Hindu cultural symbols, language or even the love of temples (Bhatnagar, 2022). Like Donald Trump, Modi provides frustrated citizens and disenfranchised voters a voice of resistance and pushback against long-time establishment elitist politicians who were perceived to be incapable of taking anyone but their own interests into consideration. Like Xi Jinping, Modi's advocation for developmental agenda and concern for the poor's welfare by promising to lift the poorest of the poor made him extremely popular. Like his Australian counterparts, Modi promises a vision of hope and a vision of his country emerging to play a far bigger and influential role in global affairs.

Modi was Gujarat's Chief Minister from 2001 to 2014 before he rose to the Prime Ministership. He was implicated in the deaths of well over 1000 Muslim deaths, organised rape, looting and infanticide during the 2002 Gujarat uprising after the death of 60 Hindu pilgrims on a train fire in a Muslim town. As Chief Minister, he was accused of inaction and the condoning of the violence, and consequently ostracised by Western politicians who shunned him for the human rights abuse. As Gujarat Chief Minister, he was only able to liaise with non-Western countries to solicit trade, investment and political capital. Modi visited Japan as Chief Minister at least twice, once in 2007 when Shinzo Abe was Prime Minister, and again in 2012, where he was hosted not only by DPJ leadership as well as the Leader of the Opposition Shinzo Abe. However, it was in China that Modi was truly welcomed. Each time Modi visited China, he was accorded treatment typically reserved for visiting Heads of State and met important (second rung leaders) leaders of the Communist Party where he was regarded as a "strong leader" with a "Chinese way", "business-oriented" and who is capable of "delivering on promises" (Mohan, 2014). Modi essentially admired the "Chinese model" arguing that India should emulate the Chinese building of a manufacturing hub He was able to return with more Chinese commitments of greater investments in Gujarat. This cultivation of Modi was probably also made in mind since the incumbent Prime Minister Singh was leaning towards an India-Japan-US axis (Mohan, 2014). Modi's orientation towards China was therefore one that was based on pure pragmatic opportunism. By the time Modi finished his Chief Minister stint, he had visited China four times. Since Modi became Prime Minister of India in 2014, he has met with Chinese Xi Jinping at least 20 times, including mutual visits and meetings on the sidelines of international summits. Modi visited China in 2015 visiting Xi Jinping's hometown in Xian, in Hangzhou in September 2016 (BRICs summit), in Wuhan (April 2018) and Chennai (October 2019). Modi did start his term and got on with the People's Republic reasonably well, with mutual state visits and personal exchanges with Chinese leader Xi Jinping. Insofar as development is concerned, the Indian Prime Minister has more in common with his Communist counterpart than with what he shares with his Global Right colleagues. As Modi said "China and its people have a special place in my heart. I admire their hard working, disciplined and resilient nature and above all, their sense of history. Our cultural bonds are very strong and deep-rooted. Over the years, our relations have further strengthened. We are committed to making them still better, fruitful and productive" (Economic Times, 2011). Modi's pragmatism however meant that despite his Chinese ties built earlier in his career, he adapted quickly to domestic realities and international circumstances upon his ascendance as Prime Minister.

In a clear sign, Modi's foreign policy was to join the high-profile Quad dialogue and the Global Right in their confrontation with the

Chinese. However, Modi did not lean to "one side" even though he was leading India towards better relations with the US and Japan completely. In essence, Modi was engaging both Shinzo Abe, the Japanese Prime Minister, who was also chief architect of the Quad, and Donald Trump the President of United States as well as leaders of China and Russia at the same time, soliciting what he possibly could from these relationships in service of India. Even though he had a fascination with the Chinese "method" in terms of entrepreneurship, investment and economic growt, this does not impede Modi's ability to make alternative judgement calls on other China-related issues pertaining to India. Whether it was confronting China further on territorial disputes, military "balancing" or joining "like-minded" friends such as Japan or the United States to confront China, Modi's consideration was first and foremost India's own interests. Modi also ran foreign policy in a way that rattled everyone in the Quad fraternity during the Ukraine War, given how India "defected" to buy energy from Russia under sanction and reselling the supplies to Europe for a huge profit. Additionally, many perceived that New Delhi has betrayed its traditional sympathy for the Palestinians to become a staunch Israeli supporter, hurting its credentials as a Global South leader. Modi's ability to "swing" to and fro both sides reflects both his pragmatism as well as a broader strategic independence that India has always been famous for. Yet to understand India's journey in becoming as a member of the Global Right, and how India's relations with China deteriorated so badly, it is essential to contextualise the domestic political and external environment that Prime Minister Modi was operating in, and how India's grand strategy was shaped by the forces at different levels. ·

Level Two: Domestic Politics

The Primacy of Local Politics: Anti-Colonialism, Statism and Rightwards Drift

Since 2017, the narratives in the West and Japan have waxed lyrical about how much India shares Western and Japanese values as the world's largest democracy. The global right politicians of the day all desired to be associated with the Indian Prime Minister to show that they were beacons of democracy, and defend "liberal" values and freedoms while standing up to China. Modi of course was still the same politician that was ostracised years before when he was the Chief Minister of Gujarat, except now he has been inducted into the Global Right fraternity and a reborn defender of freedom. Such narratives then to over-romanticise everything about the nature of India including the imperfections of the system. India does run an electoral system where some people do get a say in terms of who gets to govern via a system of votes, but it is often subjected to all sorts of influences from outright rigging to majority dominance. The vastness and diversity of an electoral system such as India's political system cannot be generalised but the dynamics of electoral politics can at best be distilled down to local politics, usually to do with bread-and-butter issues in a given electoral district. In other words, what happens in any district during an election cycle is often dominated and defined by local developments and grassroots dynamics as opposed to national issues. This importance cannot be understated as it provides Modi with such an important advantage as he has worked his entire career in grassroots politics, and is therefore a superb strategist when it comes to retail politics

For much of India's post-independence history, the National Congress party has dominated much of Indian politics premised on secularism and anti-communalism, inclusive politics and civic equality designed to protect Constitutional values. In reality, the Congress-dominated era had the effect of reinforcing the radical economic disparity and existing privileges of elites in post-colonial India. The importance of local politics and issues in each election in India meant that it was almost impossible for any party to overwhelm the dominant party, at least not until the rise of BJP 1.0 when the then Prime Minister Atal Bihari Vajpayee emerged to form a coalition government. The roots of the rise of the BJP trace back to the two parties, the Bharatiya Jana Sangh (BJS) and the Rashtriya Swayamsevak Sangh (RSS) on the ideological basis of pro-Hindu majoritarianism and economic renewal as mobilisation plank. In 2014, the BJP's victory was driven largely by the consolidation of ideological forces on two axes that govern party competition in India—the politics of statism and the politics of recognition (Verma, 2019). The former refers to the degree by which the government can intervene to effect or change societal norms or economic interactions in personal life such as marriage, inheritance, etc. and the latter refers to the efforts by the government to address the historical inequities suffered by disadvantaged communities and protect minorities from the excesses of *Hundutva* majoritarian impulses. In 2019, Modi ran a similar dominant campaign with the help of the RSS. Additionally, the BJP was observed to have redesigned and reinvented caste-based politics by stitching together winning caste coalitions (Finnigan, 2019). The targeted welfare schemes and quotas in jobs and education for the poor and nationalist narratives that played up the Pulwama attack and the Balakot airstrike certainly helped too (Sen, 2019). The BJP made inroads even in states that never had a BJP government, such as in Tripura and West Bengal (PTI, 2024). These elections have solidified three important trends in Indian politics—that the BJP is now without question the dominant party, that majoritarian politics are here to stay and most importantly, politics have shifted rightwards. Modi's increased popularity was therefore more incredulous to many. What was shocking was not so much that there was a lack of resistance, but rather the lack of a coherent response to the BJP's strategy and tactics. For many, the failings of the main political opponent prove gratifying. The defeat of the Congress party by the BJP provided a veil of satisfaction for many who are grateful to see that the erosion and defeat of what was once considered the insurmountable dynastic establishment where the government operates as a family concern as much as they are put off by the inability of the Congress party to reinvent themselves, with a significant faction still clinging onto Gandhi as legacy. The movement against the Congress Party is not only a democratic expression on behalf of many. It may also be read as an extension of anti-colonial sentiments regarding the elite families that governed India in her post-independence period.

The secret to BJP's political success was also because, under Modi, the BJP made it abundantly clear that the party would address the abject poverty, economic malaise and sense of hopelessness that the masses faced in India. This of course is intimately connected to other issues: socio-economic disparity, stalled development and reforms, gender equality, corruption, continued economic development and access to public services for all especially marginalised communities. These issues are compounded of course by India's size and ethnic make-up, which has seen fault lines drawn across the federal-regional level as well as the ethnic-religious-caste divide. Inspired by China's experience and the possibilities for India, Modi's BJP proposed a movement within India to address the very basic concerns of the people, particularly the poor. In 2014, the BJP promised to launch the "Swachh Bharat Mission" to construct toilets in each household and increase the number of household toilets from 39 to 100% by 2019. The BJP announced that India is open-defecation free, even though in reality it would appear there are contradictory reports (Sharma, 2015). The BJP also announced that liquid and solid waste management facilities as well as piped waters should be extended to rural regions. Another scheme is the Ayushman Bharat. It is the largest health care scheme in the world where more than 500 million of India's poorest have access to cashless health care through this program (PTI, 2024). In essence, under Modi's leadership, the BJP has therefore been very successful in creating and persuading coalitions of the lower caste as Modi's schemes have provided them financial relief, dignity and important basic services such as sanitation and piped water. Unfortunately, that is hardly enough. Writing on the economic catch-22 that India is facing, an economist notes that even though India shines somewhat brightly to foreign countries especially those in the West, the truth of the matter is that successive post-independence leaders, starting with its first Prime Minister, Jawaharlal Nehru, failed to confront India's true economic problems. The previous governments sought easy solutions instead. As popular discontent escalated over the decades and political corruption became widespread, India's economic expansion increasingly leaned on unregulated financial practices and environmentally harmful construction. Even though the BJP has campaigned successfully against the Congress by touching on these issues, these are massive problems that just pure political rhetoric cannot solve. There is always a constant concern regarding jobs amongst ordinary voters regarding the economic conditions, particularly in terms of regional development and job opportunities that require sustainable and ongoing investment and development. In this sense, China has become an important factor in the BJP's domestic political calculus. The Chinese path to development is an inspiration for state-led economic rejuvenation, and at the same time a potential source of political embarrassment when comparisons are made. China is ironically both a partner and a competitor all the same time for the Indian government when it comes to the questions of development and geostrategic rise.

Majoritarian Politics, Pakistan and the Muslim Question

BJP's second plank of majoritarian politics is a major and populist shift in India's politics that follows the global trend in the rise of the Global Right. The way the 200 million Muslims are treated in India is an extremely complicated and complex affair as they have faced much discrimination in employment, education and faced impediments to social mobility (Rukimini, 2021a, b) and are often subject to communal violence, most notably in Jammu and Kashmir, but also in other places such Uttar Pradesh etc (Hindustan Times, 2022). This of course is not a one-way picture, as Hindus have also complained of being on the receiving end of such intolerance, but the key difference is that today as an author argues is that "the difference lies in the patronage and State backing that the muscular Hindu majoritarianism now receives" (Rukimini, 2021a, b). Even though discrimination has existed against Muslims for decades, the political philosophy of the founding leaders has always been quite different, at least at the rhetorical level. Having experienced the horrors of the Partition War, the founders of the Congress Party and leaders of India had advocated for secularism and egalitarianism as a long-standing policy in Indian politics, even though the Indian Constitution does not explicitly require the separation of religion and government.

The Hindu nationalists, such as politician V.D. Savarkar (who authored Hundutva: Who is a Hindu?) believed that they were the "true sons of the soil", and they were following, the birth of Hindu nationalism as a political movement (Noorani, 2020) that underpins the ideal of a Hindu State. It was not until the 1980s that secularism was eroded when Indira Gandhi exploited religious divisions to help return the Congress Party to power, and this in turn created fertile ground for the rise of the BJP (Chandra, 2019). Despite that, the BJP did not quite embrace Hindu nationalism until 1989 even though it had jettisoned Gandhian socialism in 1985 (Noorani, 2020). It was widely believed that Atal Bihari Vajpayee who was the moderate face of BJP in the 1980s had actually considered leaving the Party when the BJP under the leadership of Advani transited onto a program of Hindu mobilisation through the *ekatmata yatras*, which were designed to bring out the faith and devotion of the masses towards *Bharat mata* and the *Ganga mata*, and the Ayodhya movement (Nag, 2018). By 2014, when the BJP won its first unequivocal victory in the Lok Sabha with a divisive campaign filled with anti-Muslim messaging, and soon after began to unabashedly implement its long-held agenda of promoting Hindu first policy, with the aim of making India a Hindu nation, and enshrining Hindu supremacy in law. This meant in practice minorities suffer from both direct and indirect structural violence (Biswas, 2024). Officially Muslims are discriminated against in employment, education and housing, and are often denied access to justice in seeking legal redress to fight these policies despite constitutional protection (Maizland, 2024). When political narratives—created and promoted by elected representatives—feature hate speech against Muslims on an everyday basis, it becomes natural that everyday gestures of secularism becomes eroded. There is the banning of wearing headscarves, renaming of Muslim cities, towns and buildings, removal of chapters on Muslim history from official textbooks and even riots, vigilante violence and demolition of Muslim homes (Krishnan, 2023). Modi for instance, has inaugurated a New Parliament House that is symbolic of India's new architectural nationalist symbol (Schultz et al., 2023). Eroding secularism at the political and policy level in effect means on an everyday basis, Muslims suffer from scapegoating and outright violence from social groups and the State. During the pandemic, Muslim minorities, including those working in health care were maligned and scapegoated for the spread of disease, with some going so far as to suggest that this was some sort of biological jihad (Yasir, 2020). With the demise of Vajpayee in 2018, some analysts have argued that the era of ideological moderation and the ideal of a pluralist India has truly demised (Chandra, 2018) as the BJP increasingly toughened its stance.

The question of the appeal of Hindu nationalism is not surprising. In almost every other country that has elections, politicians would utilise nationalism as a panacea in any run-up to elections. For better or worse, most parties, whether Conservative or Liberal, Left or Right leaning would seize the nationalistic narrative if they could to ensure electoral victory. The BJP under Modi used majoritarian politics to good effect, using religion to rally the electorate across caste and class lines. BJP's Hindu majoritarianism bent might appear attractive for older voters and good for politics, but the subtle curtailment of Muslim cultural symbols and enforced prejudice against Muslims do not sit well with the younger generation (Bhardwaj, 2022). Younger professional urbanites are usually less conservative, religious and more tolerant of greater multiculturalism. The advocation of majoritarian politics also creates questions of minority rights and distributive justice/politics as well as broader issues pertaining to India's neighbours such as Pakistan.

For Indians, Pakistan is a domestic political issue, more than a foreign relations one. Despite sharing close cultural heritage and colonial experience, both became sworn enemies following independence, having fought wars in 1947, 1965, 1971 and 1999. The Partition was in particular brutal, with British eyewitnesses (who had survived the Nazi camps) describing the massacres, torture and killing to be more brutal as communities who had coexisted before for a millennium started attacking each other in a terrifying outbreak of sectarian violence (Hajari, 2016).

Even though the first Islamic invasions of India took place as early as the eleventh century, and it was not before long that Persianised Turks and other Central Asians moved and established themselves across India, enabling cultural mixing that saw Hindus and Muslims living side by side. By the nineteenth century, India was a place where traditions, languages and cultures cut across religious groupings, and where people did not define themselves primary through their religious faith (Dalrymple, 2015). There are of course varying interpretations as to why the Partition came about but whether it is out of the divide and rule of the British, or natural development that came about of different groups renegotiating on power sharing or personality clashes amongst first-generation leaders the likes of Gandhi, Nehru and Jinnah. The question of Pakistan is and always will be a central component of Indian nationalism.

In this respect, India's "Muslim" problem is not unique vis-à-vis the Global Right countries, with the notable exception of Japan. There have been allegations about Islamophobia in the United States and many of her allies in Europe and Australia but what is different here is that the BJP government is now expressively "doing" something about it (Reuters 2024).

The Pakistan linkage necessitates that Muslims, even if they are of Indian ethnicity are often viewed with suspicion, and in many cases discriminated against. The partition of India and Pakistan is essentially a political and legal partition, and as such the ethnicities living in both countries essentially overlap. The common history and culture between these two nations traces back thousands of years, but the religious and political divide has created differentiated nationalisms that often create negative images in the eyes of each nation. There are lingering sentiments expressed but for the most part Indian Muslims probably feel patriotic towards India but not Pakistan. The majoritarian politics practised by the BJP creates tensions for the Muslims in India, particularly during times when it ratchets up anti-Muslim sentiments. Pakistan has enacted its own version of majoritarianism with the appearance of taking "tit for tat" measures against Hindus, but this is of course not the case that Islamabad has the welfare of Indian Muslims at heart per se. BJP's discourse on Muslim underpins their popularity in domestic politics and enables the BJP to consolidate its narrative on national security. While nationalistic tough talk on Pakistan and anti-terrorists sits extremely well with the BJP's discourse on Hindutva and anti-Muslim sentiments, it does not come without costs. Domestically, this divisive policy has actually increased dissent and violence. Internationally, it erodes Modi's image. Whether it's the democrats in the United States, NGOs in Europe or the oil-rich nations in the Middle East (Chisti, 2022), what goes in India is never exclusively India's sovereign business. The more the BJP bangs on its nationalistic drum vis-à-vis Pakistan and Muslims, the more it costs them internationally in the long run. Modi understands this, but like many of his predecessors appeared not to be doing enough to build better ties with Pakistan (Mohan 2024).

How does China fit into this dimension of Indian politics? The answer is simple: Beijing is Pakistan's major backer and looms behind many of India's policy insecurities. Beyond direct bilateral border disagreements and territorial disputes, long-term political and economic assistance and now Belt Road Initiative with Islamabad are triggering concerns about how infrastructure build-up might affect India's domestic and border security. This is a result of history, geopolitical tensions and most recently unrelenting social and corporate media coverage from India and Western media. There are thus four important dynamics as to why China is viewed negatively in India. First, China-related security issues have a lot of traction with Indian voters young and old since Indians use Western corporate and social media in their daily lives. China-related security issues are therefore being used by both the Congress Party and the BJP to taint each other by accusing each other of being soft on China. Second, the Chinese community in India is so minuscule that they are a completely insignificant force in Indian domestic politics. This means the discussions will not be moderated or restrained or balanced in any way. Third, politicians understand that articulating a strong response to China scores political points. BJP in reality won a high approval rating from how the border conflict with China was handled—and even if it actually does not do anything, the success or failure often rests on how "hard" one appears on national security (Ali & Barthwal, 2020). Fourth, the BJP perceives that India has very little to gain if it establishes good relations with China than it does if tensions are high. The logic is simple—India would be able to ingratiate herself with the United States, Japan and Europe and ride on the anti-China wave and obtain outright assistance, economic opportunities and strategic leverage from the Western camp. The real problem with China insofar as Indian domestic politics is concerned however is that China appears to stand in the way of not only as an obstacle to BJP's claim of political superiority but more importantly is an economic competitor (of sorts) in BJP's developmental blueprint.

5 INDIA'S GLOBAL RIGHT MOMENT AND ITS GRAND STRATEGY 323

BJP's Economic Conundrum: Grassroots Politics, Distributive Justice and Job Creation

India's economy had suffered drastically in the initial founding years even as India elected to adopt the democratic system of its former colonial master, without embarking on building a strong capitalistic economic system one might expect to be associated with a democracy. Nehru sought to build a non-aligned socialist state-planned economy in the new Republic by drawing technical and financial assistance from both the Soviet bloc as well as the West. With the assassination of Gandhi by Hindu nationalists, Nehru was even more determined to build a secular India that ran a system that he felt was more suited to its own conditions. In the aftermath of three Indo-Pakistani War, a border War with China, alongside a currency crisis in the 1960s, New Delhi began to move closer to Moscow strategically under the leadership of Indira Gandhi. New Delhi began emulating many aspects of the Soviet Union, including the centralisation of power and the signing of a friendship Treaty. By 1971, Gandhi had won a very tough election with an eliminate poverty "garibi hatao" slogan in March, and by May was engaged with Pakistan over the liberation of Bangladesh. Yet after a series of disastrous droughts and consequent famine in 1972–73, there was a swell of domestic dissatisfaction as inflation had a devastating impact on the lives of the people. As protests and "rebellion" broke out across the country, Indira Gandhi declared a proclamation of Emergency, that saw the authorities clamped down on the political opposition, including many members of the RSS at that time. India's third Prime Minister saw New Delhi emulating many aspects of the Soviet Union, including the centralisation of power and the signing of a friendship Treaty. By the 1970s, the Congressled government appeared to be increasingly corrupt and incompetent in terms of promoting economic growth where India's growth is pejoratively described as the "Hindu rate of growth" (Virmani, 2006). India's political neutrality and strategic inclination towards the Soviets did not help India achieve the kind of economic growth it aspired to. It wasn't until Manmohan Singh that India enacted reforms to make the country more open and receptive to foreign trade by undertaking currency stability and convertibility and import duty reduction. By the 1990s, India began to increase their engagement that saw the economic prospects improving as India began opening her doors to welcome foreign investment and engagement, drawing in part from the demonstrated success of their close neighbour China, in part because of the unprecedented opportunities accorded in a rapidly globalisation world. As an English-speaking country with cheap labour, New Delhi was able to grow its services sector significantly particularly in IT and business outsourcing operations with global firms. India began to see a slew of companies such as Infosys, Tata Consultancy Services (TCS) and Tech Mahindra globalising their products and services worldwide. Thus while China was becoming a dominant manufacturing power, India's success in the service industry saw India becoming an IT Power. There are numerous debates on development comparing India and China in the academia, media and policy circles, but the trajectory became increasingly clear as China's growth surge forward in this period. Nonetheless, there are still numerous commentaries that suggest that India would be able to catch up and surpass China in the future (such as Rockefeller International Chairman Ruchir Sharma and Columbia Economist Arvind Panagariya) provided India can overcome the obstacles ahead. India's democratic culture and younger demographics stand out as important advantages vis-à-vis China.

When Modi came to power in 2014, India was plagued by uneven growth, sluggish investment and widening disparity. There is a consensus however that the BJP has not done enough to fulfil their electoral promises to the constituents, particularly for those blue-collar workers and the young who had thought that the BJP advocated for them. By 2016, it became obvious that even though the presence of the Prime Minister is felt in India's public life across different dimensions such as the strong emphasis on international affairs, an incremental reform agenda, a political strategy relying on development-oriented discourse as well as Hindu nationalism, joblessness remains a central and important political sticking point for the BJP and Modi (Jaffrelot, 2017). In 2021, the BBC reported that as India emerged out of the pandemic, things were still grim as inflation skyrocketed while the GDP growth rate plunged to -3.1% in the last quarter of 2019–2020. This was not so much due to the pandemic but related to a disastrous currency ban in 2016 and a hasty roll-out of a new tax code. This in turn has spurred a huge spike in unemployment with more than 25 million people jobless, 75 million Indians plunged back into poverty, and only 4.3 million out of the 20 million jobs that were promised were created. India still has a sizable farming sector which employs half of India's working-age population which contributes too little to GDP. Even though spending on infrastructure has increased (Inamdar & Alluri, 2021).

The BJP government has of course tried to seek a way out of unemployment early. For a demographically expanding population, India cannot sustain its growth if the bulk of its youth working in the agriculture sector. To uplift these young people, the government would need to attract investments from the Western world, particularly the United States, Europe and Japan to increase manufacturing sector jobs. This appeared to be one of the most sensible options ahead. The desire to further open and reform India's economy made it necessary for India to totally reconcile with the West and move away from its traditional friends such as Russia. In that respect, becoming an important partner in the Global Right's Indo-Pacific strategy would help in this respect, particularly as Abe and Trump sought to "decouple" from China and relocate manufacturing and jobs away from China. Modi had then advocated an ambitious "Make in India" program for over a decade to alleviate the challenges of conducting business in India. In November 2023, the BJP instituted a production-linked incentive scheme aimed at stimulating manufacturing by providing industrial incentives to increase domestic production. The federal budget for this year allocated a further $134 billion for capital expenditure, including the construction of roads, ports, airports, and railways—a strategy that China employed more than three decades ago to promote economic growth.

In the lead-up to the 2024 elections, the mass media portrayed a rosy picture. Accordingly, when Modi took over, the GDP per capita was around $5000, but by 2022, it had arisen to over $7000. The GDP is now $3.9 trillion, going towards the BJP's previous campaign that India will have a $5 trillion economy by 2024–25. The Foreign Exchange Reserve has grown from US$304 billion in 2014 to $642 billion in February 2024. The Bombay Stock Exchange (BSE) market capitalisation is now above $4 trillion making it the 5th largest in the world behind the US, China, Germany and Japan (Firstpost, 2024). External Affairs Jaishankar highlighted that in the duration since Modi came to power, India has grown from the 5th to the 4th largest economy in the world, changing global perceptions of India (The Hindu, 2024). Finance Minister Nirmala Sitharaman in her budget address highlighted that in the previous decade, the average income of Indian people had increased by 50%, 250 million had been liberated from multi-dimensional poverty, with inflation being kept under check and build-up of infrastructure in record-time and other public welfare assistance schemes (Economic Times, 2024).

The BJP's narratives are regularly scrutinised stringently by critics and domestic political opponents as there is no definitive indication that the BJP has done an outstanding job in matching its electioneering campaign (Bhattacharya, 2022). There were questions if the rosy growth painted by the media was indeed true (Sen, 2024) and whether the success could be attributed to the performance BJP's policies or if this growth was really a case of India being buoyed by the overall growth in global economy (Misra, 2023; Ahmed, 2022). Critics also suggested that even though government statistics have shown growth in several sectors, the growth has not translated into desired job numbers (Reed, 2023) or radically better per income capita statistics (Misra, 2023) and if the real growth occurred only in corporate India (Reed, 2023). There is every indication that the discontent with unemployment had become (and will increasingly be) the key political issue that would haunt the BJP (Gandhi cited in Reed, 2023). Indeed, it does appear that unemployment and the question of distributive justice are the two most important issues domestically for the BJP (Rajvanshi, 2024).

The latter is not only creating a problem outside the BJP but also creating problems amongst its ranks. In this respect, the BJP faces a similar challenge with the Chinese Communist Party as it inducted capitalists (businessmen) into its ranks. The BJP had actually undertaken policies that has deviated from the ideal policies and economic preferences of some of the original affiliates of the Sangh Parivar, the broad Hindu nationalist Umbrella spawned by Rashtriya Swayamsevak Sangh (RSS). From the get-go, some of the affiliates such as the Swadeshi Jagaran Manch (SJM) had been opposed to the foreign investment, arguing that such capital injection do more harm than good, while the Bharatiya Mazdoor Sangh (BMS), the RSS's labour union affiliate, has contended that economic reforms have led to "jobless growth" and an "increase in [the] trade deficit", and has demanded that the government should reconsider labour policies based on liberal trade globalisation (Mehta, 2019). BJP itself started as a party with autarkic instincts even as Vajpayee and Modi moved the party away from its leftist roots and nationalistic posture and rhetoric to embrace global trade. The convincing manner by which Modi is able to persuade his constituents to support his reign through nationalistic majoritarian politics while embracing global liberal trade is a combination seen in many other authoritarian Asian countries, including China. The problem with this agenda is that it does not automatically translate into enhancing the economic well-being of the bulk of his voters, especially since he claims to represent the welfare of the lower socio-economic classes. Moreover, the BJP is adopting increasingly contradictory policies that would threaten its future viability (Verma, 2019). For instance, as the BJP flip-flopped on inducting lower caste members into leadership positions, it is increasingly relying on politicians from the upper caste in its leadership posts even as the BJP increasingly asserts representation of the lower caste. Strategy-wise, the BJP is increasingly relying on majoritarian politics and emphasising the role of religious figures might sit uneasily with its growing urban middle-class voters who might be more liberal in outlook. The BJP cannot be the protector of citizens irrespective of their caste or identity or religion if it is reliant on majoritarian politics. The emergence of a violent Hindutva movement has overridden previous standards of civic life and public responsibility but the fundamental question remains as observed:

> Why do nutrition, health and education remain afterthoughts in the Indian policy discourse, instead of rising to the top of policy priorities ? Not because we don't know what needs to be done but because the construction of dams, riverfronts and overpasses remains the focus of "development" as does the extension of mining franchises in rich forests. These activities provide more lucrative opportunities to politicians and business than does the extension of quality primary health and education … The rule of law works arbitrary. The good within the system does not break through into shared prosperity." (Mody, 2023)

While India made progress in economic growth and poverty eradication (Patnaik, 2019), other sectors such as education provision, employment and pollution remained big problems the BJP faced in 2014 (The Economist, 2024). The BJP knows that meeting their promises over the bread-and-butter issues remain central to their continued and sustained political longevity. Modi's political opponents have argued that the Prime Minister have actually aggravated on all the issues that he has raised in his political campaign (Kurshid and Muhammad 2018). Since its inception, the Modi government has therefore been under much pressure to elevate India's economy. To do this, the BJP is always keen to attract foreign investments and technological transfers so that more industries other than the software, IT backend and corporate services could be built. This would boost overall industrial capacity and generate growth opportunities to create more jobs across the secondary and tertiary sectors. Due to pre-existing tensions with the United States and the West, India's access to Western capital and technical know-how was not always possible. Generations of Indians have always aspired to study and work in the United States, but it was not always possible because of Indo-US tensions. Modi's ostracisation for his alleged involvement in the atrocities in Gujarat did not help. The key of course to India's rehabilitation lies in the plans of another member of the Global Right—Japan's Shinzo Abe. The momentum was of course put in place by Modi's predecessor as India had begun to participate in bilateral and multilateral consultations with Japan, US and Australia earlier in the first reiteration of the Quad. Yet, the state of relations between India and the United States was not as warm as it should be, and in many ways stands in stark contrast to the popular opinion of the United States in India. The United States is seen very favourably by the younger generation of Indians, many of whom would like to go to the United States to study, work and live. Cultivating closer relations with the United States has broad-based support from the public, especially the younger generation. The younger generation of politicians and strategists also recognise the importance of the United States in India's modernisation path ahead.

The Spectre of Comparison: Civilisational Enemy, Model Neighbour or Competitor

Comparatively speaking, China has always been a "foreign" entity that is perceived negatively compared to the United States in India. This is due to long-standing peripheral contact, strong civilisational pride, and stereotypes that continue to brew geopolitical tensions. With China supporting Pakistan, increasing its influence in the Indian Ocean and demonstrating its willingness to fight India in the Himalayas, Beijing has risen to become quite the challenge to India in the eyes of Indian public. At the same time, the Chinese economic growth story stands as the basis of a direct comparison to India's economic success or failure. While certainly the increased disparity in China continues to be a problem, the very fact that China has lifted millions out of absolute poverty is no mere feat. This is something that many Indians have grudgingly admired about China.

Successive governments have always argued this century will be India's century, and consequently argued there is no reason why India cannot achieve what the Chinese have done. Such comparison creates enormous pressure for India's leadership, particularly as Modi and the BJP has been articulating aloud India's ambitions of becoming a Great Power (Marshal & Yasir, 2024). The problem for Indian politicians is that they however cannot be just explained away the disparity between India and China with just an acknowledgement of the problems and challenges India faces. The poll-driven political culture necessitates a discussion of why Communist China was able to achieve this while India cannot. Whether it's the Congress or the BJP, China unwittingly becomes the elephant in the room insofar as political and economic nationalism is concerned in India. It is common place to hear explanations to hear that China has achieved this growth due to the kind of authoritarian system Beijing has in place where China tolerates inhuman working conditions for workers; discriminates against local firms in favour of local companies and corruption. Unlike India, Beijing does not have a noisy, freewheeling media that loves to blow up scandals and bad news, and in such cases, the bad news is likely to get swept under the carpet. While there are of course various explanations that can be conjured up, the fact of the matter is that such discussions would be usually politicised by the political opposition against the incumbent government, and the negative portrayals of China would likely become exaggerated.

While there is complimentary aspects of the Indo-Chinese relationship, it is also important to recognise that Beijing is a material competitor in several respects. In order for BJP to succeed in its plans, India needs to get competitive in a few domains. It has to attract and retain foreign direct investment and ensure that the capital to establish and build productive capacity. It has to uplift education, and allow for rapid urbanisation and the growing of the secondary sector to allow for more young to get better and upward socially mobile jobs. To replicate China's success, the BJP would have to lead India to entice investments and expand India's capacity across entire supple chains. The BJP also realises the enlargement of its civilian economy has also enabled China to become an innovative power that has brought significant changes to the regional strategic balance and status as a global trading power.

For the BJP, the recognition of China's increasing strategic headwinds might mean an opportunity. Over the last decade, China's domination as the World's factory has been gradually losing its shine as labour and other costs have been rising steadily. In order to manufacture in China, Western companies almost all need to have excellent after-sales service to please Chinese consumers. The problem however is that that not everything can be suitable for the Chinese market. There are also risks—from intellectual property thefts to arbitrary regulations, thus necessitating the consideration of secondary manufacturing sites outside of the PRC. There are now both foreign and Chinese manufacturing firms that have been increasingly keen to relocate their factories to cheaper inland destinations or with less regulation. Under the leadership of Modi, India increasingly positioned itself to be a viable alternative investment destination other than ASEAN, as expanding the secondary sector industries would boost manufacturing jobs and further encourage the flow of capital, technology and expertise to keep flowing into the country.

The real key to balancing China therefore cannot be based on a single-faceted strategy of acquiring more weapons and engaging in military diplomacy to perform hard balance, but rather it should be premised upon growing its own civilian economy so that its size and sophistication would provide the corresponding technological advantage. The BJP therefore is extremely keen to expand the range of industries beyond areas in which India has excelled such as IT Software and back-office operations. Consequently aligning itself with the West and offering India as an alternative venue could possibly bring more high-tech manufacturing from the West. Such a move would render real benefits reminiscent of the way China secured a role in the vital supply chain and the global strategic advantages that go with it, particularly in terms of growing high-technology industries. There is no certainty that just because of the foreign manufacturing move out of China they would naturally relocate to India. The BJP however was betting on three important dynamics. Owing to the overall climate created by the United States and its allies to secure their supply chain, New Delhi feels that it stands to benefit from the possibility of obtaining a large share of these relocations as the United States might want to beef up its new-found friend against Beijing. Delhi rather than ASEAN countries would have the incentive to compete against China in the long run. Second, like China, India is now the world's most populous nation. In the initial years of PRC's economic reforms, the compelling reason for many industries to move to China was the size of the Chinese market. Utilising this facet is a natural marketing move by India playing to its advantage.

After four decades of economic reforms, China has built up a formidable amount of reserves denominated in American dollars. This has helped underpin the strength of China's financial system and enabled China to acquire financial capabilities to defend its interests in its global strategy. It also helps Beijing underwrite its BRI investments abroad, and enables the Chinese currency to increase its steady rise as a medium of value. From the BJP's perspective, without the corresponding financial clout that China has, it would be difficult for India to achieve the corresponding great power status it seeks in its international relations. From the BJP's perspective, without the corresponding financial clout that China has, it would be difficult for India to achieve the corresponding great power status it seeks in its international relations.

The BJP perceives that China's One Belt One Road project threatens to accentuate India's domestic security problems in multifaceted. The BRI would grow and potentially lift Pakistan's economy, bringing up China's connectivity to India's borders by providing both substantial and demonstrable point of reference for India domestic politics. If China's BRI succeeds, China will improve its comprehensive strength against India. Domestically, the views of the BRI are even wider than the government—but both the BJP and the government are worried about a Chinese economic presence close to their borders: whether the presence is in Ladakh, Dolam or high up in the Himalayan plateau—all areas sensitive to India's political centre. Connectivity is only great if you can control it, and in India's case, this economic presence on the border would largely erode India's security. The BRI would confer Beijing a legitimate economic role in South Asian economies in the Himalayan and Indian Ocean as well.

India's Question for Great Power Status: China as a Political Football

China has become the most popular political football for the simple reason that this strategy has the most upsides without incurring too much domestic costs. Politicians from both the Congress Party, the BJP and other small parties have hurled abuse at each other for being "cosy" or being "soft" on China (Hindu, 2010). Like in almost every other country today, populist nationalism goes a long way in domestic politics. Stereotypes are entrenched, and there is very little incentive on the part of anyone whether in government or in the broader civil society to try and look beyond the dominant narratives in the country. If elections and policy depend on popularity and public opinion, then there is no question that there is a self-perpetuating cycle here insofar as China is concerned. There are far few calls for better relations with China as most are in agreement that closer relations with the West would enhance India's national interests in the long run. Insofar as China is concerned, the differences in the debate is the strength of confrontation and the tactics that should be deployed so that China should be "handled" or "contained", and Chinese encroachments cannot be left unanswered (Choudhary, 2023).

There are three important dynamics behind this, and this is not unique to today's world. First, conflict and criticism attract mouse clicks and attention while nationalism sells newspapers. Transnational news agencies and social media today work in tandem to create news cycles and trending topics, often perpetuating both news worthy items but also outright disinformation through skewed narratives. In an environment where the lines blur between reporters, infotainment outlets and content creators, it has almost become impossible for people to sift fact from fiction. For the majority of the people within societies, headlines provide verification to the stereotypes that exist in their head and perpetuate the realities in their minds.

Despite being non-aligned, much of India's educated and elite class are far more integrated with the Western style of life for historical and linguistic reasons. This phenomenon is true for many other countries worldwide, including elites in Russia and China too. Ordinary Indians have a far superior understanding of the West, particularly the United States and Europe but most have very limited understanding of China. To that extent, the news or opinions on current affairs they encounter online or on TV and ingest daily shape their opinions and outlook on mainstream issues. The media climate in India cannot be more cynical for China as the coverage has been consistently negative since 2016. Second, it is almost impossible for any officials, scholars and/or journalists not to take sides when writing public commentaries, news coverage or op-eds. This is true regardless of where one is, but perhaps with the key difference being the style and the way the narrative is being put forth. Most writers would not risk siding with the enemies in public narratives, rightly or wrongly. As one author notes, in a democracy such as India, public policy cannot diverge far from public sentiments (Chanakya, 2020). Third, because of this environment, those who advocate tough posture, conflict and standing up to the perceived transgressors and bullies would usually hoard the microphone, and anyone who did not join in the chime would be sidelined. This sort of collective group think pervades the public policy field—whether in democracies or dictatorships with little exception. The only difference is whether the dissent is articulated loudly in public or in private. Along with a long history of tension and little to no-contact, it is almost impossible for China's image to be upheld in India.

5 INDIA'S GLOBAL RIGHT MOMENT AND ITS GRAND STRATEGY   333

If foreign policy is an extension of domestic politics, then India's China policy is surely a function of how domestic political actors view China. The biggest headache however for the BJP is how to articulate and capitalise on this public sentiment, and achieve its political goals without getting into actual hostilities with China or driving relations to the ground. The BJP cannot reconcile or go to war with China for three important reasons: past rhetoric, current geopolitical interests and future electoral prospects. The calibration point is to maintain a suitable degree of tension with enough wriggle room for manoeuvring in case an important domestic or external variable changes. The war with Ukraine and India's refusal to side completely with the West is an important case in point. Even as India joined in the Trumpian and ultimately the US Indo-Pacific strategy, it's refusal to confront the Chinese wholeheartedly shows that the BJP's shift belies Indian interests at its core, rather than pandering to any major power's ideological leanings or political preferences. In other words, India is largely guided by both opportunity and political necessity, and its China posture is just a tool to its end. Even as India is now being courted enthusiastically by its fellow Quad members, Indian elites understand that this stems from the West's desire to contain and curb China rising prowess rather than a love for the BJP. The BJP in particular understands the value of anti-China rhetoric and appreciates such narrative in its statecraft, and therefore it does not actually mean India would ingest everything that the Global Right posits about China unquestionably.

LEVEL THREE: THE INTERNATIONAL SYSTEM

India's Historical Relations with China: Estrangement, Indifference and Détente

To appreciate the external context against the rise of India as a member of the Global Right and the rapid deterioration of Indo-China relations, this section provides a brief recap of post-War Indo-China relations for the discussion. India's contemporary post-war relations with China can be divided into four distinct and important phases. The first phase covers the post-independence romantic period until the 1962 Sino-India Border war; the second covers post 1962 conflict period till 1988 when Rajiv Gandhi visited Beijing and reconciled with Deng Xiaoping, setting in a period of détente between the two Asian giants; and the third period begins from Rajiv Gandhi's era until 2014 when the Congress Party lost the general elections; the fourth period covers India under the leadership of Modi until the present. This section will provide a brief recap of the first three phrases before discussing the fourth period in detail.

Nehru's India and Mao's China saw themselves as newly independent nations with a need to define their own identities and destinies. This romantic period is often guided by the maxim *Hindi-Chini bhai-bhai* which translates to Indians and Chinese are brothers. In a letter to his Ambassador to China Mohan Simba in 1952, Nehru indicated that he was only worried about Pakistan, and whether China is likely to provide support to India's stance on Kashmir (Namrata, 2020). Mao's subsequent neutrality on the Kashmir issue, alongside with maps used in China's textbooks that indicated Ladakh, Andaman islands and Arunachal Pradesh as "territories" seized by Imperial powers worried the Indian government about China's irredentist designs (Namrata, 2000). Nehru by 1954 had concluded a Treaty with Beijing recognising the PRC's sovereignty over Tibet while preserving India's pre-existing trade arrangements with Tibet. Notwithstanding domestic disagreements, most Indian analysts argued that this arrangement favoured the Chinese heavily. The first real challenge that came between these two Asian giants was the escape of the Dalai Lama and the creation of the Tibetan government in exile in Dharamsala in Himachal Pradesh alongside flocks of Tibetan refugees in 1959. When Zhou Enlai and Chen Yi visited India in 1960, they had an extensively long conversation with the Indian Vice President Sarvepalli Radhakrishnan by which both sides made very emotional remarks that hinted at mutual betrayal and increasing divisiveness (Zhou & Radhakrishnan, 1960). India was particularly bitter about China's inexplicable behaviour over Kashmir even as they had "overlooked" China's transgressions in Tibet and Xinjiang. The perceived Indian support for Dalai Lama as well as the deterioration in PRC's relations with the USSR triggered a change in China's support for Pakistan and underlined the rapid deterioration of India–China bilateral relations. In throwing in the proverbial towel with Pakistan wholeheartedly, Beijing's position cornered New Delhi strategically and eradicated any hope of any sort of amicable development of India–China relations. In return for China's ceding of hundreds of square miles of territory, Islamabad recognised China's sovereignty over Northern Kashmir and Ladakh. This ultimately led to the Sino-Indian clash from 22 October to 30 November 1962. This clash has decidedly militarised the 2400 km long border, part of which is in the Himalayas. Owning to the harsh geographical conditions that create a natural barrier, both nations are unable to amass a large number of troops in the area.

The 1962 Sino-Indian border war with disastrous for bilateral relations in the sense that it convinced all Indians of Chinese ambitions in Aksai Chin, in Ladakh, and Sikkim. The most serious issue for India insofar as China is concerned is the immediate threat to the Northeast Frontier. India–China relations have been on an uneasy truce since then. Needless to say, the border war ensured that any ideal of wanting to cultivate cordial relations had dissipated. The dynamics of their respective relations with other powers alongside domestic developments only allowed for relations to deteriorate. India's politicians and diplomats wanted solutions to allow both countries to achieve "self-respect" but did not materialise. Both nations were newly independent entities with relatively little foreign policy experience. Neither the Congress Party nor the Chinese Communist Party were equipped to handle these difficult disputes that came as political legacies. The Indians were keen to keep what the British said they had. The Chinese communists wanted to preserve what was left (or thought was left) of the Chinese empire after decades of warfare and struggle left ill-defined borders. Clearly, these two newly independent regimes wanted to handle and define the ill-demarcated frontiers without appearing to look weak and were exceedingly uncompromising insofar as territories disagreements were concerned. In the prelude to the 1962 border war, the Indians and Chinese were deeply unhappy with each other. This was not only the road the Chinese built in Aksai Chin, but relationship were also aggravated by over the dynamics of developing Sino-Soviet rivalry (manifested in Mao's unhappiness with Khruschev's arrogance), and the Dalai Lama's asylum in India and growing Sino-Pakistani ties.

To put things into perspective, three important developments accentuated the tensions in Indo-China relations during this period. First, China's domestic political developments had knock on effects on her foreign relations. With the Great Leap Forward developing, Chinese politics by then was taking a sharp leftist turn. What this meant was that the leaders were becoming very dogmatic, very China-centred and viewed the world in an increasingly Marxist lens where proletariat-internationalism and imperial struggles mattered more than national interests. Interactions with India were viewed through this prism of their struggle with the Soviets. Owning to the excess of her domestic politics, China reacted with little great alacrity or insightfulness over her dealings with New Delhi, particularly over the Tibetan issue. Second, China's rhetoric on India as an expansionist power continued to new heights through the 1960s. Beijing increased its support to Pakistan in her 1965 war with India and called for independence for Kashmir. This reaffirmed New Delhi's PRC's hostility to the region and further solidified India's alliance with the USSR. Third, the India–China territorial disputes increased in both intensity and range. The strategic anxiety brought about by the 1962 War had put pressure on India's leaders to prepare for a further clash. In 1967 India and China once again clashed along the Sino-Sikkim border areas of Nathu (September 1967) and Cho La (October 67). New Delhi was also extremely annoyed to find that China had built a road through Aksai Chin over the course of a few years to bolster her claim over the area. In 1987, India and China confronted each other in Sumdorong Chu Valley in Arunachal Pradesh and Cona County in Tibet. The key issue was China's challenge to India's granting of statehood to Arunachal Pradesh. It had initially looked like China and India would go to war again until diplomats met to discuss and defuse the tensions. India and China actually did not restore relations at the ambassadorial level until 1976. During the brief interlude where the Janata government came into power under Prime Minister Morarji Desai, Minister for External Affairs Atal Bihari Vajpayee (who later became Prime Minister himself) was sent to Beijing in 1979 to initiate a reconciliation of India–China relations, as Desai himself sought to avoid a repeat of the 1971 Indo-Pakistan war. Vajpayee said that he had made it clear "the unresolved boundary question must be satisfactorily settled if relations of mutual confidence are to be established", but this initial contact had "at least unfrozen the issue" (The Indian Express, 22 February 2019). This effort however was in vain as China became embroiled in the Third Indo-China War with Vietnam over PRC's support for the Pol Pot regime which New Delhi opposed. India a democratic socialist country was aligned with the Vietnamese and Soviet Communist regime, and Vajpayee had to cut short his visit (Trumbull, 1979).

After twenty-six years of confrontation, India under the leadership of Rajiv Gandhi, once again tried to reach out to Beijing. The strategic climate had changed with the ascendance of Gorbachev in USSR and Deng Xiaoping in China. The détente reached between USSR and China and the desire of the leadership in these countries to improve their economies had somewhat provided a sobering example for Rajiv Gandhi who thought that New Delhi should also take a leaf from the

USSR limited reforms. Deng's desire to create an external environment conducive to PRC's economic reforms spark an interest on the part of New Delhi to try and do the same. Rajiv Gandhi was not slavishly following the Soviets but had set his eyes on a bigger prize. The young Prime Minister had five areas of focus in terms of foreign relations: the non-aligned movement, relations with major powers, African struggle and Apartheid, nuclear disarmament and relations with neighbours, particularly with China, Pakistan and Sri Lanka. All of these were geared towards the Prime Minister's domestic plans. He was interested in achieving greater security for India, and to build an economic-technological bridge to the West, particularly the United States. By being open and listening to China's, Pakistan's and Sri Lanka's concerns, the Prime Minister thought he could yield practical insights, and might even allow him to improve relations to the best he can manage. In so doing, he would be able to reduce India's insecurities, garner political credits and enable his government to focus on what really matters to India—economic and technological modernisation. To that end, the young Indian leader was very different in his outlook, temperament and political methods. In fact, Rajiv Gandhi was seen as someone who was capable of conducting Indian foreign policy in a more pragmatic, less emotionally charged style than his predecessors, as he ultimately wanted to enhance its economic and technological ties with the West that helped India modernise and strengthen. (1985 CIA report cited by Jha, 2017). Insofar as China was concerned, mending fences with the Chinese would at minimum provide India with more strategic latitude. Gandhi therefore met Deng in 1988 on a "wall-breaking" visit, the first leader to do so in 34 years after his grandfather Nehru did so in 1954. Subsequent Prime Ministers such as P.V. Narasimha Rao, Atal Bihari Vajpayee and Manmohan Singh had all approached India–China relations with some care, all seeking to do what Rajiv Gandhi had done. Incrementally, over a period of a quarter of a century, India and China built their confidence slowly but surely. In 1993, under Narasimha Rao, India and China signed the Border Peace and Tranquility Agreement; in 2012 under Manmohan Singh, a working mechanism for consultation and coordination on India–China Border Affairs was inked (Davar, 2023).

China's Rise as a Power in India's Neighbourhood

While Rajiv Gandhi's meeting with Deng did not immediately resolve all of the India–China issues, it did lead to an overall improvement in the tone of bilateral relations. Beijing's position on Kashmir shifted to view the issue as a colonial legacy best settled by India and Pakistan on a bilateral basis. Rajiv's approach to Deng had paid off handsomely as the PRC looked as though it was bending to India's diplomatic lobbying. This of course greatly alarmed Islamabad, and the insurgency in Kashmir began to grow greatly in the 1990s. The PRC was extremely keen not to be drawn into the conflict Indo-Pakistan tensions rose. At that particular moment, China's overriding concern was to focus on its domestic economic reforms, as it had just emerged out of two decades of intense political contestation and strategic entanglements. PRC's positional shift on the issues confronting India (and Pakistan) was largely consistent with Deng's wish to cultivate the best external strategic environment so that China could concentrate on her reforms. By 1992, China has begun issuing maps without the State of Jammu and Kashmir as being part of China (Namrata, 2020). Chinese President Jiang Zemin had in fact advised Pakistan to improve ties with India through trade while allowing the Kashmir issue to be put on the back burner (Bhatt, 2019). Yet, in this decade, New Delhi's grew increasingly unhappy with Beijing owing to two new issues that created the impression that China was actively seeking to be antithetical to Indian interests. The first was China's attempt to block India's attempt to join the UN Security Council as a permanent member and Beijing's (as well as Washington's) covert attempts to tolerate Pakistani-sponsored terrorist activities as well as her not-so-secret attempts to violate the non-proliferation treaty (Bhaskar, 2015). By 1998, New Delhi had begun to openly call out the China threat as one of the reasons why India needed the bomb. The PRC revered its position by suggesting that the Kashmir issue be referred to the UN, denounced New Delhi as being "hegemonic", and began clandestinely helping Pakistan's military modernisation and missile program (Bhatt, 2019). The Chinese of course denied these accusations. The strengthening of China's relations with India's regional rivals could create greater internal and external security problems that the rapidly modernising India would have to deal with. Beyond that, a beefed-up Chinese presence in the other Himalayan state might not be entirely ruled out in the future.

Unfortunately, the real problems from China's rise are only becoming apparent from New Delhi's perspective from 2000 onwards under the leadership of the Congressional government led by Indian Prime Minister Singh. As China's economy grows exponentially, the true manifestation of China's potential now manifests itself in three important areas as India felt she needed to counter. Beijing has risen slowly and steadily over time to become a partner of significance to all the South Asian nations. This trend is not unique to South Asia and is seen across the world from Southeast Asia to the Middle East to Latin America. China's economic asymmetry with various countries in any particular region has become one of the key manifestations of China's rise. With the implementation of the One Belt One Road initiative in 2012, there is evidence to suggest that China's exponential economic growth, rapid industrialisation rate, and the closure of the development gap are all important factors that drive trade between South Asia and China (Zhou et al., 2023). Like most other regions, South Asian countries have increased their imports, particularly of capital-intensive Chinese goods largely due to the range and cost of the imports, while China imports labour-intensive products from South Asia. Even as China accounts for about 25% of the region's importance, the overall percentage of trade with the region only accounts for 5% of China's trade.

Beijing's asymmetric economic relations with South Asian countries created a deep sense of insecurity for New Delhi. Not only was India facing a more muscular and capable PLA in the Himalayas, but China's influence across much of South Asia meant India was losing direct influence in the region. Beijing's economic relations not only erode India's direct influence over the South Asian economies but also provide an alternative leverage for the South Asian nations vis-à-vis India. This economic backstop for South Asian nations would loosen New Delhi's stranglehold on their economies and provide the necessary political support for regimes that might otherwise be held hostage to New Delhi's goals. The argument is similar to the ones made by Japan in Southeast Asia, Australia with the Pacific islands and the United States in the Middle East and South America. From a geopolitical perspective, one can argue that China as an extra-regional power is what the United States is to Southeast Asia. Smaller countries in the region might tacitly appreciate an external power that can help ameliorate or balance New Delhi's clout. Having Beijing normalise her presence, economic, political or strategic would mean China would in effect become a South Asian power capable of standing up to India in her own sphere of influence. There are both practical economic and reputational costs to this development.

The most direct fear however is a nightmarish scenario that China actually gain much more influence than New Delhi in her own neighbourhood. Through her bilateral cooperation, the prospects of China gaining more than a foothold in the region. Beyond the Himalayan countries, India's more acute concerns are actually the role of China in the Indian Ocean and its littoral states (Baruah, 2023). New Delhi is concerned that Beijing might capitalise on its trade ties to secure access rights to strategic industries in the region such as port management, telecommunications and finance that would not only entrench China's presence in a way that would make Beijing a significant military power in South Asia. India's strategic nightmare of course would involve any South Asian nation hosting a Chinese strategic presence. Beijing's increased interest in development ports for instance in Sri Lanka and Pakistan have been termed by strategists in the United States as the "strings of pearl" strategy from the 1990s onwards. For the first time, India's dominance of not only South Asia but also the Indian Ocean is becoming under challenge as the PRC beefs her presence in the region (no matter how transient or "innocent" China says it is). As Baruah notes, China is the only nation to have embassies with each of the six islands in the Indian Ocean (Sri Lanka, Maldives, Mauritius, Seychelles, Madagascar and the Comoros). None of the other powers has all six. China is also a country with no sovereignty disputes and is building itself up as a credible economic and security partner in the region. For analytical purposes, South Asia here is a more confined geographical area than the greater Indian Ocean area that stretches from the Eastern Coast of Africa to the Straits of Malacca.

It is however not what the Chinese are doing on land that worries India, but rather the exponential increase of China's naval capabilities and power projection capabilities in the region. Like many other nations, China's merchant naval fleet faced many challenges from piracy threats in the South China Sea and the Gulf of Aden in the new millennium. There were many attempts (some successful) by Somali pirates to hijack Chinese cargo vessels in the Gulf of Aden. By 2008, China began to dispatch naval vessels to the Indian Ocean to protect its shipping. Building on her naval anti-piracy expeditions, China has realised that in order to protect her interests during peace or war, it is vital that she builds a navy commensurate with her political status and trading interests. The idea of a strategic presence of China in the Indian Ocean is a very new and very threatening prospect for New Delhi and other traditional naval powers such as the United States. After all, China has achieved a shipbuilding capacity that is only rivalled by the South Koreans, and it would not be far-fetched to think that China would very soon possess a carrier task force permanently assigned to the Indian Ocean. Such a task force could wreak havoc to US plans to interdict Chinese energy ships, and interfere with India's interests to ensure that it alone is the only Asian power that can dominate these waters. The containment if not exclusion of China from a viable Indian Ocean presence therefore becomes an important international public service India can perform to demonstrate her resolve and enhance her reputation and further relations with the West.

India of course has been boosting her own capabilities in the region. It has established integrated tri-service command in 2001, beefed up her naval assets and capabilities and established a naval marine presence as well as aerial assets in the region in places such as the Nicobar Islands which overlooks the Andaman Sea and the Straits of Malacca; established a listening post in Duqm Port in Oman, and building a runway on Alalega Island of Mauritius that would facilitate India's naval patrol craft to increase New Delhi's maritime domain awareness. (Ashraf, 2023).

China's interests and presence are interpreted as increasing challenges China has in effect growing ties with not just the South Asian island nations but also the Western littoral islands i.e. Sri Lanka, Maldives, Mauritius, Seychelles, Madagascar and Comoros (Bahrauh, 2023). With its view of the Indian Ocean as a whole, China is making good its stake in the Indian Ocean itself and not just South Asia. The scenario that India is fearing would become a reality as China is making good inroads with Sri Lanka (Cogan & Mishra, 2022), with the new Pro-China Maldian government as it is with Nepal in the North. This is a natural development in geopolitics. China's BRI initiatives in South Asia additionally complicates India's own plans to build and tighten her own economy's linkages with the Middle East. China is also sharpening its own power in the Himalayas particularly as it seeks to become an important extra-regional player in a region long dominated by India.

Joining the Global Right Fraternity: Bandwagoning with the United States and Japan

The BJP led by Modi assumed the leadership of India in 2014 soon after Xi Jinping officially announced the Belt Road Initiative. Coincidentally, it was also shortly the time after the United States under President Obama had announced a pivot to Asia–Pacific. Ostensibly, the Obama administration sought India out to build greater economic ties and to fight extremism but in reality, the focus of the conversation was how the United States could move strategically closer to India to counter China. Modi had met Obama no less than eight times from 2015 to 2016 (The Economic Times, 2017). Even though Obama and Trump did not see eye to eye on all issues, there is no question that the US strategic planning community had understood that China had by 2014 emerged as the United States's single greatest strategic competitor as evidenced by China's challenge to Obama's "pivot to Asia". The ascendance of Modi provided India with an important opportunity to reconsider and recalibrate India's foreign policy posture and its definition of national interests. Modi appeared to have been relatively cautious and ensured that that most of the interests pursued by the previous Prime Ministers were also pursued by the BJP government with one exception: China.

At the onset, there were great expectations of change in India's foreign policy due to Modi's high-profile personal style; his substantial political background as compared to his predecessor and his explicit linkage of Hindutva (Hindu-ness) with his political platform (Basrur, 2017: 7). The Prime Minister rousing political speeches and deep-rooted popularity with his constituents created the imagery that he was a charismatic populist outside of India, with some detractors even announcing that his "performances" were meant more for domestic consumption. Others however interpret this charisma as the newfound confidence of a rising India, and the conviction by which the new BJP government is steering India through the new and more tempestuous waters of international affairs.

By 2015, it was clear that India's foreign policy was exhibiting two new traits under Modi's leadership. The first is that India would seek deliberative engagement with leaders and countries that would bring positive results while avoiding entangling with countries and complicated issues where the outcome might be uncertain or detrimental, with the exception of China (Sidhu & Mehta, 2015). This suggests that there is a deep-seated change in India's orientation towards China. India has announced that New Delhi was willing to share its resources with the global South; and announced an assistance package to South Asian countries such as Bhutan, Nepal, Bangladesh, Maldives and Sri Lanka. India has also appeared to be increasingly interested in engaging with Africa and is increasingly tying these external development relations to India's development by getting the private sector to play a bigger role (Chopra & Joshi, 2015). Even though there is a more proactive engagement with the South, there is criticism that there is no clear evidence that India is undertaking a more concrete development agenda (Roychoudhury et al 2015). Modi has also begun to rebalance India's relations with Palestine and Israel, and signalled that India is no longer willing to go along with Palestine in all respects, particularly over its definition of East Jerusalem as its future capital, suggesting that that Israel and Palestine's conversation over their future should continue (Kumaraswamy, 2017). By 2019, India's foreign policy under Modi has been credited with three important developments—its outreach to Saudi Arabia and the United Arab Emirates a new orientation of India towards the Gulf; its upswing in relations with Japan particularly in Abe's pursuit of "free and open Indo-Pacific" and thirdly, completing India's reproachment with the United States even as Trump pursued its "America First" policy (Tellis, 2019). The second trait would be New Delhi's ability to cozy up to both Washington and Moscow all together at the same time—something that the Chinese were able to do a couple of decades earlier. As a commentator observed that in the initial years, Modi had engaged in some sort of "great power speed dating" and "diplomatic promiscuity" by boldly courting both the United States and Russia which were in effect competing powers (Jones cited by Sidhu: 19). India is now at a juncture where the key to raising its global profile is to ensure that it deepens the US–India relations and modernise its diplomatic practices to endear New Delhi to the West as well as to the Global South.

In the initial years, it is clear that the BJP was keen to acquire diplomatic achievements to garner domestic political capital and strategic credentials. This diplomatic promiscuity too extended to Modi's engagement with China. Xi and Modi had many mutual visits, where both were photographed having in-depth discussions even though US–China tensions were very apparent. Any sense of unease that the Prime Minister had at the beginning was so displaced by a newfound source of strategic opportunism that this diplomatic promiscuity had brought. With the assiduous courting by Japan, as well as the emerging opportunities with the United States, along with her allies, New Delhi began to posture herself in a way that was at odds with Beijing, as this would allow India to extract the maximum interests out of the new alignment.

The calculus was simple as discussed in the previous section. India needed technology, capital and political support from the West and Japan that were crucial to its modernisation needs. The BJP needed investments for job creation and to help boost its next electoral success. Beyond that, India needed security assurances vis-à-vis Pakistan and ultimately China across a number of issues. That was unlikely to come along just by talking to Islamabad or Beijing alone. Leaning towards the West, specifically the United States would send a signal to China that its support for Pakistan cannot be unanswered. Since there is almost no chance of driving a wedge between Islamabad and Beijing, the very least India could do was to ensure that it could remind the Chinese what this might cost them. Indeed, if the BJP got lucky, it could very well be the wedge (or leverage) that India had been looking for.

Calibrating a more confrontational (or muscular) policy towards China would certainly send powerful signals. It would help boost the Modi's and the BJP's popularity as long as New Delhi does not go into a full-scale conflict with Beijing. It would remind Indian observers that the Modi's government is not about anti-Muslim tendencies as much as they are against all of India's enemies. Aligning against China would boost BJP's and Modi's image in the Western press, as this fits with the dominant political narrative and corporate media strategy there. It would also send other South Asian nations a pre-emptive warning with regard to their dance with the "devil" here. The key here is to preserve India's hegemonic status in South Asia and the Indian Ocean, and that its position is not eroded by any other nation, particularly Pakistan which was emboldened by China (Hashmi, 2019).

By the end of 2018, when Trump's Trade War was in full swing, New Delhi's prospects looked increasingly promising. Modi's recalibration of foreign policy became more focused in courting the West and Japan while calibrating tensions in India–China relations to an optimum point. The strategy paid off, as Modi's BJP won the April 2019 elections to secure another term in government, decisively brushing aside a secular vision that governed the country 72 years before. The BJP's victory was fuelled by a relentless, data-driven and highly disciplined style of campaigning, but a survey by the Centre for the Study of Developing Societies found that more than one-third of the people who voted for the BJP did so because of Modi, notwithstanding their disappointment with their unhappiness with the economic performance of the country, with unemployment to be at record high over the last 45 years and farming income the lowest in the past 18 years. (Safi, 2019). The key to this victory is widely seen to be Modi's approval of an Indian Air Force Airstrike over the Balakot Jaish-e-Mohammad Militant camp in Pakistan in retaliation for a terrorist bombing in Indian Kashmir which left 40 dead. There is nothing like a good dose of heightened Hindu nationalism that would help at the polls. The euphoria of the political victory proved to be short-lived as the Covid pandemic severely affected most countries, India included. Even as India struggled to import vaccine raw materials from the United States, New Delhi was reticent to accept China's help in any form of matter ostensibly because of the clash in the Himalayas (Gan & Yeung, 2021).

As India emerged from the Covid, the Modi government faced severe constraints. India would have to further its interests in a world increasingly fraught with great power contention, increasingly ineffective international institutions, retreating globalisation and a very unstable neighbourhood (Joshi et al., 2020). The confrontation with China has energised the hawks across all capitals including New Delhi and pushed India strategically towards the United States and Japan. Modi had in effect demonstrated its credentials to the West in "confronting" China by giving the Chinese a "befitting" reply to the Chinese perceived naked aggression. This position helps to bolster India's value in the US-led coalition even more. Modi's first State Visit to the United States in 2019 received much fanfare at home and has been hailed as a personal as well as a diplomatic victory for the Prime Minister and for India-US relations. The reception of the Indian diaspora community in the United States was ambivalent. Ajit Sahi, the advocacy director for the Indian American Muslim Council argues that for someone with an appalling abysmal human rights record and who was once banned from the United States for his role in the Gujarat riots (where over 1000 Muslims perished), giving this person opportunity address a joint session of congress to talk about democracy ideals is mind-boggling (Sahi cited in Venkatraman, 2023). That being said, Modi's popularity received a boost across the board as the Indian nation celebrates the mending of India's relations with the United States. New Delhi's delicate handling of the United States and China, and fostering stronger ties with Japan, Australia, Russia, France, and the ASEAN region clearly demonstrates a new boldness and discipline with respect to its regional positioning and protecting its policy manoeuvrability to meet its strategic and diplomatic objectives (Hashmi, 2019).

346 V. TEO

Territorial Disputes, Threat Perceptions and Chinese Irredentism

The ongoing border dispute between India and China is a consequence of the British Empire's imperial legacy, which continues to cause problems in the present day. The Line of Actual Control (LAC), which stretches for 3440 km along the Himalayas, serves as the current border between the two nations. This LAC border was an agreement from 1993, following the reconciliation between India and China (Wagner, 2020). The current dispute centres around two significant areas of land, with several other contentious issues arising where military personnel from both sides have clashed.

In 1914, the British government reportedly held a conference with the Tibetan and Chinese governments to demarcate its borders in Shimla, Himachal Pradesh. Colonial India represented by the Colony's Foreign Secretary Henry McMahon, met Tibet's Paljor Dorje Shatra and Republic of China's negotiator Chen I-Fan. The British attempted to delineate the frontier between Tibet and China, as well as between Tibet and British India (McMahon Line), with the latter negotiated in the absence of the Chinese. The Chinese did not acknowledge this border as the British had previously declared that China had sovereignty over Tibet but not complete sovereignty, which changed in 2008 (FCO, 2008). The McMahon Line, which was determined at the Simla Convention in 1914, is still disputed by China as they did not ratify the Convention at the time, and consequently, Beijing still claims Arunachal Pradesh in its entirety (Economic Times 2021). In 1975, China killed four soldiers at Tulung La in Arunachal Pradesh, resulting in the Indian government lodging a strong diplomatic protest. From Beijing's perspective, Tibet was not "independent" when it signed the Convention with the British in 1914. This territory is referred to by the Chinese as South Tibet, and they have given Chinese names to 15 additional places in Arunachal Pradesh (Economic Times, 31 December 2021).

The second large tract of territory is Aksai Chin. This is a large tract of desolate arid territory located in Xinjiang China. This piece of desert borders the Leh District of Ladakh and Nagari Prefecture in Tibet at an elevation of around 5000 m. These 18,000 square meters of territory is claimed by India as part of the Leh District, Ladakh Union Territory but in effect controlled by China. The Colonial government of India had first proposed a "Johnson line" in 1865 to demarcate Aksai Chin to India during the time of the Dungan revolt when China did not control most of Xinjiang. By 1878, China had re-established control over Xinjiang, and Britain proposed a new boundary that modified the Johnson Line, known as the Johnson-Ardagh Line. The British did not follow up on establishing outposts, and so by the time of Indian independence, the boundary remained undemarcated until Nehru ordered that boundaries be drawn on Indian maps in 1954. By 1957 the PRC had already built a 1200 km road (China National Highway 219 and G695) that connected Xinjiang and Tibet and ran 179 km South of Aksai Chin (Panang 2022) The discovery of this highway along with the dynamics of deteriorating Sino-Soviet relations was one of the major causes of the 1962 Sino-Indian War. In 2022, there were further reports that China was planning to build another highway G695 to connect Xinjiang to Tibet by 2035 (Panang 2022). This is part of the new 345 construction plans proposed as part of the national plan designed to stimulate demand and stimulate spending on infrastructure. The problem from India's perspective is that the alignment of this road ran an average distance of 20-50 km from the Line of Actual Control and was discovered and exposed on Twitter by an amateur "Nature Desai" with the route starting going from Maza, Xinjiang (130 km northwest of Karakoram Pass) to Zanda (opposite Himachal/Uttarakhand) to Burang (south of Mansarovar and 16 km from Lipulekh Pass on the LAC) Gyriong (opposite Nepal) to Kamba (30 km north of Naku La in Sikkim) to Cona (30 km north of LAC in Tawang Sector) to Lhunze (70 km northeast of Cona), cutting across Eastern Aksai China from the new bridge at Pangong Tso (Panang, 2022).

In addition to these two large tracts of territory, India and China have at skirmishes at Nathu La and Cho La near Sikkim (1967); at Tulang La (1975 clash); Sumdorong Chu in (1987 standoff) and Dongzhang (1999 confrontation) all between Tibet and Arunachal Pradesh, Depsang (2013 standoff) in the dry river bed of Burtsa Nala/Tiannan River in Aksai Chin, Xinjiang; at Doklam (2017) between Bhutan, China and India; and finally at Galwan (2020–21) near Pagong Lake, Lakadh and Tibet. The 1962 conflict occurred during Prime Minister Jawaharlal Nehru's term, and the 1967 conflict and the 1975 confrontation occurred when Nehru's daughter, Prime Minister Indira Gandhi's leadership. The 1987 confrontation at Sumdorong Chu happened under Rajiv Ghandi's watch, while the 2013 standoff occurred under Manmohan Singh's watch. It was however in 2017 and 2020 when some of the fiercest fighting took place during Prime Minister Modi's tenure. This pattern of conflict highlighted to the Indians that China cannot be trusted.

The accounts of the incidents/skirmishes almost always vary, with sharp differences between the Chinese accounts and those of the India (and the Western) world (Maxwell, 1999; Shukla, 2020). From the start, India had propagated and believed in the naked aggression theory, particularly since Nehru had sought to decide for itself where India's borders with China should lie and impose its inherited colonial alignments without consenting to negotiation, Beijing had little choice but to react (Maxwell, 1999). At the same time, almost other narratives would picture Beijing to be the aggressive party. This is not surprising since the Chinese would have almost behaved in a hardline manner as the Indians. Additionally, the People's Republic of China had its own political problems in the late 1950s through to the 1960s, and its foreign policy was often seen as radical and extreme during this period. This is particularly so as the India–China relations were coming under the influence of the Cold War and the developing PRC–USSR antagonisms. It is important to note that it was pretty evident that both Beijing and New Delhi wanted to keep any confrontations limited, "localised" and not let them escalate into a full-blown war. By the late 1980s, both China and India sought rapprochement. In 1996, India and China jointly agreed in Article VI of an agreement that troops from: "neither side shall open fire, cause bio-degradation, use hazardous chemicals, conduct blast operations or hunt with guns or explosives within two kilometers from the line of actual control" (MEA, 1996). This is why there is a positive development that troops are deployed with medieval-like weapons such as clubs and batons instead of modern firepower. However, the existence of such non-lethal weapons might have been one of the reasons why the inhibitions of the troops to engage in skirmishes have been increased.

From the perspective of New Delhi, Chinese behaviour at the border has been nothing short of provocative, reaffirming the traditional view amongst the ruling elites and people of Chinese ambition, assertiveness and greed. Under Modi's rein, the border skirmishes happened in 2017 and 2020–21. This is not surprising given that Modi, in his first major speech as opposition leader attacked the Manmohan Singh government for being "weak" in protecting India's interests, and for encouraging neighbouring armies to encroach on Indian territory (Pradhan & MacAskill, 2013). Ironically, in the aftermath 2017 dispute at Doklam, it was the Congress politicians who turn the dispute into a political slugfest against Modi for not defending Bhutan's and India's interests, arguing that the Chinese have engaged in unprecedented military infrastructure build-up in the area, including villages and roads inside Bhutanese territory (PTI, 2023). China however has been quick to re-engage with Bhutan to enter into demarcation talks, as both countries have been negotiating since the 1970s. A significant development took place in 1996 when Beijing proposed that Bhutan cede 269 square kilometres of land in Doklam and the surrounding areas of Dromana, Sinchulung and Shakhatoe in exchange for conceding its claim to 495 square kilometres of Pasamlung and Jakarlung. For Bhutan, the main obstacle to settling the border with China is the Doklam plateau, which overlooks the Chumbi Valley and is situated near Sikkim (in India) and the 14-mile-wide Siliguri Corridor. The Indian government applied substantial pressure on Bhutan to reject the proposal, as any alteration of the status quo at Doklam would give China an advantage over New Delhi at one of India's most sensitive geographic locations (Mamgain, 2023). By 2023, it appears that the boundary demarcation between Bhutan and China are edging towards a completion, with Bhutan likely to seek solutions that would please both New Delhi and Beijing (Rajan, 2023). Retired General Singh Panag of the Indian Army has however suggested that it would be difficult for China to "choke" India's communication through the Siliguri Corridor as this was not an easy task despite popular misgivings in the mainstream media (Haidar, 2023).

The key problem for India in this territorial dispute is not just a political one where the political opponents can use territorial loss as political leverage as well as loss of credibility, prestige and legitimacy as a nationalist party, but also a strategic issue. The cause of the dispute of course originates from the differential of both parties as to which areas each control and own, and the question of what can be placed or built in those areas. The first war in 1962 was in part caused by the Chinese highway that was built in the Aksai Chin, the 2013 conflict related to the establishment of bunkers by the Indians (India Today, 2011) and the 2017 Doklam at the trilateral junction when the Chinese were attempting to extend a road southwards towards Bhutan, whom India claims to have a special relationship.

In June 2020, Indian and Chinese troops in Ladakh's Galwan Valley clashed leaving 20 Indian and 5 Chinese soldiers killed, which led to a month of lockdown and 11 rounds of fruitless military talks. Increased tensions occurred over the course of the next nine months along Pangong

Tso, Hotsprings, Gogra Post Area, and the Depsang Plans in the far north. It was only in February 2021 that there was a major breakthrough in which both sides conducted synchronised disengagement (The Indian Express, 2021). In this clash, reports suggest that Chinese troops entered the disputed territory to stop the Indians from building an extension of a road that leads into the Galwan Valley. This road is a 255 km long Darbuk-Shyokh-Daulat Beg Oldie (DSDBO) all-weather road (Subramanian, 2020). This of course was politicised by the Congress Party leader, Ahmed Patel, who in a series of high profile twits about Modi's diplomacy involved giving "a mile for an inch" when it came to the borders, particularly as Modi had travelled to China more than any of his predecessors (Hindu, 2020). It also explains the resolve of the BJP and the Modi towards these disputes.

China's BRI, Pakistan and India's Sovereign Sensitivities

The building of infrastructure and roads in the eyes of international law certainly meant exhibiting control and administration of territory, not to mention such basic infrastructure can be a prelude to establishing a more permanent presence in the form of a military garrison or a trading outpost. From India's perspective, there is tremendous concern about China's true intention as exemplified by a dated theory attributed to Mao on the idea of the "Five Fingers of Tibet". This theory (asserted by Tibetan Qing loyalists) suggest that that Tibet is akin to China's right-hand palm, with five fingers on its periphery that China should aim to liberate: Lakadh, Nepal, Sikkim, Bhutan and Northeast Frontier Agency (now Arunachal Pradesh) since China had control over Nepal, Sikkim and Bhutan during that period. In the aftermath of the 2017 conflict, a Chinese analyst at Nanjing University wrote that should Beijing lose her ability to control her border, Tibetan independence could be easily stoked, thereby engendering a national security crisis for China (Liu, 2017). Given China's determination to build its One Belt One Road projects through Pakistan and its surrounding area, New Delhi therefore sees her determination to build in the disputed areas a bigger threat than ever. The 1963 land exchange deal had removed any possibility of conflict between Pakistan and China, and diminished hopes in New Delhi that Pakistan and India would be able to settle their disputes over Kashmir.

The China-Pakistan Economic Corridor (CPEC) is one of the central connections in Beijing's BRI conception. Essentially, this is the "life-line" for goods from Western China to be transported through the Karakorum mountains via the border town of Kashgar in Xinjiang Uighur Autonomous region to the Pakistani port of Gwadar port in Baluchistan province. This allows the Chinese to reach the Arabian Sea via an alternate logistical connection. As this route joins up with the other infrastructure and roads that connect China to Central Asia, Russia and beyond, it provides a more secure route that enables vital resources such as energy to be imported and secondary goods to be exported. It is this cooperation that truly impacts India's strategic sensitivity, given Beijing's CPEC actually transverses Kashmir which India considers a disputed territory, and that this route threatens India's own non-existent or slow-to-start infrastructure projects. Beyond that, this Pakistan–China cooperation infringes New Delhi's sensibilities over the historical Pakistan-China 1863 land exchange agreement that India sees as the ultimate violation of her sovereignty. For the Indians, this is an ultimate sign of disrespect for India's views on territory integrity and sovereignty.

Today, the narratives involving Sino-Indian border disputes face the same challenges as mutual accusations persist. For most of the narratives in English, it is the Chinese who are deemed to be chipping away at Indian 'restraint" and undertaking salami-slicing tactics to remove territory bit-by-bit from India (Wagner, 2020). The Indian government has also suggested that China is incapable of observing long-standing agreements, and Beijing has been accused of having a habit of virtually ignoring India's concerns. There are also accusations that the Chinese media were whitewashing and downplaying the reports and portraying China as an innocent actor. The opposite is said in Chinese domestically in China, and collectively these dynamics have a polarising effect.

There are two important issues here. First, even though the territorial dispute is a historical legacy, one might expect that the Chinese would be willing to work with the Indians to try and resolve the issue, particularly as China has largely resolved all its border issues with most of her neighbours since the collapse of the USSR. China's hardened stance over territory conflict today extends only to her position on Taiwan, the Diaoyu/Senkaku islands (Japan) and in her disputes with the Philippines the Spratly Islands in South China Sea. The Indian-China territorial dispute is a historical legacy in inherited from colonial times. China and

India were unable to transcend their geopolitical (and probably ideological) divide then in 1962, the two countries went to war. Even then by the 1980s, New Delhi and Beijing had negotiations to manage (if not resolve) the border dispute. While very little progress had been made, although it certainly meant for almost a quarter of century after the 1987 clash at Sumdorong Chu, the border was peacefully managed without open confrontation.

Given that India and China have very similar demographic and socio-economic attributes, many researchers have regarded that they are in a strategically competitive relationship seeking to expand their influence in the region and globally. This however does not mean that the territorial dispute is predestined to be intractable, given that most of these areas are desolated no-man's land. Today, the disputed areas cannot be negotiated because both New Delhi and Beijing view the advantages conferred by these areas in zero-sum terms (Topcu, 2023), beyond the fact that the conflict has actually been crystallised for six decades and central to each country's nationalism. New Delhi is severely concerned about the overwhelming influence China might gain if Beijing succeeds in her infrastructure projects near the disputed territories, especially in her influence over Bhutan, Nepal, Sikkim, Lakdah and Arunachal Pradesh. Likewise, Beijing perceives that New Delhi is doing everything in her power to prevent China's BRI project from succeeding, and stalling the development she desires in Western China and the connected areas in South Asia and Central Asia.

This is perhaps why hostilities appear to have increased since Modi came to power. The bilateral conflicts are far more intense, of longer duration and with greater enmity than it has ever been before, with more casualties. It has worsened considerably because relations between both countries have remained aloof and distant for a better part of the last seven decades only to be punctuated by conflict and acrimony. The context is somewhat similar to the dispute in the 1960s where the Sino-Soviet rivalry provided India with an advantage. Undertaking assertive action against China would not only provide Modi personal popularity, but also help the BJP domestically and most importantly enable India to seek international support and solidarity in the eyes of the Quad community. There is really no downside to this, especially if New Delhi had already decided to sacrifice her relations with China to advance goals in so many other areas. The Panchsheel doctrine of Hindi-Chini Bhai-bhai has therefore been truly set aside. This of course is not to say the Chinese are blameless. China's systemic rise as well as her BRI initiative has unnerved not just New Delhi, but also Washington and Tokyo. Even though the Chinese government is reactive mostly in their foreign policy posture in the past decades, their hardening position today is probably a result of their perception that the US, Japan, Australia and New Delhi and other her allies in Western Europe are entering into a renewed Cold War-like structure (the Quad) to encircle China once again.

The Indian Ocean and Resecuring India's Role as the Regional Hegemon

From the Chinese perspective, the BRI initiative is essentially a strategy to help stimulate demand to absorb the excess production capacity resulting from the overinvestment and development of its industries. By focusing on the silk route countries extending from Central Asia to the Middle East, as well as further afield, China also hopes to stimulate the development of its landlocked and Western provinces. As these countries are usually not the target countries for Western investment due to their failing to meet the political-economic criteria of donor/lending countries in the developed West, they tend to embrace Chinese aid or investment with open arms. It is also a strategy by which China can expand her influence and in some ways a "coming out" project that can showcase China's rise and her commensurate "contribution" to the global south.

New Delhi naturally is extremely concerned with the expansion of Chinese BRI or bilateral-related economic activities in South Asia for fear that China might become an extremely significant economic player in her own backyard. While not necessarily a zero-sum game, Chinese economic linkages, especially if they are asymmetrical reduce India's influence in a number of ways. New Delhi might find it difficult to sway her smaller South Asian neighbours decision-making process to maintain her historical hegemonic role as these smaller powers choose to cultivate to balance their relations with an extra-regional power like China which would have her own economic and geopolitical interests to invest in her ties. Additionally, hitching their development plans to the Chinese projects might actually help accelerate their own developmental plans vis-a-vis New Delhi's own plans, not to mention put pressure on West, Japan and India to out-stake and/or out-invest Beijing in these countries - something which might be difficult in this economic climate.

The very fact that China has a BRI presence does not necessarily mean that Beijing is out to oust India from its hegemonic role in the region. This fact of course is lost in most of the discussions that Quad countries make. Despite numerous narratives that China is out to displace or encircle India in her own neighbourhood, Beijing's goals might be a lot more modest, contained and less insidious than commonly assumed. Regardless of Beijing's intention, the recent growth of China's BRI projects does pose concerns for India and US strategy planners. At the same time, they are aware that just because Beijing is determined to announce and implement these projects does not necessarily guarantee their success or that Beijing and host countries would be able to reap the geopolitical benefits for certain. BRI investments in reality are often high risk, low reward. This should not be surprising since in its earliest inception, the BRI is typically a loose coalition of private or government-linked companies all banding together under the initiative to seek opportunities overseas under the broad rubric of government sponsorship. For South Asian countries, the prospects of China's outreach in the form of BRI projects, whether in the form of outright or subsidised grants or low-interest funded long-term projects are immensely attractive as it presents a much-needed source of funds for building infrastructure, connectivity and social mobility. Viewed from a developmental perspective, the BRI is actually a positive development.

South Asian nations however are also acutely aware of the allegations and narratives pushed forth by Western and Indian think tanks and media regarding the pitfalls and perils of China's BRI: resource grab, debt trap, market dominance, asymmetrical economic dominance, political interference and control of strategic assets—but many of these nations have still signed up to partner with the Chinese. The receptivity lies not in just talk: it really depends on whether the BRI projects provide the kind of benefits as promised, and the receptivity of government and people to these projects. Insofar as South Asian and the Indian Oceanic countries are concerned, China has reached out to most of the middle and smaller countries for trade and commercial exchanges. It is important to remember that China, like India, has long been an important member of the global South, and Beijing's linkages to these countries long predate the BRI. The fact that China has developed rapidly and put herself into a position to re-establish her connections and come to the aid of many of these nations is commendable. This is particularly true when it is done without many of the arduous conditions imposed by other aid countries. There are of course alternative views. Some vocal countries have voiced out against the BRI and chose to lean towards the United States, Japan and India to balance China. Beijing however largely sees it as the sovereign prerogative of the respective governments. The World Bank has suggested in a BRI Impact report that South Asia has experienced the biggest trade cost reduction (Maliszewska & van der Mensbrugghe, 2019: 5), as well as border cost delays (Maliszewska & van der Mensbrugghe 2019: 15), socially with Pakistan (1.1 million people), Bangladesh (200,000) and Nepal (60,000 people) seeing a significant reduction in extreme poverty from the baseline statistic in the study (Maliszewska & van der Mensbrugghe 2019: 10). The same report concludes that economically, BRI is largely beneficial as global income would be increased by 0.7 per cent in 2030 relative to the baseline in the study (amounting to half a trillion dollars in 2014 prices), where the BRI areas would capture about 82 per cent of the gain. Secondly, globally the BRI could lift 7.6 million people from extreme poverty and 32 million from moderate poverty (Maliszewska & van der Mensbrugghe, 2019: 2).

China actually shares land borders with the continental/overland South Asian countries, apart from Bangladesh. Maldives and Sri Lanka which are essentially island states. Other than India and Bhutan, most of the other South Asian neighbours Pakistan, Bangladesh, Sri Lanka, Nepal, Maldives and Afghanistan have actually joined the BRI. Aside from Pakistan, the other South Asian countries are also keenly aware of the consequences this might have on their relations with India and the United States. The necessity of development, the dire need of funds as well as the need to hedge against New Delhi means that for the most part, the strategy of the smaller South Asian states mirrors those of the Southeast Asian states as they try to extract as much as possible from the larger powers competing for their affection. India has undertaken three important approaches to counter China in this regard. First, it has doubled down on its resistance to the BRI, and joined forces with the Quad countries to cast doubt on the veracity and viability of BRI projects in a very open and public manner. It would be very hard to find anything written positive about the BRI by Indian scholars and policymakers. Second, India has launched competing initiatives either by herself or in conjunction with the other initiatives launched by the United States, Japan, Australia and Europe for instance. Third, India has intensified efforts to counter China's building of the ports in Gwadar in Pakistan and Hambantota in Sri Lanka and Kyauk Phyu in Myanmar by pursuing a port project in Chabahar in

Iran (Anwar, 2019: 172). India's interest in the Quad is also a move to counter the perceived encroachment of China in the Himalayas as well as the larger South Asia neighbourhood. The expansion of Chinese activities has created certain anxieties in New Delhi as it is perceived as a sort of "encirclement". New Delhi perceives that it has little choice in the road ahead, as the Quad alliance would help both India economically and strategically, particularly in its developmental and geostrategic ambitions.

The Global Right: Reorienting India for Global Influence and Great Power Status

India's decision to join the Quad reflects a careful calibration of New Delhi's strategy to engage the countries involved—Washington, Canberra and Tokyo to address what Modi and the BJP perceives as the inadequacies of Indian foreign relations under the Congress government (Sharma & Mehta, 2020). In maintaining neutrality and sometimes leaning towards the Soviets, India has paid a steep price in her modernisation process. In order for electorate promises about living standards and jobs to be achieved, aligning with the developed West is a sure way forward. There is therefore nothing easier to demonstrate India's posture to back Japan and the United States to contain a rising China.

The road to Quad was of course first broached well before Modi became Prime Minister. It was his predecessor Manmohan Singh who agreed to join the Quad. Unfortunately, the organisation "fizzled" out after Australia's Prime Minister Rudd indicated Canberra would withdraw from its activities and Abe Shinzo stepped down subsequently stepped down. During Quad 1.0, the Indian government was still very cautious of how this would impact India–China relations and chose to be relatively careful in terms of its commitment to this dialogue. It was therefore not until 2012, when Abe became the Prime Minister of Japan again that this concept was carefully revived. Abe once enthusiastically courted Modi, and likewise, the Prime Minister reciprocated. The most important opportunity came with the election of Trump, as his campaign rhetoric and promises were music to Abe's ears even if Japan was at the receiving end of some of the jibes that Trump had made about free-riding and the US–Japan security alliance.

Prior to the ascendance of Trump, the Indian government was still relatively cautious about maintaining her relationship with China. Modi and Xi had met on many occasions starting from the time Modi was Chief

Minister in Gujarat (4 visits to China) and by June 2023, they would have met at least 20 times. As Prime Minister, Modi first visited China in May 2015 where Xi hosted him in Xian reciprocating him hosting Xi at Ahmedabad in 2014. He then visited Hangzhou in September 2016 for a G20 Summit, Xiamen in September 2017 for a BRICS Summit, Wuhan in 2018 for an informal meeting and later in April 2018 for a SCO meeting. Xi met Modi in Chennai in October 2019 (Onmanorama, 2020). In November 2022, Xi and Modi met on the sidelines of G20 summit dinner after the Galwan Valley clash in April 2020 (Times of India, 2022; Outlook India, 2022), and again in South Africa in August 2023 at the BRICS summit (Times of India, 2023). In the history of India, Modi stands out as the Prime Minister who has visited China most (Onmanorama, 2020).

With the election of Trump in November 2016, Abe was the first leader to reach out to Trump. There was great anticipation on the part of Abe that he could get the grouping to work as he was the driving force in courting India, the United States and Australia to revive the grouping. Within the first few weeks of the Trump administration, Abe's ideas on the "two oceans confluence" had entered the US State Department lexicon. India has professed to be a "non-aligned" nation for most of its post-war history, but during times of critical need has shown its willingness to strategically lean towards the USSR. Within the Quad, India is the only member not to be formally "allied" with the United States such as Japan or Australia. The latter two are linked directly via the United States with alliance obligations. India's participation was critical for the Indo-Pacific strategy to materialise. The Quad leaders—Trump, Abe, Modi and Turnbull had bilateral and multilateral meetings on the sidelines of the 30th ASEAN Summit in 2017 and agreed to revive the Quadrilateral dialogue as a response to China's belligerence in South China Sea and the Indo-Pacific region.

India therefore has a new motivation to join Quad 2.0. By 2017, India had become the most courted country. New Delhi has by then become central to the US's and Japan's strategy to contain growing Chinese power, and this situation fitted India's national interest and developmental agenda as it presents New Delhi with immense opportunities. For many American and Japanese strategists, China's power came from her ability to build asymmetrical economic relations with nations around the world, and reinvesting her economic returns into technological innovation and military modernisation. To stop China's growth, it is vital that the Quad countries collectively come to curb China's economic growth and disrupt the current political-economic role Beijing plays in the region and the world. India fitted perfectly into the United States and Japan conception of economic and tech war with China. New Delhi resembles the China the world saw forty years ago with its large population that could provide the cheap and skilled labour, the raw materials and most importantly, the market for US and Japanese MNCs. Although Trump had wanted to see industries move the manufacturing back to the United States if they could, US and Japanese planners realised that it might not be commercially feasible. If that was not feasible, it would still be better for them to relocate from China to third countries such as an ASEAN country such as Vietnam or India. The vigorous enticement by both Washington, Tokyo and other allies such as Canberra and London to bring India into their strategic fold as the central growth engine to replace China needed little prompting. New Delhi recognises it as an important opportunity. This is how India came to embrace Quad 2.0 openly as the Trump administration openly waged the Trade and Tech war against China. The euphoria did not last for long with the onset of the Covid pandemic, as the country was jolted out of its pre-pandemic inertia of moving forward in her economic plans. By May 2020, India and Japan had gotten together to offer land and funding to lure factories away from mainland China (Barrett, 2020). In June 2023, India and the United States reached a critical agreement to facilitate "greater technology sharing, co-development and co-production opportunities between the US and the Indian industry, government and academic institutions" (The White House, 2023).

It also fitted with the Prime Minister's resolve to nudge India towards a different posture towards China. India's decision is of course magnified by a corresponding worldwide media campaign backed by the United States and her allies worldwide. Narratives emerged about how India's participation could boost the Quad as an effective institution and strategic deterrent, particularly over India's commanding advantage over the Indian Ocean which further fuelled New Delhi's determination as the international public opinion was swinging in the international media. The willingness of India therefore to emphasise on her democratic credentials to join the Quad as a "like-minded" partner is part of New Delhi's response to the initiation ritual and political narrative as instituted by Japan's Shinzo Abe. India is definitely a democracy, but Modi, like his right-wing counterparts (Trump, Abe, Morrison, etc.) can hardly be considered bleeding-heart liberal democrats. The irony of Modi joining the other three strongmen on stage to talk about democracy and human rights is hardly comforting. Of course, this is part of the larger political discourse to sell the Quad to domestic and global audiences. To some of his domestic constituents, this certainly is not an accurate depiction of what Modi and his politics stand for. Globally, India is enjoying a renaissance under almost blanket positive coverage of what the Prime Minister is doing—standing shoulder to shoulder with the likes of Abe, Trump and Morrison (and later Suga/Kishida, Biden and Albanese) to defend and protect the free and open Indo-Pacific.

What these narratives provide is an esteem boost for India. Since Modi assumed Prime Ministership, India's international image and diplomacy has received a big boost. This is a result of the savviness of the BJP as a political force, as well as the merticulous planning of the Modi government, and of course the coincidence and opportunity accorded by geopolitical circumstances. By meeting the strategic needs of the United States and her allies, the collective sanitising, whitewashing and promoting of India's righteousness and importance has given New Delhi much reputational gains. This aspect is significant as China has actually dominated the news for the past two decades, but after the War on Terror, the fixation on painting China (and Russia) as public enemy no 1 in the international media has not abated. By being on the "right side" of history in international (Western) narratives, it helps with domestic politics, overcome political opposition and galvanises international support. More importantly, it provided India opportunities to compete for investment, trust and influence in geographical localities by which the United States and Japan cannot, for instance in Central Asia or in the Middle East. New Delhi might also be able to affect more influence with pariah states such as Iran and Myanmar, which China has great relations with. Iran is an important energy supplier with access to the Gulf of Aden, while Myanmar has rich resources with access to the Indian Ocean. If the United States cannot influence these two powers, perhaps India could. India is a remarkable asset to the Global Right and the Quad.

Lastly, India's move closer to the United States and Japan strategically suggests a shift in the international system where India as a rising power is choosing to bandwagon with the United States, the systemic hegemon. This is to balance against China, a perceived systemic challenger. This appears to be a move to preserve the current system in place where the United States is at the top of the pecking order. By bandwagoning with the United States, Japan and other Global Right countries,

New Delhi could pressure China to modify her behaviour, and at the same time put pressure on Russia to provide more enticement and support to New Delhi to compete for favours. It gets India out of a diplomatic rut into a position of strength and opportunity, offering her a greater role in global leadership and realpolitik in future decades. All in all, this is proverbial geostrategic "fair winds and following seas" for India in her quest for great power status. Indulging in such high-profile diplomacy appears to have all the upside for India, with only one cost: India's China policy.

The "Weak" Link: India's Propensity for Strategic Independence and Ties to Russia

Despite the appearance that India has put up in showing its resolve to join the Quad, there are still private grouses in the Western strategic community about New Delhi's commitment to the cause of containing China and its commitment to the Quad. In short, India is regarded as the "weak link" (Malhotra, 2023). New Delhi's position still shows signs of the strategic independence that India is known for. New Delhi has good reasons of course for its own posture. After all, Indian national interests, not those of United States, Japan or Australia guide India's foreign policy. The Indian posture (particular buying oil from Russia) during the Ukraine war has highlighted the differences between Western expectations and the strategic realities that New Delhi perceives. While Indian leaders would of course take every opportunity it has been offered to advance its national interests against China, particularly if it brings with it concrete benefits—may it be investments, political dialogues or strategic assistance (e.g. aircrafts, naval vessels), it does not immediately mean that when push comes to shove, New Delhi would want to get into all dimensional long standoff or a "hot" war with China. Indian strategists are familiar with the history of confronting China on a long border, drawing from their 1962 encounter and the USSR's experience. Both episodes suggested that the logistics and costs involved are certainly not worth the rewards, especially if it is over "barren" territory such as Aksai Chin.

The Western camp has reservations over India's loyalty has translated into some reluctance in sharing technology with New Delhi. Beyond concerns of entanglement resulting from misuse, conflict escalation, India's reluctance to pay full market price for the weapons; interoperation-ability issues, the US still desires to protect her sensitive military technology. As one congressional aide commented that there are concerns with technology sharing with Allies such as Australia, not to mention with India: "Australia is an ally. India wants the same privileges that allies get without having any of the same obligations or responsibilities" (Brunnstrom, 2023). Since 2018, the United States has courted India with high-tech transfers and sales such as Apache attack helicopters, drones, jet engines, semiconductors, advance drones and intelligence sharing regarding Chinese troop movements but New Delhi understands that this was done in service of US's plans to contain China rather than out of love for New Delhi. India is also aware of the cost-to-performance ratio of American versus Russian weaponry. Unless the Americans are willing to provide a huge supply of advanced tech at such a cost that renders comparable Russian offers obsolete, India would still have to rely on Russian (or other providers) arms purchases for cost-effectiveness reasons in the near future. There are ongoing talks to sell F18 Hornets and F-16s to India (Kaushik, 2023), but the political will to buy is often tempered by the ability to pay the full ticket price. Beyond, American arms sales often come with conditions and limitations (e.g. missiles are often kept by the United States, avionics cannot be upgraded or delivery delays etc.) that Russian weapons suppliers do not have. New Delhi's strategic impulses and sense of military independence might not find this agreeable. India has already indicated her preference to work with the French who have shown the flexibility to customised and supply 26 Rafael jets as well as 3 Scorpene submarines (Leali, 2023). There is also certainly the question of what each power thinks and expects of the Quad, and is willing to commit to defend her own (Misra, 2023). It is one thing to express one's participation in a joint international forum but quite another to firmly commit a nation's blood and treasure to fight on behalf of others. India's perceptions, interests and considerations might be quite different from the other three Quad members in issues that does not involve China.

As much as there might be advantages to participating in the Quad, India has shown that it clearly acts and thinks differently when it comes to Russia. There is historical affinity, strategic culture and political independence at play here that an informal Quad membership alone cannot overcome. As Russia has tightened its ties with Beijing, would it be completely wise for India to abandon her long-time security partner of sorts by throwing in the strategic towel completely with the United States to balance against a "Russia-China" alliance?

The events over the last couple of years—including the Ukraine crisis, the Nord Stream episode and how Europe has been affected by the

Ukraine War and US policies towards NATO has provided deep lessons for everyone to reflect upon, New Delhi included. The fundamental question for New Delhi is that in bandwagoning with the United States in terms going toe-to-toe with China, what would this mean for her relations with other powers such as Russia. This extends to India's role in China-Russia led forums such as the Shanghai Cooperation Organisation (SCO) and BRICS. From New Delhi's perspective, these roles lend additional counterweight to Russia to prevent the Chinese from dominating the forum and using SCO with impunity to advance its strategic goals, particularly through its partnership with Pakistan in a multilateral setting (Wani, 2023). The same could be said for BRICS. India has clearly sought to advance its goals in connectivity, counter-terrorism, anti-narcotics and stability in Afghanistan at this forum. In these respects, a good working relationship with Russia is essential to its goals. In keeping her foot in these organisations, New Delhi could enjoy the best of both worlds, and enjoyed a nimble status of being courted by both sides.

Then there is consideration of India–China relations alone. India is the only country that has actual land borders with and fought China over the course of the last decade, twice after Trump came to power in the United States in 2017 (Doklam in 2017; Galwan Valley in 2020). While this is similar in the sense to Japan with her sovereignty dispute with China over the Senkaku island, the critical difference is that Indian's long land border with China creates more of an acute security concern for New Delhi than Senkaku is with Japan. The accounts of China and India (as well as international narratives) on who started what differs (as to be expected), but the key is that both New Delhi and saw their "red-lines" violated enough to undertake the standoff. It could well be that the Chinese were reacting to India's posturing with Japan, US and Australia to contain China, and Doklam was either a reminder to New Delhi of their long border as neighbouring states and a pre-emptive move to complete further infrastructure building. Likewise, the clash could be New Delhi seeking to stoke a conflict to justify abandoning their long-held policy of maintaining relations with China, undertaking a two-prong policy to lean towards the United States and her allies while probing China on whether territorial concessions can be made. Amongst India's ruling elites, there is a deep realisation in both BJP and Congress parties that dialogue with China needs to be continued. Despite their misgivings about Beijing, the politicians feel that China can still disrupt India's modernisation plans in a big way, either via direct territorial encroachments at various levels (localised troop movements or infrastructure/settlement establishment or outright military conquest) to indirectly, such as providing support for separatists in India or supporting Pakistani military adventurism. In short, as much as India would like to hedge against China, it does not want to materialise the China threat in a big way so Beijing dedicates energy and resources to play a negative security role towards New Delhi's interests. New Delhi's concerns with Pakistan remain an important pillar in Indian foreign and security policy, and the Indian government is deeply aware of how the threat can be quickly magnified with dedicated China support. If this happens, India's neighbourhood policy might be at risk. Having hostile relations with China (as opposed to frosty) would lead to counteractions by China. At the same time, in this economic climate, New Delhi understands that it should not expect too much from the US, Japan or Australia to help, and at the same time, realises that China's economy could also contribute or harm India's well being depending on the state of bilateral relations. Beijing for instance, can choose to increase investment and commercial ties with India, but also accelerate the strategic seduction of the smaller Indian Ocean countries in a significant manner by prioritising them in the BRI initiative. Beijing and New Delhi actually also share some similar interests and goals. For one, India shares China's vision and interest in development and the eradication of poverty. Both are also heavily invested in advocating for third world countries, garnering them much respect in the region for their pursuit of anti-colonial causes and often share an unstated but common view towards issues, probably more than do with Japanese American or Australian leaders. Today through their involvement in groupings such as BRICS (Brazil, Russia, India, China and South Africa) India and China are still heavily advancing the developmental agenda for the developing world, even though they might also be jockeying for influence. Outside of BRICS and SCO, India also shares important partnerships with "pariah" states such as Iran and Myanmar which have very good relations with China, and ignoring the importance of these states would disadvantage India (Pant, 2022).

For the above reasons, India has therefore adopted a more nuanced approach to the Quad. Even though it is the only Quad member that has direct combat hostilities with China along its borders, New Delhi is still cautious when it comes to labelling China as the high-profile "enemy" or "threat" that the other Quad members have done. India's vision of the Indo-Pacific has been criticised to be distinctively "inclusive" and somewhat goes against the premise of mini-lateralism that the Quad presupposes (Mishra & Das, 2019). Due to India's supposed "hesitance", the Quad is seen as somewhat of a group that is unable to harmonise their collective vision of the group's central purpose, mission and policies. This is more so as each has their own expectations and the lack of demonstrable, tangible outcomes in the form of a formalised security structure. There is no question that India wants to be associated with the group, but at the same time wants to balance it with temperament and flexibility that is not tied to formal commitments especially if its costs to its interests are highest potentially. Therefore, analysts have suggested that India is interested in keeping the notion of "Indo-pacific" away from the idea of Quad as separate concepts. India wishes to remain engaged, not entangled in its relationship with the Quad (Malhotra, 2023).

In order to enhance its appeal as a security dialogue, as well as to market itself to more potential members, the Quad decided to remake its image explicitly as "not" an anti-China mechanism but instead to adopt the veneer of a multilateral dialogue aimed to build regional cohesion and supporting of interdependencies to adopt a pro-active agenda that involves cooperation in combating pandemics and managing challenges of maritime, climate, energy and emerging technologies in order to preserve a stable Indo-Pacific (Harsh & Basu, 2021). India's preference is thus for the Quad to remain an "issue-based partnership" (Saha, 2022).

There are also calls for India to engage in "zone-balancing" through its participation of the Quad. The idea of zone-balancing points to efforts to increase the capacity and resilience of third party-states to the inducements offered by rival states, and is distinct from efforts to match the rival state's power through internal and external balancing. The Quad's attempt to offer alternative infrastructure projects to China's BRI efforts is therefore such an exercise. In zone-balancing (Tarapore, 2023), "the balancer seeks to harden other states against the adversary's coercion or inducements, thereby limiting the adversary's opportunities to build strategic influence […] the balancing is still designed to gain an advantage over the adversary, but indirectly, by shaping the 'zone'—or geographic region—of strategic competition, rather than directly, as a dyadic race for power between rivals" (Breger, 2023). This is a good idea in practice and the spare of announcements by the Quad countries shows the intent to balance China. The overall thrust of the Indian discourse is after all to show how BRI projects are creating various difficulties for recipient countries, such as debt trap, corruption, political controversies, negative environmental implications and overall sustainability of projects (Sachdeva, 2018).

The reality however suggests that New Delhi is of course most worried about being chain-ganged into a situation where it expends a disproportionate amount of resources to compete with China without bringing the appropriate returns to itself or if promises can be upheld. There are also various debates about whether India could actually catch up with China, with the worse case scenario that India might be left to fend for itself should the US decide to strike a grand bargain with China at the expense of her allies. (Allison, 2023; Mody, 2023)

India's delivery deficit coupled with an increase in BRI projects in a particular area could pose problems for India both commercially and reputationally. For instance, India's inability to follow through on promised infrastructure projects has troubled India's effort to enhance regional connectivity through the Kaladan Multi-Model Transport Project and the Trilateral Highway (Pant, 2022). Another example would be the infrastructure project that the US has announced during the recent G20 summit to connect India, the Middle East and Europe to counter China's Belt and Road project. This is reportedly underwritten by the UAE and Saudi, and part of a diplomatic deal by Biden to ensure that Saudi Arabia mends fences with Israel (Ravid, 2023). The question is now if this can materialise, as Israel-Hamas war is in full swing at the time of publication. Beyond that, India must not be goaded into a position of overestimating the strength of their own infrastructural plans, given that cooperation with China might still be needed in many fields for development to materialise (Pal & Ray, 2013). Indeed, in April 2021, when India was severely afflicted by the Covid pandemic, the United States refused to grant exports of vaccines to India. Modi had in fact rejected Chinese offers. The US vaccines were finally granted after much ridicule in public opinion, particularly as China's state media had described the United States as an unreliable partner that treated India like a "pawn" to be discarded like used tissue when no longer useful (Gan & Yeung, 2021). Even during the supposed competitive vaccine diplomacy in South Asia, China had to step in to fill the voids when New Delhi could not fulfil her promises to administer vaccines to Sri Lanka, and Bangladesh (Ganapathy, 2021). This might be seen negatively from the Quad's perspective, but this is certainly much food for thought on how India can work with China in future to enact an improvement for human security from the recipient countries' perspective.

India's propensity to become fully committed to the Quad is now under suspicion even if the diplomatic niceties continue. From India's refusal to condemn Russia in the Ukraine War, to her profiteering activity reselling Russian oil to Europe, New Delhi was engaged in a rhetorical war of words with the United States and Europe. The differences aside, India has been accused by both the Washington and Ottawa of sending assassins to kill Punjab separatists in Canada, the latter of whom was provided by intelligence from the Five Eyes Organisation which India is not part. It raises the question if India indeed shares the same kind of values as their Quad partners. The Quad partners however have remained quiet and steadfast, largely they understand that any kind of quarrel with New Delhi is best handled in a low-profile manner. Beyond that, isolating New Delhi would only encourage India to vacillate towards Russia and China. The Quad countries would likely have to live with the Modi's India that the world has always known, an India that has practiced prudential realism of its earlier governments (Bajpai, 2019). Modi's attitude towards China is changing too. There is every indication that Modi recognises the importance of Chinese investment, and his remarks recently the importance of "put the bilateral relations forward on a sound and stable track" (Haidar, 2024).

REFERENCES

Ahmed, Aftab, "Factbox: India's Modi has Mixed Record of Economic Management", Reuters, 27 January 2022, https://www.reuters.com/world/india/indias-modi-has-mixed-record-economic-management-2022-01-27/

Ali, Asim & Barthwal, Ankita, "How BJP has Owned the National Security Issue and Why China Won't Change That", The Print, 24 June 2020, https://theprint.in/opinion/bjp-owned-national-security-issue-china-wont-change-that/447554/#google_vignette

Allison, Graham, Will India Surpass China to Become the Next Superpower?, Foreign Policy, 24 June 2023, https://foreignpolicy.com/2023/06/24/india-china-biden-modi-summit-great-powercompetition-economic-growth/

Anand, Arun, "How Narendra Modi Evaded Arrest for 19 Months by Changing His Name and Look During Emergency" The Print, 22 June 2021, https://theprint.in/india/how-narendra-modi-evaded-arrest-for-19-months-by-changing-his-name-and-look-during-emergency/681343/

Anwar, Anu, South Asia and China's Belt and Road Initiative: Security Implications and Ways Forward, Hindsight, Insight, and Foresight: Thinking About

Security in the Indo-Pacific, 1st ed., 1: pp. 161–178. Honolulu: DKI Asia-Pacific Center for Security Studies. https://dkiapcss.edu/dkiapcss25book/#contents

Ashraf, Sajjad, "Power Struggle in the Indian Ocean", ChinaUSFocus Foreign Policy Editorial, 28 April, 2023, https://www.chinausfocus.com/foreign-policy/power-struggle-in-the-indian-ocean

Bajpai, Kanti, "Modi's China challenge", East Asia Forum, 16 July 2019, https://eastasiaforum.org/2019/07/16/modis-china-challenge/

Barrett, Eamon, "India and Japan Offer Land and Funding to Lure Factories Out of China", Fortune, 7 May 2020, https://fortune.com/2020/05/07/coronavirus-india-japan-factories-china/

Baruah, Darshana M., Surrounding the Indian Ocean: PRC Influence in the Indian Ocean, 18 April 2023, Testimony for the House of Representatives Foreign Affairs Committee, Subcommittee on the Indo-Pacific Affairs, Carnegie Endownment for International Peace, https://carnegieendowment.org/2023/04/18/surrounding-ocean-prc-influence-in-indian-ocean-pub-89608

Basrur, Rajesh, "Modi's foreign policy fundamentals: a trajectory unchanged", International Affairs, Volume 93, Issue 1, Pages 7–26, 1 January 2017, https://doi.org/10.1093/ia/iiw006

Bhaskar, C. Uday, "The Forgotten India-Pakistan Nuclear Crisis: 25 Years Later", The Diplomat, 18 May 2015, https://thediplomat.com/2015/05/the-forgotten-india-pakistan-nuclear-crisis-25-years-later/

Bhardwaj, Ashutosh, "A Divided Muslim Society Faces The BJP's Challenge", Outlook, 19 August 2022, https://www.outlookindia.com/national/a-divided-muslim-society-faces-the-bjp-s-challenge-news-217036

Bhattacharya Payal, "8 Years, 8 Indicators: How Economy Fared Under Modi Government", The Times of India, 30 May 2022, https://timesofindia.indiatimes.com/business/india-business/8-years-8-reforms-how-economy-fared-under-modi-government/articleshow/91895885.cms

Bhatt, Parjanya, "Revisiting China's Kashmir Policy", *ORF Issue Brief No. 326*, November 2019, Observer Research Foundation, https://www.orfonline.org/research/revisiting-chinas-kashmir-policy-58128/

Bhatnagar, Armann, "Cultural Awakening: How PM Modi is Leading the Revival of Temples in India", Times of India, 23 October 2022, http://timesofindia.indiatimes.com/articleshow/95051485.cms?utm_source=contentofinterest&utm_medium=text&utm_campaign=cppst

Biswas, Soutik, "'Invisible in Our Own Country': Being Muslim in Modi's India," BBC, 29 April 2024, https://www.bbc.com/news/world-asia-india-68498675

BJP Tweet on Modi's Education Degrees from Amit Shah, 9 May 2016, https://twitter.com/BJP4India/status/729596646124863488?ref_src= twsrc%5Etfw%7Ctwcamp%5Etweetembed%7Ctwterm%5E7295966461248 63488%7Ctwgr%5E05609be0fd15aea77e7bb9870551e5ddb6ae0861%7Ct wcon%5Es1_&ref_url=https%3A%2F%2Fthewire.in%2Fgovernment%2Fnare ndra-modi-degree-entire-political-science

Breger, Michael, "India's Strategic Balancing Act: The Quad as a Vehicle for Zone Balancing", All FSI News, 23 January 2023, Freeman Spogli Institute for International Studies, https://fsi.stanford.edu/news/indias-strategic-balancing-act-quad-vehicle-zone-balancing

Brunnstrom, David, "Ambitious plans for US-India technology sharing face hurdles", Reuters, 24 June 2023, https://www.reuters.com/world/ambiti ous-plans-us-india-technology-sharing-face-hurdles-2023-06-23/

Chanakya, "The China Factor in Indian Politics", The Hinduistan Times, 21 June 2020, https://www.hindustantimes.com/opinion/the-china-factor-in-indian-politics/story-VEbt7c3DPlLxbX2Ua60v8M.html

Chandra, Kanchan, "The Triumph of Hindu Majoritarianism: A Requiem for an Old Idea of India", Foreign Affairs, 23 November 2018, https://www.foreig naffairs.com/india/triumph-hindu-majoritarianism

Chandra, Kanchan, "The Roots of Hindu Nationalism's Triumph in India: What the BJP Learned From the Congress Party", Foreign Affairs, 11 September 2019, https://www.foreignaffairs.com/articles/india/2019-09-11/roots-hindu-nationalisms-triumph-india

Chisti, Seema, "Foreign Anger Works on Modi—And Ensures BJP's Two-Face Act Flops", The Wire, 7 June 2022, https://thewire.in/communalism/bjp-nupur-sharma-naveen-jindal-gulf

Choudhary, Ladhu, R. "The China Question in Indian Domestic Politics", South Asian Voices, 9 February 2023, Stimson Center Publication, https://southa sianvoices.org/the-china-question-in-indian-domestic-politics/

Chowdhury, Sayandeb, "PM Modi's Educational Degree Should Neither Be a National Shame Nor a State Secret", The Wire, 12 April 2023, https://the wire.in/government/narendra-modi-degree-entire-political-science

Cogan, Mark, & Mishra, Vivek, "Sri Lanka Has Become a China-India Great Power Battleground", The National Interest, 29 August 2022, https://nationalinterest.org/feature/sri-lanka-has-become-china-india-great-power-battleground-204445

Davar, Praveen, "Recalling Rajiv Gandhi's Visit That Broke Down 'the Great Wall' Between India and China", The Wire, 21 May 2023, https://thewire. in/politics/recalling-rajiv-gandhis-visit-that-broke-down-the-great-wall-bet ween-india-and-china

Dalrymple, William, "The Great Divide: The Violent Legacy of Indian Partition", The New Yorker, 22 June 2015, https://www.newyorker.com/mag azine/2015/06/29/the-great-divide-books-dalrymple

DNAIndia, "Narendra Modi belongs to Modh-Ghanchi Caste, Which was Added to OBCs Categories in 1994, Says Gujarat Government", DNAIndia Editorial, 9 May 2014, https://www.dnaindia.com/india/report-narendra-modi-belongs-to-modh-ghanchi-caste-which-was-added-to-obcs-categories-in-1994-says-gujarat-government-1986389

CFO (Foreign and Commonwealth Office), Written Ministerial Statement on Tibet, 29 October 2008, https://web.archive.org/web/20081202021442/http://www.fco.gov.uk/en/newsroom/latest-news/?view=PressS&id=829 9838

Economic Times, "China says Arunachal Pradesh Part of it "Since Ancient Times"", The Economic Times, 31 December 2021, https://economictimes. indiatimes.com/news/india/china-says-arunachal-pradesh-part-of-it-since-anc ient-times/articleshow/88618947.cms

Economic Times, "Narendra Modi seeks Chinese investments for Gujarat", The Economic Times, 9 November 2011, https://economictimes.indiatimes. com/news/politics-and-nation/narendra-modi-seeks-chinese-investments-for-gujarat/articleshow/10667923.cms?utm_source=contentofinterest&utm_medium=text&utm_campaign=cppst

Firstpost, "10 Years of Modi Government: How Has the Indian Economy Fared?", Firstpost, 26 May 2024, https://www.firstpost.com/explainers/10-years-of-narendra-modi-government-how-indian-economy-fared-13773879. html

Finnigan, Christopher, "BJP's 2019 Victory: How Caste-based Politics has been Redefined and Reinvented", LSE South Asia Centre Blog Article 26 June 2019, https://blogs.lse.ac.uk/southasia/2019/06/26/bjps-2019-victory-how-caste-based-politics-has-been-redefined-and-reinvented/

Galonnier, Violette Graff Juliette, "Hindu-Muslim Communal Riots in India (1947–1986)", SciencesPo, Violence and Resistance of the Masses Paper, 15 July 2013, https://www.sciencespo.fr/mass-violence-war-massacre-resist ance/fr/document/hindu-muslim-communal-riots-india-i-1947-1986.html

Gan, Nectar & Yeung, Jessie, "China offered Covid aid to India while US dragged its feet, but Delhi isn't that keen", CNN World, 28 April 2021, https://edition.cnn.com/2021/04/28/china/china-india-covid-relief-mic-intl-hnk/index.html

Ganapathy, Nirmala, "India losing ground in its Covid-19 vaccine diplomacy plan in South Asia", The Straits Times, 3 June 2021, https://www.straitsti mes.com/asia/south-asia/india-losing-ground-in-its-south-asia-covid-19-vac cine-diplomacy-plan

Haidar, Suhasini, "PM Modi, President Xi Call for Speedy Disengagement Along LAC", The Hindu, 24 August 2023, https://www.thehindu.com/news/national/pm-modi-president-xi-call-for-expeditious-disengagement-de-escalation-at-lac/article67232333.ece

Haidar, Suhasini, "PM Modi's Comments on China 'Highly Significant', Denote Readiness for Post-Poll Re-engagement, Say Experts", The Hindu, 11 April 2024, https://www.thehindu.com/news/national/pm-modis-comments-on-china-highly-significant-denote-readiness-for-post-poll-re-engagement-say-exp erts/article68054334.ece

Hajari, Nisid, Midnight Furies: The Deadly Legacy of India's Partition, Boston: Mariner Books (Reprint Edition) 2016

Harris, Clare, & Gordan, Andrew, "Modi's "New India" and the Politics of Architecture", Council on Foreign Relations, Asia Program and Asia Unbound, 28 February 2023, https://www.cfr.org/blog/modis-new-india-and-politics-architecture

Hashmi, Sana, "Modi 2.0 and India's Regional Security Outlook", in CSCAP Regional Security Outlook 2020, Council for Security Cooperation in the Asia Pacific (2019), http://www.jstor.com/stable/resrep22261.7

Hindu, "Congress Targets Narendra Modi over His Visits to China", The Hindu, 13 June 2020, https://www.thehindu.com/news/national/congress-targets-narendra-modi-over-his-visits-to-china/article31823005.ece

Hindustan Times, "Kanpur violence: 36 arrested, 3 FIRs filed, property to be bulldozed, say cops", 4 June 2022, https://www.hindustantimes.com/india-news/kanpur-violence-36-arrested-property-will-be-demolished-says-top-cop-report-101654317134374.html

Inamdar, Nikhil, & Alluri, Aparna, "India Economy: Seven Years of Modi in Seven Charts", BBC News, 22 June 2021, https://www.bbc.com/news/world-asia-india-57437944

Jaffrelot, Christophe, "India in 2016: Assessing Modi Mid-Term", *Asian Survey* 57, no. 1 (2017): 21-32

Jaffrelot, Christophe, Modi's India: Hindu Nationalism and the Rise of Ethnic Democracy (Translated from L'Inde de Modi de), New Jersey: Princeton University Press, 2021

Jaffrelot, Christophe, "How Narendra Modi Transformed from an RSS Pracharak to a Full-Fledged Politician and Hindu Hridaysamrat", The Wire, 24 August 2021, https://thewire.in/politics/narendra-modi-rss-pracharak-politician

Jha, Lalit K., "Rajiv Gandhi was Genuinely Interested in US Military Ties: CIA", The Mint, 4 August 2017, https://www.livemint.com/Politics/q6x oc52bqbTg9nDU4JIvbM/Rajiv-Gandhi-was-genuinely-interested-about-US-military-ties.html

Joshi, Yogesh, Rajeev, Nishant, & Gurung, Wini Fred, "India and the World in Modi's Second Term", Institute of South Asian Studies,

December 2020, https://www.isas.nus.edu.sg/wp-content/uploads/2020/12/India-and-the-World-in-Modis-Second-Term-Full.pdf

Kaushik, Krishn, "U.S. Tries to Woo India Away from Russia with Display of F-35s, Bombers", Reuters, 17 February 2023, https://www.reuters.com/business/aerospace-defense/us-tries-woo-india-away-russia-with-display-f-35s-bombers-2023-02-17/

Krishnam, Murali, "How are Muslims Coping in India?", DW Editorial, 14 April 2023, https://www.dw.com/en/how-are-muslims-coping-in-india/a-65321878

Kumaraswamy, P.R., "Modi Redefines India's Palestine Policy", Manohar Parrikar Institute for Defence Studies and Analyses, Issue Brief, 18 May 2017, https://idsa.in/issuebrief/modi-redefines-india-palestine-policy_prkumaraswamy_180517

Kurshid, Salman, & Muhammad, Khan, "The Ten Big Failures of Narendra Modi Government", The Wire, 30 November 2018, https://thewire.in/politics/narendra-modi-government-failures

Langa, Mahesh, "PM Modi Inaugurates Revamped Temple Destroyed by 15th Century Gujarat Ruler", The Hindu 18 June 2022, https://www.thehindu.com/news/national/other-states/pm-modi-inaugurates-revamped-temple-destroyed-in-15th-century-gujarat-ruler/article65540229.ece

Leali, Giorgio, "India Buys French Fighter Jets, Submarines as Modi Visits Macron," The Politico, 13 July 2023, https://www.politico.eu/article/india-buys-french-rafale-fighter-jets-and-submarines-as-narendra-modi-visits-emmanuel-macron/

Liu, Litao, 重新审视"印度象" (Reappraising India) in Qunzhong Magazine (People's Magazine) 2017 issue 18, https://web.archive.org/web/20200716193353/http://www.qunzh.com/qkzx/gwqk/jczx/2017/201718/201709/t20170926_34043.html

Maizland, Lindsay, "India's Muslims: An increasingly Marginalised Population", Council on Foreign Relations, 18 March 2024, https://www.cfr.org/backgrounder/india-muslims-marginalized-population-bjp-modi

Malhotra, Aditi, "Engagement, not Entanglement: India's Relationship with the Quad", Georgetown Journal of International Affairs, 1 May 2023, https://gjia.georgetown.edu/2023/05/01/engagement-not-entanglement-indias-relationship-with-the-quad/

Maliszewska, Maryla, & Van der Mensbrugghe, Dominique, "The Belt and Road Initiative Economic, Poverty and Environmental Impacts", World Bank Policy Research Working Paper 8814, https://openknowledge.worldbank.org/server/api/core/bitstreams/f68d1350-e870-5a11-9d0b-d2da1849163f/content

Maizland, Lindsay, "India's Muslims: An Increasingly Marginalized Population", Council for Foreign Relations, 14 July 2022, https://www.cfr.org/backgroun der/india-muslims-marginalized-population-bjp-modi

Mamgain, Shreya, "Bhutan-China Border Dispute: Regional Security Concerns", Center for Joint Warfare Studies, 20 June 2023, https://cenjows.in/bhu tan-china-border-dispute-regional-security-concerns/#:~:text=In%20the%201 950s%2C%20Beijing%20laid,held%20by%20%27imperial%20India%27

Mashal, Mujib, & Yasir, Sameer, "China Had a 'Special Place' in Modi's Heart. Now It's a Thorn in His Side", The New York Times, 13 April 2024, https://www.nytimes.com/2024/04/13/world/asia/india-china-modi.html

Maxwell, Neville, "Sino-Indian Border Dispute Reconsidered." *Economic and Political Weekly* 34, no. 15 (1999): 905–18. http://www.jstor.org/stable/4407848

MEA (Ministry of External Affairs, India), "Agreement Between the Government of the Republic of India and the Government of the People's Republic of China on Confidence-Building Measures in the Military Field Along the Line of Actual Control in the India-China Border Areas", 1996, https://www.mea.gov.in/Portal/LegalTreatiesDoc/CH96B1124.pdf

Mehta, Gautam, "Hindu Nationalism and the BJP Economic Record in Vaishnav, Milan, The BJP in Power: Indian Democracy and Religious Nationalism", Carnegie Endownment for International Peace, 4 April 2019, https://carnegieendowment.org/2019/04/04/hindu-nation alism-and-bjp-s-economic-record-pub-78720

Mishra, Vivek & Das, "Udayan, India's understanding of the Quad & Indo-Pacific: Distinct narrative or a flawed one?", Observer Research Foundation, 19 May 2019. https://www.orfonline.org/expert-speak/indias-unders tanding-of-the-quad-indo-pacific-distinct-narrative-or-a-flawed-one-49068

Misra, Udit, "Explain Speaking: Indian Economy After 9 years of Modi Govt", The Indian Express, 30 May 2023, https://indianexpress.com/article/exp lained/explained-economics/india-economy-9-years-modi-government-863 4120/

Mody, Ashoka, India is Broken: A People Betrayed, Independence to Today, Stanford, CA: Stanford University Press, 2023

Mohan, Archis, "China Builds on "Old Ties" with Modi", The Business-Standard, 30 May 2014, https://www.business-standard.com/article/eco nomy-policy/china-builds-on-old-ties-with-modi-114053000419_1.html

Mohan, C. Raja, Elections and Foreign Policy: India's Pakistan Debate, Institute of South Asian Studies, National University of Singapore, 16 May 2024, https://www.isas.nus.edu.sg/papers/elections-and-foreign-policy-indias-pakistan-debate/

Nag, Kingshuk, "Before Vajpayee Became the BJP's Moderate Face, He Thought of Quitting the Party", https://qz.com/india/1361456/before-vajpayee-became-bjps-moderate-face-he-thought-of-quitting

Namrata, Hasija, "India-China Relations: A Shaky Road Ahead, Prospect and Exploration", Vol 18, No. 7, 2020, Republic of China Ministry of Justice Investigation Bureau, https://www.mjib.gov.tw/FileUploads/eBooks/51a2d6e529634644842e65e3f0a1f9b4/Section_file/45c806539acc47209055d33e3ddd740a.pdf

Noorani, A.G., "Savarkar & the BJ", Frontline Editorial, The Hindu, 5 January 2020, https://frontline.thehindu.com/politics/savarkar-the-bjp/article30441872.ece

Panang, Harcharanjit Singh, "China's New G695 Highway Across Aksai Chin Is a Problem. India Can't Stay Quiet", The Print 4 August 2022, https://theprint.in/opinion/chinas-new-g695-highway-across-aksai-chin-is-a-problem-india-cant-stay-quiet/1068465/

Pant, Harsh, "India and the Quad: Chinese belligerence and Indian resilience", Melbourne Asia Review, 18 March 2022, https://melbourneasiareview.edu.au/india-and-the-quad-chinese-belligerence-and-indian-resilience/

Patnaik, Ila, "Modi's Anti-poverty Schemes Work. That's Why BJP Swept the Lok Sabha Elections", The Print, 26 July 2019, https://theprint.in/ilanomics/modis-anti-poverty-schemes-work-thats-why-bjp-swept-the-lok-sabha-elections/268121/

Pradhan, Bibhudatta & MacAskill, Andrew, "Modi Attacks India Leaders Over China, Pakistan Border Disputes", The National World News, 16 September 2013, https://www.thenationalnews.com/world/modi-attacks-india-leaders-over-china-pakistan-border-disputes-1.266241

PTI (Press Trust of India), "When Will Modi Govt Respond to China's Aggression: Congress", 30 March 2023, https://economictimes.indiatimes.com/news/politics-and-nation/when-will-modi-govt-respond-to-chinas-aggression-congress/articleshow/99122527.cms?from=mdr

PTI, "BJP will win 32 Lok Sabha seats out of 42 in Bengal: Tripura CM", The Hindu, 16 May 2024, https://www.thehindu.com/elections/lok-sabha/bjp-will-win-32-lok-sabha-seats-out-of-42-in-bengal-tripura-cm/article68181975.ece

Rajvanshi, Astha, "Why Indian Voters See Job Creation as the Election's Biggest Issue"

Ranjan, Amit, "China-Bhutan Border Talks", ISAS Briefs, National University of Singapore, 25 January 2023, https://www.isas.nus.edu.sg/papers/china-bhutan-border-talks/

Ravid, Barak, "Biden Unveils Infrastructure Project to Connect India, Middle East and Europe", AXIOS, 9 September 2023, https://www.axios.com/2023/09/09/us-saudi-india-uae-railway-deal-middle-east-europe

Reed, John, "India's Narendra Modi has a problem: high economic growth but few jobs", The Financial Times, 19 March 2023, https://www.ft.com/content/6886014f-e4cd-493c-986b-1da2cfc8cdf2

Reuters, "India BJP's Election Videos Targeting Muslims and Opposition Spark Outrage", 6 May 2024, https://www.dawn.com/news/1831862

Roushan, Anurag, "Karnataka Elections 2023: PM Modi, Amit Shah Hold Roadshows in BJP's Show of Strength in Poll-Bound State", India TV editorial, 30 April 2023

Roychoudhury, Supriya; Chenoy, Anuradha; Chopra, Deepta; Joshi, Anuradha, "Is Indian Development Cooperation Taking a New Direction Under Modi?" The Institute of Development Studies and Partner Organisations. 2015 Report. https://hdl.handle.net/20.500.12413/6282

Roychoudhury, Supriya; Chenoy, Anuradha Chopra; Deepta, & Joshi, Anuradha, "Is Indian Development Cooperation Taking a New Direction Under Modi?" Policy Briefing, 1 June 2015, https://www.ids.ac.uk/publications/is-indian-development-cooperation-taking-a-new-direction-under-modi/

Rukimini, S., ""One in 7 Muslim Youth Face Discrimination": Today's India, in Numbers", The Quint, 30 December 2021, https://www.thequint.com/lifestyle/books/one-in-7-muslim-youth-faces-discrimination-todays-india-in-numbers

Rukimini, S., Whole Numbers and Half Truths: What Data Can and Cannot Tell us about Modern India, Chennai: Context Print Westland, 2021, https://carnegieendowment.org/2019/04/04/emergence-stagnation-and-ascendance-of-bjp-pub-78735

Sachdeva, "Gulshan, Indian Perceptions of the Chinese Belt and Road Initiative", International Studies, Vol. 55 No. 4, pp 285–296, https://globalindia.eu/wp-content/uploads/2019/01/BRI_Gulshan.pdf

Safi, Michael, "Indian Election Results 2019: Modi Claims Landslide Victory", The Guardian 23 May 2019, https://www.theguardian.com/world/2019/may/23/india-election-results-narendra-modi-bjp-victory

Saha, Premesha, "India and the Quad, East Asia Policy", Vol. 14 No. 3, pp 17–30, https://doi.org/10.1142/S1793930522000186

Sandefur, Justin, "The Great Indian Poverty Debate, 2.0" Center for Global Development Blog Post, 19 April 2022, https://www.cgdev.org/blog/great-indian-poverty-debate-20

Sen, Ronojoy, Indian Elections 2019: Why the BJP Won Big, Institute of South Asian Studies, ISAS Brief, 2019, https://www.isas.nus.edu.sg/wp-content/uploads/2019/06/ISAS-Briefs-No.-666.pdf

Sen, Kunal, "How India's Economy Has Fared under Ten Years of Narendra Modi", United Nations University (UNU), 7 May 2024, https://unu.edu/article/how-indias-economy-has-fared-under-ten-years-narendra-modi

Sharma, Nidhi, "Swachh Bharat Abhiyan: Survey Reveals Not Even Half the Toilets Built Being Used; Government Withheld Findings", The Economic Times, 24 November 2015, https://economictimes.indiatimes.com/news/politics-and-nation/swachh-bharat-abhiyan-survey-reveals-not-even-half-the-toilets-built-being-used-government-withheld-findings/articleshow/498 85579.cms?from=mdr

Sharma, Radhey Sham, & Mehta, Shakshi, "Foreign Policy of India Under Modi Government", *International Journal of Political Science and Governance* 2, no. 2 (2020): 123–128

Shukla, Srijan, "1975 Arunachal Ambush—The Last Time Indian Soldiers Died in Clash with China at LAC", The Print, 16 June 2020, https://theprint.in/india/1975-arunachal-ambush-the-last-time-indian-soldiers-died-in-clash-with-china-at-lac/442674/

Schultz, Kai, Biswas, Sreejam, & Sanjay, Satviki, "India's New Parliament is Symbol of Modi's Nationalist Vision", Bloomberg, https://www.bloomberg.com/news/features/2023-07-01/delhi-s-new-parliament-a-symbol-of-modi-s-nationalist-vision-for-india

Sidhu, W.P.S., & Mehta, Vikram Singh, "Modi's Foreign Policy @365: Course Correction", Brookings Institution India Center, Commentary, 9 July 2015, https://www.brookings.edu/articles/modis-foreign-policy-365-course-correction/

Subramanian, Nirupama, "Explained: The Strategic Road to DBO", The Indian Express, 16 June 2020, https://indianexpress.com/article/explained/lac-stand-off-india-china-darbuk-shyok-daulat-beg-oldie-dsdbo-road-6452997/

Onmanorama, "Despite Modi's 5 China Trips & 18 Meetings with Xi, Sino-Indian Border Dispute Escalates", Onmanorama News, 17 June 2020, https://www.onmanorama.com/news/india/2020/06/17/narendra-modi-china-sino-india-border-dispute.html

Outlook India, "G-20 Summit: PM Narendra Modi, Chinese President Xi Jinping Shake Hands On Sidelines", Outlook News 15 Nov 2022, https://www.outlookindia.com/national/g20-summit-pm-narendra-modi-chinese-president-xi-jinping-shake-hands-on-sidelines-news-237629

Tarapore, Arzan, "Zone Balancing: India and the Quad's New Strategic Logic", International Affairs, Volume 99, Issue 1, January 2023, Pages 239–25.

Tellis, Ashley, "Modi's Three Foreign Policy Wins", *The Economic Times Magazine Perspective*, 24–30 March 2019

The White House, "Joint Statement From the United States and India", 22 June 2023, https://www.whitehouse.gov/briefing-room/statements-releases/2023/06/22/joint-statement-from-the-united-states-and-india/

The Tribune, "If PM Modi's Degrees Turn Out to be Fake, He Would Lose His Lok Sabha Membership, Says AAP", 28 April 2023, https://www.tribuneindia.com/news/delhi/if-pm-modis-degrees-turn-out-to-be-he-would-lose-his-lok-sabha-membership-says-aap-493528

Times of India, "'Modi Is a Teli-Ghanchi OBC': BJP", 23 April 2014, https://timesofindia.indiatimes.com/city/ahmedabad/modi-is-a-teli-ghanchi-obc-bjp/articleshow/34084111.cms

Times of India, "PM Narendra Modi Meets Chinese President Xi Jinping at G20 Dinner", 15 November 2022, https://timesofindia.indiatimes.com/india/pm-modi-meets-chinese-president-xi-jinping-at-g20-dinner/articleshow/95536829.cms

Topcu, Neslihan, "Why Can't the Border Problem Between China and India Be Solved?", Ankara Center for Crisis and Policy Studies Commentary, 5 January 2023, https://www.ankasam.org/why-cant-the-border-problem-between-china-and-india-be-solved/?lang=en

Trumbull, Robert, "India's Visit to China Cit off in Protest", The New York Times, 19 Feb 1979, https://timesmachine.nytimes.com/timesmachine/1979/02/19/111075559.html

Wani, Ayjaz, Decoding India's Priorities at the SCO: Connectivity, Counterterrorism, and Afghanistan, Observer Research Foundation, Issue No. 406, August 2023, https://www.orfonline.org/wp-content/uploads/2023/08/ORF_OP-406_Indias-priorities-at-SCO.pdf

Wagner, Christian, The Indian-Chinese Confrontation in the Himalayas: A Stress Test for India's Strategic Autonomy, SWP Comment, No. 39, July 2020, German Institute for International and Security Affairs (Stiftung Wissenschaft und Politik), https://www.swp-berlin.org/publications/products/comments/2020C39_IndiaChina.pdf

Verma, Rahul, The Emergence, Stagnation and Ascendance of the BJP, in Vaishnav, Milan, The BJP in Power: Indian Democracy and Religious Nationalism, Washington DC: Carnegie Endowment for International Peace, 2019

Venkatraman, Sakshi, "Modi's White House Visit Hightlights Deep Diaspora Divides", NBC News 21 June 2023, https://www.nbcnews.com/news/asian-america/modis-white-house-visit-highlights-deep-diaspora-divides-rcna89275

Virmani, Arvind "India's Economic Growth History: Fluctuations, Trends, Break Points and Phases." *Indian Economic Review* 41, no. 1 (2006): 81–103. http://www.jstor.org/stable/29793855

Yasir, Sameer, "India Is Scapegoating Muslims for the Spread of the Coronavirus", Foreign Policy, 22 Apr 2020, https://foreignpolicy.com/2020/04/22/india-muslims-coronavirus-scapegoat-modi-hindu-nationalism/

Zhou, Enlai and Radhakrishnan, Sarvepalli, "Record of Conversation Between Zhou Enlai and Vice-President Sarvepalli Radhakrishnan" (21 April 1960),

Wilson Center Digital Archive, https://digitalarchive.wilsoncenter.org/doc ument/record-conversation-between-zhou-enlai-and-vice-president-sarvepalli-radhakrishnan

Zhou Ling, Mao Yanghai, Fu Qinyi, Xu Danlu, Zhou Jiaqi, & Zeng Shaolong, "A Study on the Belt and Road Initiative's Trade and Its Influencing Factors: Evidence of China-South Asia's Panel Data". *PLoS ONE* 18, no. 4 (2023): e0282167. https://doi.org/10.1371/journal.pone.0282167

CHAPTER 6

The Rise of the Global Right, Great Power Politics and The Revival of the Cold War

This volume calls for an introspective analysis that accounts for the rightward shift in global politics by focusing on the Quad countries of the United States, Japan, India and Australia from 2012 to 2022. It adopts a Waltzian three-tier analysis by focusing on how the particular combination of acrimonious domestic politics and external strategic circumstances facilitated the rise of a particular type of populist politics. This combination facilitated the rise of Conservative right-wing leaders that utilised nationalism to rally the country against a powerful external enemy—China. Whether it is the perceived decline in economic prowess vis-à-vis Beijing and the consequent increased economic asymmetry in bilateral relations or impact on other issues such as immigration, regime performance, territorial insecurities or global prestige, created an opportunity for these politicians to reinterpret international systemic changes and label Beijing to be responsible for many of the domestic ills and international problems. Blaming China (rightly or wrongly) has become a standard rally cry for many global right politicians. This is not to say that China is faultless in all respects, but rather it is important to understand the world we live in is not just shaped by Beijing's policies alone.

As in cases where nationalism becomes the dominant political force, such an environment often has the ironic effect of eroding democratic institutions, civil liberties and exacerbating more insecurities. This trend of strongmen politics in the Quad democracies mirrors the increased

© The Author(s), under exclusive license to Springer Nature
Singapore Pte Ltd. 2024
V. Teo, *Cold War Redux Amidst Great Power Rivalry*,
https://doi.org/10.1007/978-981-97-3733-8_6

379

authoritarianism seen in the People's Republic of China and the Russian Federation over the last decade. There are of course major systemic differences in how far these politicians in these democracies can go in consolidating their power compared to their counterparts in China or Russia. At the same time, it is important to understand that this trend towards authoritarian politics should be seen abnormally in the recent history of world politics. This trend is in turn a product of the very different political environment we live and operate in today. It is an environment where the social and corporate media as well as a plurality of non-state actors such as the global military-industrial complex and capital an outsized role in influencing politics and policies. It is also important to stress that within each of these countries, the way China-related issues are thought about and calculated could be vastly different but eventually these countries found it opportune to rally together against Beijing. These nuanced differences lie in how China is seen by the politicians concerned or how it is played out in domestic politics: Abe's dogmatic conservatism is very much different from Modi's

At the international level, the changes in the global balance of power have also helped to propel the rise of the global right. Even though Russia and China have since the 1990s claimed that it has been a multipolar world, the fact remains that was an era of unipolarity where the United States had undisputed pre-eminence. China today has become somewhat of a victim of her own success. Notwithstanding the numerous domestic problems she faces domestically, she is seen as the number one peer competitor that is in line to replace the United States as the global hegemon. Likewise, under Putin, Russia has thrived remarkably over the last two decades, and is now in a much better position to compete with the United States in the international system. The emergence of what looks like multipolarity (along with the European Union) has exacerbated the insecurities of US politicians and strategic planners. As the strategic balance slowly tilts towards China, the United States sees an urgent need to address this. Regardless of whether China intends (or not) to "replace" the United States in reality, the question is immaterial. Strategic planners in Washington would therefore be determined to ensure that China's rise is checked and contained to preserve the eminence of her position globally. Likewise, the Chinese cannot imagine how they can give up their development and their great power aspirations just to placate the Americans' sensitivities and desire to remain the sole global superpower. The resulting struggle we see since the end of the War on Terror is a clear manifestation of this.

In this new era, geopolitical alignment is now the primary force that guides everything from economic planning, commercial decisions to military deployments, replacing the era of free trade and globalisation in which politics served economics. The combination of the leaders' varying perceptions and interests, with the toxic mixture of intense domestic politicking contextualised against fast changing and very challenging strategic circumstances is accentuated by Great Power rivalry dressed up in Cold War rhetoric emphasising identity politics and ideological differences is amassing an uncontrollable force that will alter the trajectories of the countries concerned towards a renewal of Cold War. The American political manoeuvres behind developments in Taiwan, Hong Kong, the Korean Peninsula and Southeast Asia were to rally Asian countries behind its position in its competition with China. This is necessary not only to shore up its alliances to strengthen the San Francisco system but also necessary to reduce the influence of China in these countries. After all, it was the United States that had inducted China into working and integrating with the Asian economies from Japan to South Korea to Southeast Asia from the late 1970s. Despite its best efforts, these steps to separate and isolate China are turning out to be much more difficult than imagined. Whether it is "decoupling" or "derisking", China's manufacturing role cannot be readily replaced—whether it is by India, Vietnam or anyone else simply because the PRC is the only country that has close to complete supply chains for most consumer and industrial products. The United States weaned on a massive debt is now finding itself in great difficulties in funding its strategic influence and expansion abroad at a time when its economy is suffering from inflation. China its principal peer competitor also happens to be one of the countries that holds a significant amount of US dollars as reserves. The United States cannot weaken China significantly without hurting itself. What is more important however is that US and Western policies in recent years been that push for China and Russia to work comprehensively on the "strategic partnership" that they both had before. Such a partnership would put in place what many respected US strategists feared in the past.

China, Russia and the West in the Era of Globalisation

The Cold War was supposed to have ended with the dissolution of the Soviet Union, at least in Europe. The 1972 Sino-US reproachment put China squarely into the camp of the US-led San Francisco system in Asia. From the eyes of the Russians today, the Chinese role in the US defeat of the Soviet Union was an important but understated one. PRC's role in tying down Soviet forces along its borders created such an enormous strain for Moscow that it remains an extremely vital lesson for the Russian strategic community today. China was an important factor in the US bloc as she became the industrial hub for the United States and her allies that undertook cheap manufacturing that boosted the economies of the United States and her allies, ushering in a new era of prosperity. For China, this decade represented a sort of modern "gold rush" as Western companies and capital flooded into China to invest. This symbiotic relationship benefitted not only China but also the United States and her allies such as Japan, Australia and the region at large.

The USSR's successor state, the Russian Federation, under the leadership of its President Boris Yeltsin and Foreign Minister Andrey Kozyrev had too initially hoped to become part of the West. By the mid-1990s, Russian leaders had grown was disillusioned with the unfulfilled promises (real or perceived) of the West. Consequently, Boris Yeltsin appointed Yevgeny Primakov and re-oriented Russia's foreign policy to look east to build closer ties with her "near abroad" neighbours. The Russian Federation also began boosting ties with China which was then undertaking market reforms in earnest. With political will, Moscow and Beijing began solving issues that had plagued their relations for over three decades, beginning with the very sensitive issues of territorial demarcation as well as the sensitive question of the presence of the Chinese in the Russian Far East. These gestures were significant as relations between Russia and China were difficult because of the history of confrontation between these giants for over almost two decades from the mid-1960s to 1987. China and USSR only reach a détente when Gorbachev signalled in his 1986 Vladivostok speech to reconcile with China by addressing Beijing's concerns about the Soviet military presence that encircled China.[1] Even

---

[1] The USSR agreed to withdraw six regiments from Afghanistan, as well as a "substantial" part of the 25000 troops from Mongolia, and initiated informal arms control

though there was political will to enhance relations, China's relations with Russia did not improve all that much largely because of the stereotyping, misperceptions, distrust at both the grassroots and elite level. China and Chinese-related issues did not elicit much interestand excitement in either Russian national politics as well as in regional politics.

For most of the Cold War right through to the 2000s, the Russians themselves did not favour the Chinese, for the Chinese were seen as poor, radical and culturally inferior in comparison to Europe. The politicians in the Russian Far East also politicised the Chinese traders working and living and there were frequent acrimonies of all sorts between the people, many on either side who were neither law-abiding or well-behaved. Conversely, the perception of the Russians within China was not good as well. Every Chinese schoolchild learned that Czarist Russia had seized 1.5 million square kilometres of territory (current day Russian Far East) from China, and had committed atrocities that involved the destruction of villages and killing of innocent civilians in these hamlets. Even though the Soviet Communist Revolution happened much earlier, the Chinese Communist Party never forgot that the Soviet Cominterns played a hedging game when they were fighting against the Kuomintang and the Japanese Imperial Forces in the lead-up to the 1949 Revolution. The CCP also clearly remembered the difficult times they faced in the lead up and following the Sino-Soviet rivalry, where the Soviet Union cut off aid and withdrew Soviet technical assistance. In turn, the Russians have never forgotten the betrayal of the Chinese, whether it was them flooding the market with clone copies of Soviet weapons given to them or the ideological challenge PRC posed by claiming that they had found the genuine road to communism without the need for urbanisation or the surprise attack when Chinese forces ambushed the Soviet forces on Chenbao/Damansky Island in 1969. Most importantly, the Soviets have not forgotten how Chinese forces tied down their supply ties along the entire stretch of the Sino-Soviet border.

The collapse of the Soviet Union therefore was received with ambivalence in China. On the one hand, its old enemy and foe was gone, but on the other, the way in which the West had brought down the

talks with officials in Beijing (Lee, 1986). Gorbachev mandated in 1985 the withdrawal of Soviet backed Vietnamese troops from Cambodia that occurred in 1987–1988, and announced that the Soviets will scale down military activities in Vietnam's Cam Rahn Bay if the Americans scaled down their activities in the Philippines (Stoecker, 1989).

Soviet Communist Party left lasting and important lessons for the Chinese leaders. Given their history, the Russian Federation and the People's Republic of China therefore recognised each other as important countries to get along. For the most part, Chinese leaders (Jiang Zemin, Hu Jintao and Xi Jinping) as well as Russian leaders (Boris Yeltsin, Vladimir Putin) have put significant emphasis on ensuring that Russia and China coexisted and cooperated to keep relations on an even keel. This cooperation has been circumscribed by a steady but slow uptick in bilateral economic relations, limited people-to-people exchanges, and utilitarian strategic cooperation in terms of weapons sales. The latter means that Moscow has always been careful not to transfer its latest weapons to China, given the lessons it learned during the Sino-Soviet conflict when China used Soviet weapons against Soviet forces.

Therefore while Sino-Russia relations improved during this decade, it was largely defined by the political will of the Chinese and Russian leaders to iron out difficulties rather than a genuine reconciliation between the people. This is quite unlike what was happening with China and the West where relations were pushed forward by burgeoning economic ties, commercial interests and mutual complementarity. Russia and China did build up tolerance and respect for each other's policies and growth, and both supported each other rhetorically against perceived American encroachments. They however in reality did not have a vision that they would end up competing together in the same camp against the United States since both Beijing and Moscow had actually always envisaged and hoped for better relations with United States and Europe.

At the systemic level, the 1990s was the era of globalisation where technological advancements such as the internet, transportation and communications reduced the impact of geography and physical distances. As the world became more interconnected, political barriers were lowered and commercial firms and economics drove development across the world. We were all told that we were approaching "the end of history" as we now lived in a "global village". The increased connections and connectivity such as the United States and Europe and the remaining Communist regimes, most notably China. The international narratives showed how China was viewed by Western strategists then. Ironically, during this period, China was way more "communist", illiberal and backward than it is today. The character of the remaining Communist states (China, North Korea, Vietnam, Laos, Cuba) did not matter all that much to the United States and the West in general then. This is simply because these states were far too weak to challenge American dominance. Likewise, Moscow had lost its far-flung empire, and was dismissed as a mafia state (it was since during that period Russia was in chaos). In the international system, the United States emerged during this period undoubtedly as the pre-eminent power even though China and Russia had always maintained it was a multipolar world. In this unilateral "moment", the international system was defined by the absence of Great Power rivalry as countries were all focused on growing their economies and constructing a better world for themselves. In the Asia-Pacific, China had overall cordial relations with the US, Australia and India but increasing antagonistic relations with Japan.

Multipolarity, Return of Great Power Politics and Cold War Narratives

If one raised the prospects of a new or a renewed Cold War two decades ago (say in 2000), the person would be laughed off as insane. Today, the prospects of a new Cold War are no longer far-fetched. China's growth across all indicators has now alarmed the United States and her allies since the "China Threat" theory widely discussed since the mid-1990s now appears to be becoming reality. With the events of September 11, the US became preoccupied with the War on Terror, effectively waging wars in Iraq, Afghanistan and later Syria. By 2014, China's development had reached such a stage that many strategists in the United States lamented that they had waited too late to address the China challenge. China and Russia have truly emerged to be the important powers they said they were, and effectively ending the United States' unipolar moment. In response, the United States was therefore, understandably keen to act to preserve its hegemonic position, began undertaking a series of actions both within and outside its alliance system to "contain" China.

Back in 2014, there were some discussions in the wider strategic studies communities that a new Cold War was brewing largely because of the antagonism between the United States and Russia, this view did not gain traction because most scholars still did not see it that way. By the end of 2024, it became clear that the US and its allies are now engaged in a renewed Great Power rivalry with both Russia and China. This subject of a "new" Cold War has indeed become a subject of scholarly scrutiny, where esteemed colleagues have debated whether to-date this constituted a new Cold War. There are important reasons to understand why this is not a "new" Cold War, since the United States is not in an "ideological" conflict with either Moscow or Beijing as before. China and Russia do not operate their own political-economic command economies like the Soviet Union, and since both China and Russia share the same single political-economic system in which the majority of the world operates, it would be impossible to say that a new Cold War has emerged. Culturally, younger generations of Chinese and Russians have admired and emulated Western lifestyles for years, and most look forward to spending years in the West to live, study, and work. Therefore, there is no competition regarding which systems produce and provide the best lifestyle for people in the West. At least in the view of Western academia, the conclusion at the moment leaned towards supporting official Washington narratives of "no, we are not in the new Cold War", at least not yet. This, of course, jars squarely with the diplomatic language of the government; however, the problem is that such interpretation has little bearing on how this would be interpreted or played out in the real world.

From the standpoint of Moscow, recent geopolitical developments over the last decade and the reinvigoration of Cold War institutions, such as NATO and the San Francisco system, clearly constitute attempts to provoke a new Cold War. While there might be differing views on Putin's incursions into Crimea and the Ukraine conflict domestically and internationally, the consensus among Russian strategists is that NATO expansion is what provoked the responses from the Kremlin in the first place, not vice versa. Naturally the Chinese strategic community shares this view as well, just as Russians are sympathetic towards the Chinese on Taiwan. There are also well-established Western scholars such as John Mearsheimer in Chicago and Jeffrey Sachs at Columbia in the United States that speaks boldly and often on these topics, and usually deviating from mainstream (official) opinion. Their contrarian views of course have never been taken into consideration within the Beltway think tanks, the halls of the US Congress, or the White House.

From Beijing's perspective, what was happening looked like American strategic attempts to revive the Cold War fronts in Taiwan and the Koreas, and to undermine the ruling parties in PRC, North Korea, and Russia. The strategies and tactics used by the United States in the region and specific to Xinjiang, Hong Kong and Taiwan are right out of the Cold War playbook. Scholars affiliated with the PRC, such as Victor Gao or Wang Jisi at Beijing University, have argued that we are either entering or already in the early stages of the new Cold War. They reached their conclusions based on their assessments premised on the incessant pressure the United States, and her allies have put on a series of issues central to China's well-being and stability. From promoting "democracy" in Hong Kong, advocating for the rise of pro-independence Democratic Progressive Party in Taiwan to running a global human rights campaign against Xinjiang before launching a trade and tech war on China, there is nothing that indicates that the United States and Japan are interested in anything but toppling the Chinese Communist Party and reversing economic growth in China. Since Obama's pivot, all signals coming from the United States suggest that the Washington is not just seeking increased geopolitical competition, but rather the return of the Cold War to Asia. Chinese analysis and complaints are, of course, dismissed as "propaganda" by the US and allied think tanks, corporate and social media, and officials.

Prominent Cold War scholar Arnold Westad has argued that the lack of a deep ideological schism and a massive arms race as well as the presence of diplomatic activities indicate that there is no new Cold War brewing. Based on these indicators, he is right. The problem, however, is that the policymakers on both sides are inadvertently leading us down that path. Whatever diplomacy between the United States and her allies has with Russia and China today hardly amount to anything substantial. From Ukraine to the Hamas-Israel conflict to the South China Sea situation, there is little diplomacy to speak, except for antagonistic barbs and exchanges. After Xi Jinping's meeting with Joe Biden in Bali, where the United States underscored the importance of competing "vigorously" and "responsibly" and not veering into "conflict" and maintaining "open lines of communication" to address "transnational challenges", all it took was a stray weather balloon to be politicised to torpedo months of efforts to reset US–China relations (McDonell, 2023).

Contemporary diplomacy has, in fact, become a daily public relations exercise for conjuring up diplomatic niceties to score political points, rally domestic consensus and strengthen alliances on either side rather than addressing the genuine need to bridge the divide. Consequently, the United States and its allies on the one hand, and Russia and China on the other have been talking "past" as opposed to each other. There might be a lack of ideological schism that has characterised the United States and the USSR competition in the past, but today, the global Conservative right maintains tightly their alliance based on an identity of "like-minded partners of liberal democracies with shared values". Such ideational identification creates an "ideological" divide between liberal democracies and, by extension, non-liberal democracies. This, of course, is unlike the fixed "ideological" challenge posed by the USSR, but this label of "non-democracies' is pushing Russia and China to act more in concert just as it is solidifying the bond between the US, Western Europe, and Japan because "we are not like them". This version of state conservatism is now the main "ideological" framework for the right-wing political forces in the Quad countries. For the last 'criteria" of a massive arms race, it is difficult to quantify this as it is unclear what "massive" constitutes. There is clear evidence that in Asia, the United States and its allies alongside China are engaged in a massive competitive naval arms build-up. The United States is now trying its utmost to rejuvenate its military-industrial capacity. China, Russia and the United States are now dusting off their nuclear arsenal and actively making war preparations to build up their "defensive" weaponsarsenal. China has indicated it would increase its nuclear weapon inventory and is engaging in a massive build-up of modern submarines, naval vessels, strategic bombers and ICBMs to counter US supremacy in these areas. Russia has indicated it is actively considering deploying tactical nuclear weapons in Ukraine and has begun updating its protocol for the deployment of nuclear weapons alongside Belarus. The United States is of course preparing too for such an eventuality. Mutual trust between the United States on the one hand and Russia and China on the other is at a new low. For one, Beijing and Moscow understand that no US President can be immune to domestic politics, media narratives and public opinion polls. US policymakers likewise understand that neither the leader of Russia nor China would be willing to cede any ground to the United States.

There are signs that a renewed Cold War military competition has just restarted, and in this round, China has two important advantages. The military-industrial complex in China is state-led, and thus, is more efficient than private arms manufacturers in the United States that have gotten used to gorging on the federal budget (via lobbyists and delivering variants of systems that are often redundant and/or require numerous upgrades). Second, on a parity basis, China achieves much more for every dollar spent compared to the United States. Today, China has very quickly built a slate of hypersonic missiles capable of hitting the west coast of the United States that allied forces cannot intercept. The PLA has also established stealth bombers and fighter regiments that can defend China in a Taiwan or South China Sea confrontation, and is on track to field three aircraft carriers that would (attempt to) deny US forces into the first island chain. It is estimated that at least two additional aircraft carriers are planned. All these plans are not empty talk—and the United States understands this too well. Most analysts in the West would agree that China has the industrial capabilities to shore up its defence needs, regardless of what they say about China's economy today. What is truly worrying is the speed by which the PRC can build these capacity, and this will in turn sparked a similar trend with the United States and her allies, subject to their ability to pay and manufacture of course. Russia has, by now, massively restarted its military-industrial complex to ensure that the logistics nightmare faced in the Ukraine crisis does not repeat itself. Moscow also assists North Korea with ballistic missile technologies that Pyongyang needs to strike Japan, South Korea, and the United States. Russia has also invigorated a version of the alliance agreement that DPRK had signed with the USSR in 1962. In 2024, North Korea has effectively deployed troops to the Kursk region of Russia, creating different concerns for the United States, South Korea and Japan. The participation of DPRK elite troops has direct operation repercussions for South Korea as this is the first time North Korea's troops are gaining direct experience of the modern battlefield. However, one should not be surprised by this development, given that South Korea and Japan have become NATO's partners in the Indo-Pacific. Going forward, such actions would increasingly tie Asian security to European security.

The United States has asked all of Europe to continually help channel aid via the United States to Ukraine (minimum spending of two per cent), and the Biden administration had been increasingly raising the stakes by sending higher calibre weapons to Ukraine. In Asia, the US alliance structure is reinforced by US allies and partners spending record amounts of money importing US weaponry. Japan is now spending two per cent of its GDP, while Singapore has announced that they will spend three per cent on their GDP on defence, all ardent expressions of faith and reverence of the US presence in Asia, and in reality, increasing the geopolitical insurance premium that has Washington underwriting their security. This reflects an increased understanding that conscious strategic choices need to be made based on geopolitical alignment. There are increased discussions of multilateral cooperation at every level between the United States and its allies and partners, and one can surely expect the same between China, Russia and their partners too. If we were not on the way to a renewed Cold War a few years ago, we are today for sure. Great Power rivalry is driving the old Cold War blocs to be rejuvenated through US efforts to contain China or converse China's efforts to overcome US hegemony.

This book therefore argues that for much of the past three decades, it has been erroneous to assume that the Cold War was over. The Cold War, in fact very much alive, was just being set aside in an environment where political leadership sought to work together to improve the well-being of their people's lives. In the post-USSR world, five communist regimes remained (PRC, North Korea, Vietnam, Laos, and Cuba), with only Cuba outside of Asia. Approximately 1.5 billion people in Asia live in Communist countries, where they experience the realities of the Cold War in their everyday lives. This constitutes a little more than one-fifth of humanity. The Korean DMZ, Taiwan Straits, and monuments in Hanoi and Ho Chi Minh City are everyday reminders that the Cold War is very much alive in this part of the world. Despite the fact that the PRC, Vietnam, North Korea, and Laos have relations with the United States, none of these Communist Parties are "gamed" enough to ever have admitted that the Cold War was over just because the CPSU had collapsed over three decades ago. The control that Communist Parties of these countries have on the peoples' everyday lives today are similar to what their grandparents experienced in the 1950s and 60s and what their parents experienced in the 1980s or 1990s. All these regimes have however undertaken market reforms to varying extents (even North Korea has adopted some changes) out of necessity.

Likewise, the institutions that the United States has kept alive in Asia and Europe do not reflect the end of the Cold War. The San Francisco System, where the United States maintains the wheel-and-spoke system of bilateral alliances designed for Cold War systemic security, and the North Atlantic Treaty Organisation (NATO) have all been rejuvenated. Both Russia and China today are being "hyped" as the enemies of the United States and her allies, and of democracy and freedom-loving people worldwide. It is hard to miss the political statements, diplomatic rhetoric and the constant signalling (whether intended or not) of military exhortations, combined exercises as well increased defence spending. Likewise, it is also hard to believe in proclamations of the "absence" of the Cold War. From the viewpoint of Russians and Chinese, the frequent political statements whether in Western or Japanese corporate or social media of how China and Russia are not "freedom-loving" people or are enemies of "democracy" suggest the Cold War ideological, identity and ideational divide is ever present. Today, as the United States government rally her allies and partners to enact sanctions and laws against Russia and China for the long list of "transgressions" to force commercial firms to divest and reinvest in allied countries to "secure" their supply chains, it is hard for many to believe the diplomatic rhetoric coming out of the White House. For China, Western (US)-led covert actions public narratives and foreign policy towards Hong Kong, Taiwan and Xinjiang as well as the struggle in international public opinion over Covid, trade and tech war have all but eliminated Chinese "doves" in government or party.

Why have we come to this point? Is it because as we are told in numerous editorials Russian leader Vladimir Putin or Chinese leader Xi Jinping are inherently power hungry and and that these authoritarian countries were keen on world domination? Here is a problem. Russia and China were never liberal democracies to begin with. These two states have always had authoritarian systems, had always had "issues" with human rights in the Western sense, and have their own way of choosing their leaders and laws that differ from the developed West. In fact, this is the situation with the majority of the countries around the world today. In Southeast Asia alone, out of the eleven countries, only two countries can proudly proclaim to be "liberal democracies" in the Western sense— Indonesia and Thailand, but even then their system are far from perfect if we use Western indicators to measure the extent of their political progress. There are always allegations of rampant corruption. Southeast Asia has also somewhat an illustrious history of praetorian intervention and coups, with a "live" ongoing one now evolving in Myanmar at the time of publication. Likewise one cannot say that democracy thrives in the Middle East, Latin America or Africa by any measure.

It is true, however, that China and Russia have grown more authoritarian since 2012, but this is partly because of worsening economic conditions, domestic political struggles, and external geopolitical dynamics, which accentuated the political longevity of current leaders. In short, the increase in authoritarianism does not tell the whole story of how we are coming to a redux of the Cold War. This book argues that for us to truly understand how we are getting there it is important to examine the dynamics of the events developing in the US, Australia, India and Japan to see how the global right has become a powerful force in these countries. The Quadrilateral Security Dialogue itself is an institutional mechanism that the political leaders of these countries have come up with. The Quad however is only a small manifestation of the larger political forces at work.

The global right politicians in these countries have cultivated a particular brand of identity politics and nationalistic discourse that relies heavily on Cold War narratives to maintain an upper hand in domestic politics and to mobilise support for their foreign policy blueprint against China.

CAPITALISTIC DISPARITY, DYSFUNCTIONAL POLITICS AND ECONOMIC DIFFICULTIES

We again have to return to the 1990s to understand how the domestic imperative for today's policy evolved in the Quad countries. As stated before, the era of hyper-globalisation in the 1990s drove cooperation between China, the United States and her allies saw them entering into a period of unprecedented prosperity. During this period, there was much discussion that states to curb their sovereign rights just as governments had to curb their presence if they wanted to thrive in such a world. The global flow of capital, the transmission of data, and the power of non-state actors, such as large global multinational companies, are often at odds with the rights and interests of sovereign states and a certain segment of society. This, of course, has a particular influence on political parties and politicians across all nation-states. Pro-business politicians and parties are often at an advantage in such a globalised world since they are often the best places to grow businesses and economies. The adoption of pro-capital and pro-business policy platforms has meant that even as the economy grows, the disparity within the country increases. These economic challenges are most pronounced in the developed West, the United States, Europe, and Japan, as well as in developing Asian countries such as China and India. Therefore, there is a need to constantly deliver economic results and resolve bread-and-butter issues within the country. After two decades of hyper-globalisation and capitalistic growth, the governments concerned face some aspects of economic malfeasance and economic disparity. More advanced countries such as the United States might face other challenges such as inner city decay, breaking infrastructure, stagnant wages, and dissatisfied populations. In the age of hugely overcompensated executives and underpaid and exploited labour in menial jobs, graduates face tough job markets, retirees face escalating healthcare and living costs and discontent brews.

These tough conditions are the natural consequences of capitalistic growth and the product of development brought about by years of unbridled globalisation. The aims of the capital and national governments are not the same. Today's Global Right conservatives capitalise on such sentiments and often claim to represent the oppressed and exploited masses, often seeking to cast blame on those who have designed the economic policies of the yesteryears. They often pledge to stop the very forces of unbridled globalisation and stop the unlimited freedom of movement, people, and goods/services, as if this might reverse the effects of capitalistic growth. Whether it is Japan, the US, India, or Australia, there are economic problems associated with unbridled capitalistic development that most people find worrying or disconcerting. Such domestic circumstances are often conducive to the fermentation of nationalistic sentiments and conservative politics.

For most of the world, the most spectacular economic success and beneficiary of this system is undoubtedly China. Whether it is the Liberal Democratic Party of Japan, Republican Party in the United States, Bharatiya Janata Party of India, or Liberal-National Coalition of Australia, the economic success of the Chinese Communist Party is hard to ignore or explain particularly when it comes to questions of poverty alleviation, social welfare, infrastructure development, or global influence. Rightly or wrongly, their domestic discussions often involve China. The leaders of these parties are often individuals with attributes that could best offer a narrative on what had happened and what might be the way forward.

Conservative Leaders, Innovative Campaigning and the Aggravation of the China Problem

Japan's Abe Shinzo is probably the most "genuine" conservative politician among the Quad leaders. Due to a mixture of family circumstances and personal political outlook, Abe's concern has always been about Japan's aspirations as a great power. To that extent, his entire political universe can be defined by two ideas: to stop China from becoming an eminent Asian power and to loosen the shackles of the Peace Constitution that the Americans have hoisted on the Japanese so that the nation would become great again. The obsession with China meant that Abe had designed his entire political agenda premised upon checking Chinese economic growth and military power, making his life's mission to bear Japan's resources and external alliances to this endeavour. His envision of Quad in his first term did not find resonance with the other leaders—not the United States' Barack Obama or Australian Kelvin Rudd, or for that matter India's

Manmohan Singh. These politicians of neo-liberal democratic persuasions believe deeply in international cooperation amidst globalisation and shared visions similar to their counterpart in China. The contestation of the Senkaku/Diaoyu Islands during the time the DPJ was in office finally put Abe in power, as the Japanese sought to elect a steady hand with a clear national security agenda to protect Japan's interests. This allowed Abe to not only become the longest serving Prime Minister in Japan, but his politics also had demonstrative effects for the rest of the global right. However, by 2012, as the domestic economic circumstances deteriorated in the Quad countries, contextualised against China's growth and success, Abe's agenda found widespread popularity in Japan.

In Australia, the rise of three Conservative Prime Ministers successively saw a radical reorientation of Australia's domestic priorities and foreign policy over the course of the same decade. Tony Abbott who admittedly acknowledged that he was an admirer of Japanese Prime Minister Shinzo Abe came to power in 2013. After six years in opposition, the Conservative Liberal Party of Australia was once again back in governance. The Conservatives had lost to Kevin Rudd because Rudd for the first time (since Paul Keating) was able to persuade the Australia public that the Labour Party was just as capable of handling National Security issues as well as the Conservatives. By articulating an agenda that heavily weighed on protecting Australian borders and capitalising against Labour's perceived close ties with China, the Conservatives managed to capitalise on souring sentiments at home to capture power. For the next decade, Conservative Prime Ministers Malcolm Turnbull and Scott Morrison began to mirror Liberal Democratic Party (LDP) politicians and politicise China-related projects as national security issues detrimental to Australia's national interests at home and abroad. The means of course pulling out the rug out from under Labour's pro-business orientation, and ensuring that any politician with any form of China- or Chinese-related linkages were scrutinized with suspicion and discredited, while those that had strong pro-American and pro-UK tendencies were the only people suited to look after Australia's national interests at home or abroad. One of the critical concerns was how China and Chinese business interests channelled their support to the Labour Party during the electoral process. By securitising support from these groups, the Liberal Party was able to obtain an upper hand in electoral politics.

Likewise, the Bharatiya Janata Party's Narendra Modi became Prime Minister in 2014. As a "fixer" for the militant Hindu nationalist organisation, Modi has spent years working in grassroots politics in opposition to the Indian National Congress before finally becoming Gujarat's Chief Minister. A devout Hindu nationalist who espouses majoritarian politics based on a social exclusion agenda which was very different from his Indian Congress Party's predecessors, Modi was able to capitalize on key sentiments on the ground that propelled his popularity. During his term as Gujarat's Chief Minister, he became widely associated with certain human rights abuses and was widely criticised for his role in the suppression of the 2002 Gujarat riots. Even though Modi did have personal diplomacy with Xi Jinping of China in earlier career (as Gujarat's Chief Minister) and early on in his term as Prime Minister, New Delhi's position shifted radically as Modi responded to overtures by Shinzo Abe and later Donald Trump to align India more closely with the Quad group against China. There are several important domestic forces at play, particularly because the BJP sought to hold onto its electoral majority and needed an alternate rallying point for domestic nationalism. Consequently, the Indians decided they have to seek Western investment and capital to increase manufacturing jobs to uplift India's economy and fulfil his electoral promises. The Global Rights' support for India's bilateral issues were important particularly as China was beginning to emerge as a power in India's sphere of influence. China became an important factor in India's domestic politics as it was tied to the BJP's Pakistan-Muslim problem and territorial disputes in the Himalayas.

If Shinzo Abe was the Global Right's ideologue and intellectual force behind the Quad, it was Donald Trump that operationalised the ideas of the Quad fully. Trump's proposal to Republican voters was that China was responsible for a host of economic ills that the United States was suffering from: Beijing was responsible for intellectual thefts, economic coercion, unfair trade practices, forced technology transfers, and the terrible deficit that the United States has accumulated. It is now wielding its massive dollar holdings with much influence in international affairs, such as embarking on a Marshall plan like grand vision of the "Belt and Road Initiative" aimed at "indebting" Third World countries. The United States needs to step up to defend freedom and democracy, which essentially means taking on China. Trump had followed through on his campaign promises to bring back manufacturing and bring back jobs to the United States. His White House initiated the trade and tech war against China, backed Abe's ideas, and operationalised them fully by getting the Quad to come together for a variety of initiatives at various levels. From Covid diplomacy to securing the supply chain to conducting drills, the Quad is slowly being operationalised into an institutionalised form with partners and observers.

Thus, in Quad countries, national security has become an important key to political rhetoric and campaign strategy in Japan, the US, Australia and India. For all these Global Right conservatives, there is no threat greater than China. For Trump, his message to the Republicans was this: taking China down would somehow reduce the US deficit, bring jobs back, protect US intellectual property and reduce income inequality. What he was essentially railing at was the effects of capitalism, even though he associates China with these ills. His rhetoric promised to make all his Republican voters going through hard times "whole" again. For the Conservatives in Japan, Australia and India, it was about protecting democracy and freedoms and the preservation of their way of lives and values. Collectively they would for their own reasons want to work with the United States to protect and ensure a "free and open" Indo-Pacific and a "rules-based order world". This narrative and language emanated out of Abe's initial thinking and is reminiscent of the Cold War narratives of the yesteryears.

The only problem is that all the leaders here (Abe, Trump, Modi, Morrison, etc) are certainly not your run-of-the-mill liberal democrats. If anything they all appeared to share commonalities with China's Xi Jinping and Russia's Vladimir Putin when it came to their impulses to hold onto power and suppress any challengers with alternate visions. Unfortunately, most of these Quad politicians cannot do it as effectively as Xi or Putin. For Shinzo Abe, whose anti-China views bordered on religiosity, encircling China with the Quad would help preserve Japan's pre-eminence status and status as the single most important power in the region. It would also bind the United States tightly to Japan and facilitate Washington's willingness to support Japan's rearmament and Abe's plan to enact Constitution revision. This strategy is in fact what Gorbachev undid through his Vladivostok speech, and enabled Sino-Soviet détente to develop. For Modi, it would appeared that taking on China would help backstop New Delhi's plans to balance China's strategic and economic encroachment into the Indian Ocean and Himalayas through its BRI initiatives, economic asymmetry and increased military moves. Both Abe and Mod saw that increased multilateral engagement via the Quad would also add another tier of support in their respective territorial struggle with China. For Australian conservatives, stopping China was seen as essential to prevent Beijing from buying Australia's strategic assets (such as ports and cattle farms) and protecting Australia's way of life from foreign interference. All these leaders made campaigning on national security a premium method to ensure that any party who campaigned otherwise would be seen as "traitors" to the nationalistic cause. The rise of these global right-conservative leaders has a few common features since the first few of these politicians (Shinzo Abe and his predecessor Junichiro Koizumi) provided the demonstrative methodological gains for all those that came after. Today, we see William Lai and Bongbong Marcos Junior using the same strategy in Taiwan and Philippines' domestic politics.

These Conservative leaders understood the polity's admiration for strong leaders. They speak in liberal rhetoric, but the essence of their messages is always about the preservation of the past, of defending values and their nation's way of life. These leaders exemplify their strength through the articulation of a "clear" enemy in this case often China, and signify their common purpose and endeavour in partaking in alliance activities to defend freedom and democracy. Domestically, corporate and social media facilitate efforts that helped in the competitive demonisation of China, providing a clear and constant message to the electorate that there is extreme value in hedging against and containing China. The "free" flow of information on social media and catchy headline posts of corporate media is almost always sensational, and is certainly almost never "neutral". Beyond the fact that social media often carries factually erroneous articles, there is the conflation of facts, interpretations, and deliberately sown fake news which is often reinforced by inherent bias. Needless to say, people in India, Australia and Japan all utilised popular American social media apps and often get their news from US and Western outlets. One should not be surprised that public opinion in these countries is often aligned. While it is true that the system is open and free, it is also true that vicious partisan politics and bigoted leaders often thrive in such an environment. The implicit use of racism to taint the political opposition or anyone who argues against their messaging, of being a "traitor" to the nation is probably the singular weapon in the arsenal of these politicians.

The Strategic Need for Re-balancing and the Strengthening of the San Francisco System

Regardless of what role these politicians say China plays in their domestic politics, the fact that all four countries are affected strategically by the rise of China in at least three ways. First, as Beijing's economic clout grows and military strength increases, the capabilities of the Global Right Quad countries have decreased correspondingly in relation to those of China. Beijing has cultivated significant ties with US, Japan, Australia and even India suggesting that the independency between their country and China would create constraints on what they can do to China even as they seek to "de-risk" or "decouple". Even as the Quad countries are effectively trying to do what Gorbachev had undone in 1987 i.e. to "encircle" China from the West, East and South, it is abundantly clear that China has broken out of their attempts. By securitising the relations with China, the Quad is sending a message that national security triumphs everything else.

Second, for Australia, India, and Japan, China's growing clout has intruded into their respective spheres of influence. Whether it is the Pacific Island Nations, South Asia and the Himalayas or Southeast Asia, Canberra, New Delhi and Tokyo's influence in these spheres respectively has been reduced vis-à-vis China. Beijing has cultivated extremely asymmetric economic relations with many of these nations across these regions which have been the "traditional" backward of these nations. This is not only just a case of China coming to influence the smaller countries in these respective areas but often Beijing is "invited" by these countries to balance against perceived threats of these smaller countries. Think Myanmar and Cambodia in Southeast Asia, Pakistan, Sri Lanka and Maldives in South Asia, or Solomon Islands in the South Pacific.

For the United States, Beijing's economic clout is starting to erode the effective functioning of its San Francisco System in Asia and affect its interests in Europe, the Americas, Africa, and the Middle East. It has now increasingly difficult for the United States to lobby any government to act (even its closest Asian allies Japan or South Korea) to act against China should US–China relations deteriorate sharply. Notwithstanding China's military prowess, Beijing's economic influence is far too great for US allies not to feel its influence. The Chinese economy has grown too connected, important and influential for economies and daily lives of the people in these countries. Whether it is drones or component parts for their planes and missiles or medical supplies such as masks or respirators or the millions of different consumer products, none of these countries are capable of manufacturing everything by themselves. At the same time, there is a growing consensus among the people that they should not act as proxies to fight China on the behalf of the United States. The good news for the United States however is that the converse is true for Beijing too. Most Asian countries are reluctant to give up their ties with the United States even if they trade with Beijing. The reality is that most countries just want cordial relations with both China and the United States.

Third, there are concerns regarding the rise of China as a true blue military power, one that is seen as increasingly capable of defeating the United States in the Western Pacific. This is probably the most worrying aspect for Quad countries. Recent War Games conducted by CSIS and other think tanks, such as RAND conclude that in most scenarios, China will emerge victorious if the United States and China engage in military hostilities. While each of the Quad countries has its own domestic political circumstances with corresponding electorate preferences and leadership outlook to embrace conservatism, an all-out war between China and the United States is not something that they desire. The dangers of entanglement and entrapment are all too real and in reality too costly for any nation to get involved. The capabilities of China's Air force, Navy and Nuclear force have improved tremendously over the past decade to the extent that it is now capable of taking on the United States. The PRC has become so powerful that the United States fears that the San Francisco System is no longer effective or efficient enough to balance against or contain the People's Republic. China is now therefore threatening the smooth functioning of US-led bilateral architecture in the Asia-Pacific region. Of the Quad members, this is probably more worrying for Japan than Australia or India. The problem is that China's growing power is not something that can be wished or that will go away. Beijing for one would never intentionally retard its growth just to make any country feel "safe". Similarly, Beijing should also not expect Washington or Tokyo to stop doing things to disrupt its growth and ascendance. For China, the Quad represents the first formal attempt to address this by ensuring that China is "encircled" to the West, East, and South. This of course was the brainchild of Japanese Prime Minister Shinzo Abe. By 2017, the Quad countries brought India into the picture, and the term Indo-Pacific diluted both the centrality and the importance of "China" (as opposed to

Asia-Pacific). The Global Right's policies have increased China's insecurities to the extent that the entire nation has rallied around Xi's government to ensure that Beijing becomes an innovative military power over the course of the last decade. There is therefore an urgent need for Washington to reduce the reliance of her allies on China, and rejuvenate the San Francisco system at least to prevent it from becoming ineffective. For the United States to counter and combat China in the Indo-Pacific, her allies must first and foremost be willing to politically stand by US goals and actions. The Global Rights efforts therefore aims to keep the alliance right politically by invoking the notion of a community of "like-minded" partners who share "similar values" against those who are not "like-minded" and who do not share common values.

TRAJECTORY FOR COLD WAR REDUX

The problem however is that since the rapprochement and normalisation of US–China relations in the 1970s, Beijing has actually become a de facto (rather than de jure) partner of the US and her allies in resisting the USSR. After the demise of Mao, Beijing focused on growing its economy and improving the lives of its people, becoming an important component in the US-led system in the Cold War. To that end, the US, Japan, Australia, Europe, and the rest of the world have acknowledged, cooperated, and gained from working and trading with China. The exigencies of today's geopolitics meant that these global rights needed to explain why today is so different from previous times. Using the Cold War rhetoric helps domestically, but it is less than convincing to many who do not live in the Quad countries. This comes at a period when China's worldwide importance has grown substantially and has good ties with many countries around the world. Today, for both political and economic most countries (regardless of US allies or not) would like to cultivate good relations with China. The reason is simple: Beijing has little interest (yet) in regime change or domestic interference and seems to be wholly focused on economic growth, trading and poverty alleviation. Their cheap consumer goods and BRI projects have actually helped many developing countries. For this reason, the China model is appealing to many countries around the world as well as in Asia.

The United States today would find it difficult to balance China with its alliances alone. To protect and preserve her own (US) pre-eminence and status, China's economic growth and political influence worldwide must be scaled down. In fact, if anything, the banishment of PRC is vital to the San Francisco system, since if left unchecked, PRC might actually become more influential than the United States within the system. There is therefore a need to increase the number of groupings that the United States can mobilise under different scenarios to act against China. The scholars have termed these "mini-lateralisms" of which Quad is one. There is AUKUS where Australia is hedging onto the United Kingdom and United States to provide it with nuclear submarines, as well as attempts by South Korea and Japan to engage and bring NATO into the region. The call for "decoupling" and now "derisking" stemmed from this logic. The United States and its allies have found it almost impossible to decouple. Even though US trade with China decreased sharply in the aftermath of Trump's actions, the US deficit still increased sharply as America imported more from other countries. Today, the Biden continues this trend with the "small yard high fence" strategy to enforce the trade and tech war against China in the fields of semi-conductors, quantum computing and artificial intelligence. This would likely to continue in the post Biden era. The gamble that the tech and trade war will diminish China's capabilities and momentum does not seem to be paying off. Where do we go from here then? It is unclear what a US victory over China in the Tech and Trade war would look like. Would this mean a Chinese capitulation to agree to accepting US tariffs or having its economic growth impeded and stagnate?

Today, the policies instituted by Trump (first term) and Abe are still in force despite the change in leadership. Biden had largely kept Trump's policies on the Tech and Trade War, just as Kishida had promised to continue Abe's visions and policies. India's Modi on his third term is seeking to mend fences with China even though Sino-Indian relations are still difficult. Only Australia's Labour Prime Anthony Albanese has eased off the rhetoric against China that his Conservative predecessors used and restored trade. This however has not prevented Australia from participating in US-led freedom of navigation sailings in the South China Sea. Whether China overtakes the United States as the number economy in the world or not, US efforts to helm China in would not detract from Beijing's increasing importance in global affairs or the determination of the Chinese people to seek a higher plane of development and better their lives.

Given the through-the-roof inflation and US debt challenges, it is not even clear if the United States could be held to account for its promises to her allies in the event of a Taiwan or South China Sea contingency. During the early Cold War, the United States intervened in the Korean War and the Vietnam Wars, and in both scenarios the United States did not emerge victorious against China, which was then poor, economically backward and technologically challenged. Today's China is a peer competitor that is much better armed, and backed with an industrial capacity that has little historical parallel.

Likewise in the Ukraine conflict today, it is unclear whether there is more than what the United States can do for Ukraine beyond rallying NATO against Russia and selling arms in this conflict. China of course has its own economic challenges as always. Assuming China's economic growth is jeopardised and becomes politically unstable, would this scenario be better for Beijing's trading partners and Asian neighbours? It is unlikely that an angry and unstable China would be better off for her neighbours than a rich and prosperous one with a lot to lose. Those that advocate "decoupling" or "derisking" they are probably are not aware of the terrible pain this would have for their own country's economies. While indeed the "high fence, small yard" might be a feasible strategy, it is unclear if that is enough to stop the Chinese from technological breakthroughs.

As United States steps up its support for Ukraine, Taiwan and Philippines, such policy is driving China and Russia closer than ever before. The developments in Ukraine have driven the China–Russia partnership to the highest point ever in their recent history. They are not only cooperating in bilateral terms to defeat US sanctions on Russia but are actually taking measures to undermine US economic power through their de-dollarisation drive, building alternate institutions such as BRICs and SCO. China has stepped up its collaboration with Russia even as it strove to improve its global image and linkages with Europe, the Middle East and Africa all the while trying to overcome its economic difficulties at home. It is building up its military in a way the world has not witnessed in recent history. China appears to be planning for a fleet of six modern aircraft carriers by 2035, and has made headway in various advanced military technologies such as stealth fighters, AI-assisted drone fleets and AI enabled stealth warships of varying sizes that are extremely concerning to US and Japanese strategists. It is now the only country constructing a space station that has tremendous military applications along with its independent Beidou navigation system. The rapid build-up of such actual capabilities is making many nations in Asia nervous even as the United States and her allies try to rachet up the pressure on Beijing. In the case of Taiwan for instance, there are now open calls for the United States to shift its position away from "strategic ambiguity" by openly declaring its support for Taiwan's independence movement and for Taiwan to be incorporated as a NATO partner just like South Korea and Japan. Collectively, the United States and Japan are now lobbying for the Quad countries to cooperate at various levels to balance and nullify the power China has over various countries through its cultivation of asymmetrical economic relations. The idea of zero balancing sounds fabulous, but as with many other concepts, it is easier said than done. Going forward, the question for all countries in the region is whether these efforts to "balance" China are indeed paying off or alternatively, are they escalating tensions and creating a downward security spiral for regional security.

In order to resist the US economic and tech war, Beijing has undertaken defensive measures as it emerged out of the Covid pandemic to protect herself, by re-emphasising two elements that China considered important for her "internal circulation strategy. The first is to grow domestic firms to become dominant in the domestic market, and the second is for domestic companies to become self-reliant on technological innovation. Once these companies are able to achieve overwhelming superiority in terms of achieving market share by offering quality products at very good pricing, this would put them in good stead. This is known in China as "internal circulation". When Chinese companies could effectively compete abroad, this would allow them to achieve a certain measure of dominance in the global marketplace. For the Chinese, this is known as "external circulation'. Collectively this is known as the "dual circulation" strategy. Protectionism might shield US companies in their own markets, but it does not protect American companies in the global market. Already we are seeing the effects of Chinese EV (such as BYD) and telecommunication companies (such as Huawei) emerge globally across different markets with very good results. They are very competitive globally because these companies had in fact faced fierce domestic competition in China's large market and emerged with winning products before going abroad. China and Russia have very good relations with third-world countries in Central and South America, Africa, and the Middle East and likely have an advantage over the US in these areas for historical reasons. Using "national security" to try and secure markets would most likely fail, as market logic and consumer preferences often hinges on product usability, reliability and value other than on security. China's strategy ahead would no doubt ensure that it does not get into any military adventures which may threaten to "derail". Again for the wider Asian region, how would this affect regional economies and the lives of people living in the region?

To be sure, Russia and China have grown more authoritarian over the decade, but so have the Quad countries with the rise of the Global Right. While the US and her staunch allies appeared to be making preparations for a showdown with both Russia and China, Moscow and Beijing are tightening cooperation and undertaking intensive preparations for further conflict even as the Ukraine conflict and Israel-Hamas war rage on. Russia and China are employing various means to weaken the United States, including the establishment of trading partnerships with various countries premised on local currencies, the substitution of holdings of US Treasury Bonds with gold, and intensifying military cooperation that includes technology transfers to enhance each other's fighting capability. To prepare and fight a war, a nation would need resources, manpower and money. In that respect, China and Russia appear to have plenty of both. Moscow and Beijing is now trying to balance the influence of the US dollar in the international economic and finance system, and the US dominance in international public opinion.

There are other important strategies that China and Russia could but are unlikely to undertake. The first addresses the structural impediments that inhibit openness, debate, and feedback, which would enable them to make better policies. Due to their own responses to Western countries' narratives and information warfare, the regimes in Moscow and Beijing have always naturally been to use censorship to blackout information and propagate. This has become an important handicap in China's and Russia's systems. (This however doesn't mean that the US and her allies don't do the same but their methodology in public diplomacy is way more sophisticated). The strength of the US system is its openness for debate and the freedoms that people enjoy. Currently neither Russia nor China matches this. The PRC is losing this dimension of the "information" struggle as its internal system is handicapped. China's system inhibits ordinary Chinese people from engaging with Western traditional and social media and debating the merits or from making perfectly good arguments that might not jar squarely with official government policy. Of course, it can be argued that people could climb the Great Firewall. The thing is this: if you are as strong as you say you are, there is definitely no need to build a wall. This situation has also led to the PRC's voice being censored internationally. PRC's official channels are heavily censored in the West, particularly on social and corporate media. This also means that the PRC's presence and representation in civil societies in Quad countries are heavily circumscribed. This discrimination is structural because the West argues that since the PRC is censoring them, they should not expect to have a free hand in Western societies. China's response has thus far been defensive and rhetorical. Beijing needs to cultivate world-class companies not only in the manufacturing sector but also in the information, entertainment, and culture industries if it wants to be taken seriously globally. This is the reason why TikTok has therefore now become the latest target in US efforts to eradicate a perceived "propaganda" front for Beijing and Moscow.

The key to combating propaganda and lies is always openess, and to showcase the reality. China (and Russia) needs to take this seriously so that it would be easier to combat hatred, bias, and propaganda. Central to this is that there should be domestic reforms with regard to ensuring that bias, corruption and human rights abuses are eradicated. International criticisms should be taken seriously rather than swept under the carpet. China's recent wave of unilateral visa waivers for selected countries is a good start, but more needs to be done. In addition, the Chinese government needs to ensure a more accountable and responsive governance is put in place and to build corresponding structures to increase its soft power and messaging ability worldwide to have a better understanding of its circumstances. China should also try to build bridges with her neighbours, particularly Japan and India to reduce tensions. Their concerns must be taken seriously and addressed. There is also a need to keep communications open, particularly when times are tough rather than resort to unilateral policies that sanction or punish the partner country concerned (such as Australia). To that end, soft power approaches rather than hard power threats might work better for China's Asian neighbours.

From the eyes of those with vested interest in tensions and conflict, be it the military-industrial complex, arms lobby-funded "think tanks", the intelligence services or those that benefit from the prospecting raw materials or rebuilding of war-torn cities, a new Cold War might sound like exciting prospects. Such thinking however might backfire. At the rate China is modernising its military, it might lead to a different strategic calculus for countries in the region. The American expectation is that countries would naturally lean towards the US bilateral alliance in the region, but unless the United States can convincingly assure the region that it pays off to do so, this might not happen. Countries such as Japan and South Korea might decide to go nuclear especially if Russia arms North Korea, and ASEAN might decide to distance itself from the United States strategically if they feel that US policies harm their well-being. Certainly, for the majority of Asian people who prefer peace and prosperity in the mundane sense, a Cold War in the region would only devastate our lives as we know it. Be it the freedom to travel and work, the ability to learn cross-culturally, and to engage with friends and family all across the world, those who have lived through the 1950s to the 1990s would have remembered what the Cold War meant. It is important to recognise what this might mean for Asia before we follow the Pied Piper down the drain.

As of 2024, we are slowly and surely moving into a major conflict that would divide the world. Donald Trump's strong electoral mandate means a few things going forward. The 2.0 Trump Administration, packed with Trump loyalists is going to bring the United States into more political turmoil as it declares war on the "Deep State" to make the US government "leaner", more efficient and effective. This White House is more unlikely to compromise, given that it is Trump's second term and that the Republican have seized control of Congress and Senate for 2025. In order to rejuvenate the US economy, Trump would likely try and extract concessions out of everyone, friend or foe, ally or enemy. All the stress on better government efficiency and effectiveness would contribute to a United States much stronger and meaner than before, as Washington readies to fight a war with China, the country that Trump considers most threatening to US pre-eminence and hegemony globally. At a minimum, the Trade and Tech War is here to stay. Trump would also likely try and extract more concessions from its allies and partners in East Asia, and ensure that the countries reduce their economic engagement with China. This is already creating problems for many companies—such as Samsung, TSMC Apple, not to mention many other Chinese companies. This would be problematic for almost all the countries in the region, especially those that rely on free trade—as their economic lifelines are intimately connected with the Chinese economy and the American liberal order. When nations such as the East Asian states who rely on the United States for security and China for economic growth are told (or nudged) by Washington and Beijing to do diametrically different things, domestic turmoil would ensue. In short, the onset of a renewed Cold War would create an impossible situation for them. Even though political narratives in everyday narratives might "deny" that a renewed Cold War is brewing, unless something is done at the highest political level, the world will gradually be forced to coalesce into three groups. One would be led by the United States and her allies, and the other by China and Russia, with the rest of the world coexisting in the third. Great Power rivalry and geopolitical competition dressed in the language of identity will drive us towards a redux of the Cold War. Even if the Great Power rivalry did not start out as a Cold War, once we adopt the mantle of an "across the nation" effort to jointly label a country as the "enemy" and join blocs and target the country unconditionally, we will end up living the realities of a renewed Cold War based on ideological fault lines. This is simply because we have made up our mind that the "opposite" side is inherently evil, and adamant to prevent the rise of a "free and open" Indo-Pacific because they do not share our "values". The strange thing is that people who often articulate such views are people who have little real-world experience of what living on the "other side" is actually like. The astonishing number of people who are moved or affected by these messages on social media or the news cannot be underestimated. What is more worrying is the number of intellectuals who for various reasons are going along with the prevalent populist thinking. In strategic studies and international relations, the concept of "balancing" should be interpreted as being "flexible" both ways. The US strategic community has always tried to make the case that China should be balanced against—whether one is concerned with China's growing power or as a growing menace (threat). The rhetoric however should be taken with a pinch of salt—given that the United States has defined China has its most threatening peer competitor. We should always be conscious about how we get our knowledge of who friends are and who our enemies are, just as we should be very clear eye when parties approach with offers of help to balance or counter other parties. The pertinent question for regional countries should be this: why should a nation expend blood and treasure to help another nation balance or confront a third country? As long as we do not take stock of where we are heading, we will probably end up living in a strange world with bifurcated globalisation as the US bloc and the China–Russia bloc tries to intensify and build their economies based on their respective narratives and agenda. Without due care, we might find our circumstances change very quickly and probably for the worse. There is no question that we are "now back to the future" of seeing our world divide again. That is

408 V. TEO

unless we are wise enough to take a good hard look at ourselves and resist those who profess to be acting for our benefit when they are actually not.

References

Lee Gary, Gorbachev Makes Overture to Asia, The Washington Post, 2 August 1986

Stoecker, Sally, Clients and Commitments: Soviet-Vietnamese Relations 1978-1988, California, Santa Monica: RAND, 1989

The White House, Readout of President Joe Biden's Meeting with President Xi Jinping of the People's Republic of China, 14 November 2022, https://www.whitehouse.gov/briefing-room/statements-releases/2022/11/14/readout-of-president-joe-bidens-meeting-with-president-xi-jinping-of-the-peoples-republic-of-china/#:~:text=President%20Joseph%20R.,across%20a%20range%20of%20issues.

McDonnell, Stephen, Balloon saga deflates efforts to mend US-China relations, 6 February 2023, https://www.bbc.com/news/world-asia-china-64529922

INDEX

A

Abbott, Tony, 5, 13, 19, 50, 60, 62, 222, 224, 227–232, 234, 236, 237, 239, 241–243, 258–260, 263, 264, 273, 275, 280, 281, 284, 286, 394

Abe, Shinzo, 5–7, 10, 11, 13, 18, 19, 26, 34, 35, 39, 50–52, 54, 56, 57, 63, 64, 70, 73, 75, 77, 78, 81–83, 85, 87, 88, 91, 97, 99, 104, 105, 107, 108, 124, 148, 159, 168, 173, 183, 185, 223, 224, 231, 265, 279, 280, 312–315, 328, 358, 394–397, 399

Administration

  Biden, 37, 107, 154, 191, 194–197, 389

  Clinton, 68, 134, 164, 165

  Obama, 35, 36, 97, 129, 136, 139, 153, 156, 158–160, 170, 177, 280, 281, 342

  Trump, 35, 36, 38, 99, 104, 107–109, 148, 149, 174, 176, 182, 185, 186, 188, 189, 239, 240, 263, 282, 357, 358

Aksai Chin, 335, 336, 346, 347, 349, 360

alliance, 1, 14, 20, 22–28, 30, 34, 36–38, 56–59, 61, 62, 67–70, 77, 79, 81, 88, 90, 91, 94, 96–98, 101, 102, 104, 106, 111, 126, 133, 156, 158, 160, 161, 165, 174, 187, 195, 197, 222, 225, 230, 234, 235, 243, 268, 269, 271–274, 280, 285, 286, 336, 356, 357, 361, 381, 385, 387, 389, 390, 393, 397, 400, 405

animosity, 37, 125, 143, 236

antagonistic press, 29

anti-China

  policy, 4, 8

  rhetoric, 8, 36, 37

  sentiments, 6, 13, 36, 81, 168

ANZUS Treaty, 220, 243, 268, 269

Arbott, Tony, 10

410 INDEX

Arunachal Pradesh, 334, 336, 346, 347, 350, 352
assertiveness, 133, 157, 169, 348
asymmetric (asymmetricity), 11, 14, 23, 89, 183, 271, 339, 398
AUKUS, 279, 284–287, 401
authoritarianism, 3, 152, 380, 391
autocracy, 18, 54

B

bandwagon, 3, 11, 256, 286, 359
Beidou, 24, 402
Biden, Joe, 4, 36, 151, 153, 154, 189, 191, 194, 195, 287, 359, 365, 387, 401
bilateral
  conflict, 80
  consensus, 399
  relationship, 3, 68, 185
BJP (Bharatiya Janata Party), 39, 307–312, 316–322, 324–327, 329–331, 333, 341–344, 350, 393, 395
border, 20, 34, 37, 39, 40, 140, 163, 164, 270, 322, 323, 331, 334–336, 346, 348, 350, 351, 355, 360, 362, 383
BRI (Belt Road Initiative), 28, 40, 42, 169–172, 183, 276, 322, 330, 331, 341, 351, 353–355, 363–365, 396, 400
BRICS (Brazil, Russia, India, China, South Africa), 314, 357, 362, 363, 402
bullying, 2, 151, 169, 184, 240

C

campaign, 5, 20, 38, 72, 81, 85, 87, 88, 107, 126, 128–130, 132, 133, 135, 141–144, 147, 148, 157, 166, 172, 176, 177, 193,

234, 237, 281, 310, 313, 316, 319, 325, 326, 356, 358, 387, 395, 396
capabilities
  industrial, 389
  manufacturing, 23
  military, 96, 98, 157
charismatic, 13, 18, 20, 64, 158, 221, 222, 313, 342
China
  aggressiveness, 13, 80, 175
  assertiveness, 13, 169
  policy, 5, 11, 13, 38, 42, 91, 153, 221, 224, 239, 333, 360
  threat, 10, 12, 20, 31, 34, 36, 58, 85, 87, 158, 255, 259, 279, 282, 338, 363, 385
climate change, 5, 31, 229, 238, 264, 277
Clinton, Bill, 89, 142
Clinton, Hillary, 37, 125, 127, 128, 138, 141, 143, 146, 156
comfort women, 53, 54, 76, 106
confrontation, 27, 28, 37, 39, 41, 95, 96, 98, 100, 102, 106, 132–134, 152, 157–160, 167, 180, 197, 314, 331, 336, 345, 347, 348, 352, 382, 388
Congress, 41, 54, 137, 152, 153, 287, 311, 316, 318, 323, 329, 345, 348, 356, 362, 386
conservatism
  conservatives, 6, 7, 10, 11, 13, 17–20, 28, 32–34, 37–40, 50, 52, 54, 70, 73, 79, 95, 97, 125, 126, 129, 149, 155, 161, 177, 191, 224, 227, 232, 236, 237, 242, 264, 274, 285, 320, 393, 397
  neo, 34, 50, 126
  new, 7, 35, 86, 88
  state, 388

INDEX 411

ultra, 50, 161
containment strategy, 102
Covid
  pandemic, 6, 22, 31, 107, 110,
    153, 176, 189, 191, 193, 238,
    240, 262, 277, 282, 345, 358,
    365, 403
  vaccine, 191, 192, 194
CPEC (China-Pakistan Economic
  Corridor), 351
CPTPP (Comprehensive and
  Progressive Agreement for
  Trans-Pacific Partnership), 109

D

decoupling, 2, 23, 109, 110, 153,
  154, 195, 283, 381, 401, 402
defensive weapons, 388
deficit, 23, 36, 136, 141, 181, 184,
  186, 195, 326, 365, 395, 396,
  401
Democratic
  base, 230
  party, 19, 37, 53, 85, 125, 127,
    129, 137, 139–141, 144, 154,
    198, 244
  politics, 140, 147
departure, 153, 230, 258
derisking, 283, 381, 401, 402
development, 1, 2, 7, 13, 14, 18,
  20–22, 26, 28, 29, 31, 32, 37,
  41, 50, 59, 65, 68, 74, 77, 84,
  89, 109, 110, 123, 156, 166,
  170, 171, 173, 174, 176, 182,
  187, 191, 193, 277, 284, 307,
  308, 310, 311, 313, 314, 317,
  321, 324, 327, 334, 339–341,
  343, 348, 349, 353, 355, 358,
  363, 365, 384, 385, 392, 393,
  401
  assistance, 103, 278
  narrative, 110

diplomacy
  vaccine, 154, 191, 194, 196, 365
  values-based, 58, 62
  wolf-warrior, 107
discrimination, 238, 245, 257, 318,
  319, 405
disparity, 14, 15, 22, 32, 40, 66, 67,
  94, 136, 155, 169, 264, 316,
  317, 324, 328, 329, 392
distributive justice, 320, 326
Doklam, 347–349, 362
DPJ (Democratic Party of Japan), 82,
  86, 393
DPRK (Democratic People's Republic
  of Korea), 81, 90, 105, 106,
  132, 162, 177–180, 389

E

economic challenges, 58, 392, 402
economic clout, 103, 110, 171, 172,
  255, 398
elections, 2, 10, 19, 36, 51, 53, 57,
  72, 81, 82, 84, 85, 87, 89, 91,
  103, 104, 125, 130, 133, 137,
  138, 140, 141, 143, 145, 146,
  153, 221, 222, 224–226, 228,
  241, 262, 265, 266, 268, 270,
  274, 278, 281, 312, 316, 317,
  320, 323, 325, 331, 334, 344,
  356, 357
establishment, 8, 14, 19, 39, 64, 70,
  73, 78, 83, 87, 89, 99, 125, 130,
  132, 133, 138, 140, 141, 144,
  145, 148, 149, 156, 160, 171,
  175, 180, 182, 186, 220, 228,
  233, 239, 253, 281, 310, 313,
  317, 349, 363, 404
exclusive economic zone (EEZ), 90

F

factionalism, 70

412 INDEX

foreign interference, 177, 235, 257, 262, 263, 266, 397

G

generation
postwar, 49, 66, 308
wealth, 69
genros, 53, 78
geopolitical, 7, 14, 29, 35, 40, 41, 172, 184, 220, 322, 328, 333, 339, 353, 354, 381, 386, 387, 389, 391, 407
globalisation, 5, 12, 136, 137, 265, 324, 326, 345, 381, 384, 392–394, 407
global right
agenda, 15, 130, 144
movement, 109
politics, 5
GPS (Global Positioning Satellite System), 24
Great Power
rivalry, 8, 10, 11, 20, 172, 197, 199, 381, 385, 390, 407
status, 161, 331, 360
struggle, 196

H

Hatoyama, Yukio, 78, 82, 91, 251
Hawke, Bob, 247, 248, 270
hedge, 80, 164, 227, 283, 355, 363
high-tech, 21, 186, 187, 330, 361
Himalayas, 39, 40, 307, 309, 328, 334, 339, 341, 345, 346, 356, 395, 396, 398
Hindutva, 311, 321, 327, 342
history, 2, 5, 37, 39, 53, 54, 56, 57, 60, 65, 68, 77, 78, 88, 91, 101, 103, 107, 132, 144, 159, 160, 164, 167, 169, 178, 190, 191, 193, 222, 223, 225, 231, 233,

239, 248, 249, 257, 270, 273, 279, 281, 314, 316, 320–322, 332, 357, 359, 360, 382, 384, 391, 402
historical revisionism, 91, 160, 161
masochistic, 77, 81
Huawei, 187, 188, 228, 258, 259, 281, 403
human rights, 4, 27, 41, 156, 163, 174–177, 220, 221, 226, 228, 240, 242, 246–250, 255, 258, 271, 282, 285, 286, 314, 345, 359, 387, 391, 395, 405
hypersonic missile, 24, 99, 388

I

identity, 64, 65, 69, 225, 237, 245, 250, 257, 265, 288, 311–313, 327, 381, 387, 390, 392, 407
crisis, 49, 150
national, 5, 63, 161, 249
identity politics, 7, 14, 23, 24, 33, 38, 230, 232, 239, 267, 271, 282, 286
immigration
anti, 5
policy, 245
Indian Ocean, 39, 94, 328, 331, 340, 341, 344, 353, 358, 359, 363, 396
Indo-Pacific, 2, 25, 28, 31, 36, 102, 173, 274, 285, 343, 359, 363, 364, 396, 399, 400, 407
region, 6, 12, 31, 42, 273, 357
strategy, 29, 172, 173, 198, 325, 333, 357
inequality, 136, 137, 396
infrastructure, 24, 59, 84, 86, 103, 110, 171, 187, 192, 258, 259, 261, 277, 278, 312, 313, 322, 324, 325, 347, 349–352, 354, 362–365, 392, 393

INDEX 413

intelligence, 32, 143, 187, 231, 233, 251, 259, 273, 284, 361, 366, 401, 405

international law, 92, 101, 350

interoperability, 99, 286

irredentism, 94, 157, 168, 175, 346

isolationist, 104, 133, 135, 144, 147, 156

K

Keating, Paul, 233, 234, 248, 272, 284, 285, 288, 394

Kim, Jong-un, 12, 105, 106, 132, 147, 149, 162–164, 177–180, 282

Kirabati, 277

Kishida, Fumio, 73, 86–88, 99, 100, 111, 401

Kishi, Nobusuke, 51, 52, 64, 89, 161

Koizumi, Junichiro, 6, 18, 19, 50, 55, 56, 60, 61, 64, 66, 67, 74, 77–81, 85, 88, 91, 92, 94, 95, 104, 158, 159, 162, 231, 265, 279, 397

L

Labour party, 22, 38, 184, 244, 288, 394

LDP (Liberal Democratic Party), 26, 50, 52, 53, 56–58, 60, 65, 67–70, 72, 73, 75, 77, 78, 82, 84–89, 91, 93, 95, 97, 98, 158, 159, 394

Liberal-National coalition, 236, 238, 241, 244, 274, 393

lobby, 127, 398, 405

M

majoritarian politics, 223, 317, 318, 320, 321, 326, 327, 395

manufacturing, 17, 21, 23, 72, 107, 109, 110, 159, 169, 185, 186, 195, 314, 324, 325, 330, 358, 381, 382, 395, 399, 405

capabilities, 23

relocation, 103

media, 3, 4, 14, 17, 33, 49, 60, 74, 75, 81–83, 85, 86, 88, 102, 105, 107, 124, 126, 127, 130, 134, 137, 146, 148, 174, 189, 223, 226, 231, 234, 241, 245, 252, 257, 266, 276, 279, 283, 322, 324–326, 329, 349, 351, 354, 358, 359, 365

corporate, 33, 126, 141, 223, 251, 322, 344, 380, 397, 405

social, 6, 7, 17, 31, 33, 41, 49, 77, 81, 85, 124, 126, 175–177, 192, 194, 222, 223, 237, 243, 251, 257, 285, 322, 332, 387, 390, 397, 404, 407

methodology, 7, 12, 18, 19, 34, 50, 61, 62, 81, 88, 126, 135, 138, 147, 148, 172, 191, 279, 404

military-industrial complex, 14, 127, 141, 144, 145, 147, 153, 180, 197, 281, 380, 388, 405

mini-lateralism, 28, 363, 401

modernisation, 9, 28–30, 35, 65, 67, 94, 99, 157, 159, 164, 165, 175, 183, 186, 226, 273, 280, 328, 337, 338, 344, 356, 357, 362

Modi, Narendra, 5, 10, 11, 13, 18, 19, 39, 40, 50, 60, 62, 124, 168, 185, 221–224, 307–318, 320, 322, 324–328, 330, 334, 341–345, 348–350, 352, 356–359, 365, 366, 380, 395, 396, 401

Morrison, Scott, 10, 11, 13, 18, 19, 37, 38, 50, 60, 110, 184, 222, 235–242, 258, 260–264, 266,

414   INDEX

267, 273, 277, 282–286, 358, 359, 394, 396
multiculturalism, 232, 233, 237, 246, 249, 258, 265, 320
multilateral, 6, 98, 156, 164, 165, 328, 357, 362, 364, 396
cooperation, 389
relations, 98, 164
multipolarity, 380, 385

N

narratives, 2, 6, 8, 12, 14, 15, 18, 29, 33, 49, 60, 61, 65, 75, 80, 83, 88, 102, 110, 111, 128, 129, 133, 136, 141, 143, 146, 148, 150, 155, 168, 170, 171, 173–175, 177, 180, 189, 190, 192, 199, 241, 244, 245, 248, 265–267, 271, 315, 317, 319, 326, 331, 332, 348, 351, 354, 359, 362, 384, 386, 391, 392, 396, 404, 406
National Congress party, 316
nationalising islands, 93
nationalism
cultural, 267
economic, 329
ethnic, 313
nationalistic posturing, 81
statist, 65, 223
non-aligned, 39, 323
movement, 269, 307, 337
policy, 39, 332, 357
normalisation, 20, 98, 158, 177, 400
normalcy, 69
normal state, 68, 69
North Korea, 10, 20, 22, 25, 29, 56–58, 90, 105–107, 131, 132, 156, 160, 162, 163, 177–180, 188, 192, 197, 223, 259, 271, 282, 307, 384, 386, 389, 390, 406

O

Obama, Barrack, 4, 5, 35, 61, 62, 96, 97, 100–102, 125, 129, 135–137, 139, 141, 142, 145, 155–157, 159, 160, 162, 168, 177, 223, 226, 227, 250, 260, 273, 281, 342, 387, 393
OBOR (One Belt One Road), 40, 110, 169, 170, 331, 339, 350
option selection, 4

P

pacifism, 34, 69, 97
Pakistan, 223, 318, 320–323, 328, 331, 334, 336–338, 340, 344, 345, 350, 351, 355, 362, 363, 395, 398
peace, 6, 7, 9, 31, 43, 54, 63, 67, 70, 90, 95, 97, 101, 147, 158, 269, 274, 340, 406
international, 99
regional, 18
(PIC) Pacific Islands Countries, 276
pivot, 4, 5, 35, 36, 96, 97, 156–158, 160, 161, 168, 227, 230, 250, 270, 273, 342, 387
PLA (People's Liberal Army), 24, 30, 39, 94, 157
politics, 1, 2, 5, 7, 8, 10, 12–15, 17, 19, 20, 27, 28, 31, 33–36, 39, 41, 42, 50–54, 56, 61–64, 66–68, 70, 72–74, 77, 78, 80–83, 85, 87, 88, 95, 104, 108, 123, 125, 126, 130, 131, 135, 137, 138, 141, 145–148, 150, 152, 153, 155, 157–161, 166, 168, 171, 173, 174, 176, 186, 191, 197, 221–225, 228, 229, 232, 234, 235, 237–242, 244–246, 251, 252, 254, 256, 263, 264, 266, 267, 273, 274, 281, 308, 310, 316, 318,

320–322, 335, 359, 379, 381, 383, 392–395, 397
   domestic, 10, 12, 13, 15, 20, 28, 31, 33, 34, 36, 39, 41, 42, 50, 63, 64, 68, 72, 77, 88, 135, 137, 146, 152, 153, 155, 160, 166, 168, 173, 176, 225, 239, 242, 244, 245, 251, 252, 254, 273, 281, 308, 310, 322, 331, 333, 335, 359, 379, 380, 392, 395, 397, 398
   pork barrel, 67, 78, 81, 82, 85
populist, 5, 6, 11, 17, 33, 79, 134, 135, 148, 152, 158, 159, 221, 224, 237, 242, 265, 286, 313, 318, 331, 342, 379, 407
ports, 110, 164, 171, 260, 261, 277, 325, 340, 351, 355, 397
problem framing, 4
proxy, 106, 112, 123, 132, 153, 155, 177, 178, 180, 197, 198

Q

Quad, 4–11, 13–17, 19–23, 25–30, 32–34, 36, 37, 39–42, 49, 50, 57–59, 62, 63, 91, 102, 103, 108, 110, 133, 173, 182, 184, 185, 187, 189, 192, 194–196, 198, 221, 243, 267, 275, 279, 283–287, 308, 314, 328, 352, 355–361, 363–366, 379, 392, 393, 395, 396, 398–401, 404, 405
   Quad 1.0, 10, 356
   Quad 2.0, 22, 63, 275, 284, 357, 358

R

racism/racist, 15, 142, 220, 244, 245, 256, 257, 266, 397

Reagan, Ronald, 66, 104, 126, 129, 138, 141, 149–151, 182
   administration, 138, 269
refugees, 229, 247, 248, 252, 253, 281, 334
Republican
   base, 134, 139, 140, 142
   party, 37, 125–127, 129, 134, 137–141, 144, 148–152, 176, 238, 244, 393
   politics, 36, 125, 126, 129, 130, 137, 151, 153, 191
revisionism, 279
   constitutional, 57, 60, 81
   historical, 91, 160, 161
right-wing, 11, 13, 50, 60, 61, 76, 79, 85, 92, 125, 133, 222–224, 228, 229, 237, 239, 241, 251, 264, 279, 309, 312, 358, 379
Rudd, Kevin, 6, 22, 38, 62, 224–228, 230, 234, 235, 243, 249, 266, 270, 273, 279, 280, 286, 356, 393, 394
rules based international order, 177

S

San Francisco system, 8, 11, 12, 14, 20, 26, 29, 41, 109, 268, 271, 272, 274, 381, 382, 386, 390, 398–401
Sino-Soviet, 1, 335, 347, 383, 384, 396
Solomon Islands, 267, 277, 398
South China Sea, 2, 25, 26, 28, 30, 35, 42, 94, 95, 123, 162, 163, 165, 167, 168, 175, 228, 240, 266, 274–276, 340, 351, 357, 387, 388, 401, 402
sphere of influence, 14, 171, 278, 340, 395
strategic
   abandonment, 34, 69

416 INDEX

affinity, 243, 361
ambiguity, 403
assets, 171, 258, 260, 354, 397
circumstances, 155, 379, 381
partnership, 253, 273, 381
reproachment, 10
vantage point, 109
structural dominance, 21
submarines, 99, 102, 165, 231, 275, 280, 281, 284, 287, 361, 388, 401
supply chain, 7, 23, 108–110, 154, 187, 188, 192, 195, 196, 273, 283, 330, 381, 391, 396
systemic change, 9, 20

T

Taiwan, 2, 4, 6, 9, 20, 21, 24–26, 28–30, 42, 64, 67, 68, 84, 89, 92, 94, 95, 107, 123, 133, 163–165, 174, 176, 194, 198, 225, 240, 255, 256, 270, 271, 275, 277, 285, 351, 381, 386, 388, 390, 391, 397, 402
territorial
disputes, 4, 9, 25, 85, 107, 167, 168, 175, 315, 322, 336, 346, 349, 351, 395
infringement, 92
rights, 92
traditionalist, 53
transgressions, 4, 90, 151, 161, 180, 228, 240, 281, 334, 391
Trump, Donald, 1, 2, 4–6, 10, 11, 13, 18, 19, 22, 23, 36, 37, 50, 60, 62, 63, 103–106, 108, 109, 123, 125, 127, 128, 131, 142, 143, 178, 180, 185, 274, 281, 282, 313, 395
administration, 35, 36, 38, 99, 104, 107–109, 148, 149, 174, 176,

182, 185, 186, 188, 189, 239, 240, 282, 357, 358
doctrine, 126, 144, 148, 172, 176, 180
White House, 97, 105, 107, 133, 145, 146, 148, 172, 173, 181, 190
Turnbull, Malcolm, 10, 13, 19, 37, 60, 62, 222, 231–237, 239, 241, 242, 258–264, 273, 281, 282, 284, 286, 357, 394

U

unipolarity, 68, 380
US-Japan
alliance, 26, 34
defense guidelines, 100
relations, 89

V

vaccine, 7, 17, 153, 154, 191, 192, 194, 196, 287, 345, 365
values, 3, 4, 7, 12, 14, 17, 18, 29, 34, 38, 41, 58, 62, 69, 74, 91, 95–97, 104, 109, 126, 135, 156, 160, 174, 175, 246, 247, 249, 250, 260, 267, 274, 282, 283, 286, 307, 315, 316, 331, 333, 345, 366, 387, 396, 397, 400, 404, 407

W

war
cold, 1, 2, 4, 7, 8, 10, 12, 14, 20, 22, 25, 27, 28, 30, 31, 33–35, 37, 41–43, 67, 70, 89, 112, 123, 135, 138, 157, 161, 172, 174, 175, 193, 196–221, 268, 271–273, 307, 348, 353, 379,

381, 382, 385–392, 396, 400, 402, 405–407
diplomatic, 391
tech, 1, 4, 7, 19, 36, 107, 133, 148, 186, 188, 189, 191, 358, 387, 395, 401, 403
trade, 23, 36, 107, 108, 147, 181–186, 188, 191, 195, 282, 344, 401
War on Terror, 5, 77, 80, 90, 155, 156, 158, 167, 223, 243, 249, 250, 272, 273, 359, 381, 385
White Australia policy, 220, 245, 255

X
Xi, Jinping, 3–6, 12, 32, 39, 58, 133, 149, 169, 170, 174, 175, 193, 231, 267, 275, 285, 313, 314, 341, 343, 356, 357, 384, 387, 391, 395, 396, 400

Y
Yasukuni, 53, 77, 79, 80, 95, 279

Z
zero-balancing, 403

Printed in the United States
by Baker & Taylor Publisher Services